SEEKERS OF SCENERY

Seekers of Scenery

TRAVEL WRITING FROM
SOUTHERN APPALACHIA, 1840–1900

Edited by

KEVIN E. O'DONNELL

and

HELEN HOLLINGSWORTH

THE UNIVERSITY OF TENNESSEE PRESS / Knoxville

Library of Congress Cataloging-in-Publication Data

Seekers of scenery: travel writing from southern Appalachia, 1840–1900 /
edited by Kevin E. O'Donnell and Helen Hollingsworth.— 1st ed.
    p. cm.
Includes bibliographical references and index.
ISBN 1-57233-278-6 (hardcover)
1. Appalachian Region, Southern—Description and travel.
 I. O'Donnell, Kevin E., 1962–
II. Hollingsworth, Helen, 1930–

F217.A65S44 2004
917.4—dc22   2004012275

For Julia A. Hollingsworth,
Marie H. Vann, and Lucille B. Frizzell;
and for Cassie Coberly

—H.H.

For Eugene Owen O'Donnell

—K.O.

Contents

Figures

Maps

Acknowledgments

I n the late 1980s, Helen Hollingsworth began a project under the working title "Travelers in the Southern Highlands." In the summer of 1989,
she spent many hours in the University of Tennessee Hodges Library ware-
house buildings, browsing among the bound nineteenth-century periodicals. Helen found many southern Appalachian travel articles, including
a number of significant pieces not listed in previous bibliographies. By
the early 1990s, she had collected articles and proposed an anthology to
John H. Blair publishers. At that time, personal matters led her to set the
project aside.

Eight years later, during the fall of 1999, Helen was *Emerita* in the
English department at East Tennessee State. As an Associate Professor
with an interest in nineteenth-century nonfiction, I had been reading into
the regional travel literature. Good fortune and a conversation with
Roberta Herrin, an English department colleague, led me to find out
about Helen's project. Helen was gracious enough to give me full access
to the boxes of material she had collected. They provided the basis for the
book you now hold.

This book represents my extension of Helen's work. I selected from
her material, added articles from my own research, drew up a plan for the
anthology, wrote the general introduction, article introductions, notes,
and bibliography. I also arranged photos of the illustrations and designed
the maps and worked with the cartographer. I take responsibility for
errors or omissions.

xvi ACKNOWLEDGMENTS

Thanks to ETSU colleagues Martha Copp, Tess Lloyd, Norma Meyers, John Morefield, Catherine Murray, Ted Olson, Jeff Powers-Beck, Fred Waage, for engaging discussion and camaraderie. Thanks to Frank Burns, Donald E. Davis, David Williams, Jennifer Bauer Wilson for their correspondence. Thanks to Deanna Bryant and the English Department office staff; to the staffs in the ETSU Archives of Appalachia and Sherrod Library Circulation department; to the summer 2001 staff at the American Antiquarian Society; to Terri Simerly and Jessica Notgrass for graduate assistance; especially to Kathy Olson Hallenbeck, who scanned, typed, and edited prodigious amounts of text; to Kelly Hensley, ETSU interlibrary loan coordinator; and to the splendid people at University of Tennessee Press. Frosty Levy, ETSU Department of Biological Sciences, answered botanical questions. Larry Smith, director of ETSU University Relations photo department, photographed and scanned illustrations.

Personal thanks to the following for various mountain rambles: the above-mentioned Martha and Tess; Mike Deakins, Alan Gamble, Scott Honeycutt, Dan Kleeman, John and Ileana Slack, Jeff Supplee, Heather Yurek. Thanks also to the Constance Fenimore Woolson Society; to Cherokee Forest Voices and the State of Franklin Group/Tennessee Chapter of the Sierra Club; to the volunteer trail maintainers at the Tennessee Eastman Hiking and Canoeing Club. Thanks to the O'Donnells for pulling together during a difficult time, and especially to Tim for setting me up with a place to write during a crucial couple of weeks, and most especially to my father, to whom I've dedicated my work on this book. I wish he could be here to see the result.

Helen also wishes to thank Linda Carmichel, Martha Crowe, Roberta Herrin, and Jeri Hurd—Appalachians all!—for their contributions to this project.

The ETSU Research Development Committee made this book possible through travel money for Helen in 1989, and with travel money and a summer stipend for me in 2001.

—Kevin E. O'Donnell
Johnson City, Tennessee
July 2004

Remarks on the Texts, Notes, and Illustrations

This anthology contains nineteenth-century selections from the following American magazines: *Appalachia* (Appalachian Mountain Club, Boston), *Appleton's Journal, Atlantic Monthly, Christian Observer* (Louisville), *Cosmopolitan, Harper's Monthly, Lakeside Monthly* (Chicago), *Lippincott's, Southern Literary Messenger.* (In addition, the selection by Charles Lanman is from a newspaper, the *Daily National Intelligencer* [Washington, D.C.].)

The text of each article is from its first appearance in print. Some punctuation has been slightly modernized. Otherwise, punctuation, spelling, and use of typefaces have been preserved. Readers should expect to encounter some archaic or variant spelling and punctuation.

Notes for the articles are explanatory. They include updated travel information and notes on human and natural history, on literary studies, and on Appalachian studies. They also include glosses on botanical names, when those may be of special interest to the traveler and amateur botanist, or when there may be a question about common names or about the accuracy of a writer's observations. Sources for botanical information are primarily Justice and Bell, and Peattie. Otherwise, secondary sources for the end notes and introduction are referenced, MLA-style, to the Bibliography.

Illustrations are photographs of prints from first editions of articles. The prints are mostly woodcuts, printed from engraved composite woodblocks. (See Introduction for more about illustrations.)

A Word to Travelers

This is an academic book, but it is also designed to serve as a companion for the unhurried, historically minded automobile traveler in the southern Appalachians. At their best, the essays reprinted here can make your travel more rewarding—giving you a kind of second sight, a vision of the landscape as it is now *and* as it was in the nineteenth century.

The places described are reached via the following interstate highways and parkways—from the east: Blue Ridge Parkway, I-81, I-85, I-40; from the south: I-77, I-26, I-75; from the west: I-40, I-64; from the north: I-77, I-81.

To find essays about particular destinations:

- Peruse the itineraries shown in the table of contents.
- Refer to the index for place names.
- Browse the list of maps (see pages xiii and xx), to see if any match your destination. Hikers note that four of the five maps include segments of the Appalachian National Scenic Trail.

Also, don't miss the notes, where you'll find updated travel information and observations. For further reading to accompany this book, see the Federal Writers' Project guides, produced by the Works Projects Administration in the 1930s and 1940s. These guides are primary sources for most subsequent travel books about the southern Appalachian region. Of the many fine travel books about the region that have been published more recently, Sakowski's *Backroads* series is especially good. For general reading, Davidson, Dykeman, and Roderick Peattie are good places to start.

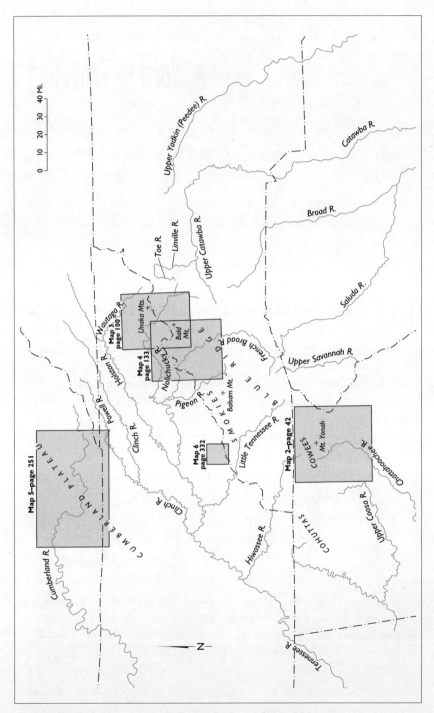

OVERVIEW OF SOUTHERN APPALACHIA, WITH INDEX TO OTHER MAPS

Introduction

SCENERY, MARKETS, AND MOUNTAINEERS

KEVIN E. O'DONNELL

Overview of Region, Time Period, and Themes

This book is a collection of writing about the highlands of the south-eastern United States, a region that begins south of the New River and extends through the mountainous parts of Virginia, Kentucky, Tennessee, and North Carolina, down to Georgia and Alabama.

The terrain includes flat, fertile valleys, as well as high "hollers" and backwoods. Here also rise the highest mountains in the east—rainy, temperate, and botanically rich. The ranges include the Cumberlands, the Blue Ridge, and the Blacks, as well as the Smoky, Unaka, Balsam, and Nantahala ranges, plus numerous smaller ranges and sub-ranges. From those high ridges, the upper Tennessee and upper Cumberland Rivers drain west, through the Ohio and Mississippi; the upper Catawba, Yadkin, and Savannah run southeast, to the Atlantic; and the upper Chattahoochee south to the Gulf of Mexico.[1]

The articles in this collection have been selected from a large body of travel writing about the region that appeared in American periodicals in the second half of the nineteenth century.[2] The articles have been chosen to cover the region with minimal redundancy, and to provide material of special interest to twenty-first-century readers. Contained herein are wonderful accounts of historic scenes and sites. Some passages read as environmental elegy: descriptions of old-growth forests that are now cut over; waterfalls now dammed; 360° views that can no longer be seen because of pollution on the high ridges.[3] Information throughout this volume is glossed, and updated where necessary, with explanatory end notes.

For readers interested in the history and culture of the region, these articles offer a glimpse of the social, economic, and political forces that shaped the region as we know it today. They describe nineteenth-century economic and domestic practices. They show how the image of the mountaineer—the idea of a distinct, white, southern Appalachian population—emerged in the national consciousness. And they detail the development of the region during a crucial period.

At the same time, the writings and illustrations reprinted here also say much about the nation as a whole. These articles were written during a turbulent era—circa 1840 to 1900—which saw the emergence of the United States as an urban, industrial, knowledge-based economy and culture.[4] During this time period, America shifted from agriculture to industry, from rural to urban society. This period straddles the Civil War and encompasses the final shift of the United States from a federation to republic.

Industrial monopoly capitalism matured during the years encompassed in this book. The period saw boom-and-bust cycles, major economic panics roughly every twenty years from 1837 to 1893. The postwar Gilded Age brought enormous creativity, and also corruption and destruction. It saw the development of a convict-leasing system, a version of slavery that used primarily African Americans—often imprisoned for vagrancy and other trumped-up charges—to build the railroads that later transported genteel tourist parties to mountain retreats. The era also saw great labor strife and the rise of the sharecropping system.

The magazines in which these articles appeared, the monthly "qualities," including *Harper's* and *Appleton's,* were America's first mass medium (Ohmann vii). The illustrations reproduced in this book are among the nation's first mass-produced images. The rise of the magazines was, in turn, made possible by the Common School movement, which originated and spread during the period covered by this anthology. Schooling and literacy gave rise to a national literary culture, which was both given form and reflected in the magazines. That same culture helped create a newly rootless professional class, members of which developed an Arcadian longing for stability that found its image in the landscape of the mountain south, even as industrialism was beginning to transform that same landscape forever.

The energy of America during this period is reflected in these travel writings. All the elements of the nineteenth-century drama of nation-building are here: genocide, colonialism and industrialism, leisure and consumption, evolving attitudes towards nature and regional and ethnic identities. Not only do these essays provide a travelogue to the region. Herein can also be read the sins and aspirations of the nation as a whole.

The Cherokee Removal: Cleansing the Landscape

This anthology begins with a dispatch from George Cooke, a painter, art critic, and contributor to the *Southern Literary Messenger*. Cooke was in Dahlonega (pronounced *duh-LON-uh-guh*), Habersham County, north Georgia, on the heels of the Cherokee removal. That infamous episode of ethnic cleansing occurred only a year before Cooke posted his article to the *Messenger*. Background about the Cherokee removal is important for an understanding of the cultural work that Cooke and others performed in the region.

After the American Revolution, surviving Cherokees found a haven in the mountains of north Georgia. Here, many Cherokees regrouped and tried to "civilize," to assimilate and adapt white culture. This post-revolutionary generation included members of mixed blood, such as John Ross, Elias Boudinot, and Sequoyah, the inventor of the Cherokee system of writing. The Cherokees maintained an independent territory until gold was discovered in 1828. Then the state of Georgia confiscated the land, and prospectors rushed in to seize Cherokee fields and homesteads, often at gunpoint. Opportunistic whites were protected by hurriedly enacted state laws prohibiting Indians from bringing suit or testifying against a white man. After several years of turmoil and violence, the state in 1835 offered the Cherokees five million dollars and new lands in the Oklahoma Territory in exchange for their Georgia holdings. A minority faction, led by John Ridge, signed the treaty of New Echota. However, the vast majority of the Cherokees were opposed to it (Foreman 269). The wider American public soon came to understand that the treaty was a fraud. Considerable political and civil opposition arose, especially in the northeast. (Ralph Waldo Emerson wrote his famous open letter to President Martin Van Buren, protesting the removal, in the spring of 1838. On opposition to removal in the northeast, see Richardson, 275–79.)

Nevertheless, that same spring, General Winfield Scott received command of all U.S. forces in the Cherokee territory, together with reinforcements, and with orders to move the Cherokees out by force. By the summer of 1838, nearly seventeen thousand Cherokees had been herded into stock-ades, at bayonet and gunpoint. By October of that year, the "Trail of Tears" was well under way. By the following spring, probably more than four thousand Cherokees had died, either in the stockades, in transit, or in the Oklahoma Territory shortly after arrival. Ethnologist James Mooney quotes a Georgia volunteer with the Federal army who was later a Confederate colonel: "I fought through the Civil War and have seen men shot to pieces and slaughtered by the thousands, but the Cherokee removal was the cru-elest work I ever knew" (130).

———— · · · ————

In 1826, several years *before* the state of Georgia first confiscated the Cher-okee territory, Elias Boudinot (aka Buck Watie [1804?–1839]), a Cherokee writer and educator, was traveling in the northeast, raising funds for a print-ing press. Boudinot was a proponent of cultural assimilation. In an address delivered in Philadelphia and elsewhere in the northeast, he told his audi-ence about the southern mountains: "Those lofty and barren mountains, defying the labour and ingenuity of man, and supposed by some as placed there only to exhibit omnipotence, contribute to the healthiness and beauty of the surrounding plains, and give to us that free air and pure water which distinguish our country" (71).

Boudinot circulated a printed version of the address. The pamphlet describes the natural beauty and climate of the region, and goes on to com-ment, "These advantages, calculated to make the inhabitants healthy, vig-orous, and intelligent, cannot fail to cause this country to become interesting. And there can be no doubt that the Cherokee Nation, however obscure and trifling it may now appear, will finally become, if not under its present occupants, one of the Garden spots of America" (71).

The tone of the address is solemn. It's hard not to hear the heartache in that rueful aside—"*if not under its present occupants.*" Yet in a sense, Boudinot brings the same message as later tourism promoters. The mountains are healthy and beautiful—and ripe for exploitation. Nevertheless, even Boudinot must have been surprised by how quickly white vacation-home builders would overtake the region in the handful of years after his address. First, there was the gold rush of 1828, during which land was confiscated under state law. That was two years after Boudinot's speech. After that, according to sociologist and historian Wilma Dunaway, wealthy second-home owners began encroaching on Cherokee lands, often under circum-stances that were questionable even under the laws of the state of Georgia.

In 1832, the state divided the territory into land lots of 160 acres, and gold lots of 40 acres. The lots were supposed to be raffled off to homesteaders. Yet, according to Dunaway, irregularities and corruption were rampant. "Despite state requirements that grantees live on the awarded parcels for at least five years," writes Dunaway, "nearly half the land was held by absentees, two years after the lottery. In spite of Georgia's 'free' acreage policy, 16 percent of the households held all the land, while the majority of Habersham County families remained landless" (*First Frontier* 64).

Sixteen percent held *all* the land. And who were these 16 percent who already controlled the coveted land, several years before Cherokees were removed at gunpoint? They were a combination of wealthy tidewater families, deep-south plantation owners, and new-money northern industrialists who had moved south. Many had British and international connections. In short, these are the people that writer and painter George Cooke sought as patrons. They are the reason he went to the southern mountains in the first place. Cooke, the artist and aesthete, traveled through the American east and southeast in search of commissions. (See Pennington for an account of Cooke's southern itinerancy.)

By the summer of 1840, Cooke's peregrinations had led him to the former Cherokee lands of Habersham County. He was in the region to sell his services. And one service he provided was cultural legitimation. In his essay for the *Southern Literary Messenger,* reprinted here, Cooke sprinkles descriptions of the north Georgia landscape with quotes and allusions from Euripides, Milton, Austen, and Byron. Cooke draws comparisons between north Georgia sites and European tourist sites that genteel readers would know. He refers to natives in terms of a romanticized myth, set in "ancient times." He thus writes the recent Cherokee occupants into an imaginary distant past. And by framing the freshly cleansed region in terms of European aesthetic traditions, he helps to secure cultural possession of the land.

———————

Charles Lanman, author of the second article in this collection, wrote from Dahlonega in 1848, eight years after Cooke's visit. Lanman's series of letters appeared in the Washington D.C.–based *Daily National Intelligencer* in the spring and early summer of 1848, at a time when that newspaper was perhaps the most influential periodical in the nation. Lanman's letters were later collected and published as *Letters from the Alleghany Mountains* (1849). The book helped him to establish a reputation in the nation's capital, and thus to secure connections and employment. After his trip to the southern mountains, Lanman obtained a War Department library position, from which he resigned in 1850 to become Daniel Webster's private secretary.

Lanman, like Cooke, was a painter. Though never a professional, Lanman studied under Asher B. Durand when he was young and continued painting and sketching all his life. (Lanman exhibited a painting entitled *Tallulah Chasm*—presumably depicting the gorge and waterfall in north Georgia—at the American Art-Union, in 1847. The painting is no longer extant [Keyes 88, n. 2].) Lanman, like Cooke, writes vivid, poetic landscape descriptions. His essays have a romantic, painterly quality not often found in later writings about this region.

In addition, Lanman addresses Native American themes in this article. In many of his other travel writings, he is a keen and often credible observer of Native American material culture, and his writings are still valued as documentary sources by historians today. Nevertheless, Lanman also appears to get at least a few things wrong. Here, for example, is the single reference Lanman includes to the Cherokee removal that took place ten years before his visit: "the digging of gold was not made a regular business until after they [Cherokees] had been *politely banished* by the General Government" [emphasis added].

Readers with even a cursory knowledge of the circumstances surrounding the removal will be disturbed by Lanman's remarks. He seems so obviously meretricious. Yet it is not to excuse Lanman to say that he participated in the ideology of his culture. Lanman, like Cooke, sells cultural legitimacy to a ruling class, a class to which he aspires. He writes to representatives of the oligarchy, the captains of America's emerging industrialism.

Consider the *Daily National Intelligencer,* in which Lanman's letters appeared. Microfilm reproductions of editions from May 1848 show long columns of small print, on the one hand, and columns of numbers, on the other. The print is filled with documentary material, such as transcripts of speeches from the U.S. Senate (usually speeches criticizing then-President James K. Polk, the nemesis of the *Intelligencer*'s whiggish editors). The numbers show real estate and stock transactions. Lanman's lyrical, even flowery romanticism—always on page 2 or 3; never on the front—seems at first incongruous, surrounded by numbers and fine print.

Yet the connection between romantic lyricism and financial data runs deep. Lanman is writing to the lettered elite, the players in the national political culture. These potential vacationers have been educated to love the picturesque, and are also potential investors. Likewise, the two functions Lanman performs—cultural legitimation, on the one hand, and documentation of resources and potential investments, on the other—are two sides of the same coin. George Cooke, the painter, also shows two sides of a coin in his dispatch to the *Southern Literary Messenger*. Cooke's article from north Georgia is divided into two sections, each with a different dateline: The first is from Habersham County, where there is scenery—waterfalls and mountains. The second dateline is from Dahlonega, site of the new gold mint.

Scenery and Postwar Investment

Eighty miles northwest of Dahlonega, the rugged area around the upper bend of the Tennessee, along Chickamauga Creek, was the last stronghold for resistant Cherokees immediately following the American Revolution. Those Cherokees who refused to assimilate to white culture aligned themselves with Dragging Canoe and became identified as the Chickamauga (Mooney 64–65). For a short period, around the turn of the nineteenth century, Chickamaugas controlled this region, a remote, isolated "mountain fastness."

Barely three generations later, however, the land around Chattanooga was a prime target for Gilded Age real estate and industrial developers. The region's coal and iron reserves, the abundant timber, the promise of raw natural resources, all were "discovered" by northerners who had seen the area as soldiers and officers during the Civil War. A portion of the Union army returned south during Reconstruction to take advantage of those resources.

General John T. Wilder, for instance, was a Union officer during the battles of Chickamauga and Chattanooga in late fall and early winter of 1863. After the worst of it was over, he noticed signs of iron ore in the area around Walden's Ridge. He returned later and founded the Roane Iron Company in 1868. The city of Rockwood, Tennessee, sprang up around his company. Wilder later also purchased land and built a hotel on Roan Mountain, Tennessee/North Carolina. (See Warner, in this volume, for a description of the hotel site.) Wilder's postwar career exemplifies the activities of the outside investor during this period. Wilder invested heavily in industry, on the one hand, and tourism, on the other. Such was to be the typical pattern in southern Appalachia: the investment dollars and the tourists tended to come hand in hand, the one promoting the other. Just as pent-up investment was finding release in the unexploited raw materials of the southern mountains, pent-up tourism was also beginning to find an outlet in the region.

From a broader point of view, postwar investment in the southern mountains reflected an international trend. This was the height of the

Victorian era. International colonialism was emerging full-blown. Britain and other European colonial powers were securing authority over much of Africa, Asia, the South Pacific, and Latin America. Britain's imperial expansion would reach its peak within the next twenty years. British and Scottish investment capital, then—in addition to northeastern money—flowed into the American south through the international bond market. Much of this capital came through New York City and was managed by firms on Wall Street, less than a half-mile walk from the Harper Brothers' publishing offices, on Pearl Street at Franklin Square. As capital loosened up and became available, northeastern and British investors established a colonial relationship with the American south—or re-established that relationship, as the case might be. C. Vann Woodward writes of this era, "So active were English investors in the region that for a time it seemed as if the mother country, after the lapse of a century, were about to renew an old relationship with the South" (118–19).

Investment capital flowing through New York was used to establish industrial concerns to extract natural resources—mainly coal, iron, and later timber. Some manufactories were set up, but for the most part the industries were extractive. Raw or lightly refined resources were shipped outside the region for manufacture elsewhere. The result would be, by the early twentieth century, "worn-out soil, cut-over timberlands, and worked-out mines" (Woodward 320).

At the same time, during the decades that followed Wilder's initial investment, the climate and scenery would attract increasing numbers of tourists from the northeast. By the turn of the next century, the end of the period covered in this anthology, the Chattanooga area was one of the most popular tourist destinations in the eastern United States.

O. B. Bunce in the Southern Mountains

After the war, as northern capitalists came south, another type of entrepreneur was also drawn to the region, a type that we might call a scenery entrepreneur. (See Dona Brown, 43–48, for a discussion of nineteenth-century writers and artists working as what Brown calls "scenic entrepreneurs" in the mountains of the northeast.) In the spring of 1871, Oliver Bell Bunce traveled south from New York to Chattanooga on a business venture.

Bunce was a top editor for *Appleton's Journal,* one of the most widely circulated national illustrated magazines to emerge after the war. His magazine was locked in tight competition with others, including *Harper's* and the upstart *Scribner's* (Rainey 56–57). Bunce had been hired specifically to make the illustrations in *Appleton's* more appealing. He had developed his skills before the war, producing illustrated books for the Christmas trade. After the war, *Appleton's* hired him and gave him free rein to commission illustrators and to oversee reproductions, in addition to assigning writers and writing many articles himself.

Bunce was not an editor in the conventional sense, but rather more of a media impresario, one of the new breed of New York–based editors who were managing the emerging technologies for mass production of images. The technology Bunce had learned to exploit was the composite-boxwood print-block. By the end of the 1860s, blocks and screws had been developed which were durable enough to be set into high-speed presses to produce runs of 200,000 copies or more. The process required teams of engravers and printers, as well as illustrators in the field. It also required a good manager, a coordinator who could handle people and business and who could decide what combinations would make a good product.

Bunce's product was the mass-produced image, the sort of image people could cut out and pin or frame on a wall after they had read a magazine. The prints are beautiful. (The reproductions that appear in this volume are from photographs of prints. To truly appreciate the high quality of the prints, readers are advised to look at the original magazines.) The wood-engraving technique, with its ability to reproduce fine textures and hatching effects, lent itself especially well to landscape images.

By the spring of 1871, as Bunce arrived in Chattanooga, he had conceived a plan to improve *Appleton's* circulation. Bunce traveled with Harry Fenn, a British-born illustrator who had immigrated to the U.S. during the Civil War. Fenn was already a minor celebrity of sorts, well known enough that *Appleton's* heavily advertised his exclusive contract with the magazine. The announcement ran in the back of the journal in March and April of 1871:

> The publishers of APPLETONS' JOURNAL have the pleasure of announcing the completion of arrangements by which Mr. HARRY FENN will for a time give his professional services exclusively to the prosecution of the series of views entitled "PICTURESQUE AMERICA," which for a few months past has been a conspicuous and attractive feature in the JOURNAL. Mr. Fenn will this spring visit SOUTH CAROLINA, GEORGIA, TENNESSEE, AND VIRGINIA, after

which he will proceed to sections North and West; and, when the summer heats are over, he will visit other Southern localities. . . . Mr. Fenn, whose vivid and graphic pencil has placed him at the acknowledged head of American draughtsmen, will for the present give his professional labors solely to the pages of APPLETONS' JOURNAL.

The resulting series of articles and prints in *Appleton's* would turn out to be one of the most widely read periodical series of the century (Overton 58).

Before advertising the exclusive contract with Fenn, *Appleton's* had already featured illustrations, by Fenn and other illustrators, of western North Carolina's mountain landscape—including a three-part series of illustrated articles in October 1869 by Charles Lanman entitled "Novelties of Southern Scenery" and a series of short features on western North Carolina by Henry Colton in 1870 and 1871. (See Rainey, 54–58, on the importance of western North Carolina in the development of the series.) Yet by the spring of 1871, Bunce had in mind something bigger than a magazine series. He would go on to convert his initial collection of articles and images into one of the most influential illustrated works of the nineteenth century, in America or anywhere. *Picturesque America,* the 900-page folio of travel essays and landscape prints—wood engravings as well as more-expensive steel plate engravings—was sold in installments, by subscription through Appleton's house, bound in two volumes, 1872–74.

Picturesque America was a taste-setting venture. Subscribers included influential writers, such as Emerson, Longfellow, Oliver Wendell Holmes, Whittier, and Harriet Beecher Stowe. They also included millionaire industrialists, statesmen, and clergymen. (See Overton, 59–60, for reproductions of subscription sheets containing signatures of many of these persons.) William Cullen Bryant is often credited as the primary editor for the project. Bryant was hired on for his celebrity status, however. His actual role was relatively minor, and came late in the project. And though Bryant signed the book's preface, he rewrote it from an earlier version written by Bunce (Rainey 83). The resulting work was a popular success. According to one source, nearly a million sets were sold (Comparato 19). And today the woodblock and steel plate prints are still popular with print dealers and collectors.

The fact that Bunce began the folio project with a trip to the southern mountains is significant. Views of southern Appalachia make up a substantial portion of the first volume. Out of thirty-four articles in that first volume, eight—including the "On Lookout Mountain" article reprinted in this anthology—feature sites in what is now considered southern Appalachia. Competing magazines had been featuring primarily western scenes in their pages. Bunce, however, gambled that portrayals of reconciliation with the South would appeal to war-weary northeastern urbanites, fatigued with compassion for blacks and anxious to reconcile. The reconciliation theme is indeed thought to be largely responsible for the success of the travel series and of the subsequent folio. "As the first publication to celebrate the entire continental nation," writes Sue Rainey, *Picturesque America* "enabled Americans, after the trauma of the Civil War, to construct a national self-image based on reconciliation between North and South and incorporation of the West" (xiii). (See also Buck, 115–44, and Rowe, 1–22, on the theme of reconciliation in politics and literature, respectively.)

Mass-Producing the Picturesque

Illustrations—mainly prints from wood engravings—were a primary feature of American literary magazines in the postwar decades of the nineteenth century. Indeed, editors put so much emphasis on illustrations that writers were often upstaged. One *Harper's* author, Lafcadio Hearn, went so far as to give up his contract to write about Japan after finding out that the artist who was to accompany him on the trip would make more than double his pay (Mott II 397). Even Henry James had reservations. James supported and admired many of the prominent magazine illustrators, and he visited with them often in the 1880s at a summer artists' colony at the village of Broadway, in the Cotswolds of Great Britain (Olson 14–17). Yet he also felt that illustrations detracted from his text. James biographer Leon Edel reports the following remarks that James wrote to an editor of *Century Magazine* in the 1880s: "Ah, your illustrations—your illustrations . . . how, as a writer, one hates 'em; and how their being as good as they are makes one hate 'em more! What one writes suffers essentially, as literature, from going with them, and the two things ought to stand alone" (156–57).

Yet it should be no surprise that during the Gilded Age illustrations often upstaged text in the literary magazines. The quality of the illustrations, as James admits, was quite good. Furthermore, mass-produced images were still, in the decades following the Civil War, something of a novelty. Though printed illustrations had been common for hundreds of years, prints of such high quality had never before been so readily available. Middle-class subscribers to the magazines could look forward to new illustrations arriving in the U.S. post every month.

In addition, the fact that the magazine illustration technology lent itself to landscape reproductions coincided happily with the interests of American middle-class readers of the Victorian era, who were eager to view landscape images. After the Civil War, the illustrated monthly magazines, with their mass-produced landscape images, brought the high-art traditions of the prewar period "down market," so to speak. The landscape traditions were brought to the masses.

Nineteenth-century landscape viewing in America has roots in British aristocratic traditions. The term "picturesque"—a term used by many of the writers in this anthology—originated in eighteenth-century British aesthetic discourse. Edmund Burke's widely circulated *Philosophical Enquiry into the Origin of Our Ideas of the Sublime and Beautiful* (1757) helped to set the stage, by establishing the meanings of two related terms: "sublime" and "beautiful." According to Burke, scenery that is wild, untamed, disordered, and terrifying is sublime. Scenery that is pastoral, lush, ordered, and serene is beautiful. A third term, "picturesque," was coined by a British cleric, William Gilpin, after Burke's treatise had circulated. In Gilpin's view, a picturesque scene contains elements both sublime *and* beautiful. Gilpin popularized the use of all three terms, roaming the countryside and using "sublime," "beautiful," and "picturesque" in a series of essays to categorize specific landscape views. To Gilpin and his late-eighteenth-century British adherents, a picturesque landscape was the most desirable.[5]

Americans were quick to adopt British aesthetics, and landscape appreciation became a badge of class status in the nineteenth century. Landscape conventions thus came both to shape and to reflect notions Americans had about what the country should be. Modern American art historians have had much to say about specifically how the idea of the picturesque informed emerging American middle-class identities in the nineteenth century. Here, for example, is an analysis by Brigitte Bailey:

> Derived from the aesthetics of a landowning gentry, the picturesque developed into a mercantile perspective as well; detached from literal landownership, this pictorial habit awarded the picturesque tourist a metaphorical, visual ownership. It became a flexible model for the gaze of a cultural elite (whether English or American) interested in finding a perspective from which the diverse and unruly growths of 19th-century representative democracies

could be integrated into a non-coerced but controlled composition, a composition that was perceived—i.e., "owned"—by the elite spectator, the carrier of the social gaze. (9)

Whether or not a well-defined political ideology necessarily accompanied landscape viewing of the era, the success of *Picturesque America* suggests that there was certainly something about landscapes that appealed deeply to middle-class readers of postwar illustrated magazines. What might have been the attraction? In a broad discussion of western landscape traditions, critic W. J. T. Mitchell discusses the "imperial" ideology of landscape paintings. Landscape images, says Mitchell, are about the viewers' desire to possess, which is tied in with a drive towards future development. "Empire moves outward in space as a way of moving forward in time," writes Mitchell. "The 'prospect' that opens up is not just a spatial scene but a projected future of 'development' and exploitation" (17).

Art historian Albert Boime develops a similar analysis in his discussion of American landscape painting of the prewar years. Boime claims that America's painting conventions expressed that era's ideology of Manifest Destiny. The thesis of Boime's influential book is implied in his title: *The Magisterial Gaze: Manifest Destiny and American Landscape Painting, 1830–1865* (1991). Boime claims that all the major movements in prewar nineteenth-century American landscape painting—the Hudson River, Luminist, and Rocky Mountain schools—reveal in "their common structural paradigm the sociopolitical ideology of expansionist thought" (5).

Expansionist ideology of some sort is not hard to find in the writings of Thomas Cole, the leading painter of the Hudson River school, whose "Essay on American Scenery" (1836) Boime quotes. In that essay, Cole celebrates the expansion of civilization and the conquest of nature: "Looking over the yet uncultivated scene, the mind's eye may see far into futurity. Where the wolf roams, the plough shall glisten; on the gray crag shall rise temple and tower—mighty deeds shall be done in the new pathless wilderness; and poets unborn shall sanctify the soil" (Cole 12).

In other words, for Cole, landscapes are to be possessed, occupied, "civilized," and developed. The promise of possession is one of the appeals of the American landscape image of the antebellum period.

A generation after Cole painted his most significant works, the magazine illustrators of the postwar era were greatly influenced by Cole and other painters of the Hudson River school. Many of the woodcut prints, especially those published during Reconstruction, borrowed the composition and vocabulary of the influential paintings that preceded them. The prints thus lend themselves to the sort of analysis Boime develops for the paintings.

Consider, for example, the third figure in this volume: "Lookout Mountain.—Cliffs East of the 'Point'" (page 67). This image of Chattanooga, from a woodblock print engraved from Harry Fenn's "vivid and graphic pencil," can be read as embodying a desire to possess the landscape of the south. One of the first things an art historian would point out is that its basic composition comes from the Hudson River school tradition. As in many of Thomas Cole's paintings, so in this Harry Fenn composition: the canvas is divided diagonally, almost but not quite into two triangles, by a mountain ridge in the near-middle ground. In the foreground is a rugged cliff, with blasted trees. The foreground shows the "sublime" part of the landscape. In the background, stretching off into the distance, is the "beautiful" portion. There the landscape is tamed: the railroad stretches, and the civilized plumes of smoke rise from the city of Chattanooga. Together, the elements of the scene are picturesque, in a formulaic way.

Fenn's drawing in fact echoes a famous 1836 painting by Cole: *View from Mount Holyoke, Northampton, Massachusetts, after a Thunderstorm (The Oxbow).* On display at the Metropolitan Museum of Art, New York, Cole's painting shows a view of the Connecticut River, with the canvas divided diagonally by the ridge at the near-middle ground. The river's oxbow meanders to the right, lazily looping away from the diagonal, into the middle and far distance. In Fenn's "Cliffs East of the 'Point,'" the Tennessee River (a river that, like the Connecticut, shares its name with a state) also loops into the middle and far distance. Yet *this* river, the Tennessee, has a surplus of snakelike loops, exuberant oxbows receding into the softly mysterious wilds. The picture presents a prospect, a land filled with promise. Given our knowledge now that the region was poised on a period of heavy development, driven by northern readers, it's hard not to see this "prospect" as the promise of industrial and tourism development. At the same time, the image was—for Reconstruction-era northern viewers schooled in the Hudson River way of seeing—familiar, even nostalgic. It promised, perhaps, the restoration of an earlier landscape, the healing of a wound or soothing of a loss.

Chattanooga and Monopoly Capitalism

Twenty years after Bunce and Fenn traveled through Chattanooga, another prominent New York magazinist visited Lookout Mountain and wrote about the region. Julian Ralph's *Harper's* article—entitled "The Industrial

Region of Northern Alabama, Tennessee, and Georgia" (March 1895)—
focuses on the industrialization that swept the area during the intervening
decades. An excerpt from the article, along with accompanying illustrations, is reprinted in this volume.

Ralph, a one-time star reporter for the *New York Sun* who was making
the transition to magazine writing, traveled to Chattanooga in the winter
of 1893. Earlier that year, he had covered the World's Columbian Exposition in Chicago and the trial of Lizzie Borden in New Bedford, Massachusetts, among other major stories. (A later account of the trial of the
accused axe murderess describes Ralph as "possibly the most distinguished
newspaper correspondent at this time" [cited in Lancaster 234].) Historian
Frederick Jackson Turner was also at the Columbian Exposition, a triumphant celebration of the four-hundredth anniversary of Columbus's
landing in the Americas. There, Turner delivered a now-famous academic
talk in which he declared the frontier "closed." America had achieved the
great work of the postwar years, according to Turner, what Theodore
Roosevelt called "The Winning of the West." Turner and others were optimistic, even triumphalist, about the nation's progress through history.

Yet at the same time, the newspapers were filled with horrible news
about the American economy. The bad news started in the spring of 1893.
By summertime, stock markets had collapsed and financial panic ensued,
a result of overextension of railroad building and other capital investments.
The collapse initiated a serious and lingering economic depression, the
worst the country had seen up to that time.

The early 1890s were also a period of extraordinary labor strife. Convict
leasing, specifically by the Tennessee Coal, Iron, and Railroad Company
(TCI)—which Ralph praises in his article—was a factor in bringing mine
workers to a boil. In the summer of 1892, tensions climaxed in Anderson
County with a battle between state militia and free coal mine workers.
The closely tied steel industry was in turmoil, as well. That same summer,
the Homestead strike, near Pittsburgh, resulted in a gun battle between
Pinkerton agents and steelworkers that left thirteen dead. Other notable
labor events of this period include the Pullman strike of 1894 that launched
Eugene V. Debs to national prominence.

In his article, Ralph is mindful of the need to promote industry and
boost economic interests. He describes Chattanooga, for example, as "a
brown and white mound of smoke and steam" and refers to the "curtain of
smoke that hides the busy city." Though nature writer Bradford Torrey,
writing in Chattanooga at about that same time, disapproves of the air on

Lookout Mountain, the smoke in Ralph's account is meant to reassure readers in the grip of financial uncertainty. Ralph's article also includes the by-now obligatory, *Oxbow*-esque view of the Tennessee River—a half-tone reproduction of a graceful drawing, "Chattanooga and Moccasin Bend, from Lookout Mountain" (page 74). This is the gesture towards nostalgia and reconciliation, a calming image to help reassure people.

Ralph was, in fact, in Chattanooga at the invitation of Chattanooga's most influential business boosters: brothers Adolph and Milton D. Ochs. Milton was the managing editor of the *Chattanooga Times*. Adolph was the paper's publisher. (Adolph would go on in 1896 to acquire the *New York Times* and transform it into one of the world's best-known newspapers.) In Chattanooga, the brothers were pillars of the community, heavily promoting civic pride as well as outside investment in the region.

Chattanooga was, by the 1890s, one of the most visited tourist sites in the country, for a number of reasons. The railroads, the city's location on north/south and east/west crossroads, and the area's scenic values and moderate climate drew visitors from all over.

In addition, visitors were drawn by the historic significance of the Civil War battlefields on the high ridges above the city. During the war, in the fall and early winter of 1863, losses had been heavy on both sides at the dramatic and bloody battles of Chickamauga and Chattanooga. The Confederates won the battle in the fall, but a Union reversal in November set the stage for Sherman's march through the south by the following spring. Chattanooga was a violent turning point, and people remembered.

The Ochs brothers understood the significance of the "sacred ground" on Lookout Mountain. They purchased most of the land where the battles were fought and donated that land to the government as part of a plan to create the nation's first national military park, to be called the Chickamauga and Chattanooga National Military Park. The brothers also helped to coordinate a series of celebrations, including the dedication ceremony in September 1895, which was attended not only by federal dignitaries but also, more poignantly, by many former Union and Confederate soldiers. The reunion was widely covered in the national media, as emotional accounts of the ceremonies appeared throughout the national press.

Meanwhile, Ralph's article, which appeared in March of that year, was, like Bradford Torrey's series in the *Atlantic* a few months later, part of the campaign of national publicity focused on the region. The Ochs brothers helped to coordinate the publicity, and Milton even escorted Ralph around town, as Ralph relates in his article reprinted in this volume. In fact, much of Ralph's data about regional industrial development appears to have come from the Ochs's staff.

Ralph plays a role as civic and economic booster for the region against a backdrop of the ascendancy of monopoly industrial capitalism in its purest American form. Indeed, the year of Ralph's visit, the financial panic had created an opportunity for investors in the Tennessee Coal, Iron, and Railroad Company (TCI). The panic allowed investors to consolidate financially troubled holdings, pulling them together under the umbrella of TCI to create "the largest single holder of ore lands and furnace plants in the U.S." (Woodward 299). Not too many years later, TCI would become the linchpin in America's most complete "horizontal and vertical" monopoly, as J. P. Morgan's acquisition of TCI in 1907 completed his monopoly over the industrial resources of the eastern United States (Woodward 300–302).

—————

Unlike Julian Ralph, Bradford Torrey, writing for the *Atlantic*, appears to hold himself apart from the business of making money. Torrey is the author of "A Week on Walden's Ridge," a series of articles that appeared in the *Atlantic Monthly* the same year as Ralph's article. The first article from Torrey's series is reprinted in this anthology. Rather than visiting with civic boosters or participating in public pomp and ceremony, the refined, perceptive New Englander retreats to the heights of Walden's Ridge, beyond Signal Mountain (almost directly to your right, north, if you are the viewer of the picture on page 66). Torrey, among his other accomplishments, was the first editor of Henry David Thoreau's journals (1906). He identified with Thoreau and wrote and promoted the sort of aesthetic naturalism that is now considered the primary American literary tradition to emerge from the nineteenth century.

Torrey was in Chattanooga not for a cultural celebration, then, but rather to escape into a sensory experience of botanical, zoological, and topographical wonders. Yet, in a sense, the article reproduced in this volume completes the cultural work of reconciliation. Torrey's nature writing is a refiguring of the landscape. The last stronghold of Chickamauga resistance emerges as an unpeopled landscape of variegated natural forms. At the same time, Torrey writes with wit, charm, and a touch of mysticism. His careful observations of nature will appeal to the modern reader tutored in the tradition that Torrey himself helped to create.

In 1910, the Grand View Coal and Timber Company was organized in order to develop 32,000 acres on Walden's Ridge (Eller 108). Grand View's acreage included much of the area whose beauty Torrey describes so rapturously. The land company was formed to cut all the timber off of the ridge. Thus, the development process initiated by Harry Fenn's rendering of the grand views from the ridges above Chattanooga moved towards a conclusion with the help of an investment syndicate named, without any apparent intentional irony, Grand View.

David Hunter Strother and the Rise of *Harper's* Magazine

The literary monthlies such as *Atlantic* and *Harper's*—which came to be called the "qualities," to distinguish them from the grittier and less-literary weekly illustrated magazines and newspapers—would achieve their greatest influence during the postwar Gilded Age. But they began their rise in the 1850s. A key figure in the emergence of the illustrated monthly was David Hunter Strother—aka "Porte Crayon"—a writer and illustrator whose work is represented in this anthology. Aside from George Washington Harris, of Knoxville, Tennessee, Strother was the only southern Appalachian writer to gain a national audience before the Civil War. Strother's writing is charming and humorous, but the key to his success was probably his ability to draw.

Born into an influential Berkeley County, (West) Virginia, family, Strother received formal artistic instruction in Philadelphia while still a child. After a teenage apprenticeship, in his early twenties he embarked on a portrait-painting career. He toured through the Ohio Valley, completing thirty-seven paintings in little more than a year. Then he set off for his European "Grand Tour." During his travels abroad, Strother entertained family members with letters home. Unbeknownst at first to Strother, the letters were also forwarded to the *Martinsburg Gazette* and printed for the amusement of the town. *An amazing or terrible mother, I'm not sure.*

Strother's talent for portraiture, it turns out, was undistinguished. Nevertheless, he did become known among fellow artists in Europe for his spirited pencil sketches of street scenes and characters (Cuthbert and Poesch 14). Upon returning to America, he discovered his talents were best suited not for oil painting but rather for the newly emerging reproduction technology. Already in the 1850s, technicians had developed the technique of assembling boxwood blocks so that they could be carved by teams of engravers and set directly onto presses. Strother's style suited the medium. He learned quickly to copy his own sketches directly onto wood blocks.

As an added benefit, Strother's style was best suited to character sketches, in the mode of the "genre" paintings that were wildly popular among American purchasers of paintings in the 1840s and 1850s (Johns xi–xii). By the mid-to-late 1840s, Strother was earning regular, and remunerative, commissions for his woodcut book illustrations.

In the early 1850s, Strother traveled with family members on a series of hunting and fishing expeditions into the Virginia mountains, packing his sketching supplies along with his hunting rifle. In the spring of 1853, he toted the resulting portfolio to New York City, where he met with the editors of what would soon be the nation's most popular periodical, *Harper's New Monthly Magazine*.

Strother's combination of skills suited the editorial formula that the Harper brothers were developing. The magazine had started in 1850 as an "eclectic," reprinting mainly pirated texts from English authors. But by 1853 it was beginning to Americanize its content and to distinguish itself with a quantity of woodcut illustrations considered lavish for the time. The new editorial policies paid off. Circulation rose from 7,500 in 1850 to more than 100,000 in less than three years (Exman 12). When Strother proposed a series of illustrated travel articles, Fletcher Harper, the magazine's manager, listened. Strother was awarded a contract, and he returned to Virginia to write and to draw—and to attempt to do for the Shenandoah Valley what Strother's literary hero, Washington Irving, had done for the Hudson River Valley. Strother adopted the pen name "Porte Crayon" as a nod to Irving, whose famous *Sketch Book* was credited to the fictional author, "Geoffrey Crayon." (A *porte crayon* is a French crayon-holder for sketch artists.)

Strother's first *Harper's* series was published as "A Visit to the Virginia Canaan" (1853). Though his literary legacy would not turn out to be as lasting as Irving's, Strother's work was immediately popular. Soon after his series began, he was awarded a standing commission and became the magazine's highest paid contributor (Cuthbert and Poesch 31). Between the time his work first appeared and the start of the Civil War, the magazine's circulation rose from below 100,000 to above 200,000, an "unprecedented circulation for a three-dollar magazine" (Mott II 391), and an increase for which Strother must share some credit. Strother's contributions during that era included the seven-part series, "A Winter in the South," an installment from which is included in this anthology. And so it was that

Strother's popular accounts of travel in the southern mountains led him to become one of America's most <u>financially successful writers</u> in the 1850s.

lol.

Tourism Trends

Strother understood that the region was appealing because it was relatively unexplored by his magazine's northeastern audience. As his fictionalized landscape painter says, in the article reproduced here, "Perhaps I am splenetic, but I never could appreciate sights or endure countries that have been so inked over with dottings and jottings, etchings and sketchings— besmoked, besmeared, bedaubed, bepainted—gaped at and slavered over, by every litterateur, artist, and snob in Europe and America."

In fact, during the 1850s, tourism to southern Appalachia rose dramatically, not only among southerners, but also among northerners and international tourists. (See Richards's 1857 national guidebook, as an indication of how well established travel routes in the southern mountains had become by that time.) The rise was partly due to magazine articles such as those produced by Strother and also due to increasing population pressures in the northeast (Schwarzkopf 35–49). The Civil War, however, greatly reduced national and international travel to the region. Southerners continued to visit the mountains, to be sure—on those occasions when they could find the respite and the resources.[6] Soon enough, however, war and economic collapse cut tourism in the southern mountains down to a trickle.

Meanwhile, as tourism languished in the south, domestic tourism in the north continued increasing up until the war, and even maintained a level during the conflict. After the war, pent-up demand for leisure and enjoyment pushed mobs of tourists to destinations accessible to northeasterners—New Hampshire's White Mountains, the Catskills, the Great Lakes region, even the Adirondacks. Domestic travelers who wanted to distinguish themselves had to find someplace else to visit.

——— · ———

When Constance Fenimore Woolson began visiting the mountain region around Asheville, North Carolina, in the early 1870s, she understood that the region was poised at the beginning of an era of great development. Woolson made her living through magazine writing, and she chose her subjects carefully. Woolson's article entitled "The French Broad" (*Harper's*, April 1875), reproduced in this volume, is named after the high-altitude river in the upper Tennessee Valley whose waters flow through a gorge that forms the only break in the high ramparts around the Great Smoky Mountains. A railroad that was planned through the gorge would connect the Tennessee River drainage with the eastern seaboard. Woolson knew full well that when the railroad was completed, the transportation corridor would open up development and tourism. Woolson's thinly fictionalized narrator, Miss Martha, refers to the area around Asheville: "'And over and around all,' I added, 'is spread the most magnificent scenery to be found in the old States—scenery which has remained undiscovered, while the White Mountains and many minor groups are crowded with visitors and dotted with easels.'"

In fact, the scenery was not so undiscovered as Woolson's narrator suggests. By 1875 the region had already been featured at length—in the numerous *Appleton's* illustrated installments, already discussed here, as well as in Edward King's "Great South" series, which ran in *Scribner's* the year before.

Still, Woolson was ahead of the tourism crowd, though not by much. The increasing national interest in the southern mountains, along with the increasing population pressures on the east coast, would soon convert Asheville and surroundings into a popular tourist destination. By the end of the 1880s, George Vanderbilt—grandson of New York's Commodore Vanderbilt and partial inheritor of the latter's vast fortune—would vacation in Asheville and begin his plans for Biltmore Estate. The enormous estate, completed in 1895, is still intact today. Run by a private organization for the enjoyment of a paying public, it is a gorgeous decorative arts museum and has become, in effect, one of the nation's shrines to the decadence and leisure made possible by Gilded Age concentrations of wealth.

The Rise of the Female Magazinists

Writers in the west have long traveled to out-of-the-way places as a first step in establishing themselves in their profession. Indeed, the notion that a writer must travel is deeply embedded in transatlantic cultural traditions associated with mercantile capitalism. Consider the career of Alexis de Tocqueville. When Tocqueville and fellow nobleman Gustave de Beaumont traveled to America in 1831, both were young and both aspired to literary achievement. They came to America ostensibly to tour and report on prisons for a commission on prison reform. However, their actual goal was to see and write about the wilds of America (George Wilson Pierson 230).

In so doing, they were following a career track in the colonial tradition. Indeed, for Tocqueville and Beaumont, the career move paid off: both returned to France and built their subsequent professional lives primarily on materials they had gathered during their nine-month American journey. (Though not read today, Beaumont's romance novels about the new world, following the model of Chateaubriand, were well received. Tocqueville, of course, is still widely quoted—if not widely read. *Democracy in America,* his two-volume work of political theory, published between 1835 and 1840 and immediately translated into many languages, has never been out of print and was the basis for his professional life, though he never returned to America.)

By the middle of the nineteenth century, the opportunities for writing careers had expanded dramatically beyond those available for nobility and the transatlantic elite. The market for New York "quality" magazines such as *Harper's* and the *Atlantic Monthly* was increasing due to rising literacy and improving printing technology. This market, along with evolving professional roles, began to create opportunities for female travel writers.

Indeed, any number of reasons may help to account for the mid-nineteenth-century emergence of women magazinists. The women's movement in America had, by 1848, enough coherence to be represented in the Seneca Falls convention. Within the publishing industry, important individuals began promoting women writers. Annie Adams Fields, for instance, the wife of *Atlantic Monthly* editor James Fields, played a strong mentoring role to younger women and persuaded her husband in the 1850s and 1860s to open his magazine to such figures as Harriet Beecher Stowe, Celia Thaxter, Rose Terry Cooke, and others. Other women writers, notably Sarah Hale, Lydia Huntley Sigourney, and Ann Stephens, had editorial influence on various magazines and published their own work as well as promoting other women writers (Wood 9). Another reason for the rise of professional female magazinist at mid-century may have been, perversely, the fact that other occupations previously open to women actually began closing off to them at that time. As Ann Douglas Wood writes, "in many other occupations, . . . ranging from medicine to industry, the professionalization process which was taking place in the early nineteenth century imposed requirements which home-bound women simply could not meet" (7).

On top of all those other reasons, however, was the unstoppable, expanding market for print culture. Between 1860 and 1880, "a literary journalist's financial compensation tripled in the United States, and it became possible to earn a living entirely through authorship" (Tichi 11). At the same time, the market was growing specifically for writing about the south. The period from the early 1870s into the 1880s marked the end of Reconstruction and the beginning of what some southerners called

"redemption." Under any name, the period was marked by a frenzy of investment and resource extraction in south.

Stepping in to fill this market demand were talented and prolific writers such as Constance Fenimore Woolson and Rebecca Harding Davis, two
of the better-known writers whose work is reprinted in this anthology. As
the Gilded Age progressed, women were more and more perceived—with
some hyperbole, no doubt, but also with some justification—as dominant
in the literary culture of the magazines. Henry James may have been exag-
gerating when he wrote, in a review of Woolson's work in 1887, "The covers of American and English periodicals tell a . . . story; in these monthly
joints of the ladder of fame the ladies stand as thick as on the staircase at a
crowded evening party" (163). But the emergence of the postwar female
magazinists was an undeniable phenomenon. The women writers of the era
were not in the vanguard, as their prewar sentimental counterparts had
been. These second- and third-generation women writers were, rather, self-
conscious about their roles as professionals (Wood 12–13).

The tone of James's essay about Woolson—alternately praising and
dismissive—points to a tension that female professional writers experienced during this era. That tension is highlighted most interestingly in
this anthology by Rebecca Harding Davis, whose contribution is a fictionalized travelogue wherein two female characters journey into the southern
mountains. In the story, Mrs. Denby, a widow from the northeast, carries
an infant, her only child, to the heights of the Black Mountains, in the
hopes of reviving the child's health. The other female traveler, Miss Cook,
is a childless professional, a reporter for the New York papers. Miss Cook
quickly becomes the object of curiosity on the part of the mother: "This
tight little person, buckled snugly into a waterproof suit, her delicate face
set off by a brown hat and feather, talking political economy and slang in
a breath, was a new specimen of human nature to [Mrs. Denby]."

Though Miss Cook, the dynamic, snappily dressed female writer, initially appears as an attractive figure, she quickly becomes the object of distrust, until she emerges as an outright villain. In one scene, for example,
Miss Cook derives petty and selfish delight from the poverty of the mountain people:

> The house also was dirty and bare, but the table was set with
> fried chicken, rice, honey and delicious butter.
> "And how—how much are we to pay for all this?" said Miss
> Cook before sitting down.

"If ten cents each would not be too much?" hesitated the woman.

Miss Cook nodded: her very portemonnaie gave a click of delight in her pocket. "I heard that these people were miserably poor!" she muttered rapturously. "Don't look so shocked. If you earned your bread by your brains, as I do, you'd want as much bread for a penny as possible."

After Miss Cook's character is established in this way, she exits the story. Shortly after the scene described above, and only about a third of the way into the story, here is how she takes her leave: The widow, Mrs. Denby, who is naively awed by Cook's writing ability, asks if the writer won't stay in order to gather more "facts." Miss Cook responds with "cool superiority":

"Why child, I have them all now—got them this morning. Oh, I can evolve the whole state of society from half a dozen items. I have the faculty of generalizing, you see. No," folding up her papers decisively, "I've done the mountains and the mountaineers. Between slavery and want of railroads, humanity has reached its extremest conditions here. I should not learn that fact any better if I stayed a week."

If it weren't clear already, the audience learns here that Miss Cook is insensitive and callous, with no appreciation for family values. Beyond her role as a foil, however, the character has no purpose in the story. She turns out to be incidental to the plot and the main action. When she leaves, she is not missed. It is almost as if Davis needed to inoculate her audience against the common negative perceptions of the professional female writer before she—Davis, herself a female professional writer—could continue with her travel tale.

The work of female writers had a great influence on the development of the southern mountains. Davis, for example, published two major illustrated travelogues about the region for *Harper's* during the 1880s. The second of these series, especially, is straightforward "New South" propaganda, designed to convince northerners that the south was a good place to invest money. During this same period, New South proponents actively solicited the support of Davis's husband, Richard, the editor of a large northeastern daily newspaper (Rose 111–12). It seems likely that Davis knew that her work had the power to influence investment and development.

Frances Fisher Tiernan's work is not represented in this anthology, but it might well have been. Tiernan was from Salisbury, North Carolina, and wrote under the name Christian Reid. Tiernan was enormously prolific. One of her most popular works was serialized in *Appleton's* in 1875. Entitled "'The Land of the Sky;' or Adventures in Mountain By-Ways," it tells the story of a party of genteel, well-to-do travelers through the mountains. They socialize, pursue romance, and occasionally comment on pretty scenery, paying absolutely no attention to mountain inhabitants, nor to economic or social matters.

This publication marked the first appearance in publication of the phrase "Land of the Sky" to refer to the mountains of western North Carolina. The phrase is not used much today, but it caught on at the time among tourist promoters and tourists. A historian of Madison County writes, of Tiernan's serial, "This novel went into edition after edition, and was read in all parts of the country with an enthusiasm which modern readers may find hard to share. *'The Land of the Sky'* became adopted as an epithet by the whole tourist-courting mountain region. And tourists came more numerously than ever, to Warm Springs and other places, in hopes of seeing the mountain landscapes as Christian Reid had seen them" (Wellman 101–2). As late as the 1930s the term was still associated with a touristic view of the region (Federal Writers' Project, North Carolina 377).

"Local Color" and Other Literary Conventions

In the 1880s, a genre associated specifically with women rose to prominence: that is, the style that became known as "local color" fiction. Local color was not a movement in the conventional sense. It had no proponents or manifestos; the term emerged only in retrospect. But the trend that "local color" names is clear and well defined. Local color stories tend to focus on region, character, and dialect, at the expense of plot (much to the disparagement of later critics). Whatever its drawbacks, the style soon became the rage. Women writers such as Mary Murfree and Rose Terry Cooke, as well as men such as Mark Twain and Bret Harte, produced work that now goes under the heading "local color" and that was very popular during the period. One prominent early-twentieth-century American literary critic goes so far as to claim that the 1880s "stand for the complete triumph of dialect and of local color" (Pattee 307).

More recently, literary scholars have revived debates over the value, meaning, and cultural function of American local color. Many critics are interested in recovering this work for the literary canon, and they argue that the genre has been unfairly disparaged because of its association with females and femininity. (See Ammons and Rohy for an overview of this scholarship.)

Whatever the canonical status of local color, the relationship between it and travel writing is often overlooked. As Strother's contribution to this anthology shows, for example, there was already established, long before the term "local color *fiction*" emerged, a well-defined if overlooked tradition of thinly fictionalized travel writing in American popular magazines. Travel writers such as Strother employed overtly "literary" devices, including fictional characters and even third-person narrators. Entertaining though these writings were, they were also read for their documentary value. Strother, for example, in his "Winter in the South" series, provides drawings and descriptions of industrial sites and processes. Such materials were taken as records of economic and political affairs in the provinces. Indeed, this material is considered part of the documentary record by historians today. (Modern travelers today can follow the route Strother's party followed down what is now Spivey Creek, along Tennessee 36/U.S. 19W, into Tennessee from the North Carolina state line, and judge for themselves the veracity of his reporting).

Other writers in this section of the anthology perform the same genre-straddling act. Constance Fenimore Woolson's piece, for example, "The French Broad," uses literary and even dramatic staging conventions (the remark overheard from the balcony, for instance). At the same time, the article contains valuable travel information, about history, economy, geology. Though most often presented as the uninteresting dialogue in the mouth of a boring "professor" character, the background information is important, nonetheless. (See Berthold for a discussion of this technique.)

Rebecca Harding Davis's story reprinted here is more overtly literary than Woolson's (like Strother's article, it is narrated in the third person) and it contains less hard data, but is nonetheless based on a true story (Sheaffer 292). Another writer whose work appears in this anthology, Charles Dudley Warner, was a prominent figure in northeastern literary circles. His essay that is reprinted here does not use fictional devices per se. But it is "literary" in the tradition of the English essayists—sprinkled liberally with wit and satire, and essayistic literary conventions.

Discovering and Inventing the Mountaineer

While images of Appalachia played an important role in the rise of American literary magazines in the nineteenth century, the significance of that role has not been widely recognized—such, at least, is one of the arguments of this introduction. On the other hand, Appalachian studies scholars *have* long recognized the important role that the national media have played in developing images of Appalachia.

Scholars such as Henry Shapiro, David Whisnant, and James Klotter have studied the way southern Appalachia as a region was "discovered" in the national magazines in the nineteenth century. The word "discovered" usually appears in quotation marks in these discussions because the common argument is that the media actually *created,* through the machinations of representation, Appalachia as a distinct region. In other words, some scholars argue that the representation preceded and gave rise to the reality. This somewhat postmodern claim is the thesis, for example, of Shapiro's well-known book, *Appalachia on Our Mind: the Southern Mountains and Mountaineers in the American Consciousness, 1870–1920* (1978).

It is possible to overstate the postmodern aspect of this argument. After all, magazine writers clearly did not simply invent the region out of whole cloth. Certainly the region does have at least some basis for identity in its geography and topography. Late-nineteenth-century railroad maps, for example, show a relatively railroad-free area that corresponds roughly to what is now considered the center of southern Appalachia. (See, for example, the maps reproduced in Ayers, 10–11.) Railroads were late to the region because of topography, not because—or certainly not solely because—of the literary tropes developed in the national media. Nonetheless, it's also true that the *meaning* of the region, in the national consciousness, emerged and was defined in the national magazines.

Significantly, the large body of travel writing on Appalachia in the national press in the nineteenth century is almost completely lacking in what might be considered a "native" Appalachian voice from the period. The region is instead always defined by outside writers. Make no mistake: plenty of southerners wrote about the region. (In this volume, they include Allen, Cooke, Strother, Meriwether, Harney, arguably Rebecca Harding Davis.) But to southerners, the region appears just as alien as it does to the northern writers.

James Lane Allen is a case in point. Born on a farm outside of Lexington, Kentucky, the boy called "Laney" was eleven years old when the Civil War began. Though the family came from well-to-do tidewater Virginia stock, it suffered setbacks during the war. Circumstances required Laney to put himself through school at nearby Transylvania University. After graduating in 1872, Allen became a schoolmaster and then college teacher, at various regional institutions. However, he was barred from the top jobs because he had no Ph.D.

Another career avenue *was* open, however, to an aspiring literary man from Kentucky. At the northeastern magazines, there was work for a Kentucky writer who was good with a pen. Allen probably understood the economic forces involved, as he traveled the rails from Kentucky up to New York, in the late spring of 1884. He planned to spend the summer shopping himself around at the offices of various publishers. (By now, the trip to the editorial offices in New York, portfolio in hand, was obligatory for the aspiring professional.)

Allen was apparently well advised about the profession. He started at the top, visiting first the Franklin Square offices of *Harper's* magazine. The Kentuckian must have been awed by the urban bustle that flowed around the Harper's offices. Over those buildings loomed the Manhattan end of the Brooklyn Bridge. (The "Great East River Bridge" had opened for traffic only the year before.) In front passed the New York Elevated Railroad. Everywhere in the old business district surged the Victorian energy of America's great metropolis.

The record shows that Henry Mills Alden, manager of *Harper's,* was impressed by the Kentuckian in his office. Only a few months earlier, a collection of local color stories had been published by a literary man from Tennessee—at least, as far as Alden knew, the author was a literary *man* from Tennessee. In fact, Charles Egbert Craddock would not reveal to her *Atlantic Monthly* editors until the following year that her real name was Mary Murfree. In the meantime, though, Craddock had just published a collection of stories entitled *In the Tennessee Mountains*. That book was already proving to be the publishing sensation of the summer. To Alden, the mustachioed, square-jawed man in front of him was the very image of what he imagined Craddock to be: "a strapping six-foot Tennessean" ("Charles Egbert Craddock" 127). No matter that Allen was from Kentucky, not Tennessee. Another distinction lost on Alden was that Allen was from the Lexington area, not from the mountains.

Nevertheless, Alden told Allen that he liked his portfolio, but that the writer needed a professional focus, a literary identity—"the discovery of a definite field" (Allen, "Henry Mills Alden" 333). Alden suggested to the young writer that he make it his business to "interpret Kentucky to the Atlantic seaboard" (Knight 56). When Allen returned to Lexington from New York at the end of the summer, he was surprised to receive a telegram from *Harper's* ordering two papers about his home state. (Allen had been similarly well received in other offices around New York. By the time he received the *Harper's* telegrams, he had already contracted with the *New York Evening Post* to write about the Cumberland Mountains [Knight 56].)

The following spring, then, 1885, Allen set out from Lexington to satisfy his contracts. Traveling to Burnside by train, he rode hack (a hack is a sturdy, four-wheeled coach pulled by a team—what northerners of the period might have called a "mud wagon") then rented a horse, to complete the journey up through Pineville to the Cumberland Gap. Back in Lexington, he compiled his notes and submitted the results to fulfill the commission for *Harper's* (not for the *Post,* as originally contracted). The selection reprinted here is Allen's first major commissioned work, though another article, "The Blue-Grass Region of Kentucky," would appear first in print, in February 1886.

Allen went on to become a highly successful magazinist and novelist. Though his New York editors were interested in mountains, however, Allen was never comfortable writing about them. Out of an enormous volume of subsequent writing, Allen only returned once to the topic, for a minor article. Unlike the Bluegrass region, the mountainous southeast of his native state was utterly unfamiliar to him.

Indeed, for Allen, the difference between the Bluegrass and the mountains is the difference between the civilized world and the savage. From his first paragraph, in the selection reprinted here, Alden emphasizes the "distinctness" of the mountaineer and frames his article as a quest for "more knowledge of that peculiar and deeply interesting people, the Kentucky mountaineers." His mountaineers are backwards and uncurious, yet also invested with a primitive nobility:

> Straight, slim, angular, white bodies; average or even unusual
> stature, without great muscular robustness; features regular and
> colorless, unanimated but intelligent, in the men sometimes fierce,
> and in the women often sad; among the latter occasional beauty of

a pure Greek type; a manner shy and deferential, but kind and fearless; eyes with a slow, long look of mild inquiry, or of general listlessness, or of unconscious and unaccountable melancholy; the key of life a low minor strain, losing itself in reverie; voices monotonous in intonation; movements uninformed by nervousness— these are characteristics of the Kentucky mountaineers.

While to the editor from New York, people in Kentucky are pretty much all the same, to the writer from Lexington, the people in the mountains are their own type, a distinct, racialized "other." Allen's verbal portraits are reinforced by the prints of "genre" sketches by E. W. Kemble, which accompany Allen's article. (See, for example, the picture on page 255, entitled "Native Types.")

Some Appalachian studies scholars consider Allen's article the first explicit representation in the national media of a trope, an early version of what would later become the hillbilly stereotype that "still influences popular and academic thought" (Billings and Blee 29). Yet other writers in this anthology, southerners and northerners alike, engage in similar representations. Louise Coffin Jones, for example, writes for *Lippincott's* (December 1879) an account of her experience as a Reconstruction-era school volunteer with white Appalachians in the upper Yadkin Valley of North Carolina. In Jones's first encounter with her new hosts, she meets "Uncle Billy," a man in butternut homespun whose characteristic verbal mannerism is "he! he! he!" and who speaks thick dialect. Uncle Billy, it turns out, is of the "better class of the region." Jones also describes "the lower class, composed of 'poor white trash'": "The civilities, courtesies, even some of the decencies, of life were dispensed with; and as a relapse from culture is always more degrading in its influence and tendencies than a corresponding state of ignorance among a people who have never been elevated, so these degenerate Anglo-Saxons compared unfavorably with the native Indians, a few of whom still lingered in the mountains."

Rebecca Harding Davis, on the other hand, portrays mountaineers as a romantic caricature of the noble savage, the flip side of the image of the backwards primitive. So Davis writes, also for *Lippincott's* (July 1875), in her story reproduced in this volume, of the Yares, a fictional family of native inhabitants of the upper North Fork Valley of the Swannanoa River: "The Yares were, in fact, a family born with exceptionally strong intellects and clean, fine instincts: they had been left to develop both in utter solitude and without education, and the result as to manner was the grave self-control of

Indians and a truthful directness and simplicity of thought and speech which seemed to grow out of and express the great calm Nature about them as did the trees or the flowing water."

The question remains, in any event, whether there isn't something more going on here than just dismissive racist caricature. What is the cultural function of these images of mountain whites? Why is there such a large body of work, especially after the Civil War, that contains such representations? The same questions can be raised in regard to local color fiction of the period. Henry Shapiro's analysis of the function of local color fiction, then, could just as well apply to the travel literature. Here is Shapiro:

> The very "exotisme" of Creoles and Cajuns, of Southern moun-
> taineers singing old English ballads, of preindustrial New Eng-
> land seen from the point of view of the present was proof of the
> victory of nationalizing and homogenizing tendencies over the
> resistance of regionalism and diversity. The American local col-
> orists embraced the present and articulated for the nation a
> vision in which the past was merely quaint, the exotic merely pic-
> turesque. Comparison functioned not to point up failure but to
> acknowledge success.
>
> What provided the focus for the sketches of the American local
> colorists was never a contrast between alternative social or cultural
> systems, but rather a perception of the peculiarity of life in the
> "little corners" of America that they described. At most those areas
> "in the country and in those sections which have been least affected
> by the progress of a growing national unity" represented exceptions
> that proved the rule of the dominance of a national culture. (14–15
> [Shapiro here is quoting a sketch by Constance Woolson.])

In other words, the apparent fascination with diversity, with regional variation, is in fact assimilationist. The local color—and presumably the travel writing, as well—with all its depiction of peculiarities and regional differences, actually performs an homogenizing function. Shapiro goes on to write, "The lessons taught [by local color sketches of peculiar regional characters] were two: the monolithic character of modern, middle-class American culture, and the pastness of the past" (15).

Is the travel writing in this anthology really just performing an assim-ilationist function, an unintentional embrace of modernity? Readers are invited to judge for themselves. For, scattered throughout the racialized and even sometimes offensive descriptions of mountain whites, there is a good deal of lovingly rendered simple detail that often seems to defy the sort of analysis that Shapiro and others would apply. Jones, for instance— for all her stubborn dismissiveness, even occasional contempt for the mountaineer—writes engagingly and at times admiringly of mountain domestic life: food, cooking, family structure, divisions of labor, all emerge with a wonderful specificity in her article. Allen, for another example, carefully records unusual details of herb gathering and mountain economy. These details, in the writings in this volume, have a cumulative effect that suggests something beyond assimilation.

What Ammons and Rohy write about local color, then, may apply to the travel literature as well: "Local color has the ability to challenge and deconstruct monolithic national, imperial, and racial agendas. The sheer display of diversity offered by local color, for all the attempts to control and hierarchize it, speaks to a multicultural reality that defies homogenization and erasure" (xvii–xviii). So, too, the writers in this anthology often express, along with a perhaps unavoidable provincialism, an underlying attitude—call it a curiosity, an attraction to what's different. The attitude suggests at least a healthy ambiguity towards difference, heterogeneity, "otherness."

Native Types, Black and White

The writings in this anthology can be used, in any event, to trace the evolution of a stereotype about mountain whites that emerged during the period covered. The stereotype arose, at least initially, from the economic relationship between the financial and cultural urban centers and the rural south, especially after the Civil War. As already discussed, the American south was in a kind of colonial relationship with the northeastern and British financial centers. So the use of the term "native" to refer to mountain whites—in the picture on page 255, and elsewhere throughout this anthology—is significant. In the nineteenth century, the word "native" had strong connotations that it has largely lost in the twenty-first century. Historian Arnold Toynbee, for instance, explains how, in the Victorian mind, the word "native" referred to a subject people, usually nonwhite people, that had come under colonial rule (I 151–53). Such a view—of mountain whites as essentially nonwhite, inferior, and colonially subject—was common in postwar nineteenth-century America.

Consider an exhibit that appeared in the World's Columbian Exposition, in Chicago, in 1893. According to a catalogue of the fair, the "ethno-

logical grounds"—site of exhibits set up by the U.S. Department of
Ethnology—featured a display entitled "The Old Kentucky Home." This
was a "primitive log cabin," originally built in Kentucky, that had been
moved and reassembled in Chicago's White City. As the catalogue explains,
"the cabin is embellished with the old oaken bucket in the yard, the shuck
mat before the door and the leather thong to lift the latch" (Cameron 332).
This display was positioned between a replica of a Viking ship, on one side,
and a replica of the homes of the mysterious Indian "cave dwellers," on the
other. (The cave dwellers, vanished occupants of the McElm Valley of the
Colorado, had left behind "crumbling shrines" and only indirect clues of
their vanished civilization [Cameron 331].)

By equating the Kentucky mountaineer with Vikings, on the one
hand, and vanished Indian civilizations, on the other, the exhibit shows
something like the attitude already held by Louise Coffin Jones in 1879,
when she writes, in her essay about western North Carolina, reprinted
here, that "I had ample leisure to study the primitive manners and customs
of the people."

Nevertheless, group stereotypes are, of course, complicated phenomena. The mountain white stereotype was multifaceted, and at least some
historians argue that it was not as pernicious or detrimental as Shapiro and
others would insist. Nina Silber, for example, argues that by the end of the
nineteenth century, attitudes towards mountain whites had changed. Far
from being constructed solely as a marginalized "other," mountaineers
came to be understood as racially British ("Anglo-Saxon"). They in fact
came to be considered American to the core—more American than most
other Americans. Silber writes,

> Initially stressing the strange and alien qualities of this isolated
> population, northerners, by the 1890s, wrote of, read about, and
> helped to cultivate the truly American qualities of the southern
> mountain people. To a great extent, they helped to initiate and
> foster a pervasive mythology of southern Appalachia in which
> unadulterated Unionism, pure and upstanding patriotism, and
> undiluted racial purity became the hallmarks of the region's inhab-
> itants. At the same time, these myths of southern mountain life
> opened a new path for northern humanitarianism that was far
> removed from the disturbing racial and social conflicts that held
> the South in its grip during this troubling period of economic and
> political turmoil. (248)

As Silber suggests, part of the reason that mountain whites came to be considered a particularly *American* racial type had to do with the circumstances of blacks in the south. Immediately after the Civil War, northerners directed educational and reformist energies southward, to help freed blacks become enfranchised. However, as Reconstruction dragged on, and then ended ignominiously, the "race problem" began to seem intractable. New England reformers and third-generation abolitionists began directing their attention away from blacks and redirecting it towards the southern mountains. As a quasi-racial "native type," mountain whites appeared to need education as much as the blacks did. Unlike blacks, however, mountain whites did not serve as reminders of the unachieved goals of abolition. What's more, against the frightening backdrop of increasing Gilded Age immigration, the mountain whites of the south provided a soothing notion of racial purity and "Anglo-Saxonism" (Klotter 840). As a result, "the white people of the southern mountains, especially in what came to be known as 'Appalachian America,' became northern culture's cause celebre in the late nineteenth century" (Silber, "What Does America Need?" 248).

Beginning around the 1890s, the mountain south thus began experiencing the influence of what David Whisnant and other scholars of Appalachia would come to call the "uplift movement." As evangelical energies turned away from blacks and towards whites, national church and evangelical publications, including the *Christian Observer,* the *Home Mission Monthly,* and publications of the American Missionary Association, began publishing countless articles about Appalachia. In this volume, Margaret Johann's "A Little Moonshiner" serves as an example of this body of writing.

Scholars such as Whisnant are undecided about the effect that the uplift movement had on mountain whites. On the one hand, uplift efforts provided documented economic and social benefits. On the other hand, like many forms of charity and missionary work, the uplift efforts were patronizing and exacted a cultural toll.

Nevertheless, the treatment of mountain whites in the magazine writing of the time seems downright positive compared to the treatment accorded to blacks. Not only are the essays in this anthology filled with potentially offensive portrayals. "As we drove into Chattanooga," writes Bradford Torrey here, "it was impossible not to smile at the pinched and woebegone appearance of the colored people. What had they to do with weather that makes a man hurry?" Louise Coffin Jones, in reference to ghost stories about

Revolutionary War dead at a gravesite north of Greensboro, writes, "these superstitions had such a hold upon the minds of the negroes that not even for his freedom would one walk across the battle-field after dark." Other examples abound, throughout this anthology.

More pernicious than the stereotypes is the outright disinformation that appears in some of these articles. O. B. Bunce, for example, writes dismissively here of rumors of Ku Klux Klan activities in the south—this at a time when Klan violence had become so bad that, even as Bunce was enjoying Chattanooga in the spring of 1871, the U.S. Congress passed an anti-Klan bill giving the president power to place "rebellious" areas under federal control. Even Rebecca Harding Davis, whom twenty-first-century readers consider enlightened, seems to downplay the serious problems of race relations in the south. "Now one of the Ku-Klux would hardly go to milking cows," thinks the northern female protagonist of Davis's story.

Perhaps the most egregious example of disinformation appears in Julian Ralph's article. Ralph blames the postwar cotton economy on "the shiftlessness of the negro, which led him to favor cotton as the easiest crop to handle on shares and to borrow money upon." In effect, this amounts to blaming the victim for the sharecropper system—a system that has been called a continuation of slavery by other means. Likewise, Ralph remarks that "the labor in this great industrial section is mainly black, of course." Ralph is referring to the worst jobs in the iron industry—the digging of iron ore and the operation of furnaces. What he fails to note is that much of that labor was performed by convicts, leased from the state. Convict leasing, like the sharecropper system, has also been called an extension of slavery by other means. Negroes were often imprisoned for phony vagrancy charges, sent to labor camps, and never heard from again. As historian Matthew Mancini writes, working conditions for leased convicts varied, but were "usually awful and sometimes murderously so" (107).

W. E. B. Du Bois's essay that is reprinted here puts debates about local color and assimilation in a different light. Du Bois's perspective is African American, separated from white experience by what he calls "the Veil," a pervasive cultural divide between the two races. Yet he is also separated from the experience of southern rural blacks about whom he writes. In comparison to them, he is almost a Yankee. Raised in western Massachusetts, he attended Fisk at a time when that institution was in the business of "producing African-American versions of New England ladies and gentlemen," writes

Du Bois biographer David Levering Lewis, "Black Puritans or Afro-Saxons, as they were sometimes half-mockingly called" (60). *Frankenstein?*

By the time Du Bois returned to Tennessee to write this article, he had become a world traveler, educated at (Heidelberg,) a participant in the transatlantic culture of the Euro-American bourgeoisie of the period. In rural Tennessee, then, he is certainly encountering some kind of "other." His prose veers towards caricature at times. Of one family he writes, for instance, "They were never vulgar, never immoral, but rather rough and primitive, with an unconventionality that spent itself in loud guffaws, slaps on the back, and naps in the corner"—echoing some of the standard stereotypes of the period. At the same time, though, Du Bois writes about these people, "primitive" and "remote" as they are, with an undeniable love and tenderness. It's not just that his political agenda leads him to embrace a black identity—though that it does. ("There was among us but a half-awakened common consciousness, sprung from common joy and grief . . . and, above all, from the sight of the Veil that hung between us and Opportunity," he writes.) But beyond or perhaps through the trope of racial solidarity, Du Bois shows in his essay the possibility of reaching across some very wide cultural and historical divides. Here is a passage that only suggests his tone; it is an account of domestic arrangements with a large family in a one-room cabin—the type of arrangements that other writers in this volume treat with scorn or disgust: "At first I used to be a little alarmed at the approach of bed-time in the one lone bedroom, but embarrassment was very deftly avoided. First, all the children nodded and slept, and were stowed away in one great pile of goose feathers; next, the mother and the father discreetly slipped away to the kitchen while I went to bed; then, blowing out the dim light, they retired in the dark."

Yankee Hikers and the Origins of the Appalachian Trail

The obsession with types and characters—with "local color" or "people of color," as the regionalist writers of the time sometimes dubbed them, using the phrase to refer to mountain whites as well as to nonwhites—was, perhaps, the American literary phenomenon of the late 1870s and 1880s. Nevertheless, one contingent of American travelers was drawn to the southern mountains during this same period, not by rural types, and not by a desire merely to view mountains, but rather by an urge to explore the highest, most remote peaks in the east.

This group is represented by the Boston-based Appalachian Mountain Club—or the Appalachian Club, as members first called it. (Early members referred to each other as "Appalachians.") Formed in 1876, the AMC is a venerable organization that is still going strong today, promoting hiking and conservation and maintaining the Appalachian Trail and the "hut" system in New Hampshire's White Mountains. In the beginning, as now, the club consisted largely of urban or semiurban professionals. Its members tended to be knowledge workers: scientists, professors, teachers, ministers. The club was formed to promote "the interests of those who visit the mountains of New England and adjacent regions, whether for the purpose of scientific research or summer recreation" ("Introductory" 1). Club members balanced the interests of science and recreation, and also of art and representation, with the desire for exploration. The club had five Councillor positions in the early years: Councillor of Explorations, Councillor of Improvements, of Natural History, of Topography—and, interestingly, Councillor of Art (a position occupied at first by Charles E. Fay, who was also first president of the club).

AMC members initially focused their prodigious energies on "improvements." That mostly meant backbreaking work digging trail. Their trail systems in fact later became the basis for sections of the Appalachian National Scenic Trail—the Appalachian Trail, or "AT," as it is now often called. One writer of an essay reprinted in this anthology, Frank O. Carpenter, was a co-founder of the North Woodstock Improvement Association and in that role blazed what is now a section of the AT in the upper Pemigawasset Valley (Waterman and Waterman 231). The devotion of AMC members to improvements expressed a martial spirit and also a New England, post-abolitionist, reformist energy. Early members included prominently placed women, some of whom were noted for adventurous exploration (Waterman and Waterman 191).

Of the three selections in the final section of this anthology, two were written by members of the AMC—Dimmock and Carpenter. Both of those essays were published in *Appalachia,* the journal of the Appalachian Mountain Club, which is the only periodical represented in this anthology that did not enjoy wide circulation.

Nonetheless, though the circulation of *Appalachia* was limited, writers in the journal had a high degree of accountability. Members were required to read their papers to other club members prior to publication. The reports were delivered to an audience that included many who had already visited the southern mountains themselves. Indeed, though the journal was focused on the northeast, every one of its first twelve volumes contains at least one substantial account of a journey to the southern peaks. So club members formed a community of inquiry. These writers are specific about the conditions they encounter, the terrain they cross, the people they meet. They name names. Their accounts of travels and travails in the southern Appalachians are likely to have a high degree of veracity.

Little is known about Jehu Lewis, the author of the last essay in this anthology, though internal evidence suggests he grew up in New England. In any case, he shares the sensibility of the "Appalachians," those early AMC members. Like the other two writers in this section—and unlike other writers in this anthology—Lewis traveled to the summit on foot. He recounts traveling for a time through bear trails or "fauna corridors," tunnels created by game or wildlife through dense laurel undergrowth on high slopes. The mode of travel, as well as the motives, of the writers in this section may be shared by many who visit the southern mountains today.

Lewis and Carpenter both describe marvelous views from the summits they reached. Such vistas are, alas, no longer. Air pollution, as mentioned earlier, has permanently reduced visibility. Now, for thirty days or more per summer, the air quality in the Great Smoky Mountains is worse than that in Los Angeles ("Equal to L.A. . . ." A1). Mountaintop clouds in the Smokies and the Black Mountains are commonly as "acidic as vinegar ("Balsam Trail" 2; "Equal to L.A. . . ." A1). The reduced air quality is rooted ultimately in the desires expressed by those nineteenth-century seekers of scenery represented in this book. The drive to "civilize" and possess the landscape has resulted, ironically, in less scenery. At the same time, these articles provide the modern traveler with a different kind of vista, an historical insight into the development of the southern mountains whose high ridges may now so often be veiled by summer ozone haze.

SECTION I

On the Heels of the Cherokees

TOURISM AND DEVELOPMENT IN THE LOWER SOUTHERN APPALACHIANS

Sketches of Georgia

GEORGE COOKE (1793–1849)

HABERSHAM CO. – TALLULAH GORGE – TOCCOA FALLS –
MT. YONAH – CLARKESVILLE – DAHLONEGA – ATHENS GA

Born in Maryland, George Cooke made his living traveling about the south and east, under commissions to paint portraits, landscapes, religious subjects, and historical narratives. He traveled in Europe, 1826–31, where he met, among others, poet Henry Wadsworth Longfellow, who became a lifelong friend. In addition to the article below, Cooke wrote a three-part series of high-Romantic art criticism for the first volume (1834–35) of the *Southern Literary Messenger.*

In the unsigned article reprinted here, Cooke describes Habersham County and the town of Dahlonega, in north Georgia. This mountainous region was part of an independent Cherokee territory until gold was discovered in 1828. The discovery set in motion a series of events that led ultimately to the notorious "Trail of Tears," the forced removal of the Cherokees, which was finished by the summer of 1839. The following summer Cooke traveled to Habersham County in search of patrons among the wealthy who were already establishing vacation homes in the region. (See O'Donnell for more about the Cherokee removal and Cooke's work in the South.)

Southern Literary Messenger, November 1840.

In 1849 Cooke died in New Orleans. At the behest of his patron—Daniel Pratt, an Alabama industrialist who was born in New Hampshire—Cooke was buried in Prattville, in what is now the Daniel Pratt Cemetery, within the Pratt Historic District, Autauga County, Alabama.

HABERSHAM COUNTY, GEORGIA, *Sept.* 15th, 1840

My Dear Sir: I have at length reached this utmost bourn of Georgia—a *terra incognita* to the people of the United States—where the great Alleghany range of mountains terminates in a thousand isolated peaks and picturesque valleys, through which the dividing waters take their

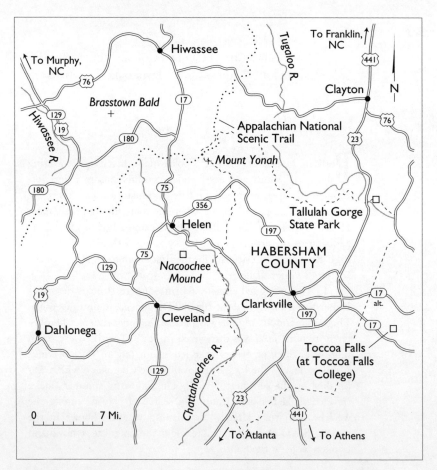

HABERSHAM CO. – TALLULAH GORGE – TOCCOA FALLS – MT. YONAH – CLARKESVILLE – DAHLONEGA – ATHENS GA, VISITED BY GEORGE COOKE, 1840

course, eastward and westward and southward. Here the Terrora Creek gushes forth, and, rending the granite hills, tumbles from cliff to cliff— forming the terrific cataracts of Tallulah—and winding its way amidst the wildest scenery, swells the current of the great Savannah, and blends its waters with the Atlantic Ocean five hundred miles south-eastward. In the same hill, and within a few steps, are the sources of the Chatahooche[1]— which, taking a south-westward direction, flow into the Gulf of Mexico at the distance of six hundred miles: and but three hundred yards from these, are the springs of the Highwassee[2] which run north-westwardly into the Tennessee, and, after a circuit of nearly a thousand miles, fall into the Ohio River. From this elevated point of land, I look down on the states of North and South Carolina, Tennessee and Georgia. To the north and west, mountains rise amphitheatrically, ridge behind ridge, until distance blends them with the azure vault of heaven. To the south, the broken fragments of the mountains lie scattered in heaps; and to the east, the alluvial plains descend to a boundless horizon, dark and blue as the sea, out of which rises the Stone Mountain in DeKalb County, like an isle in the midst of the ocean. To the geologist, nature here unfolds her secret laboratory in the deep chasm of Tallulah and the bold cliffs of Mount Yonah, rising two thousand seven hundred feet above the valley of Naucooche.[3] She invites the mineralogist to her richest arcana, where every rivulet sends forth its golden sands and gems abound, and veins yet unexplored. The lover of romance is invited here to wander amongst the scenes of adventure by "Guy Rivers",[4] and the pony club, the brigands of this Alpine region. But to the artist, and the admirer of the picturesque, these lofty hills and verdant vales, these yawning chasms and foaming cataracts, throw wide their varied beauties, and invite his wandering steps.

Toccoa,[5] or the beautiful Cascade, is indeed a scene of enchanting beauty, where fairies might dance by its sparkling light, and gem their robes with its pearly drops, or see themselves in its placid pool. It falls from the top of the Blue Ridge, in one unbroken sheet of water, twenty feet wide and one hundred and eighty-six in height, down a perpendicular wall, into a rocky basin, which it reaches in such dewy-drops as to leave unruffled the bosom of the reservoir, but fans the air with gentle zephyrs— and the ascending spray reflects an iris over the dark verdure of the embowered scene, where lofty elms mantle its beauty with a flickering veil, as if it were too modest for the vulgar gaze.

Tallulah[6] (or the terrible, in Indian parlance,) is a more masculine scene, bearing no more comparison with Toccoa, than would the Inferno of Dante with the Georgics of Virgil. It met our view, not with the smiles of its modest rival, but with the angry brow and hoarse murmurings common to the rougher sex. He looked defiance from his deep mote and granite walls, and came bounding by us, foaming and fretting in his furious course, to meet his gentle sister in the Tugalo.[7] The visitor in approaching this scene finds himself on the verge of a yawning chasm; down which he looks, perhaps a thousand feet, and near as many wide, cleaving the mountains for several miles. At one moment, he stands upon a projecting rock and clings to a stunted pine, whilst he peeps into the abyss below, where rocky ledges sustain a stately growth of forest-trees, or perpendicular cliffs extend to the bottom of the ravine. There, the water is caught into a basin of its own carving in the solid granite, and is then dashed down the precipice in the whitest foam, and whirled from side to side, meandering, until another fall engulfs it, and then another, until lost in the sinuosities of its own dark channel.

> "How profound
> The gulf! And how the giant element
> From rock to rock leaps with delirious bound,
> Crushing the cliffs, which downward worn and rent
> With his fierce footsteps, yields in chasms a fearful vent."[8]

I will not compare these falls with those of the Velino fountains,[9] which inspired the muse of Byron—for Terni combines the beauty of Toccoa with the sublimity of Tallulah;[10] but those who have seen the Natural Bridge of Virginia, may remember they are looking up a rent in the great globe, four times as deep, and ten times as wide as that spanned by the bridge, and not through a limestone formation; but the everlasting granite has yielded to the attrition of water, and laid open the bowels of this mundane sphere, where veins of purest quartz shine at the depth of a thousand feet. How came they there? What fires heaved up these mighty hills and filled them all with gold?

Mount Yonah is to Georgia as the Peaks of Otter to Virginia, but not so lofty. The view, however, from its summit, is as extensive, and very beautiful. The Unaka, or Smoky Mountain, in Tennessee, (here called the Blue Ridge,) may be seen in the north-west, rising like the clouds of a gathering storm—and around Mount Yonah on every side is the rich gold region, where this metal is found in the washings of the ravines, or in deposit upon a slate surface in meadow-lands, and in ore in veins of quartz. But the most pleasing object from this mountain, is the valley of Naucooche, through which the Chatahooche winds its way, skirted with verdant plains for many miles, and closed in between high hills, with here and there a farm-house. In the midst of this vale, there rises a mound[11] of which tradition has preserved this story. That in ancient times, the tribe of Indians calling this hunting-ground their own, were threatened with a sore calamity, which could only be averted by the sacrifice of the most precious object in the nation. The council assembled, and all eyes were turned to the bright and beautiful daughter of the Chief, Naucooche (the Evening-Star). But the offering must be voluntary. And the maiden came forth, not like Jeptha's daughter,[12] to welcome her victorious father, or like Iphigenia,[13] led as a lamb to the slaughter, but with heroic firmness mounted the funeral pile to make an atonement for her people—the victim of a superstition found among all Pagan nations. May it not have originated in the antiquity of that doctrine, "without the shedding of blood there is not forgiveness;" or in the promise of a seed that should bruise the serpent's head?

Habersham has become the summer resort of families from Augusta, Savannah and Charleston; and several gentlemen have purchased and are improving beautiful residences in these salubrious hills—and when the railroad shall be finished to Athens, within sixty miles of this place, I have no doubt that many will find it more agreeable to own little villas here, where they can enjoy the sweets of domestic life, rather than wander through the Northern States, or resort to the Virginia Springs. Already the frost has nipped the tender plants of the forest, and the mellow tints of autumn soften with purple hues the distant landscape. The gorgeous sun goes down in his chariot of gold, and the shades of evening close in with a warm fire, the hospitable hearth, the social circle, and the tale of adventures.

To the residents of Clarksville,[14] we are greatly indebted for many polite attentions; and their company in our excursions to the falls, the perils and adventures by the way, will be remembered amongst the most pleasurable hours of our lives. Indeed hospitality is characteristic of Georgia, and will compare with old Virginia in her palmy days. Everywhere we have met with a cordial reception, and that rare combination of polished politeness and undisguised sincerity.

We leave Clarksville this evening, and you shall hear from me again on my tour.

DAHLONEGAR, *Sept.* 18

The Cherokees called gold *tahlonega,* from which this place derived its name as the centre of the gold region. It is the county town of Lumpkin, and situated on a high hill, with others overlooking it, very similar in appearance to the convent of Valambrosa, in the Appenines;[16] from which, it is thought, Milton drew his description of Paradise.

> "Where Eden crowns with her inclosure green,
> As with a rural mound, the champaign head
> Of a steep wilderness, whose hairy sides
> With thicket overgrown, grotesque and wild,
> Access denied; and overhead up grew
> Insuperable height of loftiest shade,
> Cedar, and pine, and fir, and branching palm,
> A sylvan scene; and, as the ranks ascend
> Shade above shade, a woody theatre
> Of stateliest view."[17]

The surrounding country exhibits the appearance of "Ocean into tempest tost"[18] and suddenly congealed; and notwithstanding the sterility of the soil, a heavy growth of wood covers the steep acclivity and throws its dark shadow over the deep glen below—but scarcely a foot of tillable land can be found; and were it not for the hidden treasures of the mine, no human habitation would have intruded on the haunt of the wild-deer and wolf: but "nature abhors a vacuum," and supplies the deficiencies of every portion with an equivalent for what it has not—the rice field and the sea island supply provision and clothing for mankind—and the mountains supply him with mineral wealth and hygienic fountains.

This country, you know, was recovered from the Cherokees but a few years since; and that portion supposed to have gold, was divided by the state into forty acre lots, and disposed of by lottery to the people—each man and woman having one chance. As you may suppose, there was much variation in the value of these lots; but No. 52 was considered the El Dorado of the whole—and happy would that man be to whom it might fall.[19] The day came, and it was announced the portion of a poor man in Green County. Away went the speculators, Gilpin-like,[20] to gain the prize, and found the man ploughing in his field. He heard the glad tidings without emotion, and continued his ploughing; but when the offer rose to $30,000 cash, he sold it. In a few days $100,000 was offered, but the infatuated purchaser held on—and only awoke from his Utopian dream, by the ruinous discovery that No. 52 was one of the poorest lots in the region of Dahlonega. About three years since, the government established a branch mint[21] here, which coins about $120,000 annually, and probably as much more is sent away in bullion. The whole population is engaged in digging for gold; and the face of the country for many miles presents the appearance of new made graves, or like Pere la Chaise[22] after the three days revolution in Paris. The gold is found in deposit on a slate foundation: and sometimes the slate itself is rich with gold. These are called deposit mines, and are covered with a bed of pebbles or large stones, worn smooth by attrition, which must have been deposited there before the existence of any vegetable substance, for none is found below; but above them is an accumulation of alluvial many feet thick. The appearance of the gold when found, is as if it had been dropped in a melted state; but it is very probable it has been washed out of the fissures in the rock, and worn smooth by the continual action of water. It is found in the greatest abundance in the bed of the Chestatee River, by turning the current[23]—sometimes in large pieces weighing several hundred pennyweights; yet it is never found in such pieces, in the quartz veins. There, it is seldom visible to the eye: but when ground, yields from five to twenty dollars per day per hand. Whether these mines are to grow more productive, or work out, is a problem only to be solved by time; but if we are to judge from the experience of other mineral regions, the true wealth of this country is but indicated by what has been done.[24] This is the opinion of an experienced English miner here, to whom I narrated the disappointed hopes of the "Walton Company,"[25] and he assured me that it could not have been an entire deception, and that he has no doubt of there being a rich vein in that place.

ATHENS, *Sept.* 23

We arrived here last evening, and are again enjoying the hospitality of this truly Athenian people. I am now seated by the fireside of a friend, who would not allow us to remain at the hotel. We find the climate very little warmer than that we left in the mountains, and the atmosphere much dryer and more elastic. There has not been a case of fever[26] this year, and I am told that there never is any but such as may be traced to the grossest imprudence. You have therefore nothing to apprehend for our health; and as we shall remain here a month or more, and shall be at Milledgeville during the session of the Legislature, I may hereafter give you further sketches of Georgia scenes.

Dahlonega

(LETTERS FROM THE ALLEGHANY MOUNTAINS)

CHARLES LANMAN (1819–1895)

DAHLONEGA – LUMPKIN CO. – UNION CO. GA

Charles Lanman was born in the Lake Erie town of Monroe, in what was then the Territory of Michigan. His grandfather, James Lanman, of Norwich, Connecticut, was a U.S. senator from 1819 to 1825. When Charles was ten years old, he was sent east to live with the senator, so that he could be educated at the Plymouth Academy, near Norwich. At the age of sixteen, he entered an East India mercantile house in New York City. At the same time, he began his explorations of the eastern United States.

Lanman was a lifelong, adventurous traveler. He visited places that were remote at the time but later became popular tourist destinations. Over the course of his life, he found his way over the entire Appalachian range, from Georgia to the Bay of Fundy. He also traveled extensively through the Mississippi Valley and the Great Lakes and along the St. Lawrence. He was an enthusiastic sport fisherman and devotee of Izaac Walton. An entry in the 1932 *Dictionary of American Biography* claims that Lanman was also "one of the first to use the canoe as a pleasure craft."

While writing "Letters from the Alleghany Mountains," from which the present selection is taken, Lanman "rode with spring"; that is, he followed a route that parallels the southern half of what is now the Appalachian National Scenic Trail, working his way

Daily National Intelligencer, May 1848.

north as the weather warmed. His series of dispatches appeared in the whiggish *Daily National Intelligencer* in the spring and early summer of 1848, at a time when this Washington, D.C., newspaper was at nearly the peak of its influence. The exposure Lanman received from his series of articles helped him to obtain appointment to a War Department library position, from which he resigned in 1850 to become the private secretary of Daniel Webster.

Lanman was a prolific writer. In addition to a surprising amount and range of nonfiction—including *The Private Life of Daniel Webster* (1852) and *Dictionary of the United States Congress* (1859), both still considered valuable historical records—Lanman published at least five volumes of travel literature. *Letters from the Alleghany Mountains* was published in book form in 1849 and soon went through a number of reprints in England and America. It was also repackaged with other writings as part of *Adventures in the Wilds of America* (1854). Also notable is the fact that, early in his life, Lanman exhibited sketches and paintings from nature, and studied for a time under Asher B. Durand. Lanman lived the later part of his life in Georgetown, moving in Washington, D.C., political circles, securing various appointments—including one as American secretary of the Japanese legation—while continuing to travel, write, and paint.

DAHLONEGA, (GEO.) APRIL 20, 1848

The Cherokee word Dah-lon-e-ga signifies *the place of yellow metal*; and is now applied to a small hamlet at the foot of the Alleghany Mountains, in Lumpkin county, Georgia, which is reputed to be the wealthiest gold region in the United States. It is recorded of De Soto and his followers that, in the sixteenth century, they explored this entire Southern country in search of gold, and unquestionable evidences of their work have been discovered in various sections of the State. Among these testimonials may be mentioned the remains of an old furnace, and other works for mining, which have been brought to light by recent explorations.[1] But the attention of our own people was first directed to this region while yet the Cherokees were in possession of the land, though the digging of gold was not made a regular business until after they had been politely banished[2] by the General Government. As soon as the State of Georgia had become the rightful possessor of the soil (according to *law*) much contention and excitement arose among the people as to who should have the best opportunities for making fortunes; and, to settle all difficulties, it was decided by the State Legislature that the country should be surveyed and divided into lots of forty and one hundred and sixty acres, and distributed to the people by lottery. For several years subsequent to that period, deeds of wrong and outrage were practised to a very great extent by profligate adventurers who flocked to this El Dorado. In the year 1838, however, the Government established a branch Mint[3] at this place, since which time a much better state of things has existed in Dahlonega.

The appearance of this village, though not more than a dozen years old, is somewhat antiquated, owing to the fact that the houses are chiefly built of logs, and, having never been painted are particularly dark and dingy, but uncommonly picturesque in form and location. The population of the place is about five hundred. It is located upon a hill, and though the country around is quite uneven, having been deeply ravined by atmospheric agents,[4] when viewed in connection with the mountains, (some ten or fifteen miles off,) which seem to hem it in on three sides, presents the appearance of a pit to a magnificent amphitheatre. On approaching Dahlonega I noticed that the watercourses had all been mutilated with the spade and pickaxe, and that their waters were of a deep yellow; and having explored the country since then, I find that such is the condition of all the streams within a circuit of many miles. Large brooks (and even an occasional river) have been turned into a new channel,[5] and thereby deprived of their original beauty. And of all the hills in the vicinity of Dahlonega which I have visited I have not seen one which is not actually riddled with shafts and tunnels. The soil is of a primitive character, quite yellowish in color, composed of sand and clay, and uncommonly easy to excavate with the spade. Heretofore the gold ore of Lumpkin county has been obtained from what has been called the deposit beds, but the miners are now beginning to direct their attention to the veined ore, which is supposed to be very abundant in all directions. It is generally found in quartz and a species of slate stone. The gold region of Georgia, strictly speaking, is confined to a broad belt, which runs in a northeastern and southwestern direction from Dahlonega, which may be considered its centre. Several auriferous veins traverse the town, and it is common after a rain to see the inhabitants busily engaged in *hunting* for gold in the streets. That huge quantities are thus accumulated in *these* days I am not ready to believe, whatever may have been done in former years. I know not that any very remarkable specimens of gold ore have been found in the immediate vicinity of Dahlonega, but an idea of the wealth of the State in this particular may be gathered from the fact, that several lumps have heretofore been found in different sections, which were worth from five hundred to one thousand dollars. More valuable specimens have been found in North Carolina; but while Virginia, the Carolinas, and Alabama have all produced a goodly amount of gold, I have heard it conceded that Georgia has produced the largest quantity and decidedly the best quality.

And now with regard to the fortunes that have been made in this region. They are very few and far between. But, by way of illustration, I will give two or three incidents which have come to my knowledge. In passing, however, I may repeat the remark made to me by an intelligent gentleman, that the expenses of digging out the gold in this section of country had ever exceeded the gain by about one hundred per cent. Immense amounts of labor as well as money have been expended, and generally speaking, the condition of the people has not been improved; the very wealth of the country has caused the ruin of many individuals. The following story is a matter of popular history. After the State Legislature had divided the Cherokee Purchase into lots and regularly numbered them, it was rumored about the country that lot No. 1052 was a great prize, and everybody was on tiptoe with regard to its distribution by the proposed lottery. At that time 1052 *figured* in the dreams of every Georgian, and those figures were then far more *popular* than the figures 54 40 have been in these latter days.[6] Among the more crazy individuals who attended the lottery was one Mosely, who had determined either to draw the much talked of prize *or purchase it of the winner*, even though it should be at the cost of his entire property, which was quite large. The drawing took place, and 1052 came into the possession of a poor farmer named Ellison. Mosely immediately mounted his horse and hastened to Ellison's farm, where he found the child of fortune following his plough. The would-be purchaser made known the object of his visit, and Ellison only laughed at the impetuosity of his impatient friend. Ellison said he was not anxious to sell the lot, but if Mosely *must* have it, he *might* have it for $30,000. Mosely acceded to the terms, and in paying for the lot sacrificed most of his landed and personal property. The little property which was left him he was compelled to employ in working his mines; he labored with great diligence for several years, but he could never make both ends meet, for his mines were not at all distinguished for their richness. In process of time he was compelled to sell 1052 for what it would bring, and having squandered that remnant of his former wealth, he left the country for parts unknown, a veritable beggar. But, what is more singular than all, the present proprietor of 1052 is that identical man Ellison, who is annually realizing a handsome sum of money from the newly-discovered gold ore found in the bowels of his lottery lot.

Another instance of good fortune, unattended with any *alloy*, is as follows: Five years ago, a couple of brothers, who were at work upon the Georgia railroad, took it into their heads to visit Dahlonega and try their luck in the mining business. They were hard-working Irishmen, and understood the science of digging to perfection. They leased one or two lots in this vicinity, and are now reputed to be worth $15,000.

And now that it has come into my mind, I will mention another *lottery* anecdote, which was related to me by an old resident. By way of introduction, however, I ought here to mention that this region is famous for the number and size of its rattlesnakes, and that our hero had an utter abhorrence of the reptile. Among those who obtained prizes at the great drawing, before alluded to, was an individual from the southern part of the State, who drew a lot in this vicinity. In process of time he came to the north to explore his property, and had called at the house of a farmer near his land, for the purpose of obtaining a guide. In conversing with the farmer, he took occasion to express his dislike to the rattlesnake; whereupon the farmer concluded that he would attempt a speculation. Remembering that in going to the stranger's land he might (if he chose to do so) pass through an out-of-the-way ravine which abounded in the dreaded snake, the farmer beckoned to the stranger, and they took their way towards the ravine. After they had arrived at the spot, hardly a rod did the pedestrians pass without hearing the hiss of a snake or seeing its fiery tongue, and the stranger was as completely frightened as any one could possibly be by a similar cause. In his despair he turned to his companion and said:

"Are snakes as plenty as this *all* over the country?"

"I can't say about that, stranger, but one of my neighbors killed about a hundred last year, and I've hearn tell that your land is very rich in snakes."

"Now I ain't going any further in this infernal region, and I want to know if you have a horse that you'll give me for my land—gold ore, snakes, and all."

"I have, and a first-rate horse too."

"It's a bargain."

On the following morning, the stranger, like the hero of a novel, might be seen mounted on a Dahlonega steed, pursuing his devious pathway along a lonely road towards the south pole.

Of the uncounted gold mines which are found in this region, the most fruitful at the present times lies about twenty-five miles from here, in a northerly direction, and is the property of Mr. Lorenzo Dow Smith. And the success which has ever attended Lorenzo is worth recording. In a conversation that I had with him in this place, where he is now staying, I remarked that I should like to embody his history in a paragraph of my note book, and he replied to me as follows:

"I was born in Vermont; I came into this Southern country twenty-four years ago as a clock-pedler, where I drove a good business. I used to spend my summers among the mountains of the Cherokee country, partly for the purpose of keeping away from the fever, and partly with a view of living over again the days of my boyhood, which were spent among the Green Mountains. I made some money, and when the gold fever commenced I took it and went to speculating in gold lots, though I spent many years without finding lots of gold. I associated with bear hunters, and explored every corner and stream of this great mountain land, away to the north, and have seen more glorious scenery than any other live man. I'm forty years old, unmarried, love good liquor, and go in for having fun. 'Bout four years ago, it came into my thinking mug that there must be plenty of gold in the bed of Coosa creek, which runs into Coosa river. I traded for a lot there, and went to work. I found a deposit, gave up work, and went to leasing small sections, which are now worked by a good many men, and give me a decent living. I have had all sorts of luck in my day—good luck and bad luck. When I'm prosperous I always hope to be more prosperous still, and when I have bad luck, I always wish for worse luck—if it'll only come. I never allow myself to be disappointed. The longer I live the more anxious am I to do some good to my fellow-men. I've passed the blossom of my life, and I don't expect to live many years longer; I haven't lived as I ought to have lived, but I hope it'll be well with me when I come to take my final sleep. But enough. I'm going out to my mine on a visit to-morrow, and if you'll go with me, I'll show you some real Vermont trout, and mountain peaks which would shame the Camel's hump[7] of old Yankee land."

I did not accept Lorenzo's tempting invitation, but I made up my mind that he was an original. Some of the scenery to which he alluded I shall visit in due time.

In former times, as before intimated, the miners of this region were mostly foreigners and an abandoned race, but the principal deposits and veins are now worked by native Georgians, who are a very respectable class of people. Among them are many young men, who labor hard and are intelligent. The dangers of mining in this region are rather uncommon, owing principally to the lightness of the soil. Many of the accidents which occur, however, are the result of carelessness; and the most melancholy one I have heard of is as follows: A man named Hunt, together with his son and another man named Smith, were digging for gold on the side of a neighboring hill. At the end of a tunnel, which was some thirty feet long, they excavated a large cave or hall, which they had neglected to support in the usual manner. They apprehended no danger, but were told by a neighbor that their conduct was imprudent. The elder Hunt thought he would be on the safe side, and on a certain afternoon went into the woods to cut the necessary timber, while his son and Smith continued their labors in the cave. Night came on, and the father, having accomplished his task, retired to his home. On taking his seat at the supper table it came into his mind that his son and Smith were somewhat later in coming home than usual. He waited awhile, but becoming impatient, set out for the cave, and, on reaching it, to his utter astonishment and horror, he found that the roof of the cave had fallen in. The alarm was given, and the whole village was assembled, to extricate the unfortunate miners, and by the aid of torches the bodies were recovered. The boy was found in a running attitude, as if overtaken while endeavoring to escape, and the man Smith was found clinging to a single post, which had been vainly used to prop the ceiling of the cave.

With regard to the means employed by the miners I have but one word to say. The deposit gold is extracted from the gravel by means of a simple machine called a rocker, which merely shifts and washes out the metal. The vein gold is brought to light by means of what is called a pounding-mill, which reduces the rock to the consistency of sand, when the ore is separated by the use of quicksilver. In this particular department of their business the Dahlonega miners confess themselves to be comparatively ignorant; and what proves this to be the case is the fact, that some of their ore has frequently been worked over a second time with considerable profit.

But the prominent attraction of Dahlonega, I have not yet touched upon—I allude to *the Mint Establishment*. The building itself, which is quite large, has a commanding appearance. It was erected in 1837, at an expense of $70,000, and the machinery which it contains cost $30,000. It is built of brick, but stuccoed so as to resemble stone. It gives employment to nine men, who receive for their services, collectively, the sum of $12,000. The Superintendent, who also acts as Treasurer, is J. F. Cooper, (son, by the way, of the famous actor of that name;) the Coiner is D. H. Mason, who has a very interesting cabinet of minerals, and the Assayer is J. L. Todd. The Dahlonega Branch Mint and the one located at Charlottesville [*sic*],[8] North Carolina, are the only ones in the United States which coin the gold on the very spot where it is found. The New Orleans Branch, as well as the mother Mint in Philadelphia, are chiefly occupied with foreign ores. Of the two first mentioned, Dahlonega has thus far been the most successful, the coinage in one year having amounted to $600,000. At the present time, however, the business of this mint is said to be on the wane. The coinage of the three branch Mints mentioned above is uniform with that of the mother Mint, and it is all systematically tested there for approval. It thus appears that the whole establishment is a branch of the Treasury Department of the United States, and under the supervision of the Secretary of the Treasury, and an account of the progress and condition of the bureau is annually given to Congress.

The smallest amount of gold ore received at the Dahlonega Mint by law has to be worth one hundred dollars. When the miner has obtained a sufficient amount, he takes it to the Mint and delivers it to the Superintendent. That officer takes an account of it, and passes it over to the Assayer, who fixes its value, when the miner receives the allotted sum of money. The operation of coining is performed by the power of steam, and may be briefly described by the words rolling, drawing, cutting, and stamping. Some of the Dahlonega gold is said to be as pure as any in the world, but it is commonly alloyed with silver. One or two specimens were shown me, which were just one half silver: and yet it is said that silver ore is nowhere found in this section of country. The value of pure gold is one dollar per pennyweight: and I have learned since I came here that every genuine American eagle is made by law to contain one-twentieth of silver and one-twentieth of copper. The word bullion, which we hear so often mentioned among commercial men, is a misnomer, for it is legitimately applied only to unwrought gold, washed grains or gold dust, amalgamated cakes and balls, and melted bars and cakes; and the word ingot is applied to a bar of gold, which may be manufactured into two hundred half eagles, or one thousand dollars. To give a scientific account of what I have seen in the Dahlonega Mint would probably please my scientific readers, but, as I am not writing for them, they must excuse me. "What is writ, is writ; would it were worthier!"[9]

And now that I have been dwelling upon the origin of Gold, and the method of its transformation into coin, I cannot but cast a thought upon its moral power. It lies at the foundation of half the misery in the world; and yet, when judiciously employed, has power to rejoice the heart. It gave birth to the wonderful science of chemistry; and though one of the most ancient of metals, it always attracts the human eye by its beauty of color and texture. It dangles from the watch-fob of the old man, and glitters on the bosom of the young bride. For a little handful the sailor roams the stormy and soundless ocean, the mechanic toils at his bench or awl until the set of sun, and in some countries to the midnight hour; the merchant denies himself the pleasures of life; the politician quarrels with his fellow-men; and for this handful of beautiful dust, this Dah-lon-e-ga, does the poor author employ his brain. O Gold ! art thou not a strange magician—at once a curse and a blessing!

Three Important Characters:
1. The Narrator (Mr. Bonce)
2. His Companion (Mr. Fenn)
3. The Negro Preacher
4. The girl in the hotel

Three Important Places:
1. The town of Chattanooga
2. the Summit House
3. The City of Rocks

Three Important Events:
1. The ascent
2. The rain
3.

Three Important Ideas:
1. Rapid growth in the South (p.62)
2. Perceptions of Af. Am's
3. Personified Mountains

On Lookout Mountain

(WITH ILLUSTRATIONS BY HARRY FENN)

OLIVER BELL BUNCE (1828–1890)
HARRY FENN (1845–1911)

CHATTANOOGA – LOOKOUT MOUNTAIN – ROCK CITY TN

O liver Bell Bunce wrote popular histories, novels, and dramas. One of his plays, *Love in '76: An Incident of the Revolution,* first staged in New York in 1857, is still considered a notable if minor drama of the period. Yet Bunce's most influential work is *Picturesque America,* an illustrated book sold by Appleton, under subscription in forty-eight parts between 1872 and 1874. The book is now considered one of the most important American illustrated works of the nineteenth century. The following article first appeared in *Appleton's Journal* as the first of a two-part series about Chattanooga and surroundings. Both Chattanooga articles were reprinted, in slightly different form, with the same illustrations, in the first volume of *Picturesque America* under the title "Lookout Mountain and the Tennessee" on pages 52–70.

Bunce first worked in book production in the early 1860s, managing a small New York publishing house that produced illustrated gift books for the Christmas trade. There he developed his ability as a communications technology impresario—putting illustrators and writers together with teams of engravers and printers. After the war, he was hired on at the Appleton firm, one of New York's largest publishing houses at the time. By the end

Appleton's Journal, August 1871.

of the decade he was on the staff of *Appleton's Journal,* where he would
continue until the magazine's demise in 1878, first as an associate,
then as co-editor and chief editor.

Harry Fenn (1845–1911) was born in England and immigrated
to the United States during the Civil War. Trained in England as a
wood-engraver, Fenn established a national reputation as an illustrator by the end of the 1860s. His work was featured in *Picturesque
America,* as well as in *Appleton's* and other magazines.

It rained the first day we were at Chattanooga. It rained the second day.
The waters came down in ceaseless floods, and Lookout Mountain, with
its head buried in the mist, seemed, as seen from our hotel-window,
lumpish and uninteresting enough. "After all," said I, watching the
spiritless mass through the thick lances of rain, "Leigh Hunt was right.
A great mountain is a great humbug."

"Leigh Hunt was a Cockney,"[1] said mountain-loving Mr. Fenn;
"and *did* he use that word, 'humbug?'"

"No matter as to the exact phraseology," I retorted; "it is his
sentiment that I adore. A plague on your mountain! Look at it! A
huge, formless hump, a colorless, dead protuberance, that obstructs
rather than supplies a prospect! What is there about it, or of it, or in
it, that some men should come long distances to see it, and risk their
necks by climbing it?"

"People," replied my undisturbed companion, "who do not care for
the mountain for its own sake, care for its historical associations." "But,"
continued the philosophical artist, "wait until the rain ceases. Sunshine
will change your mood and your conclusions."

There was nothing, indeed, to do but wait. And Chattanooga, which
is dreary enough in the brightest sun, is forlorn beyond description in a
rain-storm. The town was denuded during the war of all its trees, a large
part of it was burned, and once it was buried up to its second-story
windows under the Tennessee. These things have not served to beautify
it. The streets are unpaved, and apparently un-worked; in wet weather
they are of unspeakable mud, in dry weather of indescribable dust, and at
all times they present a surface of ridges and chasms that make travelling
upon them a penance which one's bones long feelingly remember. The
principal business-avenue consists of little better than rudely-constructed
barracks; so, what with the bare and rude streets and the roughly-
constructed buildings, the place seems more like an extemporized

APPLETONS' JOURNAL

of LITERATURE · SCIENCE · AND ART

ENTERED, according to Act of Congress, in the year 1871, by D. APPLETON & Co., in the Office of the Librarian of Congress at Washington.

NO. 126.—VOL. VI.]   SATURDAY, AUGUST 26, 1871.   [PRICE TEN CENTS.

ROCK CITY, LOOKOUT MOUNTAIN (FRONT COVER OF *APPLETON'S* NO. 126). FROM OLIVER BELL BUNCE, "ON LOOKOUT MOUNTAIN." *APPLETON'S,* 26 AUGUST 1871.

mining-town of the far West than an old settlement of the East. But there is exhibited all the activity of a new colony; better buildings are rapidly going up; a fine new hotel has been opened; there are signs everywhere of prosperity and growth; and hence, if the Tennessee can only be persuaded to respect its legitimate boundaries, we shall find the town in good time a prosperous and possibly an agreeable place. At present there is very little that is interesting within its boundaries. There are several railroads, and many trains come and go; it is an extensive cattle-depot, and droves of horses and bovines ceaselessly fill the streets. The citizens are rather proud of their big new hotel, and they look upon Lookout Mountain with feelings of friendly interest; but I do not know that any thing delights them so much as reminiscences of the big flood that occurred about four years ago. They will show you the high-water marks with unsuppressed enthusiasm, and dwell upon the appearance of steamboats in their main street with an exhibition of pride that is very touching. But at present the town is a rude place; and it was one of its own citizens that said to us: "Yesterday I was watching a funeral-procession in our streets, and I really felt like thanking Heaven there was at least one way of getting out of Chattanooga!"

When the sun came out on the third day we set forth with all expedition for the mountain. During the regular season, which we had anticipated by a few weeks, coaches run at fixed intervals to the mountain-top, where two hotels give entertainment to all comers. As we were to remain several days on the mountain, our carriage was packed with all our effects, the most conspicuous object among which was Mr. Fenn's white sketching-umbrella, which, bound up with its iron lance-like handles, was always an object of curious speculation to beholders. I have no doubt more or less Ku-klux[2] suspicion attached to this queer-looking parcel during our entire sojourn in the South, and probably with just as much foundation as in case of many of the reports and stories current in regard to that mysterious if not mythical organization.

After a drive of about two miles, we began the long, sloping ascent of the mountain-road, and half an hour later found us, midway up the "formless hump," very much disposed, indeed, to beg the mountain's pardon for our depreciating criticism at the hotel-window. For now forms of the most varied and striking character revealed themselves in the cliffs and ravines of the mountain, and already superb prospects of the far valley and the winding Tennessee showed through glimpses of the trees. Above us hung beetling cliffs, which Mr. Fenn's pencil vividly delineates in one of the larger illustrations, while below us were precipitous reaches, here and there picturesquely marked by gigantic bowlders. I do not know but the best charm of mountain-views is in these half-glimpses that you catch in the ascent. If they do not possess the sublimity of the scene from the supreme altitude, they gain many beauties in the nicer articulation of the different objects below. The picturesque, moreover, is a little coy, and reveals itself more pleasingly in the half-glances through broken vistas than at the open stare. Our journey up the sides of Lookout was continually arrested by the charming pictures of this character that the winding road brought into view.

The first sensation of the prospect from the top is simply of immensity. The eye sweeps the vast spaces that are bounded only by the haze of distance. On three sides no obstacles intervene between your altitude and the utmost reaches of the vision. To your right stretch successive ranges of hills and mountains that seem to rise one above another until they dispute form and character with the clouds. Your vision extends, you are told, to the great Smoky Mountains of North Carolina, which lie nearly a hundred miles distant. The whole vast space between is packed with huge undulations of hills, which seem to come rolling in upon your mountain-shore, like giant waves. It is, indeed, a very sea of space, and your stand of rocks and cliffs juts up in strange isolation amid the gray waste of blending hills. Directly before you the undulations are repeated, fading away in the far distance where the Cumberland Hills of Kentucky hide their tops in the mists of the horizon. Your eye covers the entire width of Tennessee; it reaches, so it is said, even to Virginia, and embraces within its scope territory of seven States.[3] These are Georgia, Tennessee, Alabama, Virginia, Kentucky, North and South Carolina. If the view does in truth extend to Virginia, then it reaches to a point fully one hundred and fifty miles distant. To your left the picture gains a delicious charm in the windings of the Tennessee, which makes a sharp curve directly at the base of the mountain, and then sweeps away, soon disappearing among its hills, but at intervals reappearing, glancing white and silvery in the distance, like great mirrors let in to the landscape.

Lookout Mountain presents an abrupt precipice to the plain it overlooks. Its cliffs are, for half-way down the mountain, splendid palisades, or escarpments, the character of which can be altogether better conceived by the study of Mr. Fenn's drawings than by the most skilful word-painting. The mountain-top is almost a plateau, and one may wander at his ease for hours along the rugged, broken, seamed, tree-crowned cliffs, surveying the superb panorama stretched out before him in all its different aspects. The favorite post of view is called the "Point," a plateau on a projecting angle of the cliff, being almost directly above the Tennessee, and commanding to the right and left a breadth of view which no other situation enjoys. Beneath the cliff, the rock-strewed slope that stretches to the valley was once heavily wooded, but during the war the Confederates denuded it of its trees, in order that the approaches to their encampment might be watched. It was under cover of a dense mist that Hooker's men[4] on the day of the famous battle skirted this open space and reached the cover of the rocks beyond, up which they were to scale. The "battle of the clouds" is picturesque and poetical in the vivid descriptions of our historians, but the survey of the ground from the grand escarpments of the mountain thrills one with admiration. It is not surprising that Bragg believed himself secure[5] in his rocky eyrie, and the wonder must always remain that these towering palisades did not prove an impregnable barrier to the approach of his enemy.

On the summit of Lookout Mountain the northwest corner of Georgia and the northeast extremity of Alabama meet on the southern boundary of Tennessee. The mountain lifts abruptly from the valley to a height of fifteen hundred feet. It is the summit overhanging the plain of Chattanooga that is usually connected in the popular imagination with the title of Lookout, but the mountain really extends for fifty miles in a southwesterly direction into Alabama. The surface of the mountain is well-wooded, it has numerous springs, and is susceptible of cultivation. In time, no doubt, extensive farms will occupy the space now filled by the wilderness. There is a small settlement on the crest of the mountain, consisting of two summer hotels, several cottages and cabins, and a college. It is a grand place for study, and the young people of this sky-aspiring academy have certainly superb stimulants in the exhilarating air and glorious scenes of their mountain *alma mater*.

Only one of the public-houses was open at the time of our early visit to the mountain, but already the daily throng of visitors was large. People only came, however, for an hour or two; the regular summer crowds, who during the hot season sojourn among these lofty rocks, had given as yet no signs of their coming, and the principal hotel was closed and silent. The "Summit House," however, proved a pleasant little box. We were the only guests, and hence had choice of rooms, and first place in our landlord's affections. The sunshine that seduced us from Chattanooga only kept our company until we reached the mountain-top, when clouds began to obscure the scenery and winds to chill the air. Although nearly three days on the mountain, Mr. Fenn got his sketches with difficulty. There were glimpses of sunshine, and the clouds would lift and give us superb vanishing pictures of the valley and distant hills, touched in spots with sunlight; but the cold winds and the ever-recurring showers made sketching out-of-doors cold and dismal work. At the hotel we kept warm by means of blazing piles of logs, which a little negro lass of about twelve years kept continually piling upon the waiting andirons. To this diminutive daughter of Ethiopia we owe a world of thanks. The little creature was full of work, zeal, and affection; her big eyes had a melancholy contemplation, and her manner exhibited a motherly solicitude that was exceedingly amusing. We christened her after the immortal "Marchioness" of Dickens.[6] She seemed maid and master of all work. She waited on table, polished the boots, made the fires, helped cook the meals, as her regular duties, and then seemed never tired of watching over our comforts. At the first show of the sun in the morning, she entered our rooms and built up our fires for us, and the last thing at night was to heap the andirons with wood. The wind pierced through the thin timber frame of the house as if it had been pasteboard, and rendered fires at all hours necessary. The black "Marchioness's" especial ambition was to polish our boots. She promised each day they should be more brilliantly executed the next. "Won't have no more boots to black," was her mournful comment when we came to depart. "Why not?" was our reply; "there will be plenty of boots to black-in fact, too many, we should say." "No," was the inconsolable rejoinder, "people only come here to dinner. Nobody stays here all night. There will be no more boots to black," and with this lament upon her lips we left her. The spirits of Day and Martin will doubtless discover this polishing zeal, and shower benedictions upon her.[7]

The majority of visitors go to Lookout only for an hour or two, and hence miss some very striking characteristics of the mountain. There are a lake and a cascade of uncommon beauty about six miles distant from the "Point," and a singular grouping of rocks, known by the name of *Rock City*.[8] The City of Rocks would be a somewhat more correct appellation. This is a very odd phenomenon. Vast rocks of the most varied and fantastic shape are arranged into avenues almost as regular as the streets of a city. Names, indeed, have been given to some of the main thoroughfares, through which one may travel between great masses of the oddest architecture conceivable. Sometimes these structures are nearly square, and front the avenue with all the imposing dignity of a Fifth-Avenue mansion. But others exhibit a perfect license in capricious variety of form. Some are scooped out at the lower portion, and overhang their base in ponderous balconies of rock. Others stand balanced on small pivots of rock, and apparently defy the law of gravitation. I know of nothing more quaint and strange than the aspects of this mock city—silent, shadowy,

Lookout Mountain.—View From the "Point." From Oliver Bell Bunce,
"On Lookout Mountain." *Appleton's,* 26 August 1871.

LOOKOUT MOUNTAIN.—CLIFFS EAST OF THE "POINT." FROM OLIVER BELL BUNCE,
"ON LOOKOUT MOUNTAIN." *APPLETON'S,* 26 AUGUST 1871.

deserted, and suggestive, some way, of a strange life once within its borders. One expects to hear a foot-fall, to see the ponderous rocks open and give forth life, to awaken the sleep that hushes the dumb city in a repose so profound.

Our guide to this petrified city was a negro, who hung about the hotel to do chores, but solemnly announced himself as a Methodist preacher. As our journey was on a Sunday, we expressed our surprise that he should have been seduced from his sacred duties for the sake of the small lucre we could offer him; but he appeared to have satisfied his conscience, that, in serving the stranger, he was in some way doing a Christian duty. To our surprise we learned that he could neither read nor write. He drew texts from memory, and expounded upon them by the promptings of the spirit. White men, he said, had often come to hear him, and had praised his expositions greatly.

"But how do you manage about the hymns?" we asked.

"Why, you see, boss, I knows about fifty hymns—all by heart, sah—and I just thinks of one of them."

After all, it is not learning that supplies the founts of inspiration, or that fills the spiritual life of our being.

Lookout Mountain is remarkable generally for its quaint and fantastic rocks. Near the "Point" are two eccentric specimens that are pointed out to every visitor. The "Devil's Pulpit"—did one ever visit a mountain that had not borrowed Satanic phraseology for characterizing some of its features?—the "Devil's Pulpit," almost at the extreme end of the "Point," consists of a number of large slabs of rocks, piled in strange form one upon the other, and apparently in immediate danger of toppling over. The reader will readily discover this queer pile if he consults Mr. Fenn's drawing showing the view from the "Point." Another odd mass is called "Saddle Rock," from a fancied resemblance to a saddle. It consists of a great pile of limestone, that has crumbled and broken away in small particles, like scales, until in texture one may discover a likeness to an oyster-shell, and in form something of the contour of a saddle-tree. With queer rock forms, Lookout Mountain is certainly abundantly supplied. It is supposed that these rocks, jutting so far above the level of the Palisades, are remains of a higher escarpment, which, during uncounted centuries, has gradually worn away.

The lake and cascade to which I have referred are known as "Lulu Lake" and "Lulu Falls,"[9] *Lulu* being a corruption of the Indian name of Tullulah. The cascade is one of uncommon beauty. It is nearly as high as

Niagara, and far more picturesque in its setting. This lake and cascade can only be reached on foot or horseback; no vehicle can traverse the very rough road which leads to them. But their singular beauty, and the strange, quaint features of the City of Rocks, would reward unusual exertions on the part of the visitor. Lookout Mountain, indeed, is very imperfectly seen by those who make a hurried jaunt to its Palisades, glance at the prospect so superbly spread out before them, and then hurry back again. There is no mountain and no landscape that does not require its acquaintance to be cultivated somewhat, just as we must meet our friends in many intercourses before we can come to fully understand them. A mountain no more carries its beauty within the ready ken of everybody than a wise man "wears his heart on his sleeve for daws to peck at."[10] The supreme beauty, the varied features, the changing aspects, the subtle sentiments of the "rock-ribbed hills," enter the soul by many doors, and only after a complete surrender on our part to their influences. One can comfortably house himself on the great plateau of Lookout, and there give many days to wandering along its Palisades, or in search of the thousand picturesque charms that pertain to its wooded and rocky retreats.

Three Important Characters:
1. Narrator (Julian Ralph)
2. Dr. Milton Ochs
3. ——→ No other individuals

Three Important Places:
1. Lookout Mountain
2. Chattanooga
3. Sunset Rock

Three Important Events:
1.
2.   There aren't, really.
3.

Three Important Ideas:
1. Resources + Manpower
2. Civil War Mourning
3.

From "The Industrial Region of Northern Alabama, Tennessee, and Georgia"

JULIAN RALPH (1853–1903)

CHATTANOOGA – LOOKOUT MOUNTAIN TN

Julian Ralph was a newspaperman for the first part of his career, affiliated with the *New York Sun* during the 1880s. He began writing for magazines late in that decade, and by the early 1890s was among the most productive and well-known magazine writers in the country. He wrote for *Scribner's*, the *Century*, and *Scientific American*, among others, but was most closely affiliated with *Harper's Weekly* and *Monthly*.

In late 1893, Ralph visited Chattanooga and toured the region in the company of Milton D. Ochs, managing editor of the *Chattanooga Times*. Ochs's brother, Adolph, the paper's publisher, would go on in 1896 to acquire the *New York Times* and transform it into one of the world's best-known newspapers. Meanwhile, the Ochs brothers were both vigorous promoters of industry in the Chattanooga region. 1893 was a year of financial panic and stock market collapse in America. The early 1890s were also a period of extraordinary labor strife. (See Introduction for more about the political and economic contexts of Ralph's article.)

In this article, Ralph writes as a booster of industry. He also writes charmingly of the tourist industry, and of the photographer's business at the lookout. Volume 90 of *Harper's New Monthly*

Harper's New Monthly Magazine, March 1895

Magazine marked one of the first appearances of mass-reproduced half-tone prints of photographs, a technological development that led almost immediately to the demise of woodcut engraving prints. The half-tone reproductions satisfied a late-nineteenth-century desire for photo-realism, but are muddy and unappealing to twenty-first-century eyes and only a representative selection of the half-tones is reproduced here. (See pages 73, 74, 76, 79.)

One of the most remarkable curios in Uncle Sam's cabinet is Lookout Mountain, at Chattanooga, Tennessee. The traveller expects such occasional combinations of mountain and plain on the edges of the Rockies, the Selkirks,[1] and other great mountain chains, and yet it is doubtful whether any other as beautiful is to be found. For it has seldom happened that a tall mountain rises abruptly to interrupt and dominate a view so majestic and of such varied features. Glistening water, smiling farmland, forest, city, hill, and island, all lie upon the gorgeous and gigantic canvas of the Master Painter, who there invites mankind to his studio to enjoy such views as we had fancied only the stupid denizens of the air are privileged to dully scan.

To surfeit one's self with the wondrous changing, widening beauty of that splendid scene one does not have to consider the martial records that brave men wrote with their blood all over the foreground of the prospect. But when it happens that the spectator is an American whose soul has been stirred by the poor printed annals of Chickamauga and Mission Ridge,[2] the feast spread before Lookout Mountain ministers to the understanding the while it ravishes the eye.

In nothing is this wonder-spot more wonderful than in its accessibility. It is even more convenient to the tourist than Niagara Falls—almost the solitary great natural curiosity in our country for which one does not have to travel far and labor hard. In this case the grand view is one of the sights of Chattanooga, "the Little Pittsburg" of the South. The city enjoys it as a householder does his garden, by merely travelling to a back window, as it were, for the historic mountain is at the end of a five-cent trolley line. During half the year the tourist is even better served, for the railroads haul the "sleepers"[3] up the mountain-side in summer, and discharge the passengers on the very edge that divides *terra firma* and eagle's vision. Guided by Mr. Milton D. Ochs, of the Chattanooga *Times*, who could have offered a very wonderful view of his own from the towering pile in which that newspaper is housed, I took the trolley line during what the

[handwritten margin notes: "Compare to Bonner's initial description"; "Civil War mourning"]

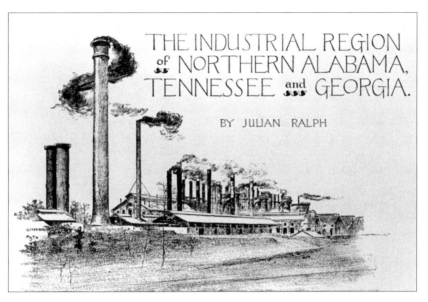

THE INDUSTRIAL REGION of NORTHERN ALABAMA, TENNESSEE and GEORGIA.

BY JULIAN RALPH

"THE INDUSTRIAL REGION . . ." [TITLE PLATE] FROM JULIAN RALPH, "THE INDUSTRIAL REGION OF NORTHERN ALABAMA, TENNESSEE, AND GEORGIA." *HARPER'S,* MARCH 1895.

Southern folk are pleased to call winter-time. The way led to just such a looking railway as one finds at Niagara Falls going down to the water's edge, though this one darts up the two-thousand-foot-high mountain-side, and is famed among professional engineers as a remarkable creation.[4] It was planned and built by Colonel W. R. King, U.S.A. It is 4500 feet in length, with an elevation of 1400 feet, and a grade of nearly one foot in three at the steepest place.

The terminus is the Lookout Point Hotel, which appears to stand upon a bowlder suspended over the remainder of creation, as if a mountain rising out of a plain had thrust out a finger and men had put up a building on the finger-nail. The biblical word-picture which tells of our Saviour being taken up on a high mountain and shown the kingdoms of the earth conveys the idea that the view from this point suggests. One can but have an idea of it, and it can only be expressed or described with a figure of speech. To be told that it commands 500 miles of the earth's surface, and that the most distant objects are parts of seven different States, is too much for the mind to master. What the eye takes in is a checker-board made up of farms, roads, villages, woods, ridges, and mountain ranges, all in miniature. The Tennessee River gladdens the scene. Though it is 1400 feet wide, it looks like a ribbon, and, like a

CHATTANOOGA AND MOCCASIN BEND, FROM LOOKOUT MOUNTAIN. FROM JULIAN RALPH,
"THE INDUSTRIAL REGION OF NORTHERN ALABAMA, TENNESSEE, AND GEORGIA."
HARPER'S, MARCH 1895.

ribbon thrown carelessly from the mountain-top, it lies in many curves
and convolutions, a dull green band everywhere fringed with a thin line
of trees that wall in the farmers' fields. You may count ten of its curves,
and three of them, immediately below the mountain, form the exact
shape of an Indian moccasin, around the toe of which a toy freight-train
crawls lazily with a muffled gasping out of all proportion to its size. A
brown and white mound of smoke and steam beyond the nearest farms
is pointed out as Chattanooga, and a rolling wooded region on the right
is spoken of as the bloodiest field of the rebellion—fearful Chickamauga.
The low dark green mound in the immediate foreground is Mission Ridge,
and between that and the curtain of smoke that hides the busy city a tiny
bit of yellow road is seen to disappear at a microscopic white gate, which
is the portal of a cemetery wherein thirteen full regiments of Northern
heroes lie—the blue who have turned to gray in the long embrace of
death—five thousand of them not remembered by name.

The rapid run by narrow-gauge road to Sunset Rock suggests a panorama in which the swiftly changing scene stands steady and the spectator whirls beside it. Coloradan views are strongly called to mind, but the memory of them is at a disadvantage, since here all nature is green and fertile instead of dead and burned. Here the land is peopled, and there it is deserted. And yet the mountain-side is precisely the same as if we were back in the Rockies, piled up with great gray rocks in mounds and giant fret-work. Sunset Rock itself is another finger or knuckle of the mountain, clinging to its side, yet seeming to hang in mid-air over the ravishing landscape far below. There are several minor battle-fields within the view from it, but at the first vantage-point the splendors of nature crowd the memories of the war out of the chief place in the mind. The charm that has made this rock the favorite rendezvous of the scores of thousands who journey to the mountain every year comes with the views at sunset when Phoebus's fires burn many-colored, and tint and tinge and illumine every distant object, from the lowly fields to the highest heavens, with slowly changing brilliant hues. I did not see it, and will not attempt a description of what I am assured is one of the most extravagant and splendid, almost daily, triumphs of nature. Let the reader imagine it, or go and be ravished by it. The stage-setting includes three ranges of hills, which even as I saw them in the early afternoon were rosy, green, and darkest blue, and behind the farthest of these the fire-god shifts his colored slides and throws his gorgeous lights from earth to sky.

Bridegrooms and beaux, and brides and *fiancees*—in a word, all lovers—make quite another use of Sunset Rock. There is a photographer there, and his exhibit of pictures shows him to be a modern Cupid, ever attendant upon Love. All around his show-room are photographs of the smitten, a pair at a time invariably, taken in the very act of being in love, seated side by side upon the gray insensate rock that juts above the diminished lands below. Each new couple that drifts along sees the portraits of all the others, and negotiations with the photographer follow close upon quick glances, hushed whispers, and coy giggling. Then out go the lovers to the rock, and out comes Cupid with his camera. He is a wag, this Cupid, for he says of his clients, "We git 'em in all stages of the disease." His collection easily divides the lovers into two classes—the self-conscious and the ecstatic. The self-conscious ones sit bolt-upright, a trifle apart, with glances fixed sternly upon nothing. The ecstatic lovers cling together, and look with sheep's eyes at one another or at Cupid. Sometimes the classes mix, and one sees an ecstatic bride leaning all her

Point Lookout, Lookout Mountain. From Julian Ralph, "The Industrial Region of Northern Alabama, Tennessee, and Georgia." *Harper's,* March 1895.

weight of love and charms upon a self-conscious groom, who frowns and pulls away. There are such pictures in the collection as would serve in a divorce court without a word of testimony on either side; but, thank Heaven, the ecstatics supply photographs that need only to be kept framed at home in order to banish discord as long as the wedded pair have sight to see how happy they had planned to be and were. Mingled discordantly with these trophies of the court of love are reminders of that class of idiots who would manage to desecrate a junk-shop if they were admitted to it. They have themselves pictured as flinging themselves off the dizzy rock; one has actually got his comrade to hold him by one too-servile trousers leg while he dangles head downwards over the precipice. That is a touch of nature that does not make the whole world kin.[5]

There are too many other points of interest on the mountain for mention here—curious freaks of nature and charming spots in abundance. It is several days' work to see them, but there are plenty of hotels and villa settlements there for those who have the time to enjoy the place in its entireness. Lookout Inn, a hotel that will accommodate three hundred boarders, is on the tip-top of the mountain, and has the reputation of being one of the very best hotels in the South. It is owned and controlled by a land and improvement company, and the principal stockholders are New-Englanders. The railways carry cars to its doors, and it is to be kept open all the year round. At the end of such a visit as I made the visitor simply tumbles back to the common-place earth on the inclined railway. The car is built in the form of an inclined plane, like the gallery in a playhouse with one side open toward the nether wall of rocks, and the other side glazed to command the marvellous view which seems to rise as the car descends, just as fairy views come up out of the stage in a transformation scene at the end of a Christmas pantomime. Then, suddenly, the car tumbles into a forest, and the only view is of the preposterous alley down which the vehicle is rolling like a ball sent back to the players in a bowling-alley.

My task here is to tell of something that lies under and in that mountain view of parts of seven Southern States, of something the eye cannot see except as a hint of it is thrown up in the clouds of smoke and steam that hang over Chattanooga. That something is the industrial awakening of the South, or more particularly of that part of that section where since the war the coal and iron buried in the rocks and soil now meet their resurrection in an activity that has connected Georgia with Pennsylvania.

[handwritten marginalia: Why is this relevant?]

[handwritten marginalia: Thread of suggested exploitation.]

A very sage writer[6] upon the industrial history of the South has shown that early in the century it promised to lead the other sections of the country, but slavery exerted the effect of humbling the artisan beneath the planter and the professional man in the general estimation. A wonderful agricultural prosperity was developed, and mechanical pursuits languished. Up to the time of the late war the South did not enthrone cotton. The South then grew its own meat and meal and flour. But after the war, when the most frightful poverty oppressed the region, the people turned to the exclusive cultivation of cotton, because that was the only staple that could be mortgaged in advance of the crop to give the planters the means of living until it could be harvested. The poverty of the planters, their dependence on the negro, and the shiftlessness of the negro, which led him to favor cotton as the easiest crop to handle on shares and to borrow money upon, were the causes of cotton's enthronement. Carpet-bag rule and the demoralization of the peculiar labor of the South added ten years to the period of Southern prostration, and it was not until 1880 that the present great industrial development of that section began. It is therefore a growth of a dozen years—a wonderful growth for so short a time.

Before the war there were a few small furnaces in this now busy district over-looked by Chattanooga's mountain, and formed of parts of Tennessee, Alabama, and Georgia. These furnaces were mainly on the Tennessee River and in eastern Tennessee, and the smelting was done with charcoal. The first coke furnace was established at Rockwood in 1868 with Northern capital on Southern credit.[7] The industry thus begun has continued to be the enterprise of Southern men, for such are the majority of the persons engaged in the business—men of the wide-awake commercial class. The Chattanooga district, so called, is in the centre of a region of coking coals and iron ores, embracing a circle of 150 miles in diameter, and covering parts of Tennessee, northern Alabama, and northern Georgia. It takes in one medium-sized furnace in northern Georgia and some smaller ones, which number nineteen, where there were none at all before the war. Its Alabama section—where there was no iron industry when the war closed, except at a few little furnaces built by the Confederates to cast their cannon—now boasts fifty-three large plants. In a word, the development has grown from the smelting of 150,000 tons of charcoal and coke irons in 1870 to the making of no less than 1,800,000 tons of pig-iron in 1889, '90, and '91. The steel industry is prospective. The name of the town of Bessemer is misleading.[8]

CHATTANOOGA FROM THE RIVER. FROM JULIAN RALPH, "THE INDUSTRIAL REGION OF NORTHERN ALABAMA, TENNESSEE, AND GEORGIA." *HARPER'S,* MARCH 1895.

Basic steel has been made in the district from the ordinary foundry ore, and has been tested by the government, and declared to be admirable. A mine of Bessemer ore has been worked at Johnson City, North Carolina [*sic*], but the capital for a steel-works to compete with those of the North has not at this time been obtained.[9]

Eighty per cent of the Tennessee iron is sold in the East, North, and Northwest—in Cleveland, Chicago, St. Louis, New York, and Philadelphia. It competes with the best foundry iron for stove plates and all sorts of foundry-work. It ranks with the best Lehigh product, and is the favorite iron with the pipe, plough, and stove makers of the East and North. Considerable foundry-work is done in the Chattanooga district. There are several stove-works there and some machine-shops that turn out both heavy and light castings. There are two large pipe-works (in Chattanooga and in Bridgeport), both owned by one corporation, and there is also in the district a very large establishment for the manufacture of railway-brake shoes and other goods.

The region in which the Chattanooga district is situated is a reach of bituminous coal and red hematite iron ore of limitless abundance that extends from Roanoke, Virginia, to Birmingham, Alabama. The coal crops out in West Virginia, crosses eastern Kentucky, where it is worked as pure cannel, semi-anthracite, and bituminous; crosses Tennessee through the Tennessee Valley to northern Alabama. It is a belt containing 26,000 square miles in three States, and everywhere the coal and iron accompany each other at pistol range. As an illustration, at Red Mountain, near Birmingham the Tennessee Coal, Iron, and Railway Company[10] gets coal on one side of a valley and iron on the other side. This great company has several plants, and made more than 400,000 tons of pig-iron in 1891. It has the largest coal plant in the Chattanooga district—one that has put out 600,000 tons of high-grade coking coal in a year. Its leading men are Southerners, and its capital is from the Northern States and England.

The labor in this great industrial section[11] is mainly black, of course. The negroes dig all the iron ore and do all the rough work at the furnaces. The coal is mainly dug by white men. The very great quantities of limestone that are quarried for smelting-flux and for building-work are taken out by negroes. It is found that with what is called "thorough foremanizing" the negro is satisfactory at these occupations. He needs strict and even sharp "bossing" to keep him at his work, and it has been found that to invest one of his own race with the authority of an overseer is to produce the strictest, even the savagest, kind of a boss.

The whole coal and iron region has suffered severely since the Baring failure in London.[12] During three years the price of iron fell from $12 to $14.50 and $15 a ton down to $8.50 and $7.75, by reason of excessive overproduction. Only the few companies that relied upon convict labor were able to make both ends meet at those prices, and it became painfully apparent that there is no decent profit in iron-making at a lower price than $10 a ton. The Southern industry suffered more severely than it should have done because not enough of the iron product was utilized in home manufactures. The transition from an agricultural to an iron-making district had been brought about too suddenly, and was allowed to go to an extreme point. The time was one of money-making in the iron industry, and the people were led to "booming" their new industry, so that nearly every one went into the manufacture of pig-iron, and too few into the conversion of it into manufactured goods. This will be fully understood when it is known that not a pound of hardware and not a pound of steel boiler plate is made in the South. Where there is room

ENTRANCE TO A COAL-MINE. FROM JULIAN RALPH, "THE INDUSTRIAL REGION OF NORTHERN ALABAMA, TENNESSEE, AND GEORGIA." *HARPER'S*, MARCH 1895.

for many large stove factories there are yet but a few small ones. But, as has been shown, the manufactures are started. Such changes[13] are brought about by one thing at a time, and already in addition to the works that have been mentioned there are large works in Chattanooga and in Atlanta for the making of ploughs and cane-mills, which contribute to a trade that already reaches into South America, the East Indies, and Australia.

The *Tradesman,* of Chattanooga, Tennessee, the leading authority upon Southern industrial affairs, published for its chief article in its

"Annual" for 1893 a paper by I. D. Imboden,[14] of Damascus, Virginia, which makes very bold and confident prophecies for the iron and steel industries of the South, and fortifies them with expert and official government reports. This is interesting and valuable, at least as showing how the leaders of opinion in the South feel upon the subject. He says that from his knowledge he forms a conclusion as strong as if it were mathematical that "the period is near when, as a group, the States of Virginia, North Carolina, Tennessee, Georgia, Alabama, and Kentucky will become the largest and most successful iron and steel producing district of like area in the world."[1]

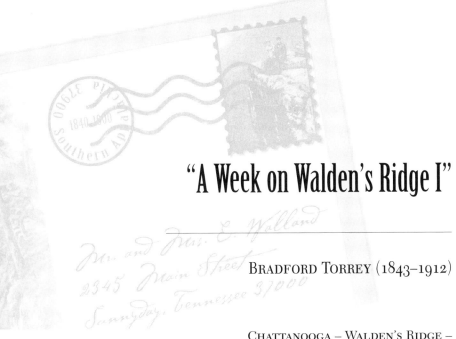

"A Week on Walden's Ridge I"

Bradford Torrey (1843–1912)

Chattanooga – Walden's Ridge – Signal Mountain – Fairmount TN

Born in Weymouth, Massachusetts, Bradford Torrey is perhaps best remembered as the first editor of Henry David Thoreau's journal, the fourteen-volume edition of which was published in 1906. A longtime admirer and promoter of Thoreau, Torrey also produced a considerable body of his own work—essays, nature writing, and literary criticism. His literary output, the equivalent of eleven books, is impressive given the fact that he earned a living as a businessman for the first half of his professional life and first appeared in print in 1883, when he was already thirty-nine years old.

Torrey visited East Tennessee in May of 1894, by which time he was writing in earnest. The resulting series of articles appeared in the *Atlantic Monthly* throughout 1895, when national attention was drawn to the region for a ceremony to designate the nation's first National Military Park at Lookout Mountain, near Chattanooga. The article reprinted here is the first of two entitled "A Week on Walden's Ridge." It was collected, along with other articles from the spring 1894 visit, as *Spring Notes from Tennessee* (1896).

Atlantic Monthly, May 1895

Another collection of Torrey articles about southern Appalachia is *A World of Green Hills: Observations of Nature and Human Nature in the Blue Ridge* (1894).

A frequent contributor to the *Atlantic Monthly* in the 1880s and 1890s, Torrey was a keen observer and earned a reputation as a naturalist. Though never formally trained as an ornithologist, he is said to have been "perhaps the world's foremost authority on hummingbirds" at the time of his death (Branch and Philippon 200). Towards the end of his life, suffering from ill health, Torrey moved to California, outside of Santa Barbara.

Throughout my stay in Chattanooga I looked often and with desire at a long, flat-topped, perpendicular-sided, densely wooded mountain, beyond the Tennessee River. Its name was Walden's Ridge,[1] I was told; the top of it was eighty miles long and ten or twelve miles wide; if I wanted a bit of wild country, that was the place for me. Was it accessible? I asked. And was there any reasonable way of living there? Oh yes: carriages ran every afternoon from the city, and there were several small hotels on the mountain. So it happened that I went to Walden's Ridge for my last week in Tennessee, and have ever since thanked my stars—as New England Christians used to say, in my boy-hood—for giving me the good wine at the end of the feast.

The wine, it is true, was a little too freely watered. I went up the mountain in a rain, and came down again in a rain, and of the seven intervening days five were showery. The showers, mostly with thunder and lightning, were of the sort that make an umbrella ridiculous, and my jaunts, as a rule, took me far from shelter. Yet I had little to complain of. Now and then I was put to my trumps, as it were; my walks were sometimes grievously abbreviated, and my pace was uncomfortably hurried, but by one happy accident and another I always escaped a drenching. Worse than the water that fell—worse, and not to be escaped, even by accident—was that which saturated the atmosphere, making every day a dogday, and the week a seven-day sweat. And then, as if to even the account, on the last night of my stay I was kept awake for hours shivering with cold; and in the morning, after putting on all the clothing I could wear, and breakfasting in a snowstorm, I rode down the mountain in a state suggestive of approaching congelation. "My feet are frozen, I know they are," said the lady who sat beside me in the wagon; but she was mistaken.

This sudden drop in the temperature seemed to be a trial even to the natives. As we drove into Chattanooga, it was impossible not to smile at the pinched and woebegone appearance of the colored people. What had they to do with weather that makes a man hurry? And the next morning, when an enterprising, bright-faced white boy ran up to me with a "Times, sir? Have a Times?" I fear he quite misapprehended the more or less quizzical expression which I am sure came into my face. I was looking at his black woolen mittens, and thinking how well he was mothered. It was the 19th of May; for at least three weeks, to my own knowledge, the city had been sweltering under the hottest of midsummer heats,— 94° in the shade, for example; and now, mittens and overcoats!

I should be sorry to exaggerate, or leave a false impression. In this day of literary conscientiousness, when writers of fiction itself are truth-tellers first,[2] and story-tellers afterwards,—if at all,—it behooves mere tourists and naturalists to speak as under oath. Be it confessed, then, that the foregoing paragraphs, though true in every word, are not to be taken too seriously. If the weather, "the dramatic element in scenery,"[3] happened not to suit the convenience of a naturally selfish man, now ten times more selfish than usual—as is the rule—because he was on his annual vacation, it does not follow that it was essentially bad. The rains were needed, the heat was to have been expected, and the cold, unseasonable and exceptional, was not peculiar to Tennessee. As for the snow, it was no more than I have seen before now, even in Massachusetts,—a week or two earlier in the month; and it lent such a glory to the higher Alleghanies, as we passed them on our way homeward, that I might cheerfully have lain shivering for two nights in that unplastered bedroom, with its window that no man could shut, rather than miss the spectacle. Eastern Tennessee, I have no doubt, is a most salubrious country; properly recommended by the medical fraternity as a refuge for consumptive patients. If to me its meteorological fluctuations seemed surprisingly wide and sudden, it was perhaps because I had been brought up in the equable climate of New England. It would be unfair to judge the world in general by that favored spot.

The road up the mountain—the "new road,"[4] as it is called—is a notable piece of work, done, I was told, by the county chain-gangs. The pleasure of the ascent, which naturally would have been great, was badly diminished by the rain, which made it necessary to keep the sides of the wagon down; but I was fortunate in my driver. At first he seemed a stolid, uncommunicative body, and when we came to the river I made sure he could not read. As we drove upon the bridge, where straight before his eyes was a sign forbidding any one to drive or ride over the bridge at a pace faster than a walk, under a penalty of five dollars for each offense, he whipped up his horse and his mule (the mule the better horse of the two), and they struck into a trot. Halfway across we met another wagon, and its driver too had let his horses out. Illiteracy must be pretty common in these parts, I said to myself. But whatever my driver's educational deficiencies, it did not take long to discover that in his own line he was a master. He could hit the ear of his mule with the end of his whip with a precision that was almost startling. In fact, it *was* startling—to the mule. For my own part, as often as he drew back his hand and let fly the lash, my eye was glued to the mule's right ear in spite of myself. Had my own ears been endowed with life and motion, instead of fastened to my head like blocks of wood, I think they too would have twitched. I wondered how long the man had practiced his art. He appeared to be not more than forty-five years old. Perhaps he came of a race of drivers, and so began life with some hereditary advantages. At all events, he was a specialist, with the specialist's motto, "This one thing I do."

We were hardly off the bridge and in the country before I began plying him with questions about this and that, especially the wayside trees. He answered promptly and succinctly, and turned out to be a man who had kept his eyes open, and, better still, knew how to say, "No, suh," as well as, "Yes, suh." (There is no mark in the dictionaries to indicate the percussive brevity of the vowel sound in "suh" as he pronounced it.) The big tupelo he recognized as the "black gum." "But isn't it ever called 'sour gum'?" "No, suh." He knew but one kind of tupelo, as he knew but one kind of "ellum." There were many kinds of oaks, some of which he named as we passed them. This botanical catechism presently waked up the only other passenger in the wagon, a modest girl of ten or twelve years. She too, it appeared, had some acquaintance with trees. I had asked the driver if there were no long-leaved pines[5] here-about. "No, suh," he said. "But I think I saw some at Chickamauga the other day," I ventured. (It was the only place I did see them, as well as I remember.) "Yes, sir," put in the girl, "there are a good many there." "Good for you!" I was ready to say. It was a pretty rare schoolgirl who, after visiting a battlefield, could tell what kind of pines grew on it. Persimmons? Yes, indeed, the girl had eaten them. There was a tree by the fence. Had I never eaten them? She seemed to pity me when I said "No," but I fancied she would have preferred to see me begin with one a little short of ripe.[6]

As for the birds of Walden's Ridge, the driver said, there were partridges, pheasants, and turkeys. He had seen ravens, also, but only in winter, he thought, and never in flocks. His brother had once shot one. About smaller birds he could not profess to speak. By and by he stopped the carriage. "There's a bird now," he said, pointing with his whip. "What do you call that?" It was a summer tanager, I told him, or summer redbird. Did he know another redbird, with black wings and tail? Yes, he had seen it; that was the male, and this all red one was the female. Oh no, I explained; the birds were of different species, and the females in both cases were yellow. He did not insist,—it was a case of a driver and his fare; but he had always been told so, he said, and I do not flatter myself that I convinced him to the contrary. It is hard to believe that one man can be so much wiser than everybody else. A Massachusetts farmer once asked me, I remember, if the night-hawk and the whippoorwill were male and female of the same bird. I answered, of course, that they were not, and gave, as I thought, abundant reason why such a thing could not be possible. But I spoke as a scribe. "Well," remarked the farmer, when I had finished my story, "some folks say they be, but I guess they ain't."

With such converse, then, we beguiled the climb to the "Brow,"— the top of the cliffs which rim the summit of the mountain, and give it from below a fortified look,—and at last, after an hour's further drive through the dripping woods, came to the hotel at which I was to put up—or with which I was to put up—during my stay on the Ridge.[7]

I had hardly taken the road, the next morning, impatient to see what this little world on a mountain top was like, before I came to a lovely brook making its devious course among big boulders with much pleasant gurgling, in the shadow of mountain laurel and white azalea,—a place highly characteristic of Walden's Ridge, as I was afterwards to learn. Just now, naturally, there was no stopping so near home, though a Kentucky warbler, with his cool, liquid song, did his best to beguile me; and I kept on my way, past a few houses, a tiny box of a post-office, a rude church, and a few more houses, till just beyond the last one the road dropped into the forest again, as if for good. And there, all at once, I seemed to be in New Hampshire. The land fell away sharply, and at one particular point, through a vista, the forest could be seen sloping down on either side to the gap, beyond which, miles away, loomed a hill, and then, far, far in the distance, high mountains dim with haze. It was like a note of sublimity in a poem that till now had been only beautiful.

From the bottom of the valley came a sound of running water, and between me and the invisible stream a chorus of olive-backed thrushes were singing,—the same simple and hearty strains that, in June and July, echo all day long through the woods of the Crawford Notch.[8] The birds were on their way from the far South, and were happy to find themselves in so homelike a place. Then, suddenly, amid the golden voices of the thrushes, I caught the wiry notes of a warbler. They came from the tree-tops in the valley, and—so I prided myself upon guessing—belonged to a cerulean warbler, a bird of which I had seen my first and only specimen a week before, on Lookout Mountain. Down the steep hillside I scrambled,—New Hampshire clean forgotten,—and was just bringing my glass into play when the fellow took wing, and began singing at the very point I had just left. I hastened back; he flew again, farther up the hill, and again I put myself out of breath with pursuing him. Again and again he sang, now in this tree, now in that, but there was no getting sight of him. The trees should have been shorter, or the bird larger. Straight upward I gazed, till the muscles of my neck cried for mercy. At last I saw him, flitting amid the dense foliage, but so far above me, and so exactly between me and the sun, that I might as well not have seen him at all.

It was a foolish half-hour. The bird, as I afterwards discovered, was nothing but a blue yellow-back, with an original twist to his song. In Massachusetts, I should not have listened to it twice, but on new hunting-grounds a man is bound to look for new game; else what would be the use of traveling? It was a foolish half-hour, I say; but I wish some moralist would explain, in a manner not inconsistent with the dignity of human nature, how it happens that foolish half-hours are commonly so much more enjoyable at the time, and so much pleasanter in the retrospect, than many that are more reasonably employed.

I swallowed my disappointment, and presently forgot it, for at the first turn in the road I found myself following the course of a brook or creek, between which and myself was a dense thicket of mountain laurel and rhododendron, with trees and other shrubs intermingled. The laurel was already in full bloom, while the rhododendrons held aloft clusters of gorgeous rose-purple buds, a few of which, the middle ones of the cluster, were just bursting into flower. Here was beauty of a new order,—such wealth and splendor of color in surroundings so romantic. And the place, besides, was alive with singing birds: hooded warblers, Kentucky warblers, a Canadian warbler, a black-throated blue, a black-throated green, a blue yellow-back, scarlet tanagers, wood pewees, wood thrushes, a field sparrow

(on the hillside beyond), a cardinal, a chat, a bunch of white-throated
sparrows, and who could tell what else? It was an exciting moment.
Luckily, a man can look and listen both at once. Here was a fringe-tree,[9]
a noble specimen, hung with creamy-white plumes; here was a magnolia,[10]
with big leaves and big flowers; and here was a flowering dogwood, not
to be put out of countenance in any company; but especially, here were
the rhododendrons! And all the while, deep in the thickest of the bushes,
some unknown bird was singing a strange, breathless jumble of a song,
note tripping over note,—like an eager churchman with his responses, I
kept saying to myself, with no thought of disrespect to either party. It
cost me a long vigil and much patient coaxing to make the fellow out,
and he proved to be merely a Wilson's blackcap, after all; but he was
the only bird of his kind that I saw in Tennessee.

On this first visit I did not get far beyond the creek, through the bed
of which the road runs, with a single log for foot-passengers. I had spent
at least an hour in going a hundred rods, and it was already drawing near
dinner time. But I returned to the spot that very afternoon, and half a
dozen times afterward. So poor a traveler am I, so ill fitted to explore a new
country. Whenever nothing in particular offered itself, why, it was always
pretty down at Falling Water Creek.[11] There I saw the rhododendrons
come into exuberant bloom, and there I oftenest see them in memory,
though I found them elsewhere in greater abundance, and in a setting
even more romantic.

More romantic, perhaps, but hardly more beautiful. I remember,
just beyond the creek, a bank where sweet bush (*Calycanthus*), wild ginger
(*Asarum*), rhododendron, laurel, and plenty of trailing arbutus (the last now
out of flower) were growing side by side,—a rare combination of beauty
and fragrance. And within a few rods of the same spot I sat down more
than once to take a long look at a cross-vine[12] covering a dead hemlock.
The branches of the tree, shortening regularly to the top, were draped
heavily with gray lichens, while the vine, keeping mostly near the trunk
and climbing clean to the tip,—fifty feet or more, as I thought,—was
hung throughout with large, orange-red, gold-lined bells. Their numbers
were past guessing. Here and there a spray of them swung lightly from
the end of a branch, as if inviting the breeze to lend them motion and a
voice. The sight was worth going miles to see, and yet I passed it three
times before it caught my eye, so full were the woods of things to look at.
After all, is it a poor traveler who turns again and again into the same path?
Whether is better, to read two good books once, or one good book twice?

A favorite shorter walk, at odd minutes,—before breakfast and between showers,—was through the woods for a quarter of a mile to a small clearing and a cabin. On a Sunday afternoon I ventured to pass the gate and make a call upon my neighbors. The doors of the house stood open, but a glance inside showed that there was no one there, and I walked round it, inspecting the garden,—corn, beans, and potatoes coming on,—till, just as I was ready to turn back into the woods, I descried a man and woman on the hillside not far away; the man leading a mule, and the woman picking strawberries. At sight of a stranger the woman fell behind, but the man kept on to the house, greeted me politely, and invited me to be seated under the hemlock, where two chairs were already placed. After tying the mule he took the other chair, and we fell into talk about the weather, the crops, and things in general. When the wife finally appeared, I rose, of course; but she went on in silence and entered the house, while the husband said, "Oh, keep your seat." We continued our conversation till the rain began to fall. Then we picked up our chairs and followed the woman inside. She sat in the middle of the room (young, pretty, newly married, and Sunday-dressed), but never once opened her lips. Her behavior was in strict accordance with local etiquette, I was afterward assured (as if all etiquette were not local); but though I admire feminine modesty as much as any man, I cannot say that I found this particular manifestation of it altogether to my liking. Silence is golden, no doubt, and gold is more precious than silver, but in cases of this figurative sort I profess myself a bimetallist.[13] A little silver, I say; enough for small change, at any rate; and if we can have a pretty free coinage, why, so much the better, though as to that, it must be admitted, a good deal depends upon the "image and superscription."[14] However, my hostess followed her lights, and reserved her voice—soft and musical, let us hope—for her husband's ear.

They had not lived in the house very long, he told me, and he did not know how many years the land had been cleared. There was a fair amount of game in the woods,—turkeys, squirrels, pheasants, and so on,—and in winter the men did considerable hunting. Formerly there were a good many deer, but they had been pretty well killed off. Turkeys still held out. They were gobbling now. His father had been trying for two or three weeks, off and on, to shoot a certain old fellow who had several hens with him down in the valley. His father could call with his mouth better than with any "caller," but so far the bird had been too sharp for him. The son laughed good-naturedly when I confessed to an unsportsmanlike sympathy with the gobbler.

The cabin, built of hewn logs, with clay in the chinks, was neatly furnished, with beds in two corners of the one room, a stone chimney, two doors directly opposite each other, and no window. The doors, it is understood, are always to be open, for ventilation and light. Such is the custom; and custom is nowhere more powerful than in small rustic communities. If a native, led away by his wife, perhaps, puts a window into his new cabin, the neighbors say, "Oh, he is building a glass house, isn't he?" It must be an effeminate woman, they think, who cannot do her cooking and sewing by the light of the door. None the less, in a climate where snow is possible in the middle of May, such a Spartan arrangement must sometimes be found a bit uncomfortable by persons not to the manner born. A preacher confided to me that in his pastoral calls he had once or twice made bold to push to a door directly at his back, when the wind was cold; but the innovation was ill received, and the inmates of the house, doubtless without wishing to hurt their minister's feelings,—since he had meant no harm, to be sure, but was simply unused to the ways of the world,—speedily found some excuse for rectifying his mistake. Probably there is no corner of the world where the question of fresh air and draughts is not available for purposes of moral discipline.

Beside the path to the cabin, on the 13th of May, was a gray-cheeked thrush, a very gray specimen, sitting motionless in the best of lights. "Look at me," he seemed to say. "I am no olive-back. My cheeks are not sallow." On the same day, here and in another place, I saw white-throated sparrows. Their presence at this late hour was a great surprise, and suggested the possibility of their breeding somewhere in the Carolina mountains, though I am not aware that such an occurrence has ever been recorded. Another recollection of this path is of a snow-white milkweed (*Asclepias variegata*),— white with the merest touch of purple to set it off,—for the downright elegance of which I was not in the least prepared. The queen of all milkweeds, surely.

After nightfall the air grew loud with the cries of batrachians and insects, an interesting and novel chorus. On my first evening at the hotel I was loitering up the road, with frequent auditory pauses, thinking how full the world is of unseen creatures which find their day only after the sun goes down, when in a woody spot I heard behind me a sound of footsteps. A woman was close at my heels, fetching a pail of water from the spring. I remarked upon the many voices. She answered pleasantly. It was the big frogs that I heard, she reckoned. "Do you have whippoorwills here?" I asked. "Plenty of 'em," she answered, "plenty of 'em." "Do you hear them right along the road?" "Yes, sir; oh yes." We had gone hardly a rod further before we exclaimed in the same breath, "There is one now!" I inquired if there was another bird here, something like the whippoorwill, meaning the chuck-will's-widow. But she said no; she knew of but one. "How early does the whippoorwill get here?" said I. "Pretty early," she answered. "By the first of April, should you say?" "Yes, sir, I think about then. I know the timber is just beginning to put out when they begin to holler."

This mannerly treatment of a stranger was more Christian-like than the stately silence of my lady of the cabin, it seemed to me. I liked it better, at all events. I had learned nothing, perhaps; but unless a man is far gone in philosophy he need not feel bound to increase in wisdom every time a neighbor speaks to him; and anyhow, that expression about the "putting out of the timber" had given me pleasure. Hearing it thus was better than finding it upon a page of Stevenson, or some other author whose business in life is the picking of right words. Let us have some silver, I repeat. I am ready to believe, what I have somewhere read, that men will have to give account not only for every idle word, but for every idle silence.[15]

The summit of the Ridge, as soon as one leaves its precipitous rocky edge,—the Brow, so called,—is simply an indefinite expanse of gently rolling country, thin-soiled, but well watered, and covered with fine open woods, rambling through which the visitor finds little to remind him of his elevation above the world. I heard a resident speak of going to the "top of the mountain," however, and on inquiry learned that a certain rocky eminence, two miles, more or less, from Fairmount (the little "settlement" where I was staying), went by that name, and was supposed to be the highest point of the Ridge. My informant kindly made me a rough map of the way thither, and one morning I set out in that direction. It would be shameful to live for a week on the "summit" of a mountain, and not once go to the "top."

The glory of Walden's Ridge, as compared with Lookout Mountain,— so the dwellers there say,—is its streams and springs; and my morning path soon brought me to the usual rocky brook bordered with mountain laurel, holly, and hemlock. To my New England eyes it was an odd circumstance, the hemlocks growing always along the creeks in the valley bottoms. Beyond this point I passed an abandoned cabin,—no other house in sight,—and by and by a second one, near which, in the garden (better worth preserving than the house, it appeared), a woman and two children were at work. Yes, the woman said, I was on the right path. I had only to keep a straight course, and I should bring up at the "top of the mountain." A little farther, and my spirits rose at the sight of a circular, sedgy, woodland pond, such a place as I had not seen in all this Chattanooga country. It ought to yield something new for my local ornithological list, which up to this time included ninety species, and not one of them a water-bird. I did my best, beating round the edge and "squeaking," but startled nothing rarer than a hooded warbler and a cardinal grosbeak.

Next I traversed a long stretch of unbroken oak woods, with single tall pines interspersed; and then all at once the path turned to the right, and ran obliquely downhill to a clearing in which stood a house,—not a cabin,—with a garden, orchard trees, and beehives. This should be the German shoemaker's, I thought, looking at my map. If so, I was pretty near the top, though otherwise there was no sign of it; and if I had made any considerable ascent, it had been as children increase in stature,—and as the good increase in goodness,—unconsciously. A woman of some years was in the garden, and at my approach came up to the fence,—a round-faced, motherly body. Yes, the top of the mountain was just beyond. I could not miss it. "You do not live here?" she asked. No, I explained; I was a stranger on the Ridge,—a stranger from Boston. "From Washington?" "No, from Boston." "Oh! from Boston!—Massachusetts!—Oh-h-h!" She would go part way with me, she said, lest I should miss the path. Perhaps she wished to show some special hospitality to a man from Massachusetts; or possibly she thought I must be more in danger of getting bewildered, being so far from home. But I could not think of troubling her. Was there a spring near by, where I could drink? "I have water in the house," she answered. "But isn't there a creek down in the valley ahead?" Oh yes, there was a creek; but had I anything to drink out of? I thanked her. Yes, I had a cup. "My husband will be at home by the time you come back," she said, as I started on, and I promised to call.

The scene at the brook, halfway between the German's house and the top, would of itself have paid me for my morning's jaunt. I stood on a boulder in mid-current, in the shadow of over-hanging trees, and drank it in. Such rhododendrons and laurel, now in the perfection of their beauty! One rhododendron bush was at least ten feet high, and loaded with blooms.

Another lifted its crown of a dozen rose-purple clusters amid the dark foliage of a hemlock. A magnolia-tree stood near; but though it was much taller than the laurel or the rhododendron, and had much larger flowers, it made little show beside them. Birds were singing on all hands, and numbers of gay-colored butterflies flitted about, sipping here and there at a blossom. I remember especially a fine tiger swallow-tail; the only one I saw in Tennessee, I believe. I remember, too, how well the rhododendron became him. Here, as in many other places, the laurel was nearly white; a happy circumstance, as it and the rhododendron went the more harmoniously together. Even in this high company, some tufts of cinnamon fern were not to be overlooked; the fertile cinnamon-brown fronds were now at their loveliest, and showed as bravely here, I thought, as in the barest of Massachusetts swamp-lands.

A few rods more, up a moderate slope, and I was at the top of the mountain,—a wall of outcropping rocks, falling off abruptly on the further side, and looking almost like an artificial rampart. Beyond me, to my surprise, I heard the hum of cicadas,—seventeen-year locusts,— a sound of which the lower country had for some time been full, but of which, till this moment, I had heard nothing on the Ridge.

As for the prospect, it was far reaching, but only in one direction, and through openings among the trees. Directly before me, some hundreds of feet below, was a piece of road, with a single cabin and a barn; and much farther away were other cabins, each with its private clearing. Elsewhere the foreground was an unbroken forest. For some time I could not distinguish the Ridge itself from the outlying world. Mountains and hills crowded the hazy horizon, range beyond range. Moving along the rocks, I found a vista through which Chattanooga and Lookout Mountain were visible. Another change, and a stretch of the Tennessee River came into sight, and, beyond it, Missionary Ridge with its settlements and its two observatories. Evidently I was considerably above the level of the Brow; but whether this was really the top of the mountain—reached, in some mysterious way, without going uphill—was more than I could say.

Nor did it matter. I was glad to be there. It was a pleasant place and a pleasant hour, with an oak root for a seat, and never an insect to trouble me. That, by the way, was true of all those Tennessee forests,—when I was there, I mean; from what I heard, the ticks and jiggers must be bad enough later in the season. As men do at such times,—for human nature is of noble origin, and feels no surprise at being well treated,—I took my immunity as a matter of course, and only realized how I had been favored when I got back to Massachusetts, where, on my first visit to the woods, I was fairly driven out by swarms of mosquitoes.[16]

The shoemaker was at home when I reached his house on my return, and at the urgent invitation of himself and his wife I joined them on the piazza for a bit of neighborly chat. I found him a smallish man, not German in appearance, but looking, I thought, like Thoreau, only grown a little older. He had been on Walden's Ridge for fifteen years. Before that he was in South Carolina, but the yellow fever[17] came along and made him feel like getting out. Yes, this was a healthy country. He had nothing to complain of; he was sixty-two years old and his doctors' bills had never amounted to "five dollar." "Do *you* like living here?" I asked his wife. "No," she answered promptly; "I never did. But then," she added, "we can't help it. If you own something, you know, you have to stay." The author of Walden would have appreciated that remark. There was no shoemaking to be done here, the man said, his nearest neighbor being half a mile distant through the woods; and there was no clover, so that his bees did not do very well; and the frost had just killed all his peach-trees; but when I asked if he never felt homesick for Germany, the answer came like a pistol shot, "No."

I inquired about a cave, of which I had heard reports. Yes, it was a good cave, they said; I could easily find it. But their directions conveyed no very clear idea to my mind, and by and by the woman began talking to her husband in German. "She is telling him he ought to go with me and show me the way," I said to myself; and the next moment she came back to English. "He will go with you," she said. I demurred, but he protested that he could do it as well as not. "Take up a stick; you might see a snake," his wife called after him, as we left the house. He smiled, but did not follow her advice, though I fancied he would have done so had she gone along with us. A half-mile or so through the pathless woods brought us to the cave, which might hold a hundred persons, I thought. The dribbling "creek" fell over it in front. Then the man took me to my path, pointed my way home-ward, and, with a handshake (the silver lining of which was not refused, though I had been troubled with a scruple), bade me good-by. First, however, he told me that if I found any one in Boston who wanted to buy a place on Walden's Ridge, he would sell a part of his, or the whole of it. I remember him most kindly, and would gladly do him a service. If any reader, having a landed investment in view, should desire my intervention in the premises, I am freely at his command; only let him bear in mind the terms of the deed: "If you own something, you know, you have to stay."

SECTION II

Vacation and Representation

WRITERS AND SKETCH ARTISTS IN "THE LAND OF THE SKY"

"A Winter in the South (4th paper of 7)"

DAVID HUNTER STROTHER - W.V.
["PORTE CRAYON"] (1816–1888)

BALD MT (YANCEY CO. NC) – SPIVEY CREEK
(UNICOI CO. TN) – JONESBOROUGH TN

David Strother, a painter and illustrator, became one of America's most financially successful writers in the 1850s. His popular travel articles about the American south—humorous, thinly fictionalized, illustrated pieces—first appeared in *Harper's,* and were mostly set in Appalachia. Strother was a Union officer in the Civil War. Though his most notable professional successes came before the war, he continued writing for *Harper's* into the 1870s. (See Introduction for more about Strother.)

Over the years, Strother's series for *Harper's* included "Virginia Illustrated" (1854); "North Carolina Illustrated" (1857); "A Winter in the South" (1857); "A Summer in New England" (1860); "Personal Recollections of the War by a Virginian" (1866); and "The Mountains" (1872).

The present selection is taken from "A Winter in the South," which appeared between September 1857 and December 1858. Here Strother adopts a literary device that he also used in his first series: the fictionalized, colorful party of travelers. The travel party here centers around one Squire Broadacre, "a Virginia Gentleman of fair lineage and good estate," and his wife, Mrs. Betty Broadacre,

Harper's Monthly, January 1858

BALD MOUNTAIN (YANCEY CO. NC) – SPIVEY CREEK (UNICOI CO. TN) – JONESBOROUGH,
ROUTE OF DAVID HUNTER STROTHER ["PORTE CRAYON"], C. 1857

and two daughters: Annette, eighteen, and Tiny, seven. Also in the
party are Leonore D'Orsay, the recently orphaned only daughter of
the Squire's sister; and Jim Bug, the Squire's "negro body servant."
Another character, Robert Larkin, is a stand-in for Strother himself.
Larkin is "a good-looking young fellow of twenty-five or older,"
whose relationship with the Broadacres is "indefinite," and who has
a "pretty talent for drawing."

In the installment that precedes this selection in the series, the
travelers set up headquarters in Jonesborough, Tennessee. Broadacre
and Larkin then ride off on horseback with a Tennessee guide named
Jones to see the highest mountains in the east. Jim Bug and the
women are left behind. As the present selection begins, the adventurers have already met with Tom Wilson, the famous Black Mountains guide, and have summited Mount Mitchell. On a return loop

through Burnsville, North Carolina, they are in a cabin, late one evening, as this installment begins.

———————

> "Good Ceres,[1] with her plump, brown hands,
> And wheaten sheaves that burst their bands,
> Is scornful of the mountain lands.

> "But mountain lands, so bare of corn,
> Have that which puts in turn to scorn
> The goddess of the brimming horn.

> "No lands of fat increase may vie
> With their brave wealth, for heart and eye,
> Of loveliness and majesty."

> P. P. COOKE.[2]

"It is astonishing," quoth Squire Broadacre, setting down his empty glass with an air of complacency, "how well I have borne these unusual hardships. What with my age and previous habits of life, I did not believe myself capable of such efforts; but, bless me, a man never knows what he can do until circumstances develop his powers."

The power of mountains to make you better.

"That is strikingly true, Sir," replied Larkin, demurely; "for who would have thought that we three could, by our unaided efforts,

AN INTERIOR. FROM DAVID HUNTER STROTHER, "A WINTER IN THE SOUTH," *HARPER'S,* JANUARY 1858.

have emptied this bottle of apple-jack at a sitting, and be none the worse for it?"

"Is it empty, Robert? God bless me; then we may as well go to bed."

Next morning, before the frost melted, our adventurers had bid adieu to Burnsville, and were on their way to the Bald Mountain[3] fourteen miles distant. This peak rises from the great ridge dividing North Carolina from Tennessee to a height but little inferior to that of its proudest neighbors. Its smooth, rounded, summit is covered with a rich growth of grass, and is entirely bare of trees; from which peculiarity it takes its name.

With the object of their journey in full view, our travelers rode rapidly along the mountain-road, discoursing pleasantly upon such subjects as were suggested by their surroundings.

"This country," said Larkin, "is certainly the grandest in its physical features that I have seen in the United States; yet by no means so savage and inaccessible as many other regions I have visited, where the elevation is much less; and while abounding in beauty and sublimity, in every element of the picturesque, the idea of sterility, the usual concomitant of mountain scenery, is not suggested here."

"On the contrary," said the Squire, "the mountains are covered with good soil and timber to their very summits; and where trees are wanting,

HARDSHIPS. FROM DAVID HUNTER STROTHER, "A WINTER IN THE SOUTH," *HARPER'S,* JANUARY 1858.

their place is supplied with fine summer pastures instead of arid and frightful rocks. The valleys and rolling hills between the great ranges appear to be well adapted to cultivation and cattle raising. There is another observation which I have made, also indicating a more genial soil and climate than belongs to our mountain regions farther north; that is, the extraordinary beauty of the children and young people we have seen. Have you not marked them, Robert?"

"Indeed I have, Sir, the girls especially; but I did not suppose you had been so observant."

"All extremes," continued the Squire, "are prejudicial to the perfect development of the human species. It is in the temperate zones that man attains his greatest perfection, and there always in that condition of life which is midway between hardship and ease, privation and luxury, and, to my eye, the greatest charm that any country can possess is a handsome, healthful and vigorous population.

> " 'Right hardy are the men, I trow,
>   Who build upon the mountain's brow,
>   And love the gun, and scorn the plow.
>
> " 'Not such soft pleasures pamper these
>   As lull the subtle Bengalese,
>   Or islanders of Indian seas.
>
> " 'A rugged hand to cast the seed,
>   A rifle for the red deer's speed,
>   With these their swarming huts they feed,
>
> " 'Such men are Freedom's body-guard;
>   On their high rocks, so cold and hard,
>   They keep her surest watch and ward.' "[4]

Mountains lead to hardy people.

"Those verses are very beautiful," said the Tennesseean, "and evidently written by one who drew his inspiration fresh from Nature, just such Nature as this by which we are surrounded. What themes for the poet lurk in these shadowy vales! how full of wild romance the history of the simple and hardy race which inhabit them!"

"Ah!" said the artist, "these mountains have a charm for me that neither Alps nor Apennines possess. One soon gets tired of the everlasting ice and snow, and sooner of the treeless, shrubless hills, and of castle-crowned rocks of Italy; but the sylvan beauty of these scenes, the glory of these virgin forests, hold my fancy with a power like fascination. Were

App mountains versus other mountains.

it not for the cold, and other engagements, I would wander about here for the next six months, and explore every part of this magnificent region."

"Nevertheless," replied the Tennesseean, "I have always entertained a great desire to see those castled rocks and snow-capped peaks of which you speak."

"Well," said Bob, thoughtfully, "they are, in truth, very grand, well worth seeing. Perhaps I am splenetic, but I never could appreciate sights or endure countries that have been so inked over with dottings and jottings, etchings and sketchings—besmoked, besmeared, be daubed, bepainted—gaped at and slavered over, by every litterateur, artist, and snob in Europe and America."[5]

"That sentiment," quoth the Squire, "is more natural than rational."

"And," said Jones, "it all only amounts to this—our friend don't admire cant: cant only disgusts us without affecting that which is intrinsic.

"'A thing of beauty is a joy forever.'"[6]

The horsemen reached the foot of the Bald Mountain about mid-day; but being entirely uninformed in regard to the neighborhood, they spent some time riding up and down in search of a guide. The first house at which they called was empty; and the next, about half a mile distant, although sufficiently populated with women and children, afforded them even less satisfactory information in regard to the object of their wishes.

At length they met a tall, wiry mountaineer, somewhat advanced in years; and on entering into conversation with him, ascertained that he was no other than Thomas Wilson, Senior, uncle to the sturdy pioneer of the Black.[7]

After some little hesitation, Uncle Tom consented to accompany them himself, and without more words they started on their way.

The ascent of the Bald, from the North Carolina side, is through an open forest; and after the savage scenes through which our adventurers had lately passed, it appeared to them a matter of no moment. It was accomplished without dismounting, and without an incident worthy of note. When they arrived at the edge of the open ground near the summit, the guide gave them some directions for descending on the western side; and, taking a friendly leave, returned from whence he came.

Left to themselves, our friends struck into a cattle-path, which led them by a circuitous route to the summit of the Bald Cone on the southern end of the mountain—its peculiar feature and highest point.

The panoramic view from this peak is similar in its general features to that obtained from the Roane;[8] but of this latter, the summit itself presents many points of grandeur and interest, with its dark groves of balsams, huge heaps of disjointed rocks, and frightful precipices; while the crown of the Bald is tame, and, instead of pictures, only affords good pasturage. In recompense for these defects, this knoll is furrowed with a rectangular ditch, or sort of intrenchment, of considerable extent, whose singular history invests it with peculiar interest. It is said to have been the work of one Davy Grier,[9] who went mad for love, fled from society, and lived a hermit on the side of this mountain, whose romantic life and death still furnish themes for the log cabin fire-side for a hundred miles around.

But the surroundings are too extensive for a sketch—too sublime for description. Our friends stood enjoying them in silence—now looking westward over the vast rolling plains of East Tennessee—now recognizing the Roane among his towering brothers to the northward—now glancing regretfully at the Black, whose peaks that day rose clean and clear against the eastern sky; then to the southward, from the magnificent valley of the French Broad, the soul, incapable of satiety, might quaff draughts of loveliness and grandeur, as it were, from a mighty bowl.

But it was long after mid-day, and the breeze cut sharper than a knife—so, leading their horses down the slope, they sought a place protected from the wind, and proceeded to refresh themselves with rolls and ham, the produce, as Squire Broadacre said, of their experience on the Black Dome.[10] This frugal repast concluded, they again mounted, and in a careless, rollicking manner, went in quest of the path by which they were to descend. The Squire took the lead, and under his guidance they rode for some distance along the open ridge without finding the object of their search. Now and then they were deluded by the appearance of cow-paths, which seemed to lead in the proper direction; but as these invariably terminated in a frozen lick or a laurel thicket, the bewildered travelers would return to the summit, after a disputatious consultation, to renew the fruitless search. As the sun was rapidly declining, and the icy north-wester hissed through the naked woods, these consultations at length degenerated into an open wrangle.

Mr. Jones declared that, if he had been consulted in the first place, they would already have been half-way down the mountain. Larkin swore that they had passed the place two miles back; that he had remarked it at the time, but no one chose to listen to him, although he knew more about mountains than any one else.

"I'll warrant you do," said the Squire, sharply. "Look you, youngster; you are my kinsman, and you came of an arrogant and conceited race— people who always knew more about every thing than every body else, and who would butt their brains out against a mountain rather than acknowledge an error."

"All true enough," retorted Larkin; "and, unfortunately, age, instead of curing, rather increases the family peculiarity."

Here the Squire began to thrash his horse, and the Tennesseean spoke up:

"Gentlemen, the heat of your argument will scarcely prevent our freezing if we remain here. We must adopt some plan of action, and that right speedily. See, the sun is setting."

The Squire's steed, impatient of the unmerited blows, had carried him under the branches of a scrub oak, which scraped his hat off. The old gentleman regarded his fallen head-gear with a look of direst vexation, and with an audible groan prepared to dismount. Before he could do so, however, Larkin sprung to the ground and politely handed him the hat.

"Gentlemen," continued Mr. Jones, "hear what I have to propose. As we ascended, the sides of the mountain appeared to be quite practicable, free from rocks and undergrowth; now let us take a free path down, and trust to fortune for the result."

"That is bold counsel, and timely," said the Squire. "Lead on!"

The last gleam of sunlight shone upon the weather-beaten and determined faces of the three travelers as they started down the steep mountain side, dodging the limbs of the dwarf oaks, and with whip and rein warily urging their horses over the loose and moss-covered rocks.

For half a mile or more they pursued their zigzag course without meeting with any serious obstacle. Soon, however, the hill-side grew steeper, and was furrowed with deep-washed gullies, half filled with ice and snow. Dark thickets of rhododendron were visible in every direction through the trees, while impenetrable abattis of fallen timber effectually closed the passages between the ravines. The horses were already panting from exhaustion, while the horsemen were wet with toil and vexation. In attempting to cross a deep gully the Squire's horse lost his footing, and with his rider went crashing into a briery thicket. By Larkin's ready aid both man and beast were presently rescued without damage.

"Bob," said the old man, "I knew your father well. The Larkins were a spirited race; and always showed best in times of trouble and danger."

It soon became manifest that such times were at hand. Precipitous ledges of rock were now seen towering above the trees, their dark faces grinning with icicles; the ravines had increased in size and depth until they were impassable. Between, a steep stair-way of loose, angular rocks, rendered more slippery and dangerous by a crust of snow, was the only road. The horsemen dismounted, and with voice and whip urged their beasts down the dangerous path, which seemed hardly safe for a practiced footman. In the patience and ingenuity with which they strove and struggled, avoiding a precipice on this side, a mass of fallen timber on that, tearing through a tangled thicket here, there forcing their reluctant steeds to some more desperate leap; in the uncomplaining fortitude with which they suffered scratches, cuts, and bruises, in the general recklessness of life and limb exhibited in their movements, one might perceive that the circumstances of our travelers were becoming well-nigh desperate. Sliding, jumping, tumbling down a break-neck declivity, Larkin was at length brought up with a jerk which threw him across a moss-covered rock at the bottom. The Black stood naked and smoking beside him; the saddle, baggage, and equipments being strewed in pieces along the steep descent. His companions arrived immediately after, hardly in better plight. The crown of the Squire's respectable hat flapped up and down like a smoke-jack, and the knees of the Tennesseean's horse were cut and bloody. They stood upon the brink of a precipice, over which poured a mountain torrent[11] with a clear leap of fifty feet.

The first movement of the travelers was to quench their fiery thirst, and the next to attend to the wants of their whinnying companions. Then they sat down quietly, face to face, to see what cheer and counsel could be gathered from communion.

The roar of the torrent made the woods tremble. The twilight was fast deepening into utter darkness, but it was still light enough to see the awful loneliness that hemmed them in, and read despair in each other's faces.

No one had any thing to suggest, so they sat still and rested, until their beards and hair were white with frost. Anon, Larkin's voice was heard, sharp and scornful, as if reading a passage from a newspaper.

"In the month of December last, three gentlemen, who had visited the Bald Mountain, attempted to descend on the Tennessee side without a guide. In so doing they lost their road, and perished, it is supposed, from cold and exhaustion. Their bodies were found half devoured by the wolves."

DESCENDING THE TUMBLING FORK. FROM DAVID HUNTER STROTHER, "A WINTER IN THE SOUTH," *HARPER'S*, JANUARY 1858.

The Squire seized the speaker's arm.

"Robert, my boy, you have aroused me from a pleasant dream."

"Friends," said the Tennesseean, "this is not a time for rest or dreams. Listen to me. We can get no farther with the horses—that is evident. I suppose they must perish; it is hard, but we can't help them. Perhaps we have still spirit and stamina enough to save ourselves."

"Skin for skin," groaned Squire Broadacre. "Yea, all that a man hath will he give for his life."[12]

"All, uncle—save his honor. Shall we desert the faithful brutes?"

"Bob Larkin," returned the Squire, "we must not sacrifice ourselves to a sentiment. Besides, boy, they are only hired horses, and I'll warrant have left no colts at home to whinny after them."

Putting their bruised and benumbed limbs again in motion, not without difficulty, our travelers gathered their gear in a heap, and tethered the horses as securely as possible to some laurels that overhung the water.

It was then resolved to follow the course of the stream until they reached the valley, where they would without doubt soon find a settlement. They would thus have a clew whereby they might return to their horses, and, with assistance from the mountaineers, possibly rescue them from their present plight.

Cheered by these new-formed hopes, they resumed their toilsome and hazardous march with an appearance of alacrity.

"Stop a moment!" cried Larkin. And hurrying back to where the baggage lay, he took his sketch-book from the saddle-bags, and bestowed it carefully in the pocket of his hunting coat. "When they find my body," he coolly soliloquized, "they will be enabled to recognize it by this." And then saying good-by to the horses, he hastily followed his companions down the precipice.

It would be a task far beyond the powers of our unskillful pen to describe that trying and hazardous tramp. To tell how they groped, in utter darkness, along the brink of that savage torrent, periling life and limb at every movement; how they crawled and struggled through dense thickets that during the passage seemed interminable; how they fell from slippery rocks, and were plunged waist-deep into foaming pools, and still kept on their way, reeking with toil, while their outer garments were frozen hard as boards; and when the stream grew larger, and they dared not attempt to stem the furious current, how they were forced to climb ragged cliffs, and creep along the verge of overhanging precipices, feeling cautiously for a place to plant each step; and when the advanced foot found no resting-place, and the turmoil of the waters rose loud and clear from a chasm of unknown depth, how the wanderer would start back with a thrill of terror, painfully and warily to seek some other road. Still they moved, for the most part, in silence. No one uttered a complaint; and when a voice was raised to call up a loiterer, or give warning of a danger, the tones were gruff and manly.

At length the cold, solemn face of the moon appeared over the awful heights from which they had descended. Although her presence was inspiriting, the few straggling and deceitful beams which reached the dark gorge threw but little light upon the path of the wanderers. Then after a time the route became more practicable. The ravine widened, and on either side of the stream were long stretches of open forest, and every heart leaped as they discovered a pathway evidently worn by human feet. Believing their toil was about to end, for awhile they gave themselves up to jollity, but the path, at length, terminated at a sugar-camp.[13] The sight of a couple of tenantless, half-ruined cabins froze their new-blown hopes, and they resumed their march, dispirited and forlorn. The valley again closed up, and they found themselves again struggling through a narrow gorge, surrounded with difficulties and dangers similar to those which had beset their way at the starting; and these even on a grander scale.

However strong may be the instinctive love of life in the human breast, it often fails men in desperate emergencies, and they will lie down quietly and die, when a spirited effort might have saved them. But we find in some characters a stubborn will, an unreasoning tenacity of purpose, which sustains when the common instinct of self-preservation has failed, and urges onward when the ordinary limits of human endurance are passed.

Thus the younger men tugged on with slow and dogged perseverance, but the good old Squire—the man of easy life and luxurious habits—what carried him through this trying night? The Squire was generally behind, and rarely spoke. Sometimes, however, he seemed to get dreamy and credulous, calling to his companions that he heard dogs barking, or had discovered paths, which, upon examination, turned out to be fancies— based, possibly, upon the distant hooting of owls, and the deceptive appearances of moonlight.

Sometimes, too, the young men were startled by the lofty strains of some old ballad resounding through the forest; but after two or three bars, this usually terminated with a crash or a splash; then some half-suppressed groans and muttered anathemas. Occasionally he would sink down upon the hill-side, lying for a time motionless, as if unconscious of his condition, or careless whether he should ever rise again. Then starting up suddenly, he would resume his march with renewed pluck and energy. What stirred him at such moments—freshened the current of his blood, and nerved his failing limbs? Who knows? Some trifling thing it may have been— a thought—a dream—a child's dimpled hand that beckoned—a blue-bird voice that whispered, "We're waiting for you, Papa! Be brave—be strong!"

THE TUMBLING FORK, BY MOONLIGHT. FROM DAVID HUNTER STROTHER,
"A WINTER IN THE SOUTH," *HARPER'S,* JANUARY 1858.

The three travelers were at length assembled upon the brow of a cliff; and one after another sunk down like men who had made their last effort.

"I'll go no farther," said the Tennesseean; "I'll lie here and take my chance."

"You'll freeze to death in an hour," said Larkin.

"Freezing, they say, is not a hard death—certainly not so hard as the life we've led for some hours."

"Now," said Squire Broadacre, "I am persuaded that I see a path there, just above us, on the hill-side."

"What's the use of a path to a man who can walk no more?" said Jones, in a tone of deep despondency.

"Uncle," said Larkin, "the tracks of the deer and wild hogs deceive you. It will lead to nothing."

"Has it come to this?" quoth the Squire; "must an old fat fogy like myself be the last to yield? Shame on you, boys! Give me a hand here, and help me to rise."

Bob sprang up in a moment and helped the Squire on his pegs. The path was examined, but whether it was worn by pigs or deer they could not make out. However, as it led down the hill by an easy grade, they agreed to follow it.

As they wound around the point of the hill, Larkin, who was in front, gave a sudden joyous whoop that made the welkin ring, exclaiming, "A light! a light!"

The shout was answered by the loud baying of dogs. Oh faithful guardians of the night, how often has that warning voice brought cheer to the heart of the midnight wanderer, turning him from dark and dangerous paths and guiding him to the welcome shelter!

The men that before could not walk broke down the hill in a lively trot, and they were soon at the cabin-door knocking for admittance. An old man opened the door, and as the firelight flashed upon the haggard faces of the travelers, he started back in terror.

"Food, fire, and rest!" cried the Tennessean, as they rushed in.

An old woman, with a grown-up boy and girl, were added to the party in a moment, all looking somewhat aghast at the new-comers.

"Whose house is this? and where are we?"

"This is Chandler's, Sir, on Indian Creek, at the foot of the Bald. And you, men, who mought you be?"

"Benighted travelers, ready to perish with cold, hunger, and fatigue. We lost our horses in the mountain, and came down this valley to the right—"

"Good Lord!" whispered the elder, in a husky voice. "Did ye come down the Tumbling Fork?"[14]

"That's it!" cried Squire Broadacre; "you've named it."

"Men alive!" screamed the old woman, holding up her hands. "Come down thar, and at night, too! and ye're not dead?"

"No," replied Jones; "but I'm afraid our horses are. We left them tied near the head of this stream."

"Then the bars and painters[15] has eat 'em certain," said the boy. "Hit's a mighty place for wild varmints up thar."

As the visitors sat by the blazing fire, picking the ice from their matted hair and beards, detailing their adventures by snatches, the cottagers stared and listened with awe-stricken countenances, as the fascinated wedding-guest hearkened to the tale of the Ancient Mariner, half doubtful of his claim to human brotherhood.

As there seemed to be no preparation for supper going on, the demand for food was reiterated in form, when, to their surprise and disappointment, old Chandler informed them that there was nothing to eat on the premises. At this the Tennesseean bent his brows and observed, fiercely, that it was as easy to take it as to ask for it. The old man looked alarmed.

"Men," said he, "you may kill me if you can find any thing to eat here, except a sack of corn in the ear, and them pumpkins in the corner there."

He was so evidently in earnest that his guests listened respectfully to the rest of his speech. Thus he continued:

"If you can wait till they are cooked, you're welcome to them; but, if you'll listen to me, you can do better, if you can make out to walk over to Kan Foster's—only a mile from here. Kan has plenty to eat; and if there's a man in these mountains that can save your horses that man is Kan Foster."

This last suggestion touched our travelers to the quick, and as the boy very civilly offered to be their guide, and promised a fair road, they concluded to go on. Their limbs had already begun to stiffen, but, under the influences of the bright moonlight and cheerful prospects, the distance was soon accomplished.

Now, with what old Chandler had told them, and the wonderful stories with which their guide enlivened the walk, the travelers approached the group of cabins which constituted the establishment of the mountain hero with feelings of lively interest and curiosity.

Although it was near midnight when they arrived, the door of the principal cabin stood open, and, by the glare of the blazing hearth, they saw two persons engaged in skinning a wild hog. The woman steadied the carcass by the hind legs, while the man, holding a bloody hunting-knife between his teeth, with arms bared and gory to the elbow, kneeled at the head of the slaughtered animal.

At the first signal whoop he sprung to his feet, took the knife out of his mouth, and shouted the welcome "Come in!"

This person was of the middle height, of a keen and wiry build, his every motion betokening promptness, activity, and resolution in the highest degree. His features, though weather-beaten, were regularly handsome, partly covered with a short black and grizzled beard, and his black eye glittered like a hawk's. His dress consisted of a nondescript hat and a well-worn suit of tawny-colored mountain jeans, made hunting-shirt fashion, and girt about the waist with a leathern belt which bore his knife-sheath. It needed not young Chandler's introduction to tell that this was Kan Foster.[16] There was a free, frank, hearty hospitality, even in the expression of his face, that warmed like the glow of his blazing chimney.

Our friends told their story briefly: "Strangers, lost in the mountains, in want of food and shelter."

"Friends," said the mountaineer, "I rejoice that fortune has led you to the door of my poor cabin. You are at home; the house and all that is in it is at your service."

His smiling dame seconded her lord's welcome with cheerful alacrity, and having aroused her eldest daughter, a comely lass of seventeen, they retired to an adjoining cabin, and in a short time the guests were invited in to supper. Now it was a pleasant sight to see the three wanderers seated at the smoking board; to mark the brave struggle between courtly politeness and hollow-eyed famine; to observe how the good dame and the lively maiden replenished the emptied dishes, and smiled to see such sincere approval of their culinary skill. Their manly host sat by and earnestly listened to the details of the night's adventures, often interrupted by swigs of coffee and mouthfuls of meat; and when at length he had obtained a clear idea of the route by which they had come, he spoke up, stoutly and cheerily,

"I think, strangers, I know the spot where your horses are at this minute—at the head of a high fall on the Tumbling Fork, a place where

KAN FOSTER. FROM DAVID HUNTER STROTHER, "A WINTER IN THE SOUTH,"
HARPER'S, JANUARY 1858.

I have often killed bar. It is an awful place, to be sure; but this I'll promise,
that if mortal man can save them I'll do it. Before light in the morning I
will take my son and start. It may be eight or ten miles distant by the way
we will go; but we'll reach them by sunrise, so as to have the whole day
before us for our work; for it's an awful country indeed."

The Squire leaned back and heaved a sigh expressive of enormous
contentment.

"I am filled, my gallant friend—"

"I'm truly glad to hear it," said Bob.

"Be quiet, Robert. I am filled with comfort by your assurances in regard to our horses. I see that in your eye which tells me they are safe."

"Now that I have room for no more provender," said Jones, "I begin to feel great sympathy for the poor brutes."

"It is the disgrace that I feel," said Larkin. "To lose our steeds and equipments is as if an army should lose its artillery and baggage. How could we return to Jonesborough in such a plight to face our ladies?"

"It will be harder to face Tom Dosser," said the Squire. "But it is now past midnight—we must to bed."

Long before the dawn Foster had equipped himself, filling his pockets with corn for the horses, and, with his eldest son, started for the mountain.

Their excessive fatigue, and the excitement incident to their position, prevented our travelers from sleeping soundly; still they enjoyed the much-needed repose until a late hour in the morning, and only left their bed in answer to a call to breakfast.

After a vigorous meal they returned to the sleeping-cabin, there, around the wide-mouthed chimney, to find what pastime they could while awaiting the return of the woodman.

The Squire got hold of an old fiddle, and having tuned it up succeeded for a time in making himself the centre of attraction. But having in a short time fiddled out the few tunes he remembered, he laid the instrument aside, and interested himself in Larkin's sketching.

Now the artist found himself in clover. There was Foster's brood to begin with—nine in number—a likely set, and the younger children endowed with singular beauty. It appeared, too, that there was a tub-mill belonging to the mountaineer's establishment, and thither came the neighbors from far and near—some mounted and some on foot—bringing their scanty grists tied up in sacks or pillow-cases, and lounging about the premises until the corn was ground.

During the progress of the sketching, these gathered around Bob, as though he were some great necromancer, performing mysterious feats far beyond the comprehension of the world at large, with winks and whispers testifying their astonishment at his skill or their approbation of his success.

First, there was the pretty girl who served them at supper on the night before. As she sat with her sleeping sister in her arms, they might have served Raphael as a model for another Madonna and Child. There was chubby-faced Dorkey running barefoot in the frost like a young

PASTIME. FROM DAVID HUNTER STROTHER, "A WINTER IN THE SOUTH,"
HARPER'S, JANUARY 1858.

partridge, cheeks all chapped, and purple with health; eyes dancing
with merriment; arms and legs shining with plumpness. She was the
pet and beauty of the family; but Bob laughed at such rustic taste.

"Pretty she is, doubtless, but look at this one."

Nancy was a year or two older—slender and graceful as the spotted
fawn, with a face whose regular beauty vied with the Greek ideal. Yet what
has the cold classic marble to compare with the fire that lights those great
romantic eyes, or the life that warms those rose-tinted cheeks?

"Verily, Robert, were she six or seven years older, we might expect
to return to Jonesborough without you!"

"Nonsense, uncle. But I can not help thinking what a superb figure
that child might make one day, if, perchance, she were taken and educated
in all the graces of civilization."

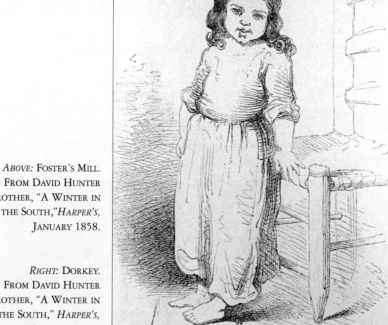

ABOVE: FOSTER'S MILL.
FROM DAVID HUNTER
STROTHER, "A WINTER IN
THE SOUTH,"*HARPER'S,*
JANUARY 1858.

RIGHT: DORKEY.
FROM DAVID HUNTER
STROTHER, "A WINTER IN
THE SOUTH," *HARPER'S,*
JANUARY 1858.

MARY FOSTER. FROM
DAVID HUNTER
STROTHER, "A
WINTER IN THE
SOUTH," *HARPER'S,*
JANUARY 1858.

CIVILIZATION.
FROM DAVID
HUNTER STROTHER,
"A WINTER IN THE
SOUTH," *HARPER'S,*
JANUARY 1858.

NANCY AND BECKY FOSTER. FROM DAVID HUNTER STROTHER, "A WINTER
IN THE SOUTH," *HARPER'S,* JANUARY 1858.

"Civilization! Robert. What do you mean by that? Hoops, the polka,
and point lace?"

"They are merely incidental, Sir. But I mean a general cultivation of
the tastes, sentiments, and intellectual faculties."

"That sounds very well for a flourish, Robert, but is not sufficiently
specific for an argument. Now let me talk a while. Have you observed our
good hostess here, how she hurries to and fro, bringing out her stores of
dried pumpkin shavings, prepared corn, maple sugar, and sweetmeats—how
she bakes, boils, and stews—striving, with all grace and cheerfulness, to do
honor to her husband's guests? Have you marked how tidy she keeps her
handsome brood—all clad in home-made of her own weaving, fashioned
and patched with her own hand? Or the elder daughter, diligent and meek,
how smilingly she skips to do her mother's bidding—to fetch dried apples
from the loft—to keep the coffee-pot from boiling over—to help off with

the big kettle—and between times to lull the little ones to sleep, or keep the wakeful out of mischief? Those who have learned so well to perform the duties of daughter, wife, and mother, I say, have been well educated, whether their dwelling is the brown-stone palace that rears its carved front on the Fifth Avenue, or the mud-chinked cottage that nestles under the magnificent shadow of the Black Dome."

"That," said the Tennesseean, "is an unanswerable *argumentum ad homminy*. Warmed, fed, and rested, what more does a man want in the world? Bless the women! they're a comfortable institution, any where or under any circumstances."

"And," said Bob, "I suppose I must abandon the idea of taming my little gazelle. Well, let her run wild; and if her life here is less brilliant, it will be more natural and poetic. In a year or two she will go to school, and pick up a little beau, who will help her to build playhouses in the rocks, and furnish them with acorn-cups and snail-shells; or make dams across the brook, to turn miniature tub-mills, framed of corn-stalks. The growing friendship will be nourished by presents of bird-eggs and pet squirrels; and when they grow up he will woo her with gay ribbons and store-goods from Jonesborough. Then, of course, they'll get married—build a cabin, hardly after the pattern of this one, and live as their fathers have done."

"A pretty little romance," said Jones; "and if, perchance, you should ride this way fifteen or twenty years after, you might see the conclusion of it."

Among the visitors at the cabin there was one that particularly attracted Squire Broadacre's attention. This was a comely young matron, whose maiden beauty had not yet entirely succumbed to the hard trials of wedded life. She of all others examined the portraits as they were turned off with the greatest interest and curiosity, and hovered around the busy limner with looks of feverish anxiety. "That's Dorkey alive! Well, it beats all!" Then she would sigh, and half whisper to Mary, "He admires to draw pretty children, does he? Well, I wish—But pshaw, no matter!" She would look up to see if the remark had been noticed, and then continue, "He thinks Nancy the prettiest, does he? Well, the child *is* handsome, but too proud and fierce-like—the very spit of her father. Dorkey is my favorite, but she is spiled with fat; and Becky's eyes are too wild, for all the world more like a rabbit's than a human's. I'd rather see a face more modest-looking, as it were. Ah me, if I thought he would like it—but no matter."

RIGHT: GOING TO SCHOOL. FROM DAVID HUNTER STROTHER, "A WINTER IN THE SOUTH," *HARPER'S,* JANUARY 1858.

CENTER: GOING TO MILL. FROM DAVID HUNTER STROTHER, "A WINTER IN THE SOUTH," *HARPER'S,* JANUARY 1858.

BOTTOM: THE ROMANCE CONCLUDES. FROM DAVID HUNTER STROTHER, "A WINTER IN THE SOUTH," *HARPER'S,* JANUARY 1858.

As Mary only laughed and shook her head, and no one else seemed to notice her, the demure little woman presently disappeared from the premises.

"Bob," said the Squire, "you should have requested that lady to sit for her portrait; she has been a great beauty, no doubt, and evidently expected the compliment."

"Who is she?" asked Bob.

"The Widow Foster—Kan's sister-in-law."

"Then bring her along."

It was too late, the widow had gone home.

The day wore on; the meridian was past; dinner over, and still no news of the horses.

As the neighbors dropped in one after another, the story of the lost horses was repeated over and over, and the subject discussed in all its bearings. It was suggested as the cause for Foster's delay that there were several branches to the Tumbling Fork, all alike in their general features, and that he might not have found the right one. Then, in their hunger, the horses might have eaten laurel and died; or have been killed by wild beasts; or, in their fear, have broken loose and tumbled over the precipices. Still the confidence in Kan Foster was universal and unlimited, and the strangers were assured that "if them horses were livin' Kan would bring them in, and if they were dead he'd bring their skins."

"Well, hit's a turrible idee," said Henderson Hensley, emphatically striking the butt of his rifle on the ground, "that of a man or a hoss being out in the Bald last night. Why, hit was cold enough to freeze the har off a bar."

This observation having been well received, he continued: "I've hunted some in all these mountains round about; but the Bald is more devilish savager than any of 'em, specially on the Tumbling Fork."

Now a gentleman, who had arrived astride of a pacing bull, put in, "If I mought be so bold, did the gentlemen come into these mountains in sarch of minerals or jist from kuriosity?"

"Simply from curiosity," replied the Squire; "to see the highest mountains in the United States."

"Well, to be sure, I have hearn say they were the highest mountains in the world; but they're no kuriosity to us folks here. We see too mighty much of 'em."

"But," said the first speaker, "I've heard there was another mountain higher than these here, somewhar in Kaintuck, or p'raps New York, or

HENDERSON HENSLEY. FROM
DAVID HUNTER STROTHER,
"A WINTER IN THE SOUTH,"
HARPER'S, JANUARY 1858.

some furrin place. My darter read it to me outen a book. It was a fire
mountain, and they called it Mount Vesy-vyous."

"Durn sich a name as that for a mountain. It sounds like gibberish;
as if it mought be a strange language, sich as Dutch or English."

Here the conversation was interrupted by a messenger from the
cabin—

"I say, mister, the Widow Foster has brung hern for ye to look at."

Bob Larkin, to whom this information was addressed, turned his
eyes upon the speaker with an expression of listless perplexity, as if
awaiting further revelations. The Squire, however, stepped into the
house and presently came back, his jolly face suffused with sentiment.

"Bob," said he, in an under tone, "come, get your pencils ready."

"I can't sketch now," replied Bob. "My fingers are cramped and my faculties wearied."

"But you must, Bob. Indeed you shall sketch them. It was not personal vanity after all, as I had supposed, but a feeling beautifully natural and true womanly. Don't you think, the poor thing went all the way to her cabin and has lugged her two children full a mile and a half over that steep ridge, on purpose that we might admire them."

Larkin followed the Squire into the house, where he saw the widow seated with her ideals beside her. After the strangers entered she modestly cast her looks upon the floor, and only raised her eyes with occasional timorous glances, to see how her babies were appreciated.

"Madam, stop—just as you are—don't move an inch! By George, that's beautiful! Hensley! you men get out of the door with your ugly mugs, and let in the light. Hist, little darling, take your finger out of your mouth. There, that will do!"

When the sketch was completed the Squire snatched the paper and handed it over to the widow, keeping his eyes fixed upon her as she examined it with tremulous eagerness.

"Hain't it like them? the sweet, little, modest-faced things!"

The gratified mother could no longer contain herself, and a tear trickled down her cheek as she clasped the little ones in her arms.

And now, Robert," said Squire Broadacre, in a coaxing tone, "one more favor. Have you noticed a poor little hard-favored child, flitting around us since morning, while no one has paid her the least attention?"

"What, that dirty, freckled, snub-nosed, ugly little imp? Uncle, it is too much."

"Bob, Bob, I shall be haunted by that forlorn forsaken child, if you don't draw her portrait. Did you never read Hans Anderson's story of the Ugly Duck?"

"May the devil fly away with her!" cried Bob. "I'd as soon think of getting sentimental on a corn-cob."

As the day waned our friends grew uncontrollably restless, and cast more anxious and frequent glances toward the road which led over the bill. Jones, who had been sleeping the greater part of the day, was now on his feet, and proposed they should take a walk up the creek. As they were about starting, a faint halloo attracted their attention to the hill. There was a man just coming over the ridge on a white horse.

"Some one coming to mill," said the Squire.

RIGHT: THE UGLY DUCK. FROM DAVID HUNTER STROTHER, "A WINTER IN THE SOUTH," *HARPER'S,* JANUARY 1858.

CENTER: THE WIDOW'S JEWELS. FROM DAVID HUNTER STROTHER, "A WINTER IN THE SOUTH," *HARPER'S,* JANUARY 1858.

BOTTOM: GOING TO MARKET. FROM DAVID HUNTER STROTHER, "A WINTER IN THE SOUTH," *HARPER'S,* JANUARY 1858.

The Tennesseean gave a signal-whoop. The horseman waved his hat, and answered the shout.

"By Heavens, it's Kan Foster!" cried Larkin, capering around like a pointer just unchained.

"And the boy?" asked the Squire, manifesting great excitement; "is he on foot?"

"Oh, smiling Fortune!" cried Jones, "there is the boy following with the black and the gray—my gray; one, two, three horses, all in a free trot, coming down the hill! Hip, hip, hip, hurrah!"

Now the whole population was out—men, women, children, and dogs all joining in the triumphant clamor. If every individual had gained a horse the rejoicing could not have been more sincere and general.

Kan Foster's manly face glowed with triumph as he rode up amidst the loud congratulations and well-merited compliments that were showered upon him from all sides. There was another cheek, too, that warmed with equal pride and pleasure, albeit its owner strove hard to appear unmoved. How could Dame Foster so chide her assistants, the widow and Mary, for neglecting the cooking and listening to the men, when she herself so often paused in her labors, ay, stood up by the chinks in the wall, that her willing ears might drink in the praises bestowed upon her lord.

"Now, Foster, my gallant friend, tell us about it all—how you found them, and how you got them out."

"Well, gentlemen," replied he, "all I can say is, that we are quite as curious to know how you ever got them down there. It's easier for a horse to go up those steep rocks than down; and that boy and I worked seven mortal hours with axe and hatchet. It was uncertain then for a while whether we could do it. But I had promised, and, by the help of Providence and that square bottle we found in your baggage, we succeeded in making my words good."

In the mean time the horses were abundantly fed, and after some sewing up of bridles, stirrup-straps, and girths, our travelers mounted.

Foster hospitably pressed them to tarry with him another night, but the Squire would not hear of it; he said they had already overstaid their time, and he wouldn't be surprised if there was a storm brewing. His fellow-travelers looked at the cloudless sky and setting sun, and speculated in silence on the intuitive knowledge which enabled the elder gentleman to foresee the tempest when the elements seemed to promise clear weather.

FORDING INDIAN CREEK. FROM DAVID HUNTER STROTHER, "A WINTER IN THE SOUTH,"
HARPER'S, JANUARY 1858.

Our adventurers started down the road at a pace that tried the
mettle of their steeds, dashing through the deep and rocky fords of
Indian Creek, and clattering over hill and dale, as if they had never
known hunger or sorrow. About nine o'clock that night they drew
rein before the mansion of Squire Irving, on the banks of the "Chucky,"[17]
about twenty-five miles from Jonesborough. Here they were received
with true Western hospitality, and here we will leave them to dream
of past perils and anticipated joys.

Indeed it is high time we were looking after our long-neglected
ladies in Jonesborough.

For some days after the departure of the gentlemen they amused
themselves indifferently well, shopping in a small way, altering the
fashion of their dresses, ripping the flounces off some, re-flouncing
others, and adjusting their brass and whalebone hoops, which had
been sadly deranged by the stage ride from Blountville.

In the course of a week these things grew tedious. Annette began
to yawn, and Madame to grow fidgety; Leonore had skimmed over a
wheelbarrow-load of British classics; Tiny had broken the limbs and
poked out the eyes of several dolls, and the disposition to ennui seemed
general. They looked out of the windows fifty times a day, and in the
afternoons, when the weather permitted, walked on the road toward

the mountains, in the hope of meeting the returning troop. As they were disappointed day after day, Madam B.'s patience at length gave way. She declared it was outrageous, vowed she didn't care if they never came back, and spoke of gathering up and returning home without them. Unfortunately the Squire had all the money, and this idea had to be abandoned. Finally, she bought another dress and seated herself to sewing, drawing the window-curtains close, and positively forbidding any allusion to the absentees. Nevertheless would the good lady start involuntarily at the sound of every footstep on the stair, or the clatter of hoofs on the street. Then she would bite her lip, sharply chide the girls for laughing, and resume her work with redoubled energy.

At length a mountaineer, who had come down to trade in Jonesborough, brought tidings that three strangers, with their horses, had perished in the mountains. As a matter of course, this report was immediately conveyed to the Eutaw.

"They're Coming!" From David Hunter Strother, "A Winter in the South," *Harper's*, January 1858.

The girls, with white lips, pronounced it nonsense. Mrs. Broadacre said it was just what they deserved; she was glad of it; and then fell into hysterics. Leonore's steadfast spirit was again in requisition, calming the matron's alarm with sensible assurances, drying the tears that trembled in Annette's eyes, and diverting Tiny's mind from the subject to renewed interest in her dolls.

Still the hours wore on heavily enough. Jim Bug was sent out on the mountain to reconnoitre, but could hear nothing except some vague rumors that went rather to confirm the story. But this the faithful servant carefully concealed; nay, on returning to the house, he even invented a soothing tale to tell instead. About the middle of the afternoon there was heard a heavy footstep on the stair. Suddenly Tiny threw aside her doll and started up:

"They're coming! they're coming!"

"Be quiet, child. It is only some one bringing up wood."

"They're here!" she cried, bounding toward the door. "I know the voice of Papa's feet."

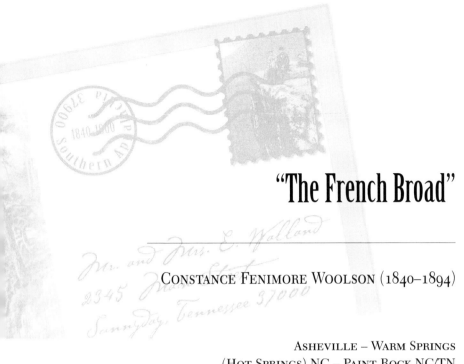

"The French Broad"

CONSTANCE FENIMORE WOOLSON (1840–1894)

ASHEVILLE – WARM SPRINGS
(HOT SPRINGS) NC – PAINT ROCK NC/TN

C onstance Fenimore Woolson was born in New Hampshire and raised in Cleveland, Ohio. After the death of her father in 1869, she began to write in earnest for the national magazines in order to provide an income for herself and her mother. She and her mother spent the next decade traveling up and down the Atlantic seaboard, dividing much of their time between St. Augustine, Florida, and Cooperstown, New York, where her mother had family ties. (Related to the Coopers of Cooperstown, Woolson is the great-niece of James Fenimore Cooper.) In 1879 her mother died, and shortly thereafter Woolson left the United States for England and Europe, never to return. She died at a hotel in Venice, in January of 1894, in a fall from a balcony that biographers believe was suicide.

Holy damn.

Woolson wrote articles, poems, short fiction, and novels. Beginning in 1870, her output was steady and would grow to include numerous magazine publications, as well as five novels (one of which was for children), a novella, a volume of travel writings, and four collections of short fiction. At the time of her death, Woolson's work, especially her fiction, was "known both in

Harper's Monthly, April 1875

the capitals of Europe and in the cities and small towns of America"
(Torsney, "Intro" 2). Her literary reputation languished after the turn
of the twentieth century but in recent decades has been revived by
scholars who now see her work as a bridge between "local color" and
later forms of American realism.

Woolson's first publications were set in Ohio and the Great
Lakes region, including fiction and also travel sketches of the Lakes
and the Ohio River for *Picturesque America* (1872–74), the influential,
Appleton's-affiliated illustrated folio sold by subscription at the end of
Reconstruction. But soon she entered what one biographer calls her
"Southern Period," which lasted most of the 1870s (Kern 46–96).
During this time, her career benefited from the competition between
national magazines for portrayals of the south. Between January
1875 and January 1876, Woolson published four travel articles
about the south in *Harper's* magazine alone. These include, in addi-
tion to the present selection, a two-part series about St. Augustine
("The Ancient City"), a sketch of Charleston, South Carolina, and
surrounding plantations ("Up the Ashley and the Cooper"), and an
account of a steamboat trip up a tributary of the St. John's River in
Florida ("The Oklawaha"). See Rowe, 148, for an overview of
Woolson's southern writing.

Woolson and her mother spent much of the summer of 1874 in
Asheville, North Carolina, and in November the two traveled by
wagon on the old drover's road along the French Broad River to Warm
Springs (now Hot Springs), and then to the railroad station at Wolf
Creek, across the state line in Tennessee (Benedict 250–52). The present selection is based on that experience. In this article, Woolson
deploys some of the same fictionalized characters that she had earlier
used in "The Ancient City" and would later use in "The Oklawaha."
The narrator, Martha Miles, is based on Woolson herself, who was, like
her narrator, <u>an enthusiastic amateur botanist and collector of ferns</u>.
The beautiful Ermine Stuart is likely based on Woolson's then-recently
widowed sister Clara, who traveled with Woolson and her mother, and
who was known to attract attention from men. Another character,
Professor Macquoid, performs the same role here that he plays in other
Woolson travel articles. The bore of the party, he recites the obligatory
history and travel information, thus providing a mouthpiece for material that would be included in a nonfiction travelogue. ⟍ ⟋ ᴹᶜ

"What is it?" asked Uncle Jack.

"A river," replied Ermine.

"Very well," said the old gentleman. Then, after a moment, "Where
is it?"

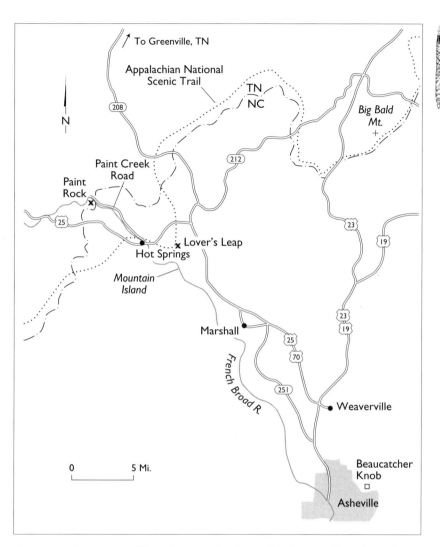

ASHEVILLE – ALEXANDER – WARM SPRINGS (HOT SPRINGS) NC – PAINT ROCK NC/TN,
ROUTE OF CONSTANCE FENIMORE WOOLSON, 1874

"In Western North Carolina."

"Very well," said the old gentleman again, taking up his newspaper. "Pray don't forget my slippers."

Later in the day, however, he took me aside.

"Do *you* know any thing about this Western North Carolina, Miss Martha?" he asked.

SUMMER SLEIGHING IN WESTERN NORTH CAROLINA. FROM CONSTANCE FENIMORE WOOLSON, "THE FRENCH BROAD." *HARPER'S,* APRIL 1875.

"Only how it looks on the map, Sir."

"And how does it look?"

"Black in the face with mountains."

"Apoplectic?"

"Decidedly. Bald Mountain,[1] you remember, had a stroke not long since."

"Are we going there?" asked Uncle Jack, resignedly.

"I don't think any one knows, Sir, exactly where we are going except Ermine," I replied.

We found it at Ashville [*sic*]. I use the word found because it was a regular game of hide-and-seek, in which the knolls, the river, and ourselves took part. It begins life down on the South Carolina border, and runs almost due north, placidly taking in small streams, and concealing its ultimate purposes with a delicate art worthy of Undine's[2] watery relations. Near Ashville is the trysting-place where it meets the Swannanoa on its way down from the Blue Ridge, but so cunningly is it all managed that no road, no path, will take you there, and unless you have the spirit and the boots of a pioneer you will miss the wedding. Having neither, we yet went, driven by the fiat of Ermine.

"I said I would witness this meeting of the waters," she began. Then, putting out a slender foot incased in a stern little double-soled boot, "Thus do I leave my mark upon the strand!"[3]

"Upon the mud," said Uncle Jack.

HAWK'S BILL MOUNTAIN.
FROM CONSTANCE FENIMORE
WOOLSON, "THE FRENCH
BROAD." *HARPER'S*, APRIL 1875.

"Witness, my friends," continued Ermine, "this is the majority of our river. Its life, so far, has been but awkward growing. It has had no definite character; no one could tell what it might come to—a swampy, a stony, or a bucolic and grassy end. Having received the Swannanoa, however, it now for the first time feels its strength. My friends let us return. Later in the day we will view it from the summit of that fern covered hill behind the town."

"Beaucatcher Knob,"[4] said Uncle Jack.

"I never hear that country-farmer name," replied Ermine. "I make it a point to not hear such titles in my rambles through Arcadia. When the dialect descends too far, I simply ignore it, and thus save myself much vexation of spirit."

Later in the day, however, although we scaled the Knob, and saw a wondrous vision of grandeur and beauty, we saw no river in all the

green valley of knolls below us, no gleam of water at the foot of the
far mountains, no flash of white through the sunset gap.

"She is hiding," said Ermine; "let us go down and find her."

The view from the Knob is one of the few that linger in memory
distinct as a painted picture. As yet it is unknown to the world at large,
but it will be famous some day, when the eager artists and tourists
discover this hidden region locked up behind mountain walls whose
peaks seem to thrust back scornfully the railroads that would penetrate
within. So far they have stood at bay, these magnificent cloud-capped
ranges, defying the world. Behind the Knob rise the rounded summits
of the Blue Ridge, singularly blue always both in sunshine and in storm.
Sitting on the grass-grown earth-works of the old Confederate fort that
crowned the summit, one faces the west, glorious in sunset tints. In the
north rise near and dark peaks leading toward the Black Mountain and its
lonely grave. No man had ever a grander sepulchre than Elisha Mitchell,[5]
who lost his life while exploring this lofty range. The mountaineers buried
him on the peak, whose height, as measured by his own hand, is cut in the
rough stone at the head of the grave—6711 feet,[6] the highest summit
east of the Mississippi. The government signal station that once stood
near has been abandoned and burned.

Looking from the Knob toward the west, we saw a crowd of peaks,
apparently endless, fading away into the horizon on the far Tennessee
border. But the southwest holds the *genius loci,* the god who guards
the valley—Mount Pisgah, solemn, grand old peak, dominant in its
gaunt majesty, although one hundred and eighty brother summits are
in sight, and the Cold Mountain beyond is counted higher.

"Physically, perhaps, but not spiritually," said Ermine. "Pisgah is
the king, the native-born god of the valley."

As the sun sank behind the mountain down into Tennessee the
one gap in the massive western wall, the gap guarded by Pisgah, began
to grow purple and soft, like a beautiful pass into some better country.
Looking through, far beyond we saw a distant mountain all tinged
with gold.

"And the building of the wall of it was of jasper, and the city was
pure gold,"[7] said Uncle Jack.

"Ashville is a very pretty village, scattered over a valley of knolls," said
Ermine, summing up her observations that evening. "Every man has an
alp for his private residence, and giants walk the streets. One fine-looking
young man I saw yesterday came up to the second-story windows."

VIEW FROM TOP OF BLACK MOUNTAIN.
FROM CONSTANCE FENIMORE WOOLSON,
"THE FRENCH BROAD." *HARPER'S*,
APRIL 1875.

"He is exactly six feet seven inches: I inquired," said practical
Uncle Jack.

"The stages coming and going are picturesque," continued Ermine,
unheeding the interruption; "the Eagle Hotel[8] chicken is tender and
unlimited; the cobble-stones are original; the Ashville dog is a mountain
animal, a sort of 'merry Swiss boy;' and the teams are a regular menagerie,
an ox and a mule behind, a small malicious steer and a particularly large
and melancholy horse in front."

"And over and around all," I added, "is spread the most magnificent
scenery to be found in the old States—scenery which has remained
undiscovered, while the White Mountains and many minor groups
are crowded with visitors and dotted with easels."

EAGLE HOTEL, ASHVILLE
[SIC], NORTH CAROLINA.
FROM CONSTANCE FENIMORE
WOOLSON, "THE FRENCH
BROAD." *HARPER'S,*
APRIL 1875.

In the morning we began our search for the river. We asked no
questions, but walked a mile to the east, a mile to the north a mile to the
south, in vain; at last we found it down in the west, hidden so cunningly
that we were on its very bridge before we saw the water. "The witch!"
said Ermine. "One might live months in Ashville without once seeing
the gleam of her silver draperies as she flits through the valley, so
hidden is her path."

"Wait till she gets around the corner and you will see a change,"
said a voice behind us. We turned. "Major Ray!" exclaimed Uncle Jack,
extending his band cordially.

"Myself in person," replied the officer. "Cause, furlough; purpose,
fishing; scene, French Broad. And you?"

"Ditto, without the fishing," replied Ermine, taking the blue-
coated arm with her graceful nonchalance. (Ermine had a way of taking
a person's arm.)

"A Regular Menagerie." From Constance Fenimore Woolson, "The French Broad." *Harper's*, April 1875.

"*I* like fishing," announced Uncle Jack, in a general way.

"A tent, you know, and hammocks," pursued the officer, as we strolled back to the village; "trouting and books and pipes, and a darky cook, one of those old fellows who can put two sticks together and give you a dinner fit for a prince."

"I'll go, Sir; say not another word—I'll go," said Uncle Jack, breezily.

"Without an invitation, uncle?"

"A truce to conventionalities, Miss Stuart. Was not my description seductively arranged to entrap not only your uncle Jack, but all of you?" said the officer, gallantly. (It was indeed, but not the only thing arranged, I thought. People do not turn up on bridges over the French Broad by chance.)

"Thank you," replied Ermine, sweetly; "nothing could be more charming. Uncle will enjoy the fishing so much, and you and I, Miss Martha, can swing in the hammocks and read the books, while the perfection of a cook serves coffee eight times a day in Sèvres cups. Then at night, telling stories around the camp fire in the tent—how romantic! Just what I have always dreamed."

"But the fire won't be in the tent, you know, niece."

"On this occasion it will be," pursued Ermine, calmly. "It was always so in my dreams."

"Then they must have been choked with smoke in your dreams, my dear."

The Major started the next morning, and we followed two days later, finding, as he had said, a great change in our river around the corner. It rushed along with tremendous speed, roaring over rocks, boiling in little pools below, swirling back again in long eddies, a rampant, foaming tide, tearing a way for itself through the very heart of the mountains, and dashing forward as though nothing should stop it short of the Pacific Ocean. The French Broad is a chief branch of the head waters of the Tennessee, and seems to take its eccentricities with it into the latter river. On its own course it flows first north, then west, then south, and the Tennessee pursues an equally exceptional path by going south across the whole of its own State and well down into Alabama, as though intent on seeking the Gulf of Mexico at Pensacola, then, suddenly seized with hesitation, it meanders off vaguely toward the west, makes a little detour into Mississippi, considers a while, and finding itself once more on the Tennessee border, away it goes straight to the north, crossing the whole State a second time, and even voyaging up seventy miles into Kentucky before it decides where it really wants to go, and, passing by the Great River with characteristic willfulness, enters the Ohio at last. We traveled slowly, loitering along the bank, stopping to gather flowers, to make very bad sketches, to drink from the ice-cold springs, to follow the brooks up their wild gorges and find the hidden falls whose voices came down to the road below, and ever and always to gaze and gaze upon the mountain walls, the rugged rocks, the islands, and the rushing, foaming river. Our road was narrow, cut out from the rock itself at the water's edge, and often the cliffs above seemed toppling over on us, so far did they lean forward, massive and bare. In places the river flowed through what might well be called a cañon. Sheerly rose the perpendicular granite walls from the water's edge, inclosing us and our pigmy road as in a gigantic well, only a little slice of blue sky far above remaining as a link between us and the outside world. It seemed as though we should never see corn fields and the broad heavens again, unless the rocs that aided Sinbad the Sailor[9] would come to our rescue.

Uncle Jack remained placid, but we saw "fishing" in his eyes.

"He will be off with the Major tomorrow, Ermine, and we shall be left alone," I said.

"If he is off, some one else will be on, Miss Martha."

"Surely you do not expect to meet any body in this remote place?"

"No," replied Ermine, idly swinging to and fro in the loop of a giant wild grapevine; "I never expect any body—it is too much trouble—but they always come, nevertheless."

They did. That night we stopped at Alexander's,[10] and found the Major awaiting us. He had pitched his tents a mile below, and came to meet us with a string of trout. With that singular mania for citizens' clothes which seems to afflict all our army officers, he had attired himself in a commonplace suit, with colored shirt and an old straw hat. Not a bright button remained, not an inch of blue. Uncle Jack examined the fish with enthusiasm.

"At dawn to-morrow," he said.

"What did I tell you, Ermine?" I said, in an under-tone, being left in a carriage drawn by two wild horses, with no other guardian than a constantly smiling and irresponsible darky named Zip, the road meanwhile but one inch wider than our wheels, and ponderous mountain wagons, drawn by oxen, thinking nothing of coming crashing and creaking around every corner. This was too much for me. After supper we strolled down toward the encampment, meeting the three-horse Tennessee stage on its way to Ashville. Two passengers were on top with the driver.

"Yes, Herr Frool," the elder man was saying, in a loud metallic voice that reminded one of tin scrapings, "the valleys of the White Mountain group are scarcely one thousand feet above the sea-level, while here, the very basin of the French Broad, along which we are now journeying, has an average elevation of more than two thousand feet."

"E-es it poss-sible!" ejaculated the companion.

"Professor Macquoid!" I exclaimed.

It was indeed that learned man himself, and with him a young German: "Herr Frool, a recent acquisition to the ranks of the foreign artists who have made this New World their home," explained the Professor.

They dismounted, returning with us to Alexander's, where they were to pass the night.

"What did I tell you?" said Ermine, when, late in the evening, we went to our room.

"But they are going on early in the morning."

"Are they?" said Miss Stuart. She was sitting before the little glass, brush in hand, her golden hair rippling over her shoulders. Her back was toward me, but I noticed that the reflection smiled. I gave it up immediately.

"Professor Macquoid is no doubt a learned man," I began, "and it is true that I did meet him in Florida last winter; still, the acquaintance was but slight, and—"

"Uncle Jack has long known him," said Ermine, brushing calmly on.

"And as to this Herr Frole—"

"Freulig is the name, Miss Martha."

"Well, Froilick, then. I don't know any thing about him."

"Do you want to know?" said Ermine, setting the stern little boots outside the door.

The next morning it was decided at the breakfast-table that we should stay a day or two at Alexander's in order that Uncle Jack might go a-fishing. The Professor had observed a remarkable dip in the strata near by, and the necessary measurements would detain him some time in

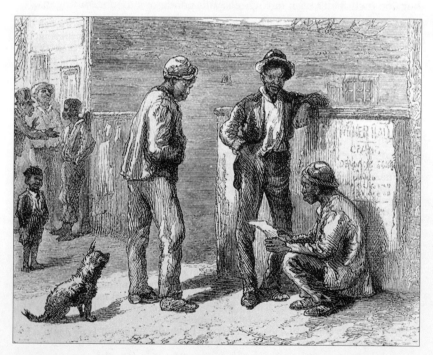

THREE MEMBERS OF THE JURY THAT WE SAW. FROM CONSTANCE FENIMORE WOOLSON, "THE FRENCH BROAD." *HARPER'S,* APRIL 1875.

the neighborhood. Miss Stuart, he observed, was interested in geology, and "Herr Frool, to whom I am showing some of the wonders of our country, Miss Martha, will be, no doubt, charmed to assist you in your search for ferns."

"Furrens?" repeated the artist.

"Yes, ferns," I replied, warming at the mention of my favorite subject; "little leaves, you know—leaves, not flowers, but *leaves*, growing on the rocks—*leaves*."

"Ah, yes, de leafs—I paint him," said the young German, vaguely. "You like leafs?"

"Indeed she does like them, Herr Fryle," said Uncle Jack, who, in high spirits, was preparing fishing tackle. "She is never happy unless she has a polly-stick-'em, or a polly-poddy, or something of the kind."

"E-es it poss-ible!" said the painter, evidently in a maze as to the meaning of these remarkable new words. Afterward I heard him saying softly over to himself, "bolly," "bolly," "bolly-boddy," as if trying them. Soon the Major appeared with fishing-rod, basket and a barefooted aboriginal boy. "He knows the bank whereon the wild thyme grows, and will pilot us thither. Ladies, pray honor the river-side tent with your presence at dinner, and inspect our spoil," said our disguised soldier.

"Will the perfection of a cook serve coffee?" asked Ermine.

"He will, fair lady. Ah, Professor, I will bid you good-by now; the stage will soon be round."

"A remarkable dip in the strata near by may compel me to remain some days in this vicinity, Sir. I shall therefore have the pleasure of seeing you again," said the learned man.

"Indeed! I am rejoiced to hear it. May I not, then, hope that you too will honor my tent with your presence to-day, you and your friend Mr.— Mr. Frawl?"

"Freulig," ejaculated the painter.

The Professor accepted with alacrity, and the fishermen started down the road, the barefooted boy who "knew the bank" going on before.

"Strange, isn't it," remarked Ermine, in her silvery voice, as we leaned over the piazza, "how suddenly an officer grows commonplace in citizen's clothes?" (When we reached the fishing ground I noticed that the Major had exchanged the old straw for his artillery cap.)

Left to ourselves, we strolled along the road down stream gathering flowers and idly talking. "I am going to climb up to the top of that rock," announced Ermine, suddenly; "I see a rosy cloud of flowers peeping over."

The *Rhododendron maximum*," said the Professor "a plant rarely found north of Pennsylvania, although growing here in thickets sometimes miles in extent. Miss Stuart, the rocks look slippery: allow me to assist you. The corolla is bell-shaped—(Have the goodness to pick up my glasses, Herr Frool)—bell-shaped, and about an inch broad—(In a moment, Miss Stuart, I shall be able to assist you if you will wait)— the color varying from rose to purple, greenish in the throat—"

"Greenish in the throat—horrible!" said Ermine from above, disappearing over the top of the rocks as she spoke.

The Professor meanwhile had stopped with his face to the cliff, clinging in a somewhat spread-out condition to four different projections; a branch had knocked his tall hat down over one eye and nearly blinded him. "Herr Frool!" he called down, "Herr Frool! will you have the goodness to step up and adjust my hat?"

RHODODENDRONS. FROM CONSTANCE FENIMORE WOOLSON, "THE FRENCH BROAD." *HARPER'S*, APRIL 1875.

The Herr, being long and lithe, stepped up, and having adjusted the hat, stepped on; we saw him no more.

"Which way did Miss Stuart go?" inquired the Professor, calling down again. Flattened against the rock he could not look up without endangering his balance.

"More to the right," I answered, putting on my glasses. "You have selected the steepest part of the cliff, Sir."

"Such has ever been my custom, madam; the path of science is the path of difficulty," replied the Professor from his perch.

"Don't you think you had better come down?" I said, watching his movements nervously. "Surely it would be better to come down rather than to fall down."

"Are you aware, madam, that I have ascended the Alps?"

"But this is more than the Alps, for you are climbing straight up toward a ledge which ends in a smooth perpendicular wall, Sir; I can see it quite plainly from here."

But the Professor, having cut loose from two of his pinnacles, made no reply, and I watched him execute a flank movement with some trepidation. Perceiving, however, that his hold was tenacious, his very feet seeming to cling like claws, I gave up the watch, and wandered on along the rocky shore, looking for ferns and finding many, including the delicate little purple-stemmed Pellæa, or cliff-brake. Meeting an advance-guard of beech-ferns coming down a gorge, I, too, in my enthusiasm was moved to climb. Before I began, however, I looked back; the Professor was still squirming up.

Is there any thing in the vegetable kingdom more beautiful than the plumy green grace of ferns? Like moonlight to the noonday sunshine, like Schubert's serenade on the violoncello to Rubinstein's Russian Hymn played by a full orchestra, like Undine to one of the French stage heroines of the day, so are the forest ferns to the ranks of the garden flowers. Robed ever in green, wild, shy, and beautiful, they nestle behind the rocks, wave by the brook-sides, and hide in the still dark glens, and the lovers of ferns are bound together the world over by that very tie that they do love them, needing no other introduction——reason sufficient for friendship between strangers, between the working gardener and the millionaire. Although a beginner, with unskilled eyes, I collected along the French Broad twelve different kinds—the polypody, the maidenhair, the bracken, the Cheilanthes, the cliff-brake, the dainty little ebony Asplenium, the lady-fern, the Filix-mas, the beech-fern, the Cystopteris, the martial

Polystichum acrostichoides, and the Mystery, so called because it positively refused to show me any seeds, so that I could not analyze it. Climbing on, half-way up the gorge I found a plateau of ferns so luxuriant, so beautiful, that I wished I might turn into tiny Tommelise, of the old fairy tale, and live down in the miniature tropic forest. Coming out at last on the top of the cliff and wandering along at random, I saw again the blaze of the rhododendrons. There in the heart of the rose-colored thicket sat Ermine, her hat thrown off, and her hands buried in blossoms.

"Herr Freulig is giving me some lessons," she said; but I saw no pencils, and I thought it looked the other way.

"Don't let me interrupt," I said, using the phrase which always signifies the deliberate intention of interrupting as much as possible. I sat down on a rock near by and began arranging my ferns. The young German sighed—(a German's sigh seems to come from the heels of his boots)—and I had the satisfaction of perceiving that the "lessons," whatever they had been, were at an end. Ermine, however, sat dreamily enjoying the rosy radiance unmindful of any change; plucking the blossoms idly, she let them fall around her until she was covered with bloom.

"What destruction, Ermine!"

"Are they not happy so?" she answered.

"Ah!" sighed the young German.

It was nearly noon before we left the rhododendrons. Going back along the cliff, we descended through the gorge of ferns, and reaching the road, strolled on down stream toward the camp.

"I wonder what has become of the Professor," I said, remembering where I had last seen him.

"Probably measuring the dip somewhere," replied Ermine.

"I left him measuring it after a fashion of his own," I said, laughing. "I only hope he got safely down again."

"E-es there danger?" inquired the artist. "I veel ho-law."

He ho-lawed, and presently we heard a sound in reply. I call it a "sound" because it was not the ordinary shout or halloo; it was more like a dignified and long-drawn "ahem." We followed the sound, and going back around the curve, discovered the Professor seated on the very ledge I had noticed, an uncomfortable little shelf with a bare granite wall rising perpendicularly behind it.

"Ah, Professor," said Ermine, calling up in her silvery voice, "how it delights me to see a real enthusiasm in the cause of science!

THE FRENCH BROAD, BELOW ASHVILLE [SIC]. FROM CONSTANCE FENIMORE WOOLSON, "THE FRENCH BROAD." *HARPER'S,* APRIL 1875.

Two hours on that ledge might have seemed tedious to any ordinary mortal; but to you—what secrets has not the eternal rock whispered in your ear ?"

"I breengs heem," said the young German, swinging himself up by an easier way; and presently we saw him walking out on the narrow ledge to his friend's assistance. But the Professor could not walk; vertigo, he explained, had seized him—the result of an overworked brain.

"R-ropes we haf not; and to carry e-es not poss-sible. You moste cr-rawl," said the Herr.

So back went the procession down the narrow ledge, the Professor crawling on his hands and knees, and his friend on the outside, tiptoeing along where there was scarcely room for a foot-hold, in order to guard against "the vertigo." For my part, I went down behind the rocks to laugh; but Ermine was equal to the occasion. Clasping her lovely hands, she went forward to meet the rescued man. "Oh, Professor!" she entreated; "we know your love for Science, yet we can not yield you entirely to her; do not, I beg, stay so long away from us again!"

The Professor thought he would not.

On a shady point we found our tent, and on the rocks in the river our fishermen, their number increased by an additional man and boy. "How they look, out on those rocks!" remarked Ermine, with the little drawl she affects at times. (Now I knew Ermine's conversational pitfalls of old: she did not say "how well," or "how ill," simply "how." The Professor, however, fell in at once.)

"Very undignified, truly," he said, supposing he was assenting.

"Yes, ver' undig," repeated the artist.

"Fishing, as an amusement, I have always condemned," continued the learned man. "It is a wanton destruction of animal life, accompanied by undue exposure to the elements; the boats, or as in this case the rocks, are apt to be singularly moist, and the effort of keeping the mind concentrated upon a stick called a rod is a waste of the nervous power."

"Do you think so?" said Ermine, languidly.

Seeing us on the bank, the fishermen came ashore, and the perfection began his savory work.

Dinner was served on the rocks at the door of the tent, and the Professor, having partaken heartily, waxed eloquent. "These mountains, my friends"—(why do we always hate a man who begins with 'my friends?')—"form the eastern margin of our continent," he began, "extending from Vermont to Alabama; the coast follows their direction, curving in at Hatteras as they trend off to the westward. The rocks in this neighborhood belong to the most ancient of the azoic series. In the language of an eloquent spokesman among our band of geologists, 'As North America is the eldest born of the continents, so the Black Mountain is the eldest born of its giant brotherhood, and was the first to emerge from the face of the water when the command went forth, Let the dry land appear!' In the group of the White Mountains, Mount Washington is the only one that rises above six thousand feet, while here there are peaks in all directions that rise above that height—yes, Sir, above that height," he continued, looking around the circle and sternly fixing the fact upon the artist, whose attention had wandered off toward Ermine.

"E-es it poss-sible!' said the Herr, hastily returning to earth again. He had no idea where the White Mountains were—(the mountains seemed to be all white or black in America); but never mind.

"Is the Bald Mountain in sight?" inquired Uncle Jack, beginning on a fresh trout.

"There are in this region many Bald Mountains so called—"

"But I mean *the* Bald, the volcano,[11] you know, Professor."

"I beg your pardon, Sir, but I do *not* know," replied the learned man, with dignity; "and science is also silent."

"Probably because she don't know either," replied Uncle Jack.

"Nobody knows," said the Major; "the people in the neighborhood of the mountain less than the outside public, who at least gained some idea, however incorrect, from the New York reporters who sat on the fences all around within sight of the peak, and dated their letters fancifully 'in the shadow of the Bald.'"

"I am tired of hearing about that mountain," said Ermine. "Who cares for a doubtful volcano? If it wants to be fiery, why does it not stop this long-drawn preparation, and go to work in earnest? It might accomplish something then besides rumbling. A wearing set they are from whom people are always 'expecting' great things; they generally remain, as Bulwer says, 'mere promising young men,' or volcanoes, to the last. And now for those hammocks."

They were brought out from the tent and soon swung from low-down branches near the water.

"Come, Miss Martha," said Ermine.

Personally, I am not very fond of a hammock; it is almost impossible to get in; and once in, it is entirely impossible to get out, at least with dignity; this "bounding in" one reads about is difficult to accomplish at my age! I did not bound, I climbed, assisted by the united strength of Uncle Jack, the Major, the Professor, and the artist. When we had finished our labors, all five of us, and I found myself safely in, Ermine issued her orders:

"Please go into the tent and take your nap, Uncle Jack. Professor, you will read aloud to us, I know. Herr Freulig, may I ask you to set my hammock swinging?"

She might indeed. Deftly attaching a rope to the tasseled net-work, the artist sat down under a pine and solemnly swung the tree-cradle to and fro, his large owl-like blue eyes fixed upon the lovely picture before him.

"And I?" said the Major.

"Go and smoke—a good way off, please. They never smoked in Arcadia, you know," replied the lady.

The Major went; but several wild flowers lost their heads *en route*, switched off remorselessly by a little branch he happened to carry.

"Oh, not that book, please," said Ermine, as the Professor brought out his pocket Guyot;[12] "the little volume on the rock, where the page is

turned down. And pray sit over there behind us; poetry sounds so much
sweeter from a distance."

> "'When buttercups are blossoming,
>   The poets sang, 'tis best to wed,'"

began the Professor, in his tin-scraping voice. The river rushed by almost
at our feet, and the sounds of the forest grew clearer. The old cook had
finished his labors and fallen asleep in the sun. Ermine swung on in her
hammock, her eyes fixed dreamily upon the opposite shore.

> "'Whereat our footsteps turned aside
>   From lord and lady of degree,
>   And bore us to that brave countree,
>   Where merrily we now abide,
>   That proud and humble, poor and grand,
>   Enchanted, golden, gypsy-land—
>   The Valley of Bohemia,'"

read the Professor, and then I too fell asleep. Time passed (at least I
supposed it passed, although I knew nothing about it). I came slowly
back from the purple oblivion mountains, hearing while yet afar off the
same rhythmic chant that echoed after me when departing.

> "'Yet still the same old dance and song
>   We found the kindly blithesome throng,
>   And joyance of Bohemia,'"

said a silvery voice, which surely was not the Professor's. I opened
my eyes, and lo! a change. The Professor had disappeared, the artist
was not, the rope trailed idly on the ground; it was Ermine who read. To
herself? I raised my head softly. On the other side, half concealed by the
hammock, I saw part of an artillery cap, and the fragrance of a cigar rose
in the air. I went to sleep again immediately. It seems they did smoke
in Arcadia after all.

"In the name of common-sense where have you been, Ermine?"
I exclaimed, the next morning, when upon first opening my eyes I
discovered my companion taking off her gypsy hat.

"Across the river, Miss Martha."

"But it is not daylight yet."

"The sun rose over the cliffs half an hour ago."

"Whom did you go with?"

"A boy; the one who knew the bank."

"What did you go for?"

"An object."

"What did you go in?"

"A cooner."

"A what?"

"A cooner. Put on your wrapper and step to the piazza door; I will show you both the cooner and the object."

Somewhat sleepily I obeyed, seeing the opposite cliffs tipped in sunshine, the dark river below, and floating on its surface a long, narrow, singularly shaped boat, its forward end raking the air; in the stern sat a man using a pole to sweep his craft along as an Indian uses his paddle.

"That boat is a cooner," said Ermine, "and that man is the object."

"Who is he?" I demanded.

"Haven't the slightest idea," replied Ermine, beginning to rebraid her hair.

The young artist came to the breakfast table portfolio in hand.

"Here it e-es, Mees Herrminia," he said, eagerly, placing a drawing in Ermine's hand. "You haf tell me to do it; I take de yesterday of afternoon, and feenish dis morn."

I looked over Ermine's shoulder. It was a sketch taken a mile back on the road toward Ashville, a point we had noticed on our way out; one of the singular, huge, boat-shaped mountain wagons was drawn up on the curve. "Excellent!" I exclaimed; "the identical keel up behind! What the mountaineers gain by having their wagons tilted forward at such an angle I can not imagine; but perhaps they model them after the sun-bonnets of their wives."

Enter the Professor, carrying a large waiter covered with fragments of rock. "I obtained them all, Miss Stuart—with difficulty, I admit. Still, I obtained them, and in such a cause I am proud to exhaust myself. I will enumerate and describe the specimens to you whenever you please."

"I am so much obliged to you," replied Ermine. "Professor Macquoid was kind enough to devote yesterday afternoon to collecting specimens of all the native rocks for my benefit," she continued, turning to me.

"Very kind indeed," I replied. "Did they study geology, do you think, in Bohemia, Ermine?"

After breakfast, as we were all sitting on the piazza, the Major came up the road, rod in hand. (He was in undress uniform now from head to foot, the gallant array of the red-legged branch of the service.)

A Mountain Wagon. From Constance Fenimore Woolson, "The French Broad."
Harper's, April 1875.

Uncle Jack was ready, eager for another day's sport.

"Wait, uncle, please," said Ermine, placidly; "I am going too."

"You are going too!" repeated the chorus, in astonishment.

"Yes. You all looked so delightfully insecure out on those rocks yesterday that I have longed to go ever since. I feel sure" (turning to the Major) "that you will take good care of me."

The Professor sat with his tray of specimens before him; he did not quite understand. Had he not given a decisive opinion against fishing only the day before? But the young artist sighed, and folded up his sketch. Now I did not care much about the disappointment of the Professor—(what is the reason that, femininely speaking, we never do care much about "the Professor?" does that honored title rob a man of all his natural aspirations toward romance?)—but the simple-hearted, solemn young Herr should not be, I resolved, so summarily dismissed. It was only too evident that Ermine was planning for a whole day with the army; this I would defeat!

"Let us all go," I suggested, affably. "Come, Professor, and you too, Herr Freulig. I will order dinner sent down to the tent."

"Well," said Uncle Jack, dubiously, "Frool might do it, and possibly Ermine, if she took a fancy; but how you and the Professor are going to climb out on those rocks, Miss Martha—"

But the Professor threw on his tall hat with *abandon*. "I will be a child for today," he cried, with enthusiasm. "Why should we labor always? For once let us be butterflies, happy butterflies!"

"Yes, de booter-fly," repeated the artist, thinking he was getting on admirably with his English.

Rods and lines were procured, and our party started down the road, Ermine in front with the Major.

"I should so much like to fish out of a cooner. Do you know any one about here who has a cooner?" she said, when we had reached the place, and were preparing to climb out to the rocks.

"Why, there was one back at Alexander's," said Uncle Jack. "Why didn't you speak before, Ermine? It has been lying there in front of the house ever since we arrived."

"Has it?" said Ermine, as innocently as though she had never seen it, much less crossed the river in it at sunrise."

"Shall I go back and get it?" asked the Major.

"Oh no; I could not think of putting you to so much trouble. See! there is a cooner now ; I wonder who is in it?"

We all looked.

"My friend of yesterday, I declare," said good-natured Uncle Jack. "Hallo there! come this way, will you?"

"Oh, uncle!"

"Why, I thought that was what you wanted, puss. But hush! here he comes."

The cooner—a mountain pronunciation of the word canoe—came slowly toward us; it was thirty feet long, barely wide enough for one person, flat-bottomed, and unpainted, a species of dug-out, although carefully shaped and planed. The man within managed the long pole skillfully, and soon floated alongside of our rock. The Major, a little vexed at the turn affairs had taken, stepped forward.

"If you will be kind enough to lend me your boat, Sir—" he began. Then stopping suddenly, "Why, Phil!" he exclaimed, "is that you?" and sprang into the cooner with extended hands.

The stranger was a man of about thirty five years, thin and prematurely old, with close-cut brown hair and brown eyes. He was dressed in the common blue jean of the country, and instead of a coat he wore a jacket belted in at the waist like a blouse. An old military cape of Confederate gray lay in the bottom of the cooner. He smiled and returned the Major's greeting, if not with equal excitement, at least with equal cordiality.

"To think now that you should have been over on that rock all yesterday morning—for it was you, wasn't it—without any recognition on my part, Phil!"

"You were too far off to see my face, George."

"You did not recognize me, of course?"

"No; I heard them call you Major, and once I thought I caught the sound of a familiar name. But I was not sure, and—and, I am not what I was, George," he added, just indicating the crutch by his side with a sad little gesture.

"Come right ashore, old fellow," cried the Major, with a sudden moisture in his dark eyes; "we'll kill the fatted calf and talk over the old days. Ladies, let me introduce to you my friend Philip Romer. We were classmates at West Point in '59."

The man took off his coarse straw hat. "I beg your pardon, ladies," he said. "I did not observe you in the shadow: my eye-sight is clouded."

By this time, of course, I had discovered that Ermine's plans had not been for "a day with the army," after all; and as for consolation, evidently the Major was as much in need of it as the Herr. Here I was, however, and a long uncomfortable day on the rocks opened before me. My only comfort lay in the thought that Ermine's sunrise-on-the-river tableau had been wasted. The man in the cooner with his dimmed eyes had probably not even seen her.

Uncle Jack, quite excited by this meeting, had climbed down to the water's edge. "But you steered the boat straight up to us when I shouted," he said, looking with sympathizing curiosity at the fine brown eyes which showed no trace of blindness.

"I guided myself by the sound of your voice, Sir; and I know every inch of the river about here. It gives me my only amusement. I won't go ashore now, George, but I will try to come and see you before you leave the neighborhood. You are at Alexander's, I suppose?"

"No, I am right here at this tent, where you will take dinner with us this noon, I hope."

"You wanted my boat—"

"It was I, Captain," said Ermine, coming forward into the sunshine. "I felt a sudden fancy to try a cooner; but now, of course—"

"You will immediately get in," interposed the Major, offering her his hand. She did not refuse, but stepping lightly in, sat down on the bottom.

"You should have this end seat," said Philip Romer, trying to rise with the aid of his crutch.

"Pray do not," said Ermine, earnestly, leaning forward and laying her hand upon his arm; "I am well placed as I am. Push off, please."

The stranger obeyed, and the long, narrow cooner floated out toward deep water.

"Don't go far away," called out Uncle Jack, uneasily.

"Needen be oneasy, Sah; de Cap'n he knows de ribber, Sah, and manage de cooner like a fiddle-string, Sah," said the old cook, who had watched the scene from his camp fire near by.

"You know him, then?" said Uncle Jack.

"'Spects I do, Sah; libs across thar in a log-cabin, Sah. My ole cousin Pomp he libs with him, Sah. Ben thar more'n eight years, Sah."

"Poor Phil!" said the major, as we slowly returned to our preparations for fishing. "He left us and joined the Southern army, being a South Carolina boy. I have heard nothing of him all these years."

"He haf no leg, and he haf not see well mit his eyes," said the artist; "I feels for heem moche peety."

"Superfluous, Herr Frool, superfluous," said the Professor, sternly. "Are you aware, Sir, that we have at the North fifteen thousand men with one leg only?"

"Feefteen t'ousand von-leg mans? E-es it poss-sible!" ejaculated the artist.

My fishing consisted principally in sitting on a safe rock near the shore reading some newspaper items about the mountain country. (I always try to read up while on the ground, having discovered that a line on the spot is worth two volumes away.) I learned, in the first place, that Buncombe County, where we then were, was named from

Colonel Buncombe, a gallant officer of the Revolution; over the door
of the family mansion once stood this legend,

> "To Buncombe Hall
> Welcome all."

It was a Congressional representative of the mountain neighborhood who
made himself and his district immortal by "only talking for Buncombe."[13]
Close upon this information came the fact that in 1871 Buncombe took
the first premium for tobacco at the Virginia State Fair, surpassing even
the celebrated yield of the Danville region. Buncombe apples were giants
of their kind, weighing from twenty-five to thirty ounces and measuring
fourteen and sixteen inches in circumference. (I was not surprised at this,
having seen the men who eat them.) The Catawba grape originated in
Buncombe, on Cane Creek, a branch of the French Broad. In the
surrounding region there were sixty mountain peaks more than six
thousand feet high, and thirty-nine over five thousand feet. I had read
as far as this, and was beginning on the climate, when the Professor fell in.
Herr Freulig, who was sitting on the shore making a sketch, dropped his
pencils. "E-es it—" he began; and then seeing the tall hat disappearing
under the water, he made a dash across the rocks to save his friend. But
the Major had already scooped him out and landed him on a slippery
knob, where he sat dripping from every angle. The tall hat, however,
was hopelessly gone, voyaging down toward the Tennessee line.

"You had better go back to the house immediately, Professor,"
shouted Uncle Jack from his rock; "you will have a chill unless you do.
And you'd better run all the way—on the double-quick, you know."

But the Professor did not know.

"I veel go mit," said the young German, with his ready good nature.
But seeing his eyes wandering regretfully toward his sketch, I interfered,
and finally we sent off our learned friend under the care of the negro
cook. The pace was a gentle amble.

"What did he try to fish for?" said Uncle Jack, in a disgusted tone.
"Do you suppose trout are going to bite when a man sits there like a
scarecrow in black clothes, tall hat, and prunella gaiters?"

Ermine came back after a time, and the Major took her place in the
cooner. She did not care to fish, however, but went off to swing in the
hammock. "No, keep your place, Herr Freulig," she said, as the young
artist rose to accompany her. "By-the-way, can you sketch heads?" she

added, carelessly. "Why not throw in the cooner and Captain Romer from this point? There is a very fine view here."

The artist set to work upon a new design.

I went on with the climate, and discovered that while in New England two hundred and fifty out of every thousand deaths are from consumption, in Minnesota and California one hundred and fifty, and in Florida fifty, here, even with an almost total lack of luxuries, the proportion was only thirty in the thousand. I was musing upon this, and wondering whether an abundance of luxuries might not do away with any necessity of dying at all, when Herr Freulig brought out his sketch for my criticism—a Hercules fiercely glaring from an Olympian cooner. "But the Captain is slighter, younger, than this," I said.

Half an hour later out he came to my rock again with another sketch, this time an Antinous,[14] fair and radiant.

"But the Captain is older and darker," I said.

"I haf not well see heem," apologized the young German, "but Mees Herrminia she say he haf a fery fine few."

"A what?"

"A fery fine few—*few*, you know. What you call heem?—dis;" and he drew a profile on the side of the paper.

"Oh!" I said, "you mean a profile. Miss Stuart said the *view* from here was very fine, but she meant the scenery."

"Did she?" said the Herr, doubtfully. "I thought she mean heem." (So did I.)

"He will be with us at dinner," I continued, aloud, "and then you can look at him."

He did look indeed. His large light blue eyes, solemn as an owl's, fixed themselves upon the stranger's face with the persistent artist stare.

"Come, come, Mr. Frowl," said Uncle Jack at last, in an under-tone, "pray eat your dinner. Why do you look at the man so?"

"Mees Herrminia she say he haf a fery fine few," replied the artist; but fortunately no one understood him.

We were all very gay at dinner. There was something so pathetic in the man sitting there with his crutch and his uncertain vision, something so mournful in this unexpected meeting with an old comrade full of health and strength, prosperous and honored, while he had lost all, that of necessity we were very gay—perhaps to keep ourselves from the other extreme. Mr. Romer (for he had said, quietly, "I have no title now")

listened to our stories, smiled when we laughed, and bore his part
pleasantly as the talk went round the table, or rather the rock on which
our cloth was spread. But after the meal was over, and Uncle Jack had gone
into the tent to take his nap, and the artist, having gazed his fill, had
withdrawn with pencils and paper for another attempt, "Come, George,"
he said, "I want to hear all about the boys. Are any of them dead?"

"All but four, Phil."

"Where did they die?"

"Fair Oaks, Gettysburg, Chancellorsville, and Drury's Bluff."

"I lost my leg at Gettysburg. Were you there?"

"Yes."

"Strange, isn't it? that we two, who were— But never mind. You
escaped unhurt, George?"

"Yes, thank God!"

"Thank Him indeed," said the stranger, baring his head. As he sat
there in the afternoon sunshine, I remembered what Ermine had said. Yes,
he had a noble head and fine outline, but he stooped slightly, and all his
movements were slow and weary. The two talked on, asking questions,
hearing and telling little histories of old comrades, too often chronicled
as "dead."

"And you, Phil?" asked the Major at last. "You see me: there is
nothing more to add," replied the other.

I glanced at my companion, suggesting with my eyes that we should
leave the friends alone together.

"No," said Ermine, replying aloud, "why should we go? Not unless
Captain Romer wishes it." For she persisted in using the title, and very
beautiful did she look as, with an unwonted flush on her cheeks and a
softened light in her steel-blue eyes, she sat leaning against an old
pine-tree. I almost wished he might see her, see her as I did, with
every tinge and outline. Perhaps he did; perhaps at times the mist
over his eyes dissolved.

At any rate, he said, gently, "Do not go; it is so long since I have
heard ladies' voices!"

"Where is your sister, Phil?" asked the Major. (He too had seen the
flush on Ermine's cheeks, and bravely made way for the victor, the poor,
maimed, unconscious victor.)

"She is dead, George. Nay, do not apologize; we are most of us
dead down here," said Romer, with a shadowy smile. "She married a

Georgian. He was shot at Gaines's Mill, and she did not long survive him. Mother died too that winter. It was a hard winter with us. Since then I have been alone."

There was a silence. "Why do you not go to Charleston or Richmond? You are buried alive here, old fellow."

"What can I do there? After I left the hospital I tried for a whole year to get some employment, and failed. Nobody wants a cripple. I did fill a small clerkship for a few months, but when my eyes began to fail— the trouble is connected in some way with an old wound near the spine— I lost even that. I am but a useless hulk, George. I can not dig, to beg I am ashamed. And so I came up to these mountains."

"And you live here?"

"Yes, in a cabin across the river. I have a little field where my man Pomp raises corn and potatoes; and then we can fish, you know. Wood costs us nothing, and—don't laugh, George—but I have learned to knit."

"Knit?"

"Yes, stockings and other things. We trade them off for supplies. I can knit quite well now, and—and the people about here are very kind," concluded the Confederate soldier, simply. We did not laugh; we could not for tears.

The next day we drove on down the river to Warm Springs.[15] In the carriage by my side, on the comfortable back seat, rode Philip Romer, while Uncle Jack and Ermine sat opposite. We had all so insisted that he had found no room for excuse. The Major accompanied us on horseback, and the Professor was some miles behind, in the stage. Herr Freulig had with difficulty obtained a mule, and now rode wherever that animal preferred, sometimes far ahead, sometimes off on side tracks up gorges, but generally close behind, the mule's head in uncomfortable proximity to my backbone. We met several country-women on horseback, going to town, with the usual white sack hung over the saddle behind.

"Now those sun-bonnets and calico dresses, if ugly, are at least comfortable," said Ermine; "but the riding dresses of the class next above are something unique both in ugliness and total want of fitness as to place and circumstance. The grim-faced wife of a well-to-do farmer, riding into town on horseback, clad in a green delaine flounced dress, a broad cotton lace collar low down on her collar-bones, and a small bonnet perched on the back of her head, with a brown veil dangling down behind, is—"

"Worth coming to see," said Uncle Jack.

Perhaps you are right, uncle. But a bonnet on horseback! Then the brown veil! Will any one explain to me why it is that in the country a veil always seems to be considered a trimming for the bonnet? In all my rambles through Arcadia I don't know that I have ever seen a veil down fair and square over the face, city fashion, where it belongs."

"Country women are sensible, and like the sunshine, niece."

"Then why wear a veil at all?"

"There are noble hearts under those gaunt, ungraceful exteriors that excite your mirth, Miss Stuart," said Philip Romer. "Those very women will come over the mountains from miles away, when you are ill, and nurse you tenderly for pure charity's sake. When the winter is hard they will share with you and bake you a cake from their last meal. They will spin their wool and dye and weave, and make you clothes from the cloth. This jacket I wear was such a gift. You must excuse its homeliness, for it is all I have."

The river grew more wildly beautiful with every western mile; the cliffs on each side were higher, towering above us almost perpendicularly hundreds of feet, with high mountains directly behind them. The swift current sped forward, now foaming over scattered rocks, now sweeping in one unbroken sheet over a smooth ledge with the green tints of Niagara, then suddenly becoming as still as a mill-pond, as if determined to surprise us. Passing Laurel Creek, with the Walnut Mountain behind, we came in sight of Mountain Island,[16] a single mountain, around whose rocky base the river flows in two streams with a tremendous rush and bustle, as though proud of its conquest from the haughty shore. The island is one rock mass, rising boldly from the water, and as our carriage wound along the little road on shore we were obliged to throw back our heads and look up, in order to see its top, with the trees against the sky.

"There is no island in the Rhine at all equal to this," said Uncle Jack, with enthusiasm.

"But it wants a castle, uncle."

"It would not be difficult to build one," said Philip Romer. "You could take the granite right out of the island itself, and labor is cheap here. Your vassals could defend you from attack by land or by water, Miss Stuart."

"And how much must I pay for my island?"

"About twenty-five cents an acre, or less. You would have not competitors," replied the soldier, smiling."

"Wildly Beautiful." From Constance Fenimore Woolson, "The French Broad."
Harper's, April 1875.

"And the title?"

"Excellent; it comes straight down from Adam."

"Behold I will build me a castle on this unknown mountain island,"
said Ermine, gazing up at the rocky heights. "Hither shall come my few
congenial souls who never make calls, or go to dinner parties, or read

Macdonald's novels.[17] We would have some of Boughton's pictures,[18] and some of Winslow Homer's, and just one of those inscrutably smiling heads from the Cesnola collection[19] to remind us that there is plenty more of life after this one is over. We would have Rhine wine, and George Eliot, and Mendelssohn, and heliotrope, and little cakes with raisins in them. No one should play games, or tell any body else what he or she 'ought to do,' and every body should he perfectly happy."

"Sejed, Prince of Ethiopia," I began, "resolved to have three days of uninterrupted happiness—"

"Begone with your ancient fables!" said Ermine. "This is the New World, and this shall be my Bohemia.

> "'Beyond, the magic valley lay,
> With glimpse of shimmering stream and fall,
> And here, between twin turrets ran
> Built o'er with arch and barbacan,
> The entrance to Bohemia.'"

"The question is," said Uncle Jack, "when they got in finally, did they have a good time?"

"How was it with you, uncle?"

"Do you mean to insinuate, Miss Puss—"

"Only a youthful excursion, uncle. The atmosphere of Bohemia is so kindly; it lingers around you yet."

"Peter's Rock," said the Major, reining in his horse alongside. "It is early. Shall we not rest here a while?" (He was but human, and he had ridden a long time alone.)

So we descended and inspected Peter's Rock with great gravity, Philip Romer remaining in the carriage.

"And who was Peter?" inquired Ermine.

She had taken the Major's arm immediately, with one of her sweetest smiles. The Major would have answered gladly had he known, or had an appropriate fiction occurred to him in time; but he could think of nothing save Mother Goose's celebrated pumpkin eater.

"Yes, who was Peter?" said Uncle Jack.

"Who vas he, dis Pete?" echoed the Herr, who had at last alighted safely from his mule.

A countryman was coming up the road with an ox team.

"I shall ask him," said Ermine, stepping forward. "Is this Peter's Rock, Sir?"

"Ya-as," replied the man, staring solemnly at our party.

"And who was Peter?"

"Wa'al," said the man, reflecting, "I reckon he was an Injun."

"But Peter is not an Indian name?"

"Oh, the whites gave 'em all sorts of names, marm. This Peter he come out on that thar rock with his bows an' arrers, an' he shot some whites a-comin' along the bank goin' west."

"Why?"

"Didn't want 'em thar, I reckon; said 'twas Injun country. What mout be yer name, folks, an' whar be yer from?"

"Our family name is Dolce-far-niente, and we are from Bohemia," replied Ermine.

"Never heerd of it. Is it fur away?"

"Friend, the glimmering glories of our land are far yet ever close at hand. Will you go with us?"

"Wa'al, no; I reckon I can't jes now. Yer see, I'm goin' to Ashville. But yourn must be a mighty nice country, I reckon," replied the mountaineer, stimulated to unwonted praises by the lovely vision of Ermine; then, seized with sudden embarrassment, he urged on his team and disappeared.

"No doubt he will often tell of the singular people he met on the river who said they came from Bohemia," remarked Ermine, laughing. "But we have our legend. What a picture it would make! Herr Freulig, look at that rock, and imagine the noble form of the Indian chieftain on the summit outlined against the sky, his arrow aimed at the destroyers of his race!"

"Of hees rase, yes," replied the artist, eagerly. "I makes heem Miss Herrminia. Here e-es de r-roke, so;" and seating himself on a log, he began sketching rapidly.

While we were loitering in the shade we heard the rumble of the stage behind us and presently it came into view jolting over the rocky road. The yellow face of the Professor looked from one of the windows. "I will alight," he said, seeing us. "Driver, do you hear? I will alight. There being no one in the coach save myself," he explained, as he climbed slowly down, "I have been most unpleasantly jolted. I assure you, ladies, that I have been bounded up and down like a rubber ball. It is but a short distance to the Springs; I will walk."

Ermine was sitting in a little leafy nook with the Major. The Professor, always serenely confident, directed his steps thither.

"Who was Peter?" demanded Ermine, barring the entrance with a long wand of mountain ivy.

"Who was Peter?" repeated the Professor in a bewildered tone.

"Yes; this is his rock, you know. I can allow no one to enter until he has solved my riddle."

The learned man invested himself with all his gallantry as with a garment. "Fair Sphinx," he replied, affecting with some trouble a playful smile, "your orders shall be obeyed. Know, then, that it was a—a geologist named Peter, an ardent votary of science, who, penetrating into these unknown mountains, measured that rock, and—and—"

"Fell over," suggested the Major.

"And was killed," concluded Uncle Jack. "They always are, you know. That is one comfort about geologists."

"But the mountaineers, who in this case must have been Indians, in their enthusiastic admiration for science, made him a solitary grave on the top of the rock, where he now lies alone with—with the sky," I added.

"Precisely what I was about to say," observed the Professor, bowing airily to us all.

"How beautiful!" said Ermine enthusiastically; "and above all, how new! Science hath gilded the rock. Imagine the lonely figure of the geologist suspended by a rope, engaged in the noble work of measuring. Sublime!" And taking the Major's arm again, she walked off down the road, leaving the learned man to the exclusive enjoyment of the little leafy nook.

But Herr Freulig sat dejectedly on his log; his pencil had stopped. "I moste alter," I heard him murmur; "it e-es not Indeens at all." And the rubber came into play.

After another half hour spent on the shore we drove on toward the Springs, leaving the Professor walking youthfully along, with an impromptu alpenstock. He had replaced his lost hat with an old straw, purchased from a rich wagoner who had two, and this head-gear he had adorned with a large bunch of rhododendrons, as much as to say, "I too can be pastoral;" he wore it tilted over on one side, and hummed to himself as he walked. The tune was *Old Hundred*; but never mind.

"Why should this foaming, rapid river be burdened with such a name?" said Ermine, as we drove on, each curve showing us new vistas of grandeur and beauty. "French Broad!—you have to take two breaths to finish it! The river is neither broad nor French that I can see."

"It was named by a party of hunters," said Philip Romer. "They were exploring the mountains, and the first river they met they called the Broad, the next they called Second Broad, and the third Main Broad; finding still a fourth, they called it French's Broad, after their captain, whose name was French."[20]

"What a poverty-stricken set of minds!" said Ermine. "Why could they not take the Indian names? Or if they must baptize things for themselves, they should at least have chosen a characteristic ugliness. They managed these things better along the Great Lakes. What grand names are Thunder Bay and Porphyry Point! What unwritten stories of the past belong to Misery River and Death's Door! Then, descending to the rude, every-day life of the hunter, what could be better than Knife River, Kettle Point, and Pie Island? For my part, I have always cherished a liking for the man who sent that Lake Huron town down to posterity labeled 'Bad Axe.' No doubt it commemorated the day when, alone on the edge of the boundless forest, the struggling settler found that his axe, the most precious treasure of the pioneer, was a bad one."

"The Indian name of the French Broad is Tockeste, the Racing River," said the soldier.

"There," said Ermine, "that is what I mean. How entirely appropriate! The Indians were poets."

"Did you know that some of the Cherokees still reside in the State?" continued Philip. "Their settlement is not very far from here—more to the south. I suppose they are by far the wildest Indians left within the borders of the old States. These mountains still give them many a free hunting ground. Singularly enough, too, they are not without their public spirit. Before the war, when the mountain people were trying to build a railroad through their country, these redskins brought out their shovels and picks, and actually graded and prepared voluntarily two miles of the road near their village. It still remains there in fair order, although the road is but a ghost."

"I have noticed a phantom pursuing us all the way from the other side of the Blue Ridge," said Uncle Jack. "Ruined culverts, half-excavated tunnels, shadowy grading, and lines of levels. I have even fancied that I hear a spirit whistle."[21]

"The ghost of the poor mountain railroad, Sir. Swindlers made off with all the money, and the robbed mountaineers gloomily make fences of the ties—all that is left to them."

NORTH CAROLINA INDIANS. FROM CONSTANCE FENIMORE WOOLSON, "THE FRENCH
BROAD." *HARPER'S,* APRIL 1875.

"By-the-way, Captain Romer, can *you* tell us who Peter was?" said
Ermine, as we drove on. "We were discussing the subject at the rock. So
far, he has been an Indian-chief and a geologist.

"He was neither, Miss Stuart," replied Philip, with ready invention.
"He was a British officer under Cornwallis, who, falling madly in love
with a beautiful maiden on the march along the Carolina coast, deserted
and fled to these mountains. On the summit of that rock, a miniature
Gibraltar, he built his cabin, and there the two lived until death suddenly
smote the fair young wife, and subaltern Peter was left alone. It is said
that her body, embalmed with spices and wrapped in bark, Indian fashion,
was fastened aloft in one of those pine trees you saw, and often at sunset
Peter was seen sitting on the edge of the cliff, with his eyes fixed
mournfully on the dark object held aloft by the green boughs—all
that remained of his love."

CASCADE NEAR WARM SPRINGS, NORTH CAROLINA. FROM CONSTANCE FENIMORE
WOOLSON, "THE FRENCH BROAD." *HARPER'S*, APRIL 1875.

"That," said Ermine, "is by far the best, and is adopted from this
time forth. Herr Freulig" (for the mule was close at my backbone again),
"did you hear that? He must be sitting on the edge of the cliff—in his
uniform, of course—with his eyes fixed upon the dark object swaying in
the green far above. The very thing for a sketch! I don't know that I ever
met a finer subject straying around loose in Arcadia."

"E—es it—" began the artist, trying to take out his portfolio on the
spot. Then, slowly shaking his head, he stopped, and dismounting from
his mule, tied that playful animal to a tree. The last I saw of him he was
sharpening his numerous pencils.

The approach to Warm Springs is very lovely. Crossing the river on
a long bridge, we drove up to the large hotel which stands here alone,

WARM SPRINGS HOTEL, ARRIVAL OF STAGE. FROM CONSTANCE FENIMORE WOOLSON, "THE FRENCH BROAD." *HARPER'S,* APRIL 1875.

maintained in the heart of the wilderness by the maimed and the halt and the blind who come here to bathe in the magical waters. The springs bubble up from the ground in a large pool near the river's edge; the temperature of the water varies from ninety-eight to one hundred and two degrees Fahrenheit. Although, unlike the Virginia resorts, the Warm Springs of North Carolina are scarcely known at the North, they are well patronized by the people of Tennessee, Alabama, and Mississippi, and of the surrounding country. As we drove up to the entrance the long piazza was gay with ladies attired in the bright colors the Southerners love so well. The universal black, so fashionable at the North, is hardly seen at the South except in mourning, and when accepted in a modified form is always lighted up with some sash or knot of gay ribbons.

"Tropical," said Ermine, alighting.

The Major had ridden by himself during the latter part of the afternoon. Once or twice we saw him, but he seemed lost in thought. As we sat on the piazza in the evening, however, he disburdened himself of his load. "I have finally unearthed the story of Peter's Rock, Miss Stuart" he began, with a careless air. "It seems Peter was a negro, and

VIEW FROM THE TOP
OF PAINT ROCK. FROM
CONSTANCE FENIMORE
WOOLSON, "THE
FRENCH BROAD."
HARPER'S, APRIL 1875.

when Stoneman rode through from Tennessee, he gave them warning
with a flaming torch, standing on the top of the rock—"

"Ah!" interrupted Herr Freulig, excitedly; "it e-es too moche. I
haf make heem von Indeen, I haf make heem von geologer, I haf make
heem a Breetish officer, and now you vants me to make heem a neeg! I
can no more."

LAST GLIMPSE OF THE FRENCH BROAD. FROM CONSTANCE FENIMORE WOOLSON,
"THE FRENCH BROAD." *HARPER'S,* APRIL 1875.

I burst into an irrepressible fit of laughter as the unhappy Herr
concluded the story of his wrongs. The sketch of the "Breetish officer"
was accepted and ratified on the spot, and Ermine resolved herself into
a consoler-general. The Major's story remains unfinished to this day.

Our river pilgrimage was drawing to a close; four miles to the west ran the Tennessee line, and beyond were the low countries and railroads. Professor Macquoid concluded to try the effect of his rhododendron hat and alpenstock in the neighborhood of Warm Springs for a few days, Ermine remaining singularly blind to their shepherd-like charm. He mentioned that he had discovered a remarkable dip in the neighborhood, which he thought it his duty to measure. (The Professor, it was understood, was engaged upon the composition of a Great Work.) Herr Freulig was of course obliged to remain with his traveling companion; but I overheard Ermine saying something about "next winter," and I thought I caught a glimpse of a sketch in her hand which looked very much like that "fery fine few."

The Major was going as far as Chattanooga, and Philip Romer said he would accompany us to the State line, and then return homeward on his friend's horse.

"But can you?" I asked, remembering the narrow road and the fords.

"The horse knows the way, and all the people about here know me, Miss Martha," said the soldier, smiling. "I am not entirely blind yet; I can see a little."

Then, as we were all silent through our great compassion for him, he turned the tide of talk into another channel. "Do you see that road across the river?" he asked. "It goes to Greenville,[22] twenty-five miles distant. In that little village, on the 4th of September, 1864, died John Morgan the raider, shot through the heart in a garden, his place of refuge having been discovered and pointed out by a woman.

"He was a bold rider," said Ermine, gently.

"I beg your pardon, niece," began Uncle Jack in some heat; "John Morgan was a rebel, and deserved his—" Then remembering Philip Romer, he paused suddenly.

"The fortunes of war, Sir. He took his fate into his own hands; we all did that, and must now bear the consequences," said the Confederate soldier, quietly.

Some distance below Warm Springs we found Paint Rock—a singular cliff marked with streaks of a dark red color, supposed by the imaginative to be Indian picture writing.[23]

"Are we in the Great Smoky Mountains?" asked Ermine.

"In their very heart, Miss Stuart; all the peaks you see belong to that chain. You are going through with the French Broad, which has cut a pathway for itself to the low countries."

We lingered on the border, but the farewells came at last. "Good-by," we said, and found ourselves strangely saddened by the breaking of this tie of a day. The Major had many a plan for future meetings with his old comrade, and he detailed them all with his hearty cordiality. Philip Romer listened, but I noticed that he did not echo the confident hope.

The Major helped him to mount, and turned the horse's head in the right direction. "Good-by," we said again, and our carriage started westward. At a curve in the road we all looked back. The solitary figure was riding slowly up into the dark cañon of the French Broad; another moment and it was lost in the pine-trees.

Beyond the mountains the river loses its wildness; tranquilly it flows along on its way to the Tennessee, and our last view of it was fair and peaceful. We heard the whistle of the locomotive, and the cars bore us rapidly away; but we watched as long as we could see them the peaks of the Great Smoky, and thought silently of that solitary figure riding back along the bank of the wild French Broad.

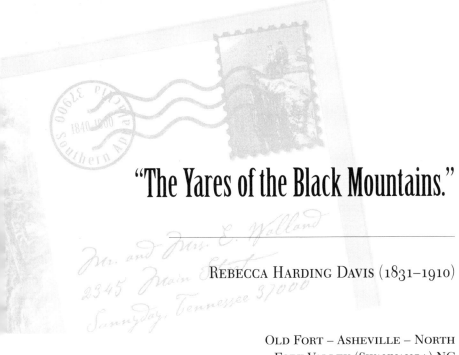

"The Yares of the Black Mountains."

Rebecca Harding Davis (1831–1910)

Old Fort – Asheville – North Fork Valley (Swannanoa) NC

R ebecca Harding Davis traveled widely throughout the United States, and many of her magazine pieces—including both "local color" fiction and travel writing—are set in the south. Of those, a significant portion are set in the mountains, mostly in North Carolina. (See Sheaffer, 292–316; see also Collins's annotated bibliography.) Davis's mountain stories include short fiction, essays for children, and what Davis biographer Helen Sheaffer calls "story-essays"—that is, fictionalized travel narratives, including, most notably, "By-paths in the Mountains," an illustrated three-part series and conventional travelogue that appeared in *Harper's* in the summer of 1880.

Unlike "By-paths" and other conventional fictionalized travelogues of the period, the present selection uses a third-person narrator. And rather than feature an ensemble of characters, it focuses on one main character, and on her perception of the region's inhabitants as she travels into the Black Mountains. The story is of special interest to students of "local color" fiction, since it may well be the first such story, featuring southern mountaineers, to appear in a national magazine. This story first appeared in

Lippincott's, July 1875

Lippincott's, July 1875, while another contender for the title, Constance F. Woolson's "Crowder's Cove: A Story of the War," appeared eight months later (*Appleton's,* March 1876). Meanwhile, Mary Noailles Murfree's "The Dancin' Party at Harrison's Cove"— the story usually regarded as seminal—appeared almost three years later (*Atlantic,* May 1878). (See Sheaffer, 306–8; Kern, 65; Collins, 37.) Though Murfree is still the best-known author of southern mountain fiction, Davis's "Yares of the Black Mountains" probably inspired Murfree to write about the region. Indeed, Murfree's first biographer, Edd Winfield Parks, speculates that Davis's essay "may well have changed the course of Mary's entire literary life" (Parks 71).

Rebecca Harding Davis was raised in Wheeling, (West) Virginia, along the Ohio River, on the border between the industrial north and the rural south. After graduating as valedictorian from Washington Female Seminary in Pennsylvania, she returned to accept an apprenticeship on the *Wheeling Intelligencer* in the late 1850s. In 1861, on the eve of the Civil War, her "Life in the Iron Mills" was published to national acclaim in the *Atlantic Monthly.* During the war she traveled to the northeast, married, moved to Philadelphia, became a regular contributor to the *Atlantic* and other national magazines, and gave birth to her first child, Richard, who would grow up to become a famous journalist. By the time of her death, Rebecca Harding Davis had published ten novels and more than one hundred shorter works of fiction and nonfiction. During her lifetime, her professional reputation came to be overshadowed by that of her son. However, in the early 1970s, Tillie Olsen published an edition of "Iron Mills" that sparked renewed interest in Davis. Now Davis is considered one of the canonical American writers of the nineteenth century.

"OLD FORT!"

The shackly little train jolted into the middle of an unploughed field and stopped. The railway was at an end. A group of Northern summer-tourists, with satchels and water-proofs in shawl-straps, came out of the car and looked about them. It was but a few years after the war, and the South was unexplored ground to them. They had fallen together at Richmond, and by the time they had reached this out-of-the-way corner of North Carolina were the best of boon companions, and wondered why they had never found each other out in the world before. Yet, according to American habit, it was a mere chance whether the acquaintance strengthened into lifelong friendship or ended with a nod in the next five minutes.

It bade fair just now to take the latter turn.

Nesbitt, who had been in consultation with two men who were ploughing at the side of the station, came hurrying up: "Civilization stops here, it appears. Thirty miles' staging to Asheville, and after that carts and mules. The mails come, like the weather, at the will of Providence. I think I shall explore no farther. When does your train go back, conductor?"

"The scenery disappoints me," said Miss Cook, bridging her nose with her eye-glasses. "It lacks the element of grandeur."

"You'll find it lacking in more than that beyond," said a Detroit man who had come down to speculate in lumber. "Nothing but mountains, and balsam timber as spongy as punk. A snake couldn't get his living out of ten acres of it."

Across the field was a two-roomed wooden house, over which a huge board was mounted whereon was scrawled with tar, "Dinner and BAR-ROOM." They all went, stumbling over the lumpy meadow, toward it. Miss Cook, who was always good-humored except on aesthetic questions, carried the baby's satchel with her own.

"Shall you go on?" she asked the baby's mother. "The conductor says the mountains are inaccessible to women."

"Of course. Why, he has slept every night since we came on to high land."

"I doubt very much whether the cloud-effects will be as good as in the White Mountains. The sky is too warm." This was said thoughtfully.

"He has one stomach-tooth almost through. The balsam-air will be such a tonic! We'll go up if it is on foot, won't we, Charley?" And she buried her face in the roll of blanket.

There was a fine odor of burnt beans and whiskey in the hot little parlor of the house, with its ragged horsehair chairs and a fly-blown print of the "Death of Robert E. Lee" on the wall. On the other side of the hall was the bar-room, where a couple of red-faced majors in homespun trousers and shirts were treating the conductor. It was a domestic-looking bar-room after all, in spite of red noses and whiskey: there were one or two geraniums in the window, and a big gray cat lay asleep beside them on the sill.

One of the majors came to Baby's mother in the parlor. "There is a rocking-chair in the—the opposite apartment," he said, "and the air will be better there for the child. A very fine child, madam! very fine, indeed!"

She said yes, it was, and followed him. He gave Baby a sprig of geranium, bowed and went out, while the other men began to discuss a Methodist camp meeting, and the barkeeper shoved a newspaper over his bottles and worked anxiously at his daybook. The other passengers all went to dinner, but Nesbitt was back at her side in five minutes.

"I'm glad you stayed here," he said. "There is a bare wooden table set in a shed out yonder, and a stove alongside where the cooking goes on. You would not have wanted to taste food for a month if you had seen the fat pork and corn-bread which they are shovelling down with iron forks. Now, if I thought—if we were going to rough it in the mountains—camp-fire, venison, trout cooked by ourselves, and all that sort of thing, I'd be with you. But this civilized beastliness I don't like—never did. I'll take this train back, and strike the trunk-line at Charlotte, and try Texas for my summer holiday. I must be off at once."

"Good-bye, then, Mr. Nesbitt. I am sorry you are not going: you've been so kind to Charley."

"Not at all. Good-bye, and God bless you, little chap!" stopping to put his finger in the baby's thin hand. He was quite sure the little woman in black would never bring her child back from the mountains.

"I'm glad he's gone," said Miss Cook, coming in from the shed. "It's absurd, the row American men make about their eating away from home. They want Delmonico's table set at every railway-station."

"You will go up into the mountains, then?"

"Yes. I've only three weeks' vacation, and I can get farther from my usual rut, both as to scenery and people, here than anywhere else. I've been writing on political economy lately, and my brain needs complete change of idea. You 'know how it is yourself.'"

"No, I—" She unlocked her satchel, and as she took out Baby's powder looked furtively at Miss Cook. This tight little person, buckled snugly into a waterproof suit, her delicate face set off by a brown hat and feather, talking political economy and slang in a breath, was a new specimen of human nature to her.

She gave the powder, and then the two women went out and deposited themselves and their wraps in a red stage which waited at the door. A fat, jolly-faced woman, proprietor of the shed and cooking-stove, ran out with a bottle of warm milk for the child, the Carolinian majors and barkeeper took off their hats, the Detroit man nodded with his on his head, and with a crack of the whip the stage rolled away with them. It lurched on its leather springs, and luffed and righted precisely like a ship in a chopping sea, and threw them forward against each other and back into dusty depths of curled hair, until even the baby laughed aloud.

Miss Cook took out her notebook and pencil, but found it impossible to write. "There is nothing to make note of, either," she said after an hour or two. "It is the loneliest entrance to a mountain-region I ever saw. These glassless huts we see now and then, the ruins of cabins, make it all the more forlorn. I saw a woman ploughing with an ox just now on the hillside, where it was so steep I thought woman, plough, and ox would roll down together. —Is there no business, no stir of any sort, in this country?" she called sharply to the driver, who looked in at the window at that minute.

"I don't know," he said leisurely. "Come to think on't, it's powerful quiet ginerally."

"No mining—mills?"

"Thar war mica-mines. But ther given over. An' thar war a railroad. But that's given over too.[1] I was a-goin' to ask you ladies ef you'd wish to git out an' see whar the traveller was murdered last May, up the stream a bit. I kin show you jest whar the blood is yet; which, they do say, was discovered by the wild dogs a-gnawin' at the ground."

The baby's mother held it closer, with her lips unusually pale. "No, thank you," she said cheerfully. "Probably we can see it as we come back."

"Well, jest as *you* please," he replied, gathering up the reins with a discontented air. "Thar's been no murder in the mountings for five years, an' 'tisn't likely there'll be another."

A few miles farther on he stopped to water his horses at a hill-spring. "Thar's a house, yonder, ef you ladies like to rest an hour," he said, nodding benignantly.

"But the mail?—you carry the mail?"

"Oh, the mail won't trouble itself," taking out his pipe and filling it. "That thar child needs rest, I reckon."

The two women hurried up the stony field to the large log hut, where the mistress and a dozen black-haired children stood waiting for them.

"Something to eat?" cried Miss Cook. "Yes indeed, my good soul; and the sooner the better. Finely-cut face, that," sketching it rapidly while the hostess hurried in and out. "Gallic. These mountaineers were all originally either French Huguenots or Germans. It would be picturesque, dirt and all, under a Norman peasant's coif and red umbrella, but in a dirty calico wrapper—bah!"

The house also was dirty and bare, but the table was set with fried chicken, rice, honey and delicious butter.

"And how—how much are we to pay for all this?" said Miss Cook before sitting down.

"If ten cents each would not be too much?" hesitated the woman.

Miss Cook nodded: her very portemonnaie gave a click of delight in her pocket. "I heard that these people were miserably poor!" she muttered rapturously. "Don't look so shocked. If you earned your bread by your brains, as I do, you'd want as much bread for a penny as possible."

The sky began to darken before they rose from the table, and, looking out through the cut in the wall which served for a window, they saw that the rain was already falling heavily. A girl of sixteen, who had been spinning in the corner, drew her wheel in front of the window: the square of light threw her delicately-lined face and heavy yellow hair into relief. She watched the baby with friendly smiles as she spun, giving it a bit of white wool to hold.

"What a queer tribe we have fallen among!" said Miss Cook in scarcely lowered tones. "I never saw a spinning-wheel before, except Gretchen's in Faust, and there is a great hand-loom. Why, it was only Tuesday I crossed Desbrosses Ferry,[2] and I am already two centuries back from New York. Very incurious, too, do you observe? The women don't even glance at the shape of our hats, and nobody has asked us a question as to our business here. People who live in the mountains or by the sea generally lack the vulgar curiosity of the ordinary country farmer."

"Do they? I did not know. These are the kindest people *I* ever met," said the little woman in black with unwonted emphasis.

"Oh, they expect to make something out of you. Travelers are the rarest of game in this region, I imagine," observed Miss Cook carelessly, and then stopped abruptly with a qualm of conscience, remarking for the first time the widow's cap which her companion wore. These people had perhaps been quicker than she in guessing the story of the little woman— that the child, dying as it seemed, was all that was left to her, and that this journey to the balsam mountains was the last desperate hope for its life.

She looked with a fresh interest at the thin, anxious face, the shabby black clothes, and then out of the window to where the high peaks of the Black Range were dimly visible like cones of sepia on the gray horizon. She had read a paper in some magazine on the inhospitable region yonder, walled by the clouds. It was "almost unexplored, although so near the seaboard cities;" the "haunt of beasts of prey;" the natives were "but little raised above the condition of Digger Indians."[3] All this had whetted Miss Cook's appetite. She was tired of New York and New Yorkers, and of the daily grinding them up into newspaper correspondence wherewith to earn her bread. To become an explorer, to adventure into the lairs of bears and wolves, at so cheap a cost as an excursion ticket over the Air-Line Railroad,[4] was a rare chance for her. As it rained now, she gathered her feet and skirts up on the chair-rungs from the dirty floor and confided some of these thoughts to her companion, who only said absently, she did not know. Doctor Beasly—perhaps Miss Cook had heard of Doctor Beasly?—had said Charley must have mountain-air, and that the balsams were tonics in themselves. She did not suppose the Diggers or animals would hurt *her*.

The truth was, the little woman had been fighting Death long (and vainly, as it proved) over a sick bed. She knew his terrors there well enough: she had learned to follow his creeping, remorseless fingers on clammy skin and wasted body, and to hear his coming footsteps in the flagging beats of a pulse. She had that dry, sapless, submissive look which a woman gains in long nursing—a woman that nurses a patient who holds part of her own life and is carrying it with him, step by step, into the grave. The grave had closed over this woman's dead, and all that he had taken with him from her: even to herself she did not dare to speak of him as of yet. The puny little boy on her arms was the only real thing in life to her. There was a chance in these mountains of keeping him—a bare chance. As for wild beasts or wild people, she had thought of them no more than the shadows on the road which passed with every wind.

The rain beat more heavily on the roof: the driver presented himself at the door, dripping. "Ef we don't go on, night'll catch us before we make Alexander's," he said. "Give me that little feller under my coat. I'll kerry him to the stage."

Miss Cook shivered in the chilly wind that rushed through the open door. "Who would believe that the streets in New York were broiling at 105° this minute?"

"That baby's not wrapped warm enough for a night like this," said the woman of the house, and forthwith dragged out of a wooden box a red flannel petticoat, ragged but clean, and pinned it snugly about him.

"She'll charge you a pretty price for it," whispered Miss Cook; "and it's only a rag."

"No, no," laughed the woman, when the widow drew out her portemonnaie. "Joe kin bring it back some day. That's all right."

"You seem as touched by that as though it were some great sacrifice," said Miss Cook tartly after they were settled again in the stage.

"It was all she had." Adding after a pause, "I have been living in New York for five years. My baby was born there, and—and I had trouble. But we came strangers, and were always strangers. I knew nobody but the doctor. I came to look upon the milkman and baker who stopped at the door as friends. People are in such a hurry there. They have not time to be friendly."

"You are a Southerner? You are coming back to your old home?"

"No, I never was in the South before."

The stage tossed and jolted, the rain pelted against the windows. Miss Cook snored and wakened with jumps, and the baby slept tranqilly. There was a certain purity in the cold damp air that eased his breathing, and the red petticoat was snug and warm. The touch of it seemed to warm his mother too. The kind little act of giving it was something new to her. It seemed as if in the North she too had been in a driving hurry of pain and work since her birth, and had never had time to be friendly. If life here was barbarous, it was at ease, unmoving, kindly. She could take time to breathe.

It was late in the night when the stage began to shiver, like the one-horse shay in its last gasp of dissolution, over the cobble-stoned streets of the little hill-village of Asheville. It drew up in front of an inn with wooden porches sheltered by great trees;[5] there were lights burning inside, and glimpses of supper waiting, and a steam of frying chicken and coffee pervading the storm. One or two men hurried out from the office with umbrellas, and a pretty white-aproned young girl welcomed them at the door.

"Supper is ready," she said. "Yours shall be sent to your room, madam. We have had a fire kindled there on account of the baby."

"Why how *could* you know Charley was coming?" cried the widow breathlessly.

"Oh, a week ago, madam. While you stopped at Morganton. The conductor of the Salisbury train sent on a note, and afterward the clergyman at Linville. We have been warned to take good care of you," smiling brightly.

The baby's mother said nothing until she was seated in her room before a wood-fire which crackled and blazed cheerfully. The baby lay on her lap, its face red with heat and comfort.

"Since I left Richmond one conductor has passed me on to another," she said solemnly to Miss Cook. "The baby was ill at Linville, and the train was stopped for an hour, and the ladies of the village came to help me. And now these people. It is just as though I were coming among old friends."

"Pshaw! They think you have money. These Southerners are impoverished by the war, and they have an idea that every Northern traveler is overloaded with wealth, and is fair game."

"The war? I had forgotten that. One would forgive them if they were churlish and bitter."

The woman was a weak creature evidently, and inclined to drivel. Miss Cook went off to bed, first jotting down in her notebook some of the young girl's queer mistakes in accent, and a joke on her yellow dress and red ribbons. They would be useful hereafter in summing up her estimate of the people. The girl and the widow meantime had grown into good friends in undressing the boy together. When his mother lay down at last beside him the firelight threw a bright glow over the bed, and the pretty young face came again to the door to nod goodnight.

It was only a hotel, and outside a strange country and strange people surrounded her. But she could not rid herself of the impression that she had come home to her own friends.

The sun rose in a blue dappled sky, but before he was fairly above the bank of wet clouds Miss Cook was out, notebook in hand. She had sketched the outline of the mountains that walled in the table-land on which the village stood; had felt the tears rise to her eyes as the purple shadow about Mount Pisgah flamed into sudden splendor (for her tears and emotion responded quickly to a beautiful sight or sound); she had discovered the grassy public square in which a cow grazed and a woman was leisurely driving a steer that drew a cart; she had visited four emporiums of trade—little low-ceiled rooms which fronted on the square, walled with calicoes and barrels of sugar, and hung overhead with brown crockery and tin cups; she had helped two mountaineers trade their bag of flour for shoes; had talked to the fat postmaster through the open pane in his window, to the negro woman milking in the sheds, to a gallant Confederate colonel hoeing his corn in a field, to a hunter bringing in a late lot of peltry from the Smoky Range. As they talked, she portioned out the facts as material for a letter in the *Herald*. The quaint decaying houses, the swarming blacks, the whole drowsy life of the village set high in the chilled sunshine and bound by its glittering belt of rivers and rampart of misty-mountain heights, were sketched in a sharp effective bit of word-painting in her mind.

She trotted back to the Eagle Hotel to put it on paper; then to breakfast; then off again to look up schools, churches and editors.

Late in the afternoon, tramping along a steep hill-path, she caught sight of two women in a skiff on a lonely stream below. It was the baby's mother and the pretty girl from the inn. No human being was in sight; the low sunlight struck luminous bars of light between the trunks of the hemlocks into the water beneath the boat as it swung lazily in the current; long tangled vines of sweetbriar and the red trumpet-creeper hung from the trees into the water; the baby lay sound asleep on a heap of shawls at his mother's feet, while she dipped the oars gently now and then to keep in the middle of the stream.

"How lazy you look!" called Miss Cook. "You might have been made out of the earth of these sleepy hills. Here, come ashore. D'ye see the work I've done?" fluttering a sheaf of notes. "I've been at the jail. A den! an outrage on the civilization of the nineteenth century! Men have been branded here since the war. Criminals in this State are actually secured in iron cages like wild beasts! I shall use that fact effectively in my book on the *Causes of the Decadence of the South:* one chapter shall be given to 'The Social and Moral Condition of North Carolina.'"

"You will need so many facts!" ejaculated the little woman, awestruck, yet pityingly. "It will take up all your summer's holiday to gather them up."

Miss Cook laughed with cool superiority: "Why child, I have them all now—got them this morning. Oh, I can evolve the whole state of society from half a dozen items. I have the faculty of generalizing, you see. No," folding up her papers decisively, "I've done the mountains and the mountaineers. Between slavery and want of railroads, humanity has reached its extremest conditions here. I should not learn that fact any better if I stayed a week."

"You are not going back?"

"Back? Emphatically, yes. I go to Georgia to-morrow morning. This orange I have sucked dry."

Miss Cook posted to the hotel, and passed the night in making sketches to illustrate her article from a bundle of photographic views which she found in possession of the landlady.

Looking out of the parlor-window next morning, she saw half the inmates of the house gathered about a cart drawn by two oxen in which sat the widow and Charley. A couple of sacks of flour lay at her feet, and a middle-aged man, a giant as to height and build, dressed in butternut homespun, cracked his long whip at the flies.

"Where can she be going?" asked Miss Cook of a young woman from Georgia whom she had been pumping dry of facts all the morning. The Georgian wore a yellow dress with a coarse frill about her swarthy neck: she sat at the piano and played "Love's Chidings."

The man, she said, was Jonathan Yare, a hunter in the Black Mountains. Her brother had told her his terrible history. Her brother had once penetrated into the mountains as far as the hut where the Yares lived, some thirty miles from here. Beyond that there were no human beings: the mountains were given up to wild beasts. As for these Yares, they had lived in the wilderness for three generations, and by all accounts, like the beasts.

Miss Cook rushed out: political economist and author though she might be, she had a gossip's keen enjoyment in a piece of bad news. "Do you know these Yares?" she whispered. "They have a terrible history: they live like wild beasts."

The little woman's color left her. Her head filled instantly with visions of the Ku-Klux and the Lowery gang. "I never asked what they were," she gasped. "I only wanted to take Charley among the balsams."

The man looked back at this moment, and seeing that the valise and box and baby's bottle of milk were in the cart, cracked his long whip over the near ox, and the next moment the widow and her baby were jolting up the rocky hill-street, abandoned to the tender mercies of the middle-aged man in butternut and his gang.

Nobody need laugh if we say that she felt a sudden spasm of fear. When Death laid his hand on her child she had taken him up and fled to these mountains without a second thought, as the women in the times of the apostles carried their dead and dying to be cured by miraculous aid. But she was a woman like the rest of us, used to jog along the conventional paths to church, to market, to the shops; her only quarrels with the departed David had been about his unorthodox habits in business and politics; and she never could be easy until she was sure that her neighbors liked her new bonnet. What would her neighbors—any neighbor— David himself, have said at seeing her in league with this desperate character, going into frightful solitudes "inaccessible to women"?

The man spoke to her once or twice, but she answered with an inaudible little chirp, after which he fell into silence, neither whistling nor speaking to his oxen, as she noticed.

She could not help observing how unusually clear the light about her was from the thinness of the air, although the sun was out of sight in a covered, foreboding sky, and black, ragged fragments of cloud from some approaching thunderstorm were driven now and then across the horizon. The road, if road you chose to call it, crept along beside the little crystal-clear Swannanoa River,[6] and persisted in staying beside it, sliding over hills of boulders, fording rushing mountain-streams and dank, snaky swamps, digging its way along the side of sheer precipices, rather than desert its companion. The baby's mother suddenly became conscious that the river was a companion to whom she had been talking and listening for an hour or two. It was narrow, deep, and clear as the air above it: it flowed with a low, soothing sound in which there came to her somehow an assurance of security and good will. But she was bewildered by the multitudes of trailing vines hedged in the river; they covered the banks, and threw long, clutching branches into the water; they crept out on projecting trees on either side and leaped across the stream, ridging it with arches of wreaths and floating tendrils. There were the dark, waving plumes of the American ivy, the red cornucopias of the trumpet-creeper, morning-glories with great white blossoms, the passion-flower trailing its mysterious purple emblems through the mud beneath the oxen's feet,—all creeping or turning in some way toward the river. Surely there were airy affections, subtle friendlinesses, among these dumb living creatures! They all seemed alive to her, though she was a prosaic woman, who read little beyond her cookery-book and Bible. It was as though she had come unbidden into Nature's household and interrupted the inmates talking together. The Carolina rose stretched in masses for miles along the road— the very earth seemed to blush with it: here and there a late rhododen-dron hung out its scarlet banner. The tupelo thrust its white fingers out of the shadow like a maiden's hand, and threw out into the air the very fragrance of the lilies-of-the-valley which used to grow in the garden she made when she was a little girl. The silence was absolute, except when a pheasant rose with a whirr or a mocking-bird sounded its melancholy defiant call in the depths of the forest. Long habit of grief had left her heart tender and its senses keen: these things, which were but game or specimens for the naturalist, were God's creatures to her, and came close to her. Charley woke, and looking up saw her smiling down on him with warm cheeks. She did not know the name of a plant or tree or bird, but she felt the friendliness and welcome of the hills, just as she used to be comforted and lifted nearer to God by distant church music, although she could not hear a word of the hymn.

Leaving the road, they entered deep silent gorges, and followed the bed of mountain-streams through cañons walled in by gray frowning rocks, over which the sky bent more darkly each moment. At last there was a break in the gorge. About her was a world of gigantic mountains. There was no sign of human habitation—nothing but interminable forests that climbed the heights, and, failing half-way, left them bare to pierce the clouds.

She had started on this journey with a vague notion of reaching some higher land where balsam trees grew, the air about which would be wholesome for Charley. She had penetrated to the highest summits of the Appalachian Range, the nursery or breeding-place from which descend the Blue Ridge, the Alleghanies, the Nantahela—all the great mountain-bulwarks that wall the continent on its eastern coast. The mighty peaks rose into the sky beyond her sight, while the gathering storm-clouds clung to their sides, surging and eddying with the wind. How petty and short-lived was wind or storm. She looked up at the fixed, awful heights, forgetting even the child on her knee. It was as if God had taken her into one of the secret places where He dwelt apart.

She came to herself suddenly, finding that the cart had stopped and the driver was standing beside examining the baby's milk.

"I reckon," he said, "it's sour, and the little chap's hungry. I'll get some fresh, an' you kin look at the mountings."

He went into the laurel, and with a peculiar whistle brought some of the wild cattle to him, and proceeded to milk one of the cows, returning with a cupful of foaming warm milk. Now one of the Ku-Klux would hardly go to milking cows, she thought; and there was something in the man's steady grave eyes that looked as if he too understood the meaning of the "mountings." They jogged on in silence.

Half an hour later the clouds closed about them and the rain fell heavily. The cart was dragged through the bed of a mountain-stream, and then stopped in front of a low log house built into the ledge of the mountain. A room on either side opened into a passage, through which a wagon might be driven, and where the rain and wind swept unchecked. An old woman stood in it looking up the stream. Her gray hair hung about her sallow face, her dress was a dirty calico, her feet were bare. Behind her was the kitchen, a large forlorn space scarcely enclosed by the log and mud walls. A pig ran unnoticed past her into it. Another woman, tall and gaunt, was fording the stream: she was dripping wet, and carried a spade. Surely, thought the baby's mother, human nature could reach no lower depths of squalor and ignorance than these.

"Mother," said Jonathan Yare, "here is a friend that has come with her baby to stay with us a while."

The old woman turned and instantly held out her arms for the child. "Come in—come to the fire," she said cordially. "I am glad Jonathan brought you to us."

If a princess had been so taken by surprise, her courtly breeding could not have stood her in better stead.

"We are waiting for father," said the woman who had carried the spade. Both men and women had peculiar voices. One could never grow used to hearing such gentle tones from such great sons of Anak.[7] At the same moment an old man of eighty, whose gigantic build dwarfed all of his sons, came into the doorway. His eyes were closed, and he groped with his staff. The widow, as soon as she saw his face, went directly up to him and took his hand.

"My name is Denby," she said. "I brought my baby here to be cured. He is all I have, sir."

"You did right to come." She guided his hand to Charley's, and he felt his skin, muscles and pulse, asking questions with shrewder insight than any physician had done. Then he led her to the table. "Boys, Mistress Denby will like to sit beside me, I think," he said.

She had an odd feeling that she had been adopted by some ancient knight, although the old man beside her wore trousers covered with patch on patch that left his hairy ankles and feet bare. Before the meal was over another strange impression deepened on her. She saw that these people were clothed and fed as the very poorest poor; she doubted whether one of them could read or write; they talked little, and only of the trivial happenings of the day—the corn or the ox that had gone lame; but she could not rid herself of the conviction that she had now, as never in her life, come into the best of good company. Nature does not always enoble her familiars. Country-people usually are just as uneasy and vulgar in their cheap and ignorant efforts at display or fashion as townsmen. But these mountaineers were absolutely unconscious that such things were. A man was a man to them—a woman, a woman. They had never perhaps heard either estimated by their money or house or clothes. The Yares were, in fact, a family born with exceptionally strong intellects and clean, fine instincts: they had been left to develop both in utter solitude and without education, and the result as to manner was the grave self-control of Indians and a truthful directness and simplicity of thought and speech which seemed to grow out of and express the great calm Nature about them as did the trees or the flowing water.

Little Mrs. Denby was conscious of this in half an hour. These were the first human beings whom she had ever met between whom and herself there came absolutely no bar of accident—no circumstance of social position or clothes or education: they were the first who could go straight to something in her beneath all these things. She soon forgot (what they had never known) how poor they were in all these accidents.

After that Charley and his mother were adopted into the family. At night, when the child was asleep, the old hunter always sat with her and his wife beside the fire, telling stories of bear-hunts, of fights with panthers, of the mysterious Rattlesnake Valley, near which no hunter ventures. He had been born in this house, and passed the whole of his eighty years in the mountains of the Black Range. One night, noticing the scars which his encounters with bears had left on him, she said, "It is no wonder that the townspeople in Asheville talked to me of the 'terrible history of the Yares.'"

The old man smiled quietly, but did not answer. When he had gone to bed his wife said with great feeling, "It was not their fights with wolves and bears that turned the people at Asheville agen the name of my boys and their father. They were the ony men anigh hyar that stood out fur the Union from the first to last. They couldn't turn agen the old flag, you see, Mistress Denby."

"They should have gone into the Federal army and helped to free the slaves," cried the widow with rising color, for she had been a violent abolitionist in her day.

"Waal, we never put much vally on the blacks, that's the truth. We couldn't argy or jedge whether slavery war wholsomest for them or not. It was out of our sight. My lads, bein' known as extraordinar' strong men an' powerful bearfighters, hed two or three offers to join Kirk's Loyal Rangers[8] in Tennessee. But they couldn't shed the blood of their old neighbors."

"Then they fought on neither side? Their old neighbors most probably called them cowards."

"Nobody would say that of the Yares," the woman said simply. "But when they wouldn't go into the Confederate army, they was driv out— four of them, Jonathan first—from under this roof, an' for five years they lay out on the mounting. It began this a-way: Some of the Union troops, they came up to the Unaka Range, and found the house whar the Grangers lived—hunters like us. The soldiers followed the two Granger lads who was in the rebel army, an' had slipped home on furlough to see their mother. Waal, they shot the lads, catchin' them out in the barnyard, which was to be expected, p'raps; an' when their ole father came runnin' out they killed him too. His wife, seein' that, hid the baby (as they called him, though he was nigh onto eight year old) under a loose board of the floor. But he, getting' scart, runs out and calls, 'Gentlemen, I surrender,' jest like a man. He fell with nine bullets in his breast. His mother sees it all. There never was a woman so interrupted as that pore woman that day. She comes up to us, travelin' night an' day, talkin' continual under her breath of the lads and her ole man's gray hair lyin' in a pool of blood. She's never hed her right mind sence. When Jonathan heard that from her, he said, 'Mother, not even for the Union will I join in sech work as this agen my friends.' He knowed ony the few folks on the mountings, but he keered for them as if they war his brothers. Yet they turned agen him at the warnin' of a day, and hunted him as if he was a wild beast. He's forgot that now. But his sister, she's never forgot it for him agen them. Jonathan's trouble made a different woman of Nancy."

But Mrs. Denby had felt but little interest in the gaunt, silent Nancy.

"You say they hunted your sons through the mountains?"

"Jest as if they war wolves. But the boys knowed the mountings. Thars hundreds of caves and gullies thar whar no man ever ventured but them. Three times a week Nancy went—she war a young girl then: she went up into Old Craggy and the Black miles and miles to app'inted places to kerry pervisions. I've seen her git out of her bed to go (fur she hed her aches and pains like other wimmen), and take that pack on her back, when the gorges war sheeted with snow and ice, an' ef she missed her footin' no man on arth could know whar she died."

"But five years of idleness for your sons—"

The old woman's high features flushed.

"You don't understan', Mistress Denby," she said calmly. "My sons' work in them years was to protect an' guide the rebel deserters home through the mountings—people at the North don't know, likely, what crowds of them thar war—an' to bring the Union prisoners escaped from Salisbury and Andersonville[9] safe to the Federal lines in Tennessee. One of the boys would be to Salisbury in disguise, an' the others would take them from him and run them into the mountings, an' keep 'em thar, bringin' them hyar when they could at night fur a meal's good victuals. About midnight they used to come. Nancy an' me, we'd hear a stone flung into the river yonder—seems as ef I stop listenin' fur that stone—an' we'd find them pore starved critters standin' in the dark outside with Jonathan. In ten minutes we'd have supper ready—keepin' the fire up every night—an' they'd eat an' sleep, an' be off before dawn. Hundreds of them hev slep' in this very room, sayin' it was as ef they'd come back to their homes out of hell. They looked as ef they'd been thar, raally."

"In *this* room?" Mrs. Denby stood up trembling. Her husband had been in Salisbury at the same time as Albert Richardson,[10] and had escaped. He might have slept in this very bed where his child lay. These people might have saved him from death. But Mrs. Yare did not notice her agitation.

"Thar was one winter when Major Gee[11] sent guards from Salisbury to watch the mounting-passes, 'specially about this house, knowin' my boys' work. Then they couldn't come anigh: thar was nigh a year I couldn't hear from them ef they were alive or dead. I'd hear shots, an' the guards 'ud tell me it was 'another damned refugee gone'—p'raps one of my boys. I'd set by that door all night, lookin' up to the clouds coverin' the mounting, wonderin' ef my lads was safe an' well up thar or lyin' dead an' unburied. I'd think ef I could only see one of my lads for jest once—jest once!" The firelight flashed up over her tall, erect figure. She was standing, and held her arm over her bony breast as if the old pain were intolerable even now. She said quietly after a while, "But I didn't begrudge them to their work. One night—the soldiers were jest yonder: you could see the camp-fire in the fog—thar war the stone knockin' in the stream. I says, 'Nancy, which is it?' She says, 'It's Charley's throw. Some-ut ails Jonathan. An' Charley hed come to say his brother war dyin' in a cave two mile up: they'd kerried him thar. I found my lad thar, worn to a shadder, an' with some desease no yerbs could tech. Wall, fur a week we came an' went to him, past the guards who war sent to shoot him down when found like a dog; an' thar he was lyin' within call, an' the snow an' sleet driftin' about him. One day Nancy was dumb all day—not a word. I said to father, 'Let her alon: she's a-studyin' powerful. Let her alone.' 'Mother,' she says at night, 'I've been thinkin' about Jonathan. He must hev a house to cover him, or he'll die.' 'Yes, Nancy, but what house?' 'I'll show you,' says she. 'You bide hyar quiet with father. The guard is used to seein' me come an' go with the cattle.' She took an axe an' went out, an' didn't come home till mornin'. In three days she hed cut down logs an' built a hut, six feet by ten, among the laurels yonder, haulin' an' liftin' them logs herself, an' floored it, an' kivered it with brush, an' brought him to it; an' thar she stayed an' nursed him. The snow fell heavy an' hid it. Yes, it seems impossible for a woman. But not many's got my Nancy's build," proudly. "One day, when Jonathan was growin' better, Colonel Barker rode up: he war a Confederit. 'Mrs. Yare,' says he, 'thar's word come your boys hev been seen hyarabouts, an' the home guard's on its way up.' An' then he tuk to talkin' cattle an' the like with father, an' turned his back on me. An' I went out an' give the signal. An' in ten minutes Nancy came in with the milk-pail as the guard rode up. I knowed the boys war safe. Waal, they sarched the laurel for hours, an' late in the afternoon they came in. 'Colonel,' says they, 'look a-here!' So we went out, an' thar war the house. 'Who built this?' says he. 'I did,' says Nancy, thinkin' the ownin' to it was death. The tears stood in his eyes. 'God help us all!' says he. 'Men, don't touch a log of it.' But they tore it to the ground when he was gone, an' took Nancy down to Asheville, an' kep her in the jail thar for a month, threatenin' to send her to Salisbury ef she'd not tell whar the boys war. They might hev hung her: of course she'd not hev told. But it wore her— it wore her. She'd be a prettier girl now," thoughtfully, "ony for what she's gone through for her brothers. Then they arrested father an' took him to Richmond, to Libby Prison. As soon as Nancy heard that, she sent for the commandant of the post. 'Give me,' she says, 'a written agreement that my father shall be released when his four sons come into Richmond, and let me go.' So they did it."

"And the boys went?"

"Of course. They reported themselves at Asheville, hopin' that would release their father sooner. But they hed to be forwarded to Salisbury, an' held there until he was brought on."

"They were in that prison, there?"

"Yes. But they was well treated, bein' wanted for soldiers. It was in the last year, when the men war desertin' and the drafts war of no use. On the fourth day the lads war brought into the guard-house before the officers.

"'Mr. Yare,' says the major very pleasantly, 'I believe you an' your brothers are reputed to be unusually daring men.'

"'That I don't know,' says Jonathan.

"'You hev certainly mistaken the object of the war and your duty. At any rate, you hev incurred ten times more risk an' danger in fighting for refugees than you would have done in the army. We have determined to overlook all the offences of your family, and to permit you to bear arms in our service.'

"'I will never bear arms in the Confederit service,' says Jonathan quietly. You know he's a quiet man, an' slow.

"A little man, a young captain, standing by, says in a heat, 'Bah! Why do you waste words with such fellows? The best use to make of the whole lot is to order them out to be shot.'

"'I agree with you, Mac,' says the colonel. 'It's poor policy, at this stage of the game, to tax the commissariat and put arms into the hands of unwilling soldiers.—But'—then he stopped for a minute—'you have no right to answer for your brothers, Yare,' he said. 'I give you half an hour,' taking out his watch. 'You can consult together. Such of you as are willing to go into the ranks can do so at once: the others—shall be dealt with as Captain McIntyre suggests.'

"They took the lads back into the inside room. When the half hour was up, all but five minutes, they saw a company drawn up in a hollow square outside. They were led out thar, facin' them, an' thar war the officers. It was a sunshiny, clar day, an' Jonathan said he couldn't help but think of the mountings an' his father an' me.

"Charley, he spoke first. 'Jonathan is the oldest,' he says. 'He will answer for us all.'

"'You will go into the service?' says the major.

"'No,' said Jonathan, 'we never will.'

"The major made a sign. My lads walked down and the soldiers presented arms. The major was lookin' curiously at Jonathan.

"'This is not cowardice,' said he. 'Why will you not go into the ranks? I believe, in my soul, you are a Union man!'

"Jonathan says he looked quick at the guns leveled at him, and couldn't keep his breath from comin' hard.

"'Yes,' he says out loud. 'By God, I am a Union man!'

"Captain McIntyre pushed his sword down with a clatter and turned away. 'I never saw pluck like that before,' he said.

"'Corporal,' said the major, 'take these men back to jail.'

"Two weeks after that Lee surrendered, an' my lads came home."

The women talked often in this way. Mrs. Denby urged them again and again to come out of their solitude to the North. "There are hundreds of men there," she said, "of influence and distinction whose lives your sons have saved at the peril of their own. Here they will always pass their days in hard drudgery and surrounded by danger."

The mother shook her head, but it was Nancy who answered in her gentle, pathetic voice: "The Yares hev lived on the Old Black for four generations, Mistress Denby. It wouldn't do to kerry us down into towns. It must be powerful lonesome in them flat countries, with nothing but people about you. The mountings is always company, you see."

The little townswoman tried to picture to herself these mountaineers actually in the houses of the men whom they had rescued from death— these slow speaking giants clad in cheap Bowery clothes, ignorant of art, music, books, bric-a-brac, politics. She understood that they would be lonesome, and that the mountains and they were company for each other.

She lived in their hut all summer. Her baby grew strong and rosy, and the mountains gave to her also of their good-will and comfort.

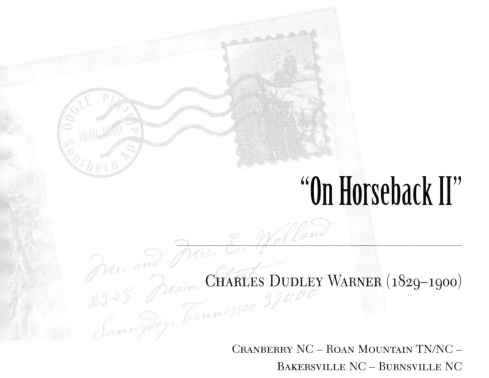

"On Horseback II"

CHARLES DUDLEY WARNER (1829–1900)

CRANBERRY NC – ROAN MOUNTAIN TN/NC –
BAKERSVILLE NC – BURNSVILLE NC

C harles Dudley Warner is best remembered for co-writing *The Gilded Age* with Mark Twain. Though Twain is usually credited as the primary author, Warner and Twain in fact divided the work nearly evenly, writing the novel tag-team style in five months (Paine I, 479). Though Twain is now the more significant figure in American letters, it was plausible for a leading American critic to argue while the two were still alive that Warner's work would endure longer (Vedder 94).

Warner was born in Massachusetts, earned a law degree from the University of Pennsylvania, and worked as a lawyer in Chicago before returning east and taking employment with the *Hartford Courant* as a contributor, associate editor, and then publisher. Later a frequent contributor to *Harper's*, the *Atlantic*, and *Scribner's*, Warner went on to control the "Editor's Drawer" section of *Harper's* from 1886 to 1892, and then succeeded W. D. Howells in that magazine's "Editor's Study" until 1898 (Lounsbury xxxi). Warner also wrote for the *Century*, the *New England Magazine*, and the *North American Review*.

Atlantic Monthly, August 1885

Warner's house in Hartford was at Nook Farm, abutting the properties of both Mark Twain and Harriet Beecher Stowe. By the late 1870s the Nook Farm community sat at the center of middle-class New England literary life as it had emerged after the war—decorous, polite, and eschewing the intense religious and political commitments of the prewar era (Andrews 110). An active abolition-ist before the war, Warner retained an interest in education and prison reform (reflected in the present selection's attention to jails in Bakersville and Burnsville, North Carolina). As a traveler, Warner was adventurous in the fashion of his day. He journeyed up the cataracts of the Nile and throughout the Middle East, as well as in western Europe, the American south and west, and Mexico.

In June and July of 1884, Warner traveled on horseback through the southern mountains with a companion, Thomas Raynesford Lounsbury (1838–1915), a longtime friend and a professor of Eng-lish literature at Yale University. (Lounsbury would later write a biographical sketch of Warner and edit the complete edition of Warner's works.) Beginning in Abingdon, Virginia, the travelers rode southeast to the vicinity of Boone, North Carolina, then up and over Roan Mountain through Bakersville to Burnsville, as related here. From Burnsville they rode across Mount Mitchell to Asheville. From there they traveled down the French Broad, over the Bald Moun-tains to the Wautaga and upper Holston Valleys in Tennessee, and back to Abingdon.

The selection reprinted here is the second in a series of four arti-cles about the trip entitled "On Horseback" that appeared in the *Atlantic Monthly,* July through October 1885. As the selection begins, Warner and his companion have arrived at Cranberry, North Carolina, near Elk Park, where U.S. 19E now crosses the state line. Throughout, Warner refers to himself as "The Friend of Humanity," and to his Shakespeare-quoting companion as "The Professor."

CRANBERRY FORGE is the first wedge of civilization fairly driven into the northwest mountains of North Carolina. A narrow-gauge railway, starting from Johnson City, follows up the narrow gorge of the Doe River and pushes into the heart of the iron mines at Cranberry,[1] where there is a blast furnace, and where a big company store, rows of tenement houses, heaps of slag and refuse ore, interlacing tracks, raw embankments, denuded hillsides, and a blackened landscape are the signs of a great devastating American enterprise. The Cranberry iron is in great esteem, as it has the peculiar quality of the Swedish iron. There are remains of old furnaces lower down the stream, which we passed on our way. The present "plant" is that of a Philadelphia company, whose enterprise has infused new life into all this region, made it accessible, and spoiled some pretty scenery.

When we alighted, weary, at the gate of the pretty hotel, which crowns a gentle hill and commands a pleasing, evergreen prospect of many gentle hills, a mile or so below the works and wholly removed from all sordid associations, we were at the point of willingness that the whole country should be devastated by civilization. In the local imagination this hotel of the company is a palace of unequaled magnificence, but probably its good-taste, comfort, and quiet elegance are not appreciated after all. There is this to be said about Philadelphia—and it will go far in pleading for it in the Last Day against its monotonous rectangularity and the Babel-like ambition of its Public Building—that wherever its influence extends there will be found comfortable lodgings and the luxury of an undeniably excellent cuisine. The visible seal that Philadelphia sets on its enterprise all through the South is a good hotel.

This Cottage Beautiful has on two sides a wide veranda, set about with easy chairs; cheerful parlors and pretty chambers, finished in native woods, among which are conspicuous the satin stripes of the cucumber tree;[2] luxurious beds, and an inviting table, ordered by a Philadelphia landlady, who knows a beefsteak from a boot-tap. Is it "low" to dwell upon these things of the senses, when one is on a tour in search of the picturesque? Let the reader ride from Abingdon through a wilderness of cornpone and rusty bacon, and then judge. There were, to be sure, novels lying about, and newspapers, and fragments of information to be picked up about a world into which the travelers seemed to emerge. They, at least, were satisfied, and went off to their rooms with the restful feeling that they had arrived somewhere, and no unquiet spirit at morn would say "to horse." To sleep, perchance to dream of Tatem and his household cemetery,[3] and the Professor was heard muttering in his chamber,

> "Weary, with toil, I haste me to my bed,
> The dear repose for limbs with travel tired;
> But then begins a journey in my head,
> To work my mind, when body's work's expir'd."[4]

The morning was warm (the elevation of the hotel must be between 2500 and 3000 feet), rainy, mildly rainy; and the travelers had nothing better to do than lounge upon the veranda, read feeble ten-cent fictions, and admire the stems of the white birches[5] glistening in the moisture, and the rhododendron trees, twenty feet high, which were shaking off

their last pink blossoms, and look down into the valley of the Doe. It
is not an exciting landscape, nothing bold or specially wild in it, but
restful with the monotony of some of the wooded Pennsylvania hills.

Sunday came up smiling, a lovely day, but offering no church
privileges, for the ordinance of preaching is only occasional in this region.
The ladies of the hotel have, however, gathered in the valley a Sunday-
school of fifty children from the mountain cabins. A couple of rainy days,
with the thermometer rising to 80°, combined with natural laziness to
detain the travelers in this cottage of ease. They enjoyed this the more
because it was on their consciences that they should visit Linville Falls,
some twenty-five miles eastward, long held up before them as the most
magnificent feature of this region, and on no account to be omitted. Hence
naturally a strong desire to omit it. The Professor takes bold ground
against these abnormal freaks of nature, and it was nothing to him that
the public would demand that we should see Linville Falls. In the first
place we could find no one who had ever seen them, and we spent two days
in catechizing natives and strangers. The nearest we came to information
was from a workman at the furnace, who was born and raised within three
miles of the Falls. He had heard of people going there. He had never seen
them himself. It was a good twenty five miles there, over the worst road
in the State—we 'd think it thirty before we got there. Fifty miles of such
travel to see a little water run down hill! The travelers reflected. Every
country has a local waterfall of which it boasts; they had seen a great many.
One more would add little to the experience of life. The vagueness of
information, to be sure, lured the travelers to undertake the journey;
but the temptation was resisted—something ought to be left for the
next explorer—and so Linville remains a thing of the imagination.

Towards evening, July 29th, between showers, the Professor and
the Friend rode along the narrow-gauge road, down Johnson's Creek, to
Roan Station,[6] the point of departure for ascending Roan Mountain. It was
a ride of an hour and a half over a fair road, fringed with rhododendrons,
nearly blossomless; but at one point on the stream this sturdy shrub
had formed a long bower whereunder a table might have been set for a
temperance picnic, completely overgrown with wild grape, and still gay
with bloom. The habitations on the way are mostly board shanties and
mean frame cabins, but the railway is introducing ambitious architecture
here and there in the form of ornamental filigree work on flimsy houses;
ornamentation is apt to precede comfort in our civilization.

Roan Station is on the Doe River (which flows down from Roan Mountain), and is marked at 2650 feet above the sea. The visitor will find here a good hotel, with open wood fires (not ungrateful in a July evening), and obliging people. This railway from Johnson City, hanging on the edge of the precipices that wall the gorge of the Doe, is counted in this region by the inhabitants one of the engineering wonders of the world.[7] The tourist is urged by all means to see both it and Linville Falls.

The tourist on horseback, in search of exercise and recreation, is not probably expected to take stock of moral conditions. But this Mitchell County [sic],[8] although it was a Union county during the war and is Republican in politics (the Southern reader will perhaps prefer another adverb to "although"), has had the worst possible reputation. The mountains were hiding-places of illicit distilleries; the woods were full of grog-shanties, where the inflaming fluid was sold as "native brandy," quarrels and neighborhood difficulties were frequent, and the knife and pistol were used on the slightest provocation. Fights arose about boundaries and the title to mica mines, and with the revenue officers; and force was the arbiter of all disputes. Within the year four murders were committed in the sparsely settled county. Travel on any of the roads was unsafe. The tone of morals was what might be expected with such lawlessness. A lady who came up on the road on the 4th of July, when an excursion party of country people took possession of the cars, witnessed a scene and heard language past belief. Men, women, and children drank from whiskey bottles that continually circulated, and a wild orgy resulted. Profanity, indecent talk on topics that even the license of the sixteenth century would not have tolerated, and freedom of manners that even Teniers[9] would have shrunk from putting on canvas made the journey horrible. The unrestrained license of whiskey and assault and murder had produced a reaction a few months previous to our visit. The people had risen up in their indignation and broken up the groggeries. So far as we observed temperance prevailed, backed by public opinion. In our whole ride through the mountain region we saw only one or two places where liquor was sold.

It is called twelve miles from Roan Station to Roan Summit. The distance is probably nearer fourteen, and our horses were five hours in walking it. For six miles the road runs by Doe River, here a pretty brook shaded with laurel and rhododendron, and a few cultivated patches of ground and infrequent houses. It was a blithe morning, and the horsemen would have given full indulgence to the spirit of adventure but for the attitude of the Professor towards mountains. It was not with him a matter of feeling, but of principle, not to ascend them. But here lay Roan, a long, sprawling ridge, lifting itself 6250 feet up into the sky. Impossible to go around it, and the other side must be reached. The Professor was obliged to surrender, and surmount a difficulty which he could not philosophize out of his mind.

From the base of the mountain a road is very well engineered, in easy grades for carriages, to the top; but it was in poor repair and stony. We mounted slowly through splendid forests, specially of fine chestnuts and hemlocks. This big timber continues till within a mile and a half of the summit by the winding road, really within a short distance of the top. Then there is a narrow belt of scrubby hardwood, moss-grown, and then large balsams, which crown the mountain. As soon as we came out upon the southern slope we found great open spaces, covered with succulent grass, and giving excellent pasturage to cattle. These rich mountain meadows are found on all the heights of this region. The surface of Roan is uneven, and has no one culminating peak that commands the country, like the peak of Mount Washington, but several eminences within its range of probably a mile and a half, where various views can be had. Near the highest point, sheltered from the north by balsams, stands a house of entertainment, with a detached cottage, looking across the great valley to the Black Mountain range.[10] The surface of the mountain is pebbly, but few rocks crop out; no ledges of any size are seen except at a distance from the hotel, on the north side, and the mountain consequently lacks that savage, unsubduable aspect which the White Hills[11] of New Hampshire have. It would, in fact, have been difficult to realize that we were over 6000 feet above the sea, except for that pallor in the sunlight, that atmospheric thinness and want of color which is an unpleasant characteristic of high altitudes. To be sure, there is a certain brilliancy in the high air—it is apt to be foggy on Roan—and objects appear in sharp outline, but I have often experienced on such places that feeling of melancholy, which would, of course, deepen upon us all if we were sensible that the sun was gradually withdrawing its power of warmth and light. The black balsam is neither a cheerful nor a picturesque tree; the frequent rains and mists on Roan keep the grass and mosses green, but the ground damp. Doubtless a high mountain covered with vegetation has its compensation, but for me the naked granite rocks in sun and shower are more cheerful.

The advantage of Roan is that one can live there and be occupied for a long time in mineral and botanical study. Its mild climate, moisture, and great elevation make it unique in this country for the botanist. The variety of plants assembled there is very large, and there are many, we were told, never or rarely found elsewhere in the United States. At any rate the botanists rave about Roan Mountain and spend weeks on it at a time. We found there ladies who could draw for us Grey's lily[12] (then passed) and had kept specimens of the rhododendron[13] (not growing elsewhere in this region), which has a deep red, almost purple color.

The hotel is a rude mountain structure, with a couple of comfortable rooms for office and sitting-room, in which big wood fires are blazing; for though the thermometer might record 60°, as it did when we arrived, fire was welcome. Sleeping places partitioned off in the loft above gave the occupants a feeling of camping out, all the conveniences being primitive; and when the wind rose in the night and darkness, and the loose boards rattled and the timbers creaked, the sensation was not unlike that of being at sea. The hotel was satisfactorily kept, and Southern guests, from as far south as New Orleans, were spending the season there, and not finding time hang heavy on their hands. This statement is perhaps worth more than pages of description as to the character of Roan, and its contrast to Mt. Washington.

The summer weather is exceedingly uncertain on all these North Carolina mountains; they are apt at any moment to be enveloped in mist; and it would rather rain on them than not. On the afternoon of our arrival there was fine air and fair weather, but not a clear sky. The distance was hazy, but the outlines were preserved. We could see White Top, in Virginia; Grandfather Mountain, a long serrated range; the twin towers of Linville; and the entire range of the Black Mountains, rising from the valley, and apparently lower than we were. They get the name of Black from the balsams which cover the summits.

The rain on Roan was of less annoyance by reason of the delightful company assembled at the hotel, which was in a manner at home there, and, thrown upon its own resources, came out uncommonly strong in agreeableness. There was a fiddle in the house, which had some of the virtues of that celebrated in the history of old Mark Langston;[14] the Professor was enabled to produce anything desired out of the literature of the eighteenth century; and what with the repartee of bright women, big wood fires, reading, and chat, there was no dull day or evening on Roan. I can fancy, however, that it might tire in time, if one were not a botanist, without the resource of women's society. The ladies staying here were probably all accomplished botanists, and the writer is indebted to one of them for a list of plants found on Roan, among which is an interesting weed, catalogued as *Humana, perplexia negligens.* The species is, however, common elsewhere.

The second morning opened, after a night of high wind, with a thunder shower. After it passed, the visitors tried to reach Eagle Cliff,[15] two miles off, whence an extensive western prospect is had, but were driven back by a tempest, and rain practically occupied the day. Now and then through the parted clouds we got a glimpse of a mountainside, or the gleam of a valley. On the lower mountains, at wide intervals apart, were isolated settlements, commonly a wretched cabin and a spot of girdled trees. A clergyman here, not long ago, undertook to visit some of these cabins and carry his message to them. In one wretched hut of logs he found a poor woman, with whom, after conversation on serious subjects, he desired to pray. She offered no objection, and he kneeled down and prayed. The woman heard him, and watched him for some moments with curiosity, in an effort to ascertain what he was doing, and then said:—

"Why, a man did that when he put my girl in a hole."

Towards night the wind hauled round from the south to the northwest, and we went to High Bluff,[16] a point on the north edge, where some rocks are piled up above the evergreens, to get a view of the sunset. In every direction the mountains were clear, and a view was obtained of the vast horizon and the hills and lowlands of several States— a continental prospect, scarcely anywhere else equaled for variety or distance. The grandeur of mountains depends mostly on the state of the atmosphere. Grandfather loomed up much more loftily than the day before, the giant range of the Blacks asserted itself in grim inaccessibility, and we could see, a small pyramid on the southwest horizon, King's Mountain in South Carolina, estimated to be distant one hundred and fifty miles. To the north Roan falls from this point abruptly, and we had, like a map below us, the low country all the way into Virginia. The clouds lay like lakes in the valleys of the lower hills, and in every direction were ranges of mountains wooded to the summits. Off to the west by south lay the Great Smoky Mountains, disputing eminence with the Blacks.

Magnificent and impressive as the spectacle was, we were obliged to contrast it unfavorably with that of the White Hills. The rock here is a sort of sand or pudding stone; there is no limestone or granite. And all the hills are tree covered. To many this clothing of verdure is most restful and pleasing. I missed the sharp outlines, the delicate artistic sky lines, sharply defined in uplifted bare granite peaks and ridges, with the purple and violet color of the northern mountains, and which it seems to me that limestone and granite formations give. There are none of the great gorges and awful abysses of the White Mountains, both valleys and mountains here being more uniform in outline. There are few precipices and jutting crags, and less is visible of the giant ribs and bones of the planet.

Yet Roan is a noble mountain. A lady from Tennessee asked me if I had ever seen anything to compare with it—she thought there could be nothing in the world. One has to dodge this sort of question in the South occasionally, not to offend a just local pride. It is certainly one of the most habitable of big mountains. It is roomy on top, there is space to move about without too great fatigue, and one might pleasantly spend a season there, if he had agreeable company and natural tastes.

Getting down from Roan on the south side is not as easy as ascending on the north; the road for five miles to the foot of the mountain is merely a river of pebbles, gullied by the heavy rains, down which the horses picked their way painfully. The travelers endeavored to present a dashing and cavalier appearance to the group of ladies who waved good-by from the hotel, as they took their way over the waste and wind-blown declivities, but it was only a show, for the horses would neither caracole[17] nor champ the bit (at a dollar a day) down hill over the slippery stones, and, truth to tell, the wanderers turned with regret from the society of leisure and persiflage to face the wilderness of Mitchell County. "How heavy," exclaimed the Professor, pricking Laura Matilda to call her attention sharply to her footing:—

> "How heavy do I journey on the way,
>   When what I seek—my weary travel's end—
>   Doth teach that ease and that repose to say,
>   'Thus far the miles are measur'd from thy friend!'
>   The beast that bears me, tired with my woe,
>   Plods dully on, to bear that weight in me,
>   As if by some instinct the wretch did know
>   His rider loved not speed, being made from thee:
>   The bloody spur cannot provoke him on
>   That sometimes anger thrusts into his hide,

> Which heavily he answers with a groan,
> More sharp to me than spurring to his side;
>> For that same groan doth put this in my mind;
>> My grief lies onward and my joy behind."[18]

This was not spoken to the group who fluttered their farewells, but poured out to the uncomplaining forest, which rose up in ever statelier and grander ranks to greet the travelers as they descended—the silent vast forest, without note of bird or chip of squirrel, only the wind tossing the great branches high overhead in response to the sonnet. Is there any region or circumstance of life that the poet did not forecast and provide for? But what would have been his feelings if he could have known that almost three centuries after these lines were penned, they would be used to express the emotion of an unsentimental traveler in the primeval forests of the New World? At any rate he peopled the New World with the children of his imagination. And, thought the Friend, whose attention to his horse did not permit him to drop into poetry, Shakespeare might have had a vision of this vast continent, though he did not refer to it, when he exclaimed: —

> "What is your substance, whereof are you made,
> That millions of strange shadows on you tend?"[19]

Bakersville, the capital of Mitchell County, is eight miles from the top of Roan, and the last three miles of the way the horsemen found tolerable going, over which the horses could show their paces. The valley looked fairly thrifty and bright, and was a pleasing introduction to Bakersville, a pretty place in the hills, of some six hundred inhabitants, with two churches, three indifferent hotels and a court-house. This mountain town, 2550 feet above the sea, is said to have a decent winter climate, with little snow, favorable to fruit-growing, and, by contrast with New England, encouraging to people with weak lungs.

This is the centre of the mica mining, and of considerable excitement about minerals. All around, the hills are spotted with "diggings." Most of the mines which yield well show signs of having been worked before, a very long time ago, no doubt by the occupants before the Indians. The mica is of excellent quality and easily mined. It is got out in large irregular-shaped blocks and transported to the factories, where it is carefully split by hand, and the laminae, of as large size as can be obtained, are trimmed with shears and tied up in packages for market. The quantity of refuse, broken, and rotten mica piled up about the factories is immense, and all the roads round about glisten with its scales. Garnets are often found imbedded in the laminae, flattened by the extreme pressure to which the mass was subjected. It is fascinating material, this mica, to handle, and we amused ourselves by experimenting on the thinness to which its scales could be reduced by splitting. It was at Bakersville that we saw specimens of mica that resembled the delicate tracery in the moss-agate, and had the iridescent sheen of the rainbow colors—the most delicate greens, reds, blues, purples, and gold, changing from one to the other in the reflected light. In the texture were the tracings of fossil forms of ferns and the most exquisite and delicate vegetable beauty of the coal age. But the magnet shows this tracery to be iron. We were shown also emeralds and "diamonds," picked up in this region, and there is a mild expectation in all the habitants of great mineral treasure. A singular product of the region is the flexible sandstone. It is a most uncanny stone. A slip of it a couple of feet long and an inch in diameter each way bends in the hand like a half frozen snake. This conduct of a substance that we have been taught to regard as inflexible impairs one's confidence in the stability of nature and affects him as an earthquake does.

This excitement over mica and other minerals has the usual effect of starting up business and creating bad blood. Fortunes have been made, and lost in riotous living; scores of visionary men have been disappointed; lawsuits about titles and claims have multiplied, and quarrels ending in murder have been frequent in the past few years. The mica and the illicit whiskey have worked together to make this region one of lawlessness and violence. The travelers were told stories of the lack of common morality and decency in the region, but they made no note of them. And, perhaps fortunately, they were not there during court week to witness the scenes of license that were described. This court week, which draws hither the whole population, is a sort of Saturnalia. Perhaps the worst of this is already a thing of the past; for the outrages a year before had reached such a pass that by a common movement the sale of whiskey was stopped (not interdicted, but stopped), and not a drop of liquor[20] could be bought in Bakersville nor within three miles of it.

The jail at Bakersville is a very simple residence. The main building is brick, two stories high and about twelve feet square. The walls are so loosely laid up that it seems as if a colored prisoner might butt his head through. Attached to this is a room for the jailer. In the lower room is a wooden cage, made of logs bolted together and filled with spikes, nine

feet by ten feet square and perhaps seven or eight feet high. Between
this cage and the wall is a space of eighteen inches in width. It has a
narrow door, and an opening through which the food is passed to the
prisoners, and a conduit leading out of it. Of course it soon becomes
foul, and in warm weather somewhat warm. A recent prisoner, who
wanted more ventilation than the State allowed him, found some means,
by a loose plank, I think, to batter a hole in the outer wall opposite the
window in the cage, and this ragged opening, seeming to the jailer a
good sanitary arrangement, remains. Two murderers occupied this
apartment at the time of our visit. During the recent session of court,
ten men had been confined in this narrow space, without room enough
for them to lie down together. The cage in the room above, a little
larger, had for tenant a person who was jailed for some misunderstanding
about an account, and who was probably innocent—from the jailer's
statement. This box is a wretched residence, month after month, while
awaiting trial.

We learned on inquiry that it is practically impossible to get a jury
to convict of murder in this region, and that these admitted felons would
undoubtedly escape. We even heard that juries were purchasable here, and
that a man's success in court depended upon the length of his purse. This
is such an unheard of thing that we refused to credit it. When the Friend
attempted to arouse the indignation of the Professor about the barbarity
of this jail, the latter defended it on the ground that as confinement was
the only punishment that murderers were likely to receive in this region,
it was well to make their detention disagreeable to them. But the Friend
did not like this wild-beast cage for men, and could only exclaim, "Oh,
murder! what crimes are done in thy name."

If the comrades wished an adventure, they had a small one, more
interesting to them than to the public, the morning they left Bakersville
to ride to Burnsville, which sets itself up as the capital of Yancey. The
way for the first three miles lay down a small creek and in a valley fairly
settled, the houses, a store, and a grist-mill giving evidence of the new
enterprise of the region. When Toe River was reached there was a choice
of routes. We might ford the Toe at that point, where the river was wide,
but shallow, and the crossing safe, and climb over the mountain by a
rough but sightly road, or descend the stream by a better road and ford
the river at a place rather dangerous to those unfamiliar with it. The
danger attracted us, but we promptly chose the hill road on account
of the views, for we were weary of the limited valley prospects.

The Toe River, even here, where it bears westward, is a very respectable stream in size, and not to be trifled with after a shower. It gradually turns northward, and joining the Nollechucky[21] becomes part of the Tennessee system. We crossed it by a long, diagonal ford, slipping and sliding about on the round stones, and began the ascent of a steep hill. The sun beat down unmercifully, the way was stony, and the horses did not relish the weary climbing. The Professor, who led the way, not for the sake of leadership but to be the discoverer of laden blackberry bushes, which began to offer occasional refreshment, discouraged by the inhospitable road and perhaps oppressed by the moral backwardness of things in general, cried out:—

"Tired with all these, for restful death I cry,—
As, to behold desert a beggar born,
And needy nothing trimm'd in jollity,
And purest faith unhappily forsworn,
And gilded honor shamefully misplaced,
And maiden virtue rudely strumpeted,
And right perfection wrongfully disgraced,
And strength by limping sway disabled,
And art made tongue-tied by authority,
And folly (doctor-like) controlling skill,
And simple truth miscall'd simplicity,
And captive good attending captain ill:
    Tired with all these, from these would I be gone,
    Save that, to die, I leave my love alone."[22]

In the midst of a lively discussion of this pessimistic view of the inequalities of life, in which desert and capacity are so often put at disadvantage by birth in beggarly conditions, and brazen assumption raises the dust from its chariot wheels for modest merit to plod along in, the Professor swung himself off his horse to attack a blackberry bush, and the Friend, representing simple truth, and desirous of getting a wider prospect, urged his horse up the hill. At the top he encountered a stranger, on a sorrel horse, with whom he entered into conversation and extracted all the discouragement the man had as to the road to Burnsville.

Nevertheless, the view opened finely and extensively. There are few exhilarations comparable to that of riding or walking along a high ridge, and the spirits of the traveler rose many degrees above the point of restful

death, for which the Professor was crying when he encountered the
blackberry bushes. Luckily the Friend soon fell in with a like temptation,
and dismounted. He discovered something that spoiled his appetite for
berries. His coat, strapped on behind the saddle, had worked loose, the
pocket was open, and the pocket-book was gone. This was serious business.
For while the Professor was the cashier, and traveled like a Rothschild,
with large drafts, the Friend represented the sub-treasury. That very
morning, in response to inquiry as to the sinews of travel, the Friend
had displayed, without counting, a roll of bills. These bills had now
disappeared, and when the Friend turned back to communicate his
loss, in the character of needy nothing not trimm'd in jollity, he had
a sympathetic listener to the tale of woe.

Going back on such a journey is the woefulest experience, but
retrace our steps we must. Perhaps the pocket-book lay in the road
not half a mile back. But not in a half a mile, or a mile, was it found.
Probably, then, the man on the sorrel horse had picked it up. But who
was the man on the sorrel horse, and where had he gone? Probably the
coat worked loose in crossing Toe River and the pocket-book had gone
down stream. The number of probabilities was infinite, and each more
plausible than the others as it occurred to us. We inquired at every house
we had passed on the way, we questioned every one we met. At length it
began to seem improbable that any one would remember if he had picked
up a pocket-book that morning. This is just the sort of thing that slips
an untrained memory.

At a post-office, or doctor's shop, or inn for drovers, it might be
either or neither, where several horses were tied to the fence, and a group
of men were tilted back in cane-chairs on the veranda, we unfolded our
misfortune and made particular inquiries for a man on a sorrel horse.
Yes, such a man, David Thomas by name, had just ridden towards
Bakersville. If he had found the pocket-book, we would recover it.
He was an honest man. It might, however, fall into hands that would
freeze to it. Upon consultation, it was the general verdict that there were
men in the county who would keep it if they had picked it up. But the
assembly manifested the liveliest interest in the incident. One suggested
Toe River. Another thought it risky to drop a purse on any road. But
there was a chorus of desire expressed that we should find it, and in this
anxiety was exhibited a decided sensitiveness about the honor of Mitchell
County. It seemed too bad that a stranger should go away with the
impression that it was not safe to leave money anywhere in it. We

felt very much obliged for this genuine sympathy, and we told them that if a pocket-book were lost in this way on a Connecticut road, there would be felt no neighborhood responsibility for it, and that nobody would take any interest in the incident except the man who lost, and the man who found.

By the time the travelers pulled up at a store in Bakersville they had lost all expectation of recovering the missing article, and were discussing the investment of more money in an advertisement in the weekly newspaper of the capital. The Professor, whose reform sentiments agreed with those of the newspaper, advised it. There was a group of idlers, mica acquaintances of the morning, and philosophers in front of the store, and the Friend opened the colloquy by asking if a man named David Thomas had been seen in town. He was in town, had ridden in within an hour, and his brother, who was in the group, would go in search of him. The information was then given of the loss, and that the rider had met David Thomas just before it was discovered, on the mountain beyond the Toe. The news made a sensation, and by the time David Thomas appeared a crowd of a hundred had drawn around the horsemen eager for further developments. Mr. Thomas was the least excited of the group as he took his position on the sidewalk, conscious of the dignity of the occasion and that he was about to begin a duel in which both reputation and profit were concerned. He recollected meeting the travelers in the morning.

The Friend said, "I discovered that I had lost my purse just after meeting you; it may have been dropped in Toe River, but I was told back here that if David Thomas had picked it up it was as safe as if it were in the bank."

"What sort of a pocket-book was it?" asked Mr. Thomas.

"It was of crocodile skin, or what is sold for that, very likely it is an imitation, and about so large"—indicating the size.

"What had it in it?"

"Various things. Some specimens of mica; some blank checks; some money."

"Anything else?"

"Yes, a photograph. And, oh, something that I presume is not in another pocket-book in North Carolina,—in an envelope, a lock of the hair of George Washington, the Father of his Country." Sensation, mixed with incredulity. Washington's hair did seem such an odd part of an outfit for a journey of this kind.

"How much money was in it?"

"That I cannot say, exactly. I happen to remember four twenty dollar United States notes, and a roll of small bills, perhaps something over a hundred dollars."

"Is that the pocket-book?" asked David Thomas, slowly pulling the loved and lost out of his trousers pocket.

"It is."

"You'd he willing to take your oath on it?"

"I should be delighted to."

"Well, I guess there ain't so much money in it. You can count it (handing it over); there hain't been nothing taken out. I can't read, but my friend here counted it over, and he says there ain't so much as that."

Intense interest in the result of the counting. One hundred and ten dollars! The Friend selected one of the best engraved of the notes, and appealed to the crowd if they thought that was the square thing to do. They did so think, and David Thomas said it was abundant. And then said the Friend: —

"I'm exceedingly grateful to you besides. Washington's hair is getting scarce, and I did not want to lose these few hairs, gray as they are. You've done the honest thing, Mr. Thomas, as was expected of you. You might have kept the whole. But I reckon if there had been five hundred dollars in the book and you had kept it, it wouldn't have done you half as much good as giving it up has done; and your reputation as an honest man is worth a good deal more than this pocket-book. [The Professor was delighted with this sentiment, because it reminded him of a Sunday-school.] I shall go away with a high opinion of the honesty of Mitchell County."

"Oh, he lives in Yancey," cried two or three voices. At which there was a great laugh.

"Well, I wondered where he came from." And the Mitchell County people laughed again at their own expense, and the levee broke up. It was exceedingly gratifying, as we spread the news of the recovered property that afternoon at every house on our way to the Toe, to see what pleasure it gave. Every man appeared to feel that the honor of the region had been on trial and had stood the test.

The eighteen miles to Burnsville had now to be added to the morning excursion, but the travelers were in high spirits, feeling the truth of the adage that it is better to have loved and lost, than never to have lost at all. They decided, on reflection, to join company with the mail-rider, who was going to Burnsville by the shorter route, and could pilot them over the dangerous ford of the Toe.

The mail-rider was a lean, sallow, sinewy man, mounted on a sorry sorrel nag, who proved, however, to have blood in her, and to be a fast walker and full of endurance. The mail-rider was taciturn, a natural habit for a man who rides alone the year round, over a lonely road, and has nothing whatever to think of. He had been in the war sixteen months, in Hugh White's regiment,—reckon you've heerd of him?

"Confederate?"

"Which?"

"Was he on the Union or Confederate side?"

"Oh, Union."

"Were you in any engagements?"

"Which?"

"Did you have any fighting?"

"Not reg'lar."

"What did you do?"

"Which?"

"What did you do in Hugh White's regiment?"

"Oh, just cavorted round the mountains."

"You lived on the country?"

"Which?"

"Picked up what you could find, corn, bacon, horses?"

"That's about so. Didn't make much difference which side was round, the country got cleaned out."

"Plunder seems to have been the object?"

"Which?"

"You got a living out of the farmers?"

"You bet."

Our friend and guide seemed to have been a jayhawker and mountain marauder—on the right side. His attachment to the word "which" prevented any lively flow of conversation, and there seemed to be only two trains of ideas running in his mind: one was the subject of horses and saddles, and the other was the danger of the ford we were coming to, and he exhibited a good deal of ingenuity in endeavoring to excite our alarm. He returned to the ford from every other conversational excursion, and after every silence. "I do' know's there's any great danger; not if you know the ford. Folks is carried away there. The Toe gits up sudden. There's been right smart rain lately. If you're afraid, you can git set over in a dugout, and I'll take your horses across. Mebbe you're used to fording? It's a pretty bad ford for them as don't know it. But you'll get along, if you mind your eye. There's some rocks you'll have to look out for. But you'll be all right, if you follow me."

Not being very successful in raising an interest in the dangers of his ford, although he could not forego indulging a malicious pleasure in trying to make the strangers uncomfortable, he finally turned his attention to a trade. "This hoss of mine," he said, "is just the kind of brute-beast you want for this country. Your hosses is too heavy. How'll you swap for that one o' yourn?" The reiterated assertion that the horses were not ours, that they were hired, made little impression on him. All the way to Burnsville he kept recurring to the subject of a trade. The instinct of "swap" was strong in him. When we met a yoke of steers, he turned round and bantered the owner for a trade. Our saddles took his fancy. They were of the army pattern, and he allowed that one of them would just suit him. He rode a small flat English pad, across which was flung the United States mail pouch, apparently empty. He dwelt upon the fact that his saddle was new and ours were old, and the advantages that would accrue to us from the exchange. He didn't care if they had been through the war, as they had, for he fancied an army saddle. The Friend answered for himself that the saddle he rode belonged to a distinguished Union general, and had a bullet in it that was put there by a careless Confederate in the first battle of Bull Run, and the owner would not part with it for money. But the mail-rider said he didn't mind that. He wouldn't mind swapping his new saddle for my old one and the rubber coat and leggins. Long before we reached the ford we thought we would like to swap the guide, even at the risk of drowning. The ford was passed, in due time, with no inconvenience save that of wet feet, for the stream was breast high to the horses; but being broad and swift and full of sunken rocks and slippery stones and the crossing tortuous, it is not a ford to be commended. There is a curious delusion that a rider has in crossing a swift broad stream. It is that he is rapidly drifting up stream, while in fact the tendency of the horse is to go with the current.

The road in the afternoon was not unpicturesque, owing to the streams and the ever noble forests, but the prospect was always very limited. Agriculturally, the country was mostly undeveloped. The travelers endeavored to get from the rider an estimate of the price of land. Not much sold, he said. "There was one sale of a big piece last year; the owner enthorited Big Tom Wilson[23] to sell it, but I d' know what he got for it."

All the way along the habitations were small log cabins, with one room, chinked with mud, and these were far between; and only occasionally thereby a similar log structure, unchinked, laid up like a cob house, that served for a stable. Not much cultivation, except now and then a little patch of poor corn on a steep hillside, occasionally a few apple-trees, and a peach-tree without fruit. Here and there was a house that had been half finished and then abandoned, or a shanty in which a couple of young married people were just beginning life. Generally the cabins (confirming the accuracy of the census of 1880) swarmed with children, and nearly all the women were thin and sickly.

In the day's ride we did not see a wheeled vehicle, and only now and then a horse. We met on the road small sleds, drawn by a steer, sometimes by a cow, on which a bag of grist was being hauled to the mill, and boys mounted on steers gave us good evening with as much pride as if they were bestriding fiery horses.

In a house of the better class, which was a post-house, and where the rider and the woman of the house had a long consultation over a letter to be registered, we found the rooms decorated with patent–medicine pictures, which were often framed in strips of mica, an evidence of culture that was worth noting. Mica was the rage. Every one with whom we talked, except the rider, had more or less the mineral fever. The impression was general that the mountain region of North Carolina was entering upon a career of wonderful mineral development, and the most extravagant expectations were entertained. Mica was the shining object of most "prospecting," but gold was also on the cards.

The country about Burnsville is not only mildly picturesque, but very pleasing. Burnsville, the county-seat of Yancey, at an elevation of 2840 feet, is more like a New England village than any hitherto seen. Most of the houses stand about a square, which contains the shabby court-house; around it are two small churches, a jail, an inviting tavern, with a long veranda, and a couple of stores. On an overlooking hill is the seminary. Mica mining is the exciting industry, but it is agriculturally a good country. The tavern had recently been enlarged to meet the new demands for entertainment, and is a roomy structure, fresh with paint and only partially organized. The travelers were much impressed with the

brilliant chambers, the floors of which were painted in alternate stripes
of vivid green and red. The proprietor, a very intelligent and enterprising
man, who had traveled often in the North, was full of projects for the
development of his region and foremost in its enterprises, and had formed
a considerable collection of minerals. Besides, more than any one else we
met, he appreciated the beauty of his country, and took us to a neighboring
hill, where we had a view of Table Mountain to the east and the nearer
giant Blacks. The elevation of Burnsville gives it a delightful summer
climate, the gentle undulations of the country are agreeable, the views
noble, the air is good, and it is altogether a "livable" and attractive place.
With facilities of communication, it would be a favorite summer resort.
Its nearness to the great mountains (the whole Black range is in Yancey
County), its fine pure air, its opportunity for fishing and hunting, commend
it to those in search of an interesting and restful retreat in summer.

But it should be said that before the country can attract and retain
travelers, its inhabitants must learn something about the preparation of
food. If, for instance, the landlord's wife at Burnsville had traveled with
her husband, her table would probably have been more on a level with
his knowledge of the world, and it would have contained something that
the wayfaring man, though a Northerner, could eat. We have been on the
point several times in this journey of making the observation, but have
been restrained by a reluctance to touch upon politics, that it was no
wonder that a people with such a cuisine should have rebelled. The
travelers were in a rebellious mood most of the time.

The evidences of enterprise in this region were pleasant to see,
but the observers could not but regret, after all, the intrusion of the
money-making spirit, which is certain to destroy much of the present
simplicity. It is as yet, to a degree, tempered by a philosophic spirit.
The other guest of the house was a sedate, long-bearded traveler for some
Philadelphia house, and in the evening he and the landlord fell into a
conversation upon what Socrates calls the disadvantage of the pursuit of
wealth to the exclusion of all noble objects, and they let their fancy play
about Vanderbilt,[24] who was agreed to be the richest man in the world,
or that ever lived.

"All I want," said the long-bearded man, "is enough to be comfortable.
I wouldn't have Vanderbilt's wealth if he'd give it to me."

"Nor I," said the landlord. "Give me just enough to be comfortable.
[The tourist couldn't but note that his ideas of enough to be comfortable
had changed a good deal since he had left his little farm and gone into

the mica business, and visited New York, and enlarged and painted his tavern.] I should like to know what more Vanderbilt gets out of his money than I get out of mine. I heard tell of a young man who went to Vanderbilt to get employment. Vanderbilt finally offered to give the young man, if he would work for him, just what he got himself. The young man jumped at that—he 'd be perfectly satisfied with that pay. And Vanderbilt said that all he got was what he could eat and wear, and offered to give the young man his board and clothes."

"I declare," said the long-bearded man. "That's just it. Did you ever see Vanderbilt's house? Neither did I, but I heard he had a vault built in it five feet thick, solid. He put in it two hundred millions of dollars, in gold. After a year, he opened it and put in twelve millions more, and called that a poor year. They say his house has gold shutters to the windows, so I've heard."

"I shouldn't wonder," said the landlord. "I heard he had one door in his house cost forty thousand dollars. I don't know what it is made of, unless it's made of gold."

Sunday was a hot and quiet day. The stores were closed and the two churches also, this not being the Sunday for the itinerant preacher. The jail also showed no sign of life, and when we asked about it, we learned that it was empty, and had been for some time. No liquor is sold in the place, nor within at least three miles of it. It is not much use to try to run a jail without liquor.

In the course of the morning a couple of stout fellows arrived, leading between them a young man whom they had arrested,—it didn't appear on any warrant, but they wanted to get him committed and locked up. The offense charged was carrying a pistol; the boy had not used it against anybody, but he had flourished it about and threatened, and the neighbors wouldn't stand that; they were bound to enforce the law against carrying concealed weapons.

The captors were perfectly good-natured and on friendly enough terms with the young man, who offered no resistance, and seemed not unwilling to go to jail. But a practical difficulty arose. The jail was locked up, the sheriff had gone away into the country with the key, and no one could get in. It did not appear that there was any provision for boarding the man in jail; no one in fact kept it. The sheriff was sent for, but was not to be found, and the prisoner and his captors loafed about the square all day, sitting on the fence, rolling on the grass, all of them sustained by a simple trust that the jail would be open some time.

Late in the afternoon we left them there, trying to get into the jail. But we took a personal leaf out of this experience. Our Virginia friends, solicitous for our safety in this wild country, had urged us not to venture into it without arms—take at least, they insisted, a revolver each. And now we had to congratulate ourselves that we had not done so. If we had, we should doubtless on that Sunday have been waiting, with the other law-breaker, for admission into the Yancey County jail.

SECTION III

Discovering, Inventing, Uplifting

MOUNTAINEERS IN THE BACKWOODS

"A Strange Land and a Peculiar People"

WILLIAM WALLACE HARNEY (1832–1912)

CUMBERLAND GAP REGION: SOUTHEASTERN KY, EAST TN

William Wallace Harney was raised and educated in Louisville, Kentucky, where his father, John Hopkins Harney, was the editor of the *Louisville Daily Democrat* from 1844 to 1868. William taught school and practiced law for a time in Louisville, and became one of the editors at his father's newspaper. In 1860, he moved to Florida and is now considered the founder of the town of Pine Castle, on Lake Conway in Orange County. He was among the "southern school" of writers popular in northern magazines during the late nineteenth century, and much of his work is set in Florida. His contributions to national magazines such as *Harper's* and the *Atlantic* include poems, stories, and articles. Highlights of his work were collected in book form as *The Spirit of the South,* published in Boston in 1909.

Harney's work is read little, if at all, today. However, the present selection is known among Appalachian studies scholars largely because of Henry Shapiro's influential 1978 book, *Appalachia on Our Mind: The Southern Mountains and Mountaineers in the American Consciousness, 1870–1920.* Shapiro begins the first chapter of that book with an account of Harney's article, claiming that the article

Lippincott's, October 1873

217

is an important landmark in the emergence of the "idea of Appalachia" in American culture. Writes Shapiro, "In a real sense it was
Harney and the editors of *Lippincott's* who 'discovered' Appalachia,
for they were the first to assert that 'otherness' which made of the
mountainous portions of eight southern states a discrete region, in
but not of America" (4). Since Shapiro's book has been published,
comments about Harney's title and the existence of his article have
appeared frequently in other Appalachian studies scholarship. The
title is much better known than the article itself, and has come to
serve as a shorthand for a certain way of representing Appalachia.

Shapiro may have been overstating the influence of this one
article. And, in any event, as Shapiro acknowledges, Harney's article
does little "to justify so striking a title" (3). Rather than being a
touristic account of the people of the region, the article serves primarily as a framework for three dramatic stories about the Civil War
era in the southern mountains.

A nodule of amygdaloid,[1] a coarse pebble enveloped in a whitish semi-
crystalline paste, lies on the table before me. I know that a blow of the
hammer will reveal the beauties of its crystal interior, but I do not crush
it. It is more to me as it is—more than a letter plucked from the stone
pages of time. Coarse and plain, it is an index to a chapter of life. In the
occupations of a busy existence we forget how much we owe to the sweet
emotional nature which, by mere chance association, retains the dearer
part of the past fixed in memory, just as the graceful volutes of a fossil
shell are preserved in the coarse matrix of a stony paste. In this way the
nodule connects itself with my emotional life, and recalls the incidents
of this sketch.

We were journeying over the mountains in the autumn of 1869. Our
camp was pitched in a valley of the ascending ridges of the Cumberland
range, on the south-east border of Kentucky. At this point the interior
valley forms the letter J, the road following the bend, and ascending at
the foot of the perpendicular.

It is nearly an hour since sunset, but the twilight still lingers in
softened radiance, mellowing the mountain-scenery. The camp-wagons
are drawn up on a low pebbly shelf at the foot of the hills, and the kindled
fire has set a great carbuncle in the standing pool. A spring branch oozes
out of the rocky turf, and flows down to meet a shallow river fretting
over shoals. The road we have followed hangs like a rope-ladder from
the top of the hills, sagging down in the irregularities till it reaches the

river-bed, where it flies apart in strands of sand. The twilight leans upon the opposite ridge, painting its undulations in inconceivably delicate shades of subdued color. Although the night is coming on, the clear-obscure of that dusk, like a limpid pool, reveals all beneath. A road ascending the southern hill cuts through a loamy crust a yellow line, which creeps upward, winding in and out, till nothing is seen of it but a break in the trees set clear against the sky. No art of engineer wrought these graceful bends: it is a wild mountain-pass, followed by the unwieldy buffalo in search of pasturage. Beyond, the mountain rises again precipitously, a ragged tree clinging here and there to the craggy shelves. Around and through the foliage, like a ribbon, the road winds to the top. A blue vapor covers it and the hills melting softly in the distance. At the base of the hills a little river winds and bends to the west through a low fertile bottom, the stem of the J, which is perhaps a mile in width. It turns again, its course marked by a growth of low water-oaks[2] and beeches, following the irregular fold in the hills which has been described.

Leaning against the bluffs hard by the camp is a low white cottage, with its paddock and pinfold, and the cattle are coming up, with bells toning irregularly as they feed and loiter on the way. The supper-horn sends forth a hoarse but mellow fugue in swells and cadences from the farm-house. Over all this sweet rural scene of mountain, valley, river and farm, and over the picturesque camp, with stock, tent and wagons, now brightened by the grace of a young girl, the twilight lingers like love over a home. As I listen and look a soft voice from the carriage at my side says, "Is the ground damp? May I get out?"

I turn to my little prisoner, and as the mingled lights cross her features I see that her wide, dark-gray eyes are swimming in tears. "Why, what is it?" I ask.

"Nothing: everything is so sweet and tranquil. I was wondering if our new home would be like this—not the hills and valleys, you know, but so quiet and homelike."

So homelike! With that vague yearning, we, like so many Southerners of the period, were wagoning from old homesteads, a thousand miles of travel, to a resting-place.

"It will be like home if you are there," I think as I assist her to alight—the burden daily growing lighter in my arms and heavier on my heart—but I say nothing.

Pretty soon she is at her usual relaxation, looking for shells, ivy berries and roots of wild vines to adorn that never-attainable home. The kindly, generous twilight, so unlike the swift shrift of the Florida levels, still lingers; and presently, amid bits of syenite, volcanic tuff and scoria,[3] she has found this nodule of amygdaloid. It differs from the fossil shells and alluvial pebbles she is used to find, and she is curious about it.

I tell the story of the watershed of the Ohio as well as I can—how it was the delta of a great river, fed by the surface of a continent lying south-eastwardly in the Atlantic; of the luxuriant vegetation that sprang up as in the cypress-swamps of her old home in Louisiana, passing, layer by layer, into peat, to be baked and pressed into bituminous coal, that slops over the flared edges of the basin in Pennsylvania, like sugar in the kettles, and is then burnt to anthracite. I promise her that in some dawn on the culminating peak, when the hills below loom up, their tops just visible like islands in a sea of dusk, I will show her a natural photograph of that old-world delta, with the fog breaking on the lower cliffs like the surf of a ghostly sea. She listens as to a fairy tale, and then I tell her of the stellar crystals concealed in the rough crust of the amygdaloid. She puts it away, and says I shall break it for her when we get home. We have traveled a long way, by different paths, since then, but it has never been broken—never will be broken now.

In addition to the geological and botanical curiosities the mountains afford, my companion had been moved alternately to tears and smiles by the scenes and people we met—their quaint speech and patient poverty. We passed eleven deserted homesteads in one day. Sometimes a lean cur yelped forlorn welcome: at one a poor cow lowed at the broken paddock and dairy. We passed a poor man with five little children—the eldest ten or twelve, the youngest four or five—their stock on a small donkey, footing their way over the hills across Tennessee into Georgia. It was so pitiful to see the poor little babes-in-the-wood on that forlorn journey; and yet they were so brave, and the poor fellow cheered them and praised them, as well he might. Another miserable picture was at the white cottage near our camp. The lawn showed evidences of an old taste in rare flowers and vines, now choked with weeds. I knocked, and a slovenly negress opened the door and revealed the sordid interior—an unspread bed; a foul table, sickly with the smell of half-eaten food and unwashed dishes; the central figure a poor, helpless old man sitting on a stool. I asked the negress for her master: she answered rudely that she had no master, and would have slammed the door in my face. Why tell the story of a life surrounded by taste and womanly adornments, followed by a childless, wifeless old age? The poor, wizened old creature was rotting in life on that low stool among his former dependants, their support and scorn. The Emancipation Proclamation did not reach him. But one power could break his bonds and restore the fallen son and the buried wife—the great liberator, Death.

The natives of this region are characterized by marked peculiarities of the anatomical frame. The elongation of the bones, the contour of the facial angle, the relative proportion or disproportion of the extremities, the loose muscular attachment of the ligatures, and the harsh features were exemplified in the notable instance of the late President Lincoln.[4] A like individuality appears in their idiom. It lacks the Doric breadth of the Virginian of the other slope, and is equally removed from the soft vowels and liquid intonation of the southern plain. It has verbal and phraseological peculiarities of its own. Bantering a Tennessee wife on her choice, she replied with a toss and a sparkle, "I-uns couldn't get shet of un less'n I-uns married un." "Have you'uns seed any stray shoats?"[5] asked a passer: "I-uns's uses about here." "Critter" means an animal—"cretur," a fellow-creature. "Long sweet'nin'" and "short sweet'nin'" are respectively syrup and sugar. The use of the indefinite substantive pronoun *un* (the French *on*), modified by the personals, used demonstratively, and of "done" and "gwine" as auxiliaries, is peculiar to the mountains, as well on the Wabash and Alleghany, I am told, as in Tennessee. The practice of dipping—by which is meant not baptism, but chewing snuff—prevails to a like extent.

In farming they believe in the influence of the moon on all vegetation, and in pork-butchering and curing the same luminary is consulted. Leguminous plants must be set out in the light of the moon—tuberous, including potatoes, in the dark of that satellite. It is supposed to *govern* the weather by its dip, not *indicate* it by its appearance. The cup or crescent atilt is a wet moon—*i.e.*, the month will be rainy. A change of the moon forebodes a change of the weather, and no meterological statistics can shake their confidence in the superstition. They, of course, believe in the water-wizard and his forked wand; and their faith is extended to the discovery of mineral veins. While writing this I see the statement in a public journal that Richard Flannery of Cumberland county (Kentucky) uses an oval ball, of some material known only to himself, which he suspends between the forks of a short switch. As he walks, holding this extended, the indicator announces the metal by arbitrary vibrations. As his investigations are said to be attended with success, possibly the oval ball is highly magnetized, or contains a lodestone whose delicate suspension is affected by the current magnetism, metallic veins being usually a magnetic center. Any mass of soft iron in the position of the dipping-needle is sensibly magnetic, and a solution of continuity is thus indicated by the vibrations of the delicately poised instrument. Flaws in iron are detected with absolute certainty by this method. More probably, however, the whole procedure is pure, unadulterated humbug. In all such cases the failures are unrecorded, while the successes are noted, wondered at and published. By shooting arrows all day, even a blind man may hit the mark sometimes.

During this journey it was a habit with me to relate to my invalid companion any fact or incident of the day's travel. She came to expect this, and would add incidents and observations of her own. In this way I was led to compile the following little narrative of feminine constancy and courage during the late war.

It begins with two boys and a girl, generically divided into brother and sister and their companion, living on the divide-range of mountains between Kentucky and Tennessee. The people raised hogs, which were fattened on the mast of the range, while a few weeks' feeding on corn and slops in the fall gave the meat the desired firmness and flavor. They cultivated a few acres of corn, tobacco and potatoes, and had a kitchen-garden for "short sass" and "long sass"—leguminous and tuberous plants. Apples are called "sour sass." The chief local currency was red-fox scalps, for which the State of Kentucky paid a reward: the people did not think of raising such vermin for the peltry, as the shrewder speculator of a New England State did. They sold venison and bear meat at five cents a pound to the lame trader at Jimtown, who wagoned it as far as Columbia, Kentucky, and sold it for seventy-five cents. They went to the log church in the woods on Sundays, and believe that Christ was God in the flesh, with other old doctrines now rapidly becoming heretical in the enlightened churches of the East. Living contentedly in this simple way, neither rich nor poor, the lads grew up, nutting, fishing, hunting together, and the companion naturally looked forward to the day when he would sell enough peltry and meat to buy a huge watch like a silver biscuit, such as the schoolmaster wore, make a clearing and cabin in the wild hills, and buy his one suit of store clothes, in which to wed the pretty sister of his friend.

Then came the war. Although it divided the two friends, the old kindness kept their difference from flaming forth in the vendetta fashion peculiar to the region. It was a great deal that these two young fellows did not believe that military morality required them to shoot each other on sight. Yet, on reconsideration, I will not be so sure of their opinion on this point. Perhaps they thought that, morally and patriotically, they ought to do this, and were conscious of weakness and failure of duty in omitting to do it. Perhaps the old goodwill survived for the girl's sake; and if so, I do not think the Union was the worse preserved on that account.

The young lover went into the ranks of Wolford's regiment[6] of loyal mountaineers, and rose—slowly at first, more rapidly as his square sense and upright character became known.

The girl, in her retirement, heard of her lover's advancement with pride and fear. She distrusted her worth, and found the hard menial duties of life more irksome than before. Not that she shrank from labor, but she feared its unfitting her for the refinement required by her lover's new social position. She had few examples to teach her the small proprieties of small minds, but a native delicacy helped her more than she was conscious of. She read her Bible a great deal, and used to wonder if Mary and "the other Mary" were ladies. She thought Peter was probably an East Tennessean, or like one, for when he denied his Lord they said he did not talk like the others. It seemed hard that to say "we-uns" and "you-uns," as she habitually did, though she tried not, and to use the simple phrases of her childhood, should be thought coarse or wrong. Such matters were puzzles to her which she could not solve. She got an old thumbed Butler's *Grammar* and tried hard to correct the vocables of her truant tongue. I am afraid she made poor progress. She had a way of defying that intolerable tyrant, the nominative singular, and put all her verbs in the plural, under an impression, not without example, that it was elegant language. She had enough hard work to do, poor girl! to have been quit of these mental troubles. Her brother was away, her parents were old, and all the irksome duties of farm-house and garden fell upon her. She had to hunt the wild shoats on the range, and to herd them; to drive up the cows, and milk them; to churn and make the butter and cheese. She tapped the sugar trees and watched the kettles, and made the maple syrup and sugar; she tended the poultry, ploughed and hoed the corn-field and garden, besides doing the house-work. Her old parents could help but little, for the "rheumatiz," which attacks age in the mountains, had cramped and knotted their limbs, and they were fit for nothing except in fine dry weather. Surely, life was hard with her, without her anxieties about her lover's constancy and her own defects. Letter-writing was a labor not to be thought of. She tried it, and got as far as "I am quite well, and I hope these few lines will find you the same," and there stopped. She ascribed the difficulty to her own mental and clerical defects, but I think it lay quite as much in the nature of the relation! How was she to express confidence when she distrusted? How express distrust when her maidenly promptings told her it was an indelicate solicitation? She could say Brindle had gone dry and the blind mare had foaled, or that crops were good; but what was that to say when her heart was thirsting and drying up? She blotted the paper and her eyes and her hands, but she could not write a line. She was a sensible girl, and gave it up, leaving her love to grow its own growth. The tree had been planted in good ground, and watered: it must grow of itself.

By and by military operations brought her lover into the old neighborhood. I cannot say he put on no affectations with his new rank, that he did not air his shoulder-straps a taste too much; but the manly nature was too loyal to sin from mere vanity. He seemed natural, easy, pleased with her, and urged a speedy wedding.

We may guess how the Lassie—we must give her a name, and that will do—worshiped her King Cophetua[7] in shoulder-straps. Had he not stooped from his well won, honorable height, the serene azure of his blue uniform, to sue for her? In all the humility of her pure loving heart she poured out her thankfulness to the Giver of all good for this supreme blessing of his love.

In the midst of this peace and content her brother appeared with a flag of truce. He was hailed as a prosperous prodigal, for he too was a lad of metal, but he brought one with him that made poor Lassie start and tremble. It was a lady, young and beautiful, clad in deep mourning. Although sad and retiring, there was that dangerous charm about her which men are lured by, and which women dread—a subtle influence of look and gesture and tone that sets the pulses mad. She was going for the remains of her husband, and told a pathetic story, but only too well. She used always the same language, cried at the same places, and seemed altogether too perfect in her part for it to be entirely natural. So, at least, Lassie thought, even while reproaching herself for being hard on a sister in affliction. Yet she could not escape the bitterness of the thought that the widow, Mrs. G——, was "a real lady"—that ideal rival she had been so long dreading in her lover's absence; and now that he had come, the rival had also come.

Her brother dropped a hint or two about the lady: Mrs. G—— had the "shads," "vodles" of bank-stock and niggers, and she paid well for small service. If King Cophetua could get leave to escort her to head-quarters,

Mrs. G—— would foot the bills and do the handsome thing. It was hard such a woman should have to go on such a sad business alone.

What could his sister say? She had herself put off the wedding a month: she wanted to get her ample store of butter, eggs and poultry to the trader at Jimtown, or, better still, to the brigade head-quarters at Bean's Station. With her own earnings she could then buy such simple muslins for her wedding-dress as became her and would not shame her lover. She wished she had married him, as he had urged, in her old calico gown. If he had asked her now, if he had pressed a little, she would have yielded; but he did not. He seemed to accept the proprieties and woman's will as unalterable. In fact, he did follow Mrs. G——'s motions with only too lively an admiration. Perhaps he did not know himself what his feelings were—what this new fever in his pulses meant. Besides the calm, holy connubial love there is a wild animal passion that tears through moral creeds and laws. Once, Lassie saw her brother give him a half-angry stare, that passed into a laugh of cool scorn. "Take care of Mrs. G——," he said to King Cophetua. "You will get bit there if you don't look out."

How the sister would have pressed the warning had she dared! Innocent as her lover might be, she believed that Mrs. G—— saw the growing passion and encouraged it. But there was nothing to take hold of. There was nothing bold, forward or inviting in her manner. If a lady has long lashes, must she never droop them lest she be charged with coquetry? May not a flush spring as naturally from shy reserve as from immodesty?

Lassie's lover did take charge of this dangerous siren to escort her to the headquarters at Louisville. But just before starting he came to Lassie with a certain eagerness, as one who is going into battle might, and assured her, again and again, of his faith. Did he do this to assure her or himself? I think the last.

How weary the month was! She occupied herself as well as she could with her sales and purchases, making a very good trade. The brigade had been at Bean's Station long enough to eat up all the delicacies to be found there, so that the little maid, who was a sharp marketer, got fabulous prices. She made up her simple wedding furniture, gave her mother a new gown and underwear, and pleased her old father with a handsome jean suit, the labor of her own nimble fingers. All that belonged to her would appear well on that day, as became them and her.

At any other time she would have followed up that thrifty market at Bean's Station. She would have huckstered around the neighborhood, and made a little income while it lasted; but now she had no heart for it. Her lover's leave was out, yet his regimental associates knew nothing about him.

A week after the day set for her marriage her brother came again with the flag of truce. He too was vexed—not so much at Cophetua's absence as at not meeting the widow, whom he had been sent to escort to the Confederate lines. But he treated his sister's jealous suspicions with a dash of scorn: "There was nothing of that kind, but if Cophetua would fool with a loaded gun, he must expect to be hurt. If ever there was a hair-trigger, it was Mrs. G——."

"Who is she?" asked his sister eagerly. "Tell me: you say there is something strange, dangerous about her, and I can see it. Who is she?"

"Humph!" said her brother. "She is a lady, and that is enough. If she is dangerous, keep out of her way."

This only deepened the mystery. But she had no time to think. Her brother left in the morning. In the afternoon the colonel of her lover's regiment came to see her with a very grave face. The young man had been arrested for dealing with the enemy, harboring spies and furnishing information of the disposition and number of the Federal forces. "If we could get at the true story of his connection with that woman," said the colonel, "I am satisfied he has only been indiscreet, not treacherous. He is one of my best, most trusted officers, and his arrest is a blot on the regiment. If he will tell anybody, he will tell you. Can you go to Louisville at once?"

Yes, at once. The traveling-dress, made up for so different an occasion, was donned, and under escort she went, by a hundred miles of horseback ride, to the nearest railway station. There was no tarrying by the way: the colonel's influence provided relays. On the evening of the third day she was with her lover.

It was as the colonel had supposed: the woman had got her lover in her toils, and he had been imprudent. He had every reason for believing that her story of her husband's remains was false. She was a dealer in contraband goods: this much he knew. Other officers, of higher rank, knew as much, and corresponded with her. If they chose to wink at it, was he, a subordinate, to interfere? She had trusted him, depended on him, and he had a feeling that it would be disloyal to her confidence to betray her, to pry into what she concealed, and expose what his superiors seemed to know. But after she was gone the story leaked out: she was not only a smuggler, but a very dangerous spy. Some one must be the scapegoat, and who so fit as the poor, friendless Tennesseean who had escorted her to head-quarters and acted for her in personal matters?

That was his story, but what a poor story to tell to a court-martial! What was she to do? Poor, simple child of the woods! What did she know of the wheels within wheels, and the rings of political influence by which a superior authority was to be invoked! She knew nothing of these things, and there was no one to tell her. She thought of but one plan: her brother could find that woman. She would seek her out—she would appeal to her.

We need not follow her on that return journey and her visit to the Confederate camp. Fortunately, the Confederates were nearer than she supposed. She came upon their pickets, and was taken into the commanding officer's presence. Her brother was sent for, and when he came she told him she was looking for his friend, Mrs. G——.

"Looking for her!" said her brother. "Why, that is what we moved out this way for! She is in camp now. We brought her and her luggage in last night."

She eagerly entreated to be taken to her, and was carried to a pavilion, or marquee, a little apart from the officers' quarters. Mrs. G—— came in richly but simply dressed, attended by a portly, handsome, but rather dull-looking officer.

"Why, Lassie!" said Mrs. G—— in surprise. "So you have come to see me? Here are the remains of my poor dear," she added with a little laugh, presenting the gentleman. "Do you think he is worth all the trouble I took to get him?"

"Ha! Much pleased! Devilish proper girl!" said the man with a stupid blush, justifying the stolidity of his good looks.

"But where is your *preux chevalier*,[8] Captain Cophetua? I declare, I almost fell in love with him myself. Frank here is quite jealous."

"Oh, Mrs. G——," broke out the poor girl, "you have killed him! They are going to try him and hang him for helping you to spy."

"Nonsense!" said the lady with a little start. "The poor fellow did nothing but what, as a gentleman, he was compelled to do. But how can I help you?"

"Save him," said Lassie. "You have your wealth, your wit, your husband: I have but him!" and she sank down in tears.

"Stupid," said the lady, turning sharply on her husband, "tell me what to do? Don't you see we must not let them hang the poor fellow?"

"Of course not," said the big man dryly. "Just countermand the order of execution. No doubt the Yankees will obey: I would."

"Of course you would: a precious life you would lead if you did not," said his wife, who evidently commanded that squad. "Never mind: there is more sense in what you said than I expected of you.—Jane," to the smart maid who attended on her, "pen, ink, paper and my portfolio."

Opening the last, she took out a bundle of letters, and, running them rapidly over as a gambler does his cards, she selected one. "This," she said to Lassie, "is a note from General ————. It is written without the slightest suspicion of my character as a spy; but you will see it involves him far more dangerously than your friend. He cannot well explain it away. Keep the letter. I will write to him that you have it to deliver over in return for his kind assistance in effecting the release of your friend. Don't fear: I ask him to do nothing he ought not to do without asking, and you give him a letter that would be misconstrued if it fell into other hands."

Armed with these instructions and the letters, Lassie returned home, passed on to Louisville, and delivered her message. The general promptly interfered, thanking her for calling his attention to the matter. His influence, and a more exact understanding of the means and appliances of the artful widow in obtaining information, effected her lover's acquittal and restoration to his former position.

"I owe her my life and good name," said the tall Tennesseean, taking Baby No. 2 from her arms. "I-uns ain't wuth such a gal."

"No," say I drily. "What did you take him for?" to her. Then I get the answer before quoted. But my companion, with a truer perception, went quietly up and kissed her Tennessee sister, a little to the surprise of both, I think, but they seemed touched by the silent little tribute more than by any words.

I have spoken of the character of the hostilities in that "debatable land." War is a bad thing always, but when it gets into a simple neighborhood, and teaches the right and duty of killing one's friends and relatives, it becomes demoniac. Down about Knoxville they practiced a better method. There it was the old game of "Beggar your Neighbor," and they denounced and "confiscated" each other industriously. Up in the poor hills they could only kill and burn, and rob the stable and smoke-house. We were shown the scene of one of these neighborhood vengeances. It is a low house at the side of a ravine, down whose steep slope the beech forest steps persistently erect, as if distrusting gravitation. Thirty Confederates had gathered in that house at a country-side frolic, and the fiddle sang deep in the night. The mountain girls are very pretty, having dark, opalescent eyes, with a touch of gold in them at a side glance, slight, rather too fragile figures, and the singular purity of complexion peculiar to high lands.

The moon went down, and the music of the dance, the shuffle of feet on the puncheon floor, died away into that deep murmurous chant, the hymn of Nature in the forest. The falling water, sleeping in the dam or toiling all day at the mill, gurgles like the tinkling of castanets. Every vine and little leaf is a harp-string; every tiny blade of grass flutes its singly inaudible treble; the rustling leaves, chirping cricket, piping batrachian, the tuneful hum of insects that sleep by day and wake by night, mingle and flow in the general harmony of sound. The reeds and weeds and trunks of trees, like the great and lesser pipes of an organ, thunder a low bass. The melancholy hoot of the owl and the mellow complaint of the whippoorwill join in the solemn diapason of the forest, filling the solitudes with grand, stately marches. There are no sounds of Nature or art so true in harmony as this ceaseless murmur of the American woods. So accordant is it with the solemn majesty of form and color that the observer fails to separate and distinguish it as an isolated part in the grand order of Nature. He has felt an indescribable awe in the presence of serene night and unbounded shadow, but to divide and distinguish its constituent causes were as vain as in the contour and color of a single tree to note the varied influence of rock, soil and river.

Over the little farm-house in the ravine in the fall of 1863 there fell with the sinking moon these solemn dirges of the great dark woods. The stars brightened their crowns till *Via Lacteal* shone a highway of silver dust or as the shadow of that primeval river rolling across the blue champaign of heaven. The depths of repose that follow the enjoyment of the young irrigated their limbs, filling the sensuous nerves and arteries with a delicious narcotism—a deep, quiet, healthful sleep, lulled by the chant of the serene mother-forest.

Hush! A light step, like a blown leaf: the loose wooden latch rises at the touch of a familiar hand; familiar feet, that have trodden every inch of that poor log floor, lead the way; and then all at once, like a bundle of Chinese crackers, intermingled with shrieks and groans and deep, vehement curses, the rapid reports of pistols fill the chambers. The beds, the floors, the walls, the doors are splashed with blood, and the chambers are cumbered with dead and dying men in dreadful agony. Happy those who passed quietly from the sweet sleep of Nature to the deeper sleep of death! Of thirty young men in the flush of youth, not one escaped. Six

Federal scouts had threaded their way since sunset from the Federal lines to do this horrible work. Oh, Captain Jack,[9] swart warrior of the Modocs! Must we hang you for defending your lava-bed home in your own treacherous native way, when we, to preserve an arbitrary political relation, murder sleeping men in their beds?

Let me close with an incident of that great game of war in which the watershed of the Ohio was the gambler's last stake.

The Confederacy was a failure in '62, held together by external pressure of hostile armies. It converted civil office into bomb-proofs for the unworthy by exempting State and Federal officials; it discouraged agriculture by levying on the corn and bacon of the small farmers, while the cotton and sugar of the rich planter were jealously protected; it discouraged enlistment by exempting from military service every man who owned twenty Negroes, one hundred head of cattle, five hundred sheep—in brief, all who could afford to serve; it discouraged trade by monopolies and tariffs. But for the ubiquitous Jew[10] it would have died in 1862-'63, as a man dies from stagnation of the blood. It was the rich man's war and the poor man's fight.

This suicidal policy had its effect. Cut off from all markets, the farmer planted only for family use. At the close of the war the people of Georgia, Alabama and the Carolinas had to be fed by the government. The farmers in 1864 refused to feed the Southern army. Seventy thousand men deserted east of the Mississippi between October 1, 1864, and February 3, 1865. They were not recalled: the government could not feed them. The Confederacy was starved out by its own people—rather by its own hideous misgovernment, for the people were loyal to the cause.

One fact was apparent as early as 1863: the South would not feed the armies—the North must. That plan, so far as the Atlantic coast States were involved, was foiled at Gettysburg. The only resource left was in the West, the watershed of the Ohio, which Sherman was wrenching out of General Johnston's[11] fingers. In a military point of view, the great Confederate strategist was right: he was conducting the campaign on the principle Lee so admirably adopted in Virginia. But President Davis had more than a military question to solve. If he could not seize the granaries of the watershed, the Confederacy would die of inanition.

That was what caused the change of commanders in Georgia, and the desperate invasion that blew to pieces at Nashville; and it introduces a little scouting incident upon which the event of that campaign may have partially turned. General Hood was in camp at Jonesborough:[12]

Forrest and Wheeler were detached to destroy Sherman's single thread of supplies. Prisoners pretended to have been on half rations, and the sanguine opinion at head-quarters was that Sherman was on the grand retreat. That able strategist had disappeared, enveloping himself in impenetrable vidette swarms of cavalry. He had pocketed one hundred thousand men in the Georgia hills, and no one could find them; at least, General Hood could not.

But others were not sanguine about Sherman's falling back. General Jackson selected a major, a trusted scout, with twenty-five men, with instructions to find Sherman. Again and again the scout and his little band tried to pierce that impenetrable cloud, and could not. Then he tried another plan. He snapped up a Federal squad, clothed a select part of his little band in their uniform, and sent the others back with the prisoners. Then he plunged boldly into the cloud, a squad of Federals, bummers, pioneers. Does the reader reflect upon the fine fibre of the material requisite for such an exploit? It is not strength, courage or tactical cunning that is most wanted, but that most difficult art, to be able to put off your own nature and put on another's—to play a part, not as the actor, who struts his hour in tinsel and mouths his speeches as no mortal man ever walked or talked in real life, but as one who stakes his life upon a word, an accent; requiring subtlety of analytic sense and quickness of thought. Polyglot as was the speech of the Federal forces, suspicion, started by that test, would run rapidly to results. Then there was the danger of collision with the regiment whose uniform they had assumed. Swift, constant motion was required. They swept to the head of the column, and, to be brief, the first Federal pontoon thrown across the Chattahoochee was laid with the assistance of these spies. The leader threw himself on the bank and counted the regiments by their insignia as they passed, until he saw the linen duster and the glittering staff of the great commander himself as they clattered over the bridge. Then to Campbellton, hard by, where their horses were rendezvoused, and whip and spur to Jonesborough.

A council of war was sitting when the scout arrived. He was hurried into its presence, and told his story with laconic, military precision. Sherman's whole force was across the Chattahoochee and marching on Jonesborough, twenty miles away.

"I have sure information to the contrary," said the commanding general, singularly deceived by a strong conviction, enforced by scouts who depended on rumor for authority. "It is some feint to cover the general movement."

"I counted the flags, guidons, regimental insignia—such force of cavalry, artillery, infantry," giving the numbers. "I saw and recognized General Sherman," said the scout briefly.

His report was not, even then, credited, but, as a precaution, a brigade of cavalry, with his battalion in the van, was sent out to beat up the enemy. A short distance beyond Flint River they struck the Federal line, which attacked at once, without feeling—a sure indication of strength. The battalion was hurled back on the brigade, the brigade rushed across the Flint River, and back into the infantry line, now throwing up tardy entrenchments at Jonesborough. The rest is historical. It was but one of the rash throws of the dice for that great stake, the watershed of the Ohio, and helps to show the principles of military action by which it was lost.

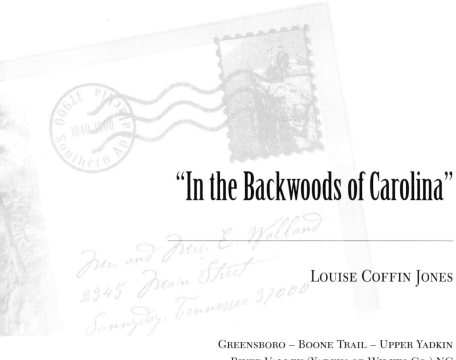

"In the Backwoods of Carolina"

LOUISE COFFIN JONES

GREENSBORO – BOONE TRAIL – UPPER YADKIN
RIVER VALLEY (YADKIN OR WILKES CO.) NC

The narrator of the following article is a stock character from Reconstruction-era stories: She is the northern teacher in the south, a soldier in what W. E. B. Du Bois calls the "crusade of the New England school-ma'm" (25). After the Civil War, northern teachers went south to teach mainly newly freed blacks, but also poor whites. Writes Du Bois:

> Behind the mists of ruin and rapine waved the calico dresses of women who dared, and after the hoarse mouthings of the field guns rang the rhythm of the alphabet. Rich and poor they were, serious and curious. Bereaved now of a father, now of a brother, now of more than these, they came seeking a life work in planting New England school-houses among the white and black of the South" (25).

Though later southern historians are cynical about the educational efforts of northerners in the south, Du Bois praises them. Nonetheless, educational opportunity remained scarce for southern blacks. As Reconstruction dragged on and then ended ignominiously, the "race problem" began to seem intractable. The "New England school-ma'm" began directing her attention away from blacks and redirecting it towards the southern mountains. Mountain whites,

Lippincott's, December 1879

a quasi-racial "native type," appeared to need education as much as the blacks did. Unlike blacks, however, mountain whites did not serve as reminders of the unachieved goals of abolition. What's more, against the frightening backdrop of increasing Gilded Age immigration, the mountain whites of the south provided a soothing notion of racial purity and "Anglo-Saxonism" (Klotter 840).

In the following article, Louise Coffin Jones does not give the specific location of the remote western North Carolina area where she taught school for six months in the 1870s. However, internal evidence indicates she was in the upper Yadkin River valley, in Yadkin or Wilkes County. Not much is known about Jones herself, beyond what can be gleaned from the small handful of articles she contributed to the national magazines in the 1870s and 1880s. One of her contributions, an 1883 *Lippincott's* article entitled "In the Highlands of North Carolina," like the present selection, focuses on domestic activities and women's clothing and occupations.

It was once my lot to spend six months in the pine woods of Western North Carolina, on the border of that region known to lovers of grand scenery as "The Land of the Sky."[1] Here, shut away from books, from society, from all the distractions of the outer world, I had ample leisure to study the primitive manners and customs of the people.

My journey into the backwoods began at Greensboro', a central town of North Carolina. Many traditions and associations cluster about this place. It is the home of the Worths and Vances and Moreheads, and in the palmy days of Southern prosperity the stately brick mansions with wide piazzas, set back from the street and shaded by noble oaks, were the scenes of profuse and graceful hospitality.

Still older traditions date back to the times of the Revolution. A few miles to the northward the battle of Guilford Courthouse[2] was fought between the British forces under Cornwallis and the Americans under Greene. Mounds and trenches where the British soldiers were buried are still shown, the old trees about the ancient village of Martinsville bear marks of cannon-ball, and bullets and buttons were until within a few years ploughed up on the battle-field. The dread inspired among the negroes and lower classes of whites by the current ghost-stories has died out only during the present generation. According to these stories, spectral troops of cavalry, or "King's Light-horse," rode at night across the field, the groans of wounded and dying sounded on the night air, lights were seen moving, words of command and the clash of arms were heard.

These superstitions had such a hold upon the minds of the negroes that not even for his freedom would one walk across the battle-field after dark.

The country about Greensboro' has been generally cleared and cultivated, though many forests of oak and chestnut still stand, and many old fields have been abandoned to a growth of sedge-grass and young pines.

I had been in Greensboro' two or three days, and was wondering in what kind of a place and among what people I was destined to spend the next half year, when one afternoon a large, antique-looking covered wagon drawn by two horses stopped at the gate, and a lively old man in home-spun clothes crawled out of the forward end and jumped over the front wheel to the ground. A fringe of scanty gray hair showed under his hat; a stubbly beard of two or three days' growth adorned his chin; he had shrewd, twinkling gray eyes, a hooked nose, and teeth that met on the edges. Low cowhide shoes, tied with leather strings, displayed woollen stockings the color of his butternut clothing. This was my first sight of Uncle Billy L——, a character who afforded me continual entertainment during the six months that followed.

He came up to the door, other faces in the mean while peering out of the front of the wagon or from under the curtain at the side. In a high-pitched voice he said, "I reckon our teacher's hyar—one of them Northern teachers that the superintendent brought down the other day. If she's hyar I want her. We're jist a-startin' home, and we'll take her with us. Reckon she's got a chist of clothes to go."

I presented myself, and pointed out my trunk, a large Saratoga[3] which stood in the hall.

He looked at it a minute, with his eyebrows and upper lip elevated and his teeth set on edge, then burst into a shrill prolonged "He! he! he! Reckon you've got a man in thar," he said, "but you've no need to bring a feller down here with you from the North. We've got plenty of likely ones here: I've got six boys myself. But come to the wagon and git in; I'll send the boys in for your chist."

I followed him to the gate, feeling that the leafless oaks and blue November sky suddenly and strongly suggested home-sickness.

"'Light, boys, 'light!" Uncle Billy said. "This is our new teacher.— This is my son Jeems; this is my son John; this is my son Thomas; this my son Levi; and I've got two more at home. John's married, but you can have your pick of the rest. He! he! he!"

"Now, William," said a reproving voice from the interior of the wagon, "what d'ye want to plague the young woman for? She ain't used to your ways."

"That's my old woman," said Uncle Billy. "Come, git inside, and she'll make a good place for ye in the hay."

Just then a lady and gentleman whose acquaintance I had made in the last few days came to bid me good-bye. They seemed to be the last link that bound me to the enlightenment of the nineteenth century, and it was with a gulp of homesick longing that I took leave of them, and with Uncle Billy's assistance mounted into the front part of the wagon, feeling that the Dark Ages had yawned to take me in.

Aunt Betsy, Uncle Billy's wife, sat in the middle of the wagon on an old bed-quilt spread on the hay. She was stout, round-shouldered and short-waisted, and wore a little cape of old-fashioned indigo-blue calico stretched across her shoulders. Her dress was of homespun, made in the most primitive fashion; her calico sun-bonnet, stiffened with splints of cornstalk instead of pasteboard, hung from one of the ribs or staves which supported the wagon-cover overhead. Her faded brown hair was parted crookedly on top of her head, drawn violently back and fastened with a horn comb. No garniture of white was visible about her neck or wrists. Her face had evidently been fair in youth, and still showed traces of former comeliness, but the effect was spoiled by a solitary lower tooth, which closed on the outside of her upper lip, when her mouth was shut, like a yellow tusk.

The four sons, varying in age from eighteen to thirty, were tall and loose-jointed, with the bright eyes, good color and free expression of mountaineers. They were dressed in homespun like their father.

They returned with my trunk, or "chist," and after much rearranging of their purchases, which had been stowed away for the journey, room was made for it in the back part of the wagon. Aunt Betsy and I leaned against it; in front of us on the hay sat Uncle Billy and his oldest son, facing each other; Jeems was driver, and his two younger brothers sat beside him on the seat. The string that drew the curtain behind was closely tied, and the opening in front was nearly filled: our view of the outer world was restricted to glimpses we caught between the heads of Jeems and his brothers. So we rode out of Greensboro' and began our slow journey to the mountains.[4] The wagon was one of a kind I have seen nowhere outside of North Carolina. The bed was longer than the bed of an average farm-wagon, and, instead of being straight along the sides, it presented a concave curve, being low in the middle and high in front and behind. The white cover followed the outline of the wagon-bed; it ran up in front, up behind, and had a corresponding depression in the middle. There were no springs, and we jolted along over the dirt-road, which had been washed into gullies here and there, the horses going all the while at a slow walk.

The glimpses we obtained through the opening in front showed us withered November woods, brown oak trees and yellow chestnuts, and old field where the faded sedge-grass waved in the wind and the dark green of the pine-thickets contrasted vividly with the red soil of the numerous gullies.

Toward dusk Uncle Billy sprang out of the wagon with the agility of a boy, and walked on ahead of the team, now and then shouting back directions to Jeems about driving; and just before dark we turned off the road, drove through a gap in the fence, across a field of sedge-grass, and stopped in front of a low wooden house with a tumble-down piazza. The people who lived here were acquaintances of Uncle Billy's, and according to the Southern custom we were to avail ourselves of their hospitality for the night. I was cramped and stiff from sitting in one position so long, and was glad to crawl over the front seat, through the opening and down over the wheel to the ground. Noisy greetings were exchanged between the two families, and Uncle Billy's shrill "He! he! he!" rang out as he uttered some joke which he thought intensely funny. The wood was piled higher in the huge fireplace, and we sat around the ruddy blaze, while children with long white hair and one finger in their mouths stood on the hearth in front of us and stared at us. The girls wore homespun dresses with narrow skirts that reached to their heels: the boys' clothes were cut just like their father's, and made them look like little old men.

When summoned to supper we went out through the darkness several yards to the kitchen, where we sat down to fried pork, soda biscuits, strong coffee, persimmon pudding—or "simmon puddin'," as it was called—and honey. The men-folks talked, and sometimes Aunt Betsy spoke of her visit to Greensboro', but the women of the family stood abashed and mute by the fireplace or brought more hot biscuits and coffee.

When bedtime came I was ushered into a room with two beds in it, and told which I was to occupy. Some members of the family slept in the other, but they came in after I was asleep, and were up and gone before I awoke. We started early next morning, after eating breakfast by candlelight. The blue November sky became overclouded, and a drizzling rain fell. The wind sighed drearily through the withered brown leaves of the oak woods, and the road was full of sticky red mud. Inside the wagon Aunt Betsy and I shivered, in spite of the bed-quilt we had wrapped around us, and Uncle Billy turned up his coat-collar, pulled down his hat-brim and set his teeth on edge. His tall sons took turns in walking up the hills, for the heavy load and thick mud made it hard pulling for the horses. We passed farms so rocky that one might walk from one side of a field to the other without stepping off the rocks, old fields washed into gullies and partly overgrown with pines and patches of scrubby oak timber, and crossed Deep River and several swift-running streams. We toiled up one muddy hillside and down another all the forenoon, and saw in this half day's journey only two large, comfortable-looking houses with extensive grounds. The other houses we passed were low, unpainted wooden structures, with rickety piazzas in front and no front yards or ornamental shrubbery.

We stopped at noon at a house in the wet brown November woods. Several lean, hungry-looking hounds skulked around the door. No one was at home but a woman and two little children, and they were huddled over a fire in the bare, comfortless kitchen. The woman seemed afraid of strangers, and said scarcely a word, but gave us the use of her fireplace. Aunt Betsy prepared a hasty lunch from some materials she had in the wagon: she made a johnny-cake of Indian meal and baked it on a board in front of the fire, and boiled coffee in a coffee-pot set on the coals. As she bent over the fire, her face red with heat, giving the coffee-pot a spiral twirl or beating a final pat upon the johnny-cake with her broad hand, I thought I could see why she was short-waisted and round-shouldered. Fifty years' cooking by a fireplace, stooping over the hearth an hour or two three times a day, was enough to warp any form.

We passed few houses that afternoon, and few patches of cleared land. The woods seemed endless: from the top of each hill we climbed we saw an horizon of forest. The chestnuts had disappeared, and tall pines, fit for "the mast of some great ammiral," mingled with the oaks. As the wind swept through their branches a long, slow, mournful sound was borne to our ears, bringing some indefinable association of sadness and longing. Great bunches of dark-green mistletoe grew in the oak trees. There was a thick undergrowth of chinquapin, persimmon and holly, the latter a beautiful tree with clusters of bright red berries and glossy green leaves set around the edge with thorns. The persimmon boughs were laden with fruit, some smooth, full and bright yellow, others shriveled and purple. The latter were delicious to the taste, resembling dates in flavor, but it was a favorite practical joke among the natives to press the former upon strangers, telling them that the more tempting fruit was the better. Whoever tasted it rarely cared to repeat the experience, remembering the smarting puckered sensation it left in his mouth. Uncle Billy presented some yellow persimmons to me with a sober face, but Aunt Betsy said, "Now, William!" and he burst into his usual shrill "He! he! he!" then went on to relate a number of familiar sayings and stories connected with the persimmon, beginning with the proverb, "It's the longest pole that knocks the persimmon," and ending with a story of his own about one of his neighbors trying to catch a 'possum which was up in persimmon tree feeding on the fruit.

Toward the end of the day's journey the hills grew steeper and rose into mountains, and the road wound along their base or zigzagged up their sides. The country was wild and lonely. It seemed that we had left all traces of the busy, progressive world behind, having penetrated into the forest beyond the farthest echo of the railroad. Darkness came upon us while we were yet several miles from our journey's end. The jolting of the springless wagon and the confinement produced a feeling akin to sea-sickness, and I spent the last hour in a state of half unconsciousness, half misery, with my head in Aunt Betsy's lap.

She roused me by saying, "We've got thar;" and the next minute we turned off the main road into a short lane leading to a house. As soon as the sound of wagon-wheels greeted the inmates the door opened, firelight streamed out, three large dogs came rushing down to the big gate, figures filled the lighted doorway, and clamorous greetings were exchanged between the members of the family. The younger children shouted, "Pap and mam's come!" and called off the dogs, who were leaping up to the horses' heads and getting in everybody's way: "Down, Towse! down, Bull! down, Pup!"

When I was seated in front of the huge fireplace these children, five in number, ranged themselves on the broad stone hearth before me, and proceeded to take a deliberate survey of me from head to foot. This was no intentional rudeness on their part, but simply an expression of childish curiosity; nor was it considered a breach of manners by the parents, for no reproof was offered. The girls had long hair, white as flax, which was permitted to hang straight down from the line of parting: when it fell over their eyes they put it back behind their ears. The skirts of their homespun dresses were long and narrow, and were finished at the bottom with a little hem.

A little shed-room attached to the back of the house, with a small four-paned window and a door that was warped so that it would not shut by several inches, was set apart for my room; and though it contained no toilet conveniences—no wash-bowl or pitcher, no looking-glass or stand—in fact, nothing but a bed and a chair, I learned to be thankful for the comparative privacy it afforded me. Many of the houses in the neighborhood had no spare room for guests, and when I went visiting I had to sleep in the same room with the whole family. The feather bed in my room was so high that it was necessary to mount on a chair to get to it, and when the plunge was made I sank down half buried.

The next morning, when I awoke, there was a row of children's faces, one above another, peeping in though the warped door. Aunt Betsy came presently with a pewter basin of water, and sent them away. She set the basin on the chair in my room and threw a towel over the back. I learned to be thankful for these accommodations and to regard myself as a pampered Sybarite.[5]

A look from the front door showed me the character of the surroundings. In front of the house, a few rods away, was the red muddy road, and beyond it rose a hill covered with scrubby oaks, withered and brown, interspersed with a few pines. Between the road and house were the woodpile, a soap-kettle, an outdoor oven for drying persimmons and blackberries, the loom-house, and a small log building wherein were some blacksmith's tools, several old wagon-wheels and some rusty horseshoes. On one side was the garden, looking dreary and forlorn, as gardens usually do in November, with turnip-tops visible on the muddy surface, and two or three embankments marking the place where cabbage had been stowed away for the winter. On the other, in close proximity, were the barn and two or three corn-cribs. Back of the house the ground sloped steeply to a creek bordered with hazelnut bushes, then rose as steeply on the other side to an unbroken forest of leafless oaks and dark-green pines. The opposite slope was covered with white skeletons of trees, and was called "the deadenin':" the nearest slope was marked with cornstalks, showing that it was a part of the farm. I marveled how horses and ploughs went up and down these steep slopes when preparing the ground, or horses and wagons in corn-gathering time. At the openings of the valley through which the creek flowed were mountains beyond mountains, blue with the haze of distance. And this was all there was to be seen—no sign of neighbors' houses, no sight of neighborly smoke.

Uncle Billy's house was made of logs, weatherboarded on the outside and ceiled on the inside with planed boards, which had grown brown with smoke and time. It consisted of one large room, with a loft overhead and two shed-rooms attached to the back. At the front of the house was a long porch—or "peazzer," as it was called—with a shelter and a railing. A continuation of its floor led to the kitchen, a few yards distant, but there was no protection against rain or snow. In bad weather the family made a rush from the "big house" to the kitchen, accepting without protest an inconvenience which they seemed to regard as irremediable.

The kitchen was of logs, and glimpses of surrounding scenery could be obtained through the chinks. There were two doors, one on each side, but no windows. A long table, made of two wide boards, occupied the greater part of the room, and here at meal-time Uncle Billy and Aunt Betsy sat at the opposite ends, with their sons and daughters ranged on two long benches between them, like Job and his wife before their calamities. A huge fireplace, with the pots, pans, kettles, long-handled ovens and other articles used in cooking, filled one end of the room, and the other was occupied by unused spinning-wheels, reels, quilting-frames and side-saddles. Some shelves which hung against the wall held the blue-edged dishes and yellow platters, and bundles of dried herbs and miscellaneous articles of household use, such as candle-moulds, gourd dippers and bunches of red peppers, depended from the beams overhead.

The dish-washing was not done on the table, but at the hearth, the women preferring to bend over with their heads to the fire while they washed the dishes in a "keeler." A keeler is a wooden vessel resembling a foot-tub, and a "piggin," used for carrying water from the well, is another, which resembles a pail, except that it has no movable handle, a stave which projects above the rest serving for that purpose.

The food of which these hardy mountaineers partook was produced on their own land, the usual dishes being pork in various forms, mush, crackling, cornbread, stewed pumpkin, blackberry pies served in yellow earthen dishes, and persimmon pudding.

One day will serve as a sample of many. Early in the morning, while it was yet dark, Uncle Billy got up and dressed himself in front of the fire, which he replenished by throwing on a piece of fat pine; then, opening the door of the short crooked stairs that led to the loft, he called, "Jeems!

Thomas! Levi!" in a voice that must have come like a shot to the ears of the sleepers. Then, with many long yawns and groans and ho-hums, he sat before the fire until breakfast was ready, looking into the blaze with elevated eyebrows. He was not always hilarious, but had occasional spells of low spirits, and intimated by gloomy remarks that he thought everything was going to destruction. Aunt Betsy in the mean time had risen and waked her girls, and was now rattling the pots and dishes in the kitchen. Breakfast was eaten by candlelight, then the members of the family dispersed to their various tasks. Jeems and two or three of his brothers took their axes and went into the woods, whence the echoes of their "riving" of shingles or their chopping sounded all the forenoon. Levi, in obedience to his father's orders to take a grist (long *i*) to mill, put a sack of corn on a horse, mounted bareback before it, and rode off whistling through a path in the woods to a mill miles away on the creek. Uncle Billy betook himself to husking corn in the barn or wandered, with his hands behind his back, through his turnip-patch and cornfields, planning the next year's crops. Aunt Betsy went to the loom-house, whence the sound of her vigorous industry soon came: one daughter washed dishes in the log kitchen, and another went to sweep the floor and make the beds. She who did the sweeping had no light task. This had always been associated in my mind with carpets and dust, but here it related to bare floors and mud which had been carried in on the feet of the family. The broom was a bundle of sedge-grass about as long as one's arm, tied tightly at the stems with a string and wielded with one hand. The sweeper had to stoop with a one-sided motion at every stroke, and the energy of her efforts to get the floor clean sent the airy, thistle-like seeds of the sedge-grass floating through the room. At noon the members of the family gathered from their various tasks to dinner, then went back again and worked till nightfall.

After supper there was an irregular procession from the log kitchen into the house, and whoever shut the "peazzer"-door had to get up and open it for the next comer, for the string was broken and the latch could be lifted only from the inside. This was a slight inconvenience, but they had become accustomed to it, and did not seem to think of remedying it. With a great clattering the splint-bottomed chairs were dragged into a semicircle in front of the hearth: a knot of fat pine from a pile in the corner was thrown into the fire, and the rich flame brightened the whole room. Lamps were unknown and candles rarely used. A pine-knot answered the purpose of lamps within and lanterns without. Uncle Billy and his sons sat around the fire with their hats on, and discussed farm or neighborhood matters. Aunt Betsy busied herself with knitting, and the younger children, bending over to shade their eyes from the light, pored over some schoolbook or "ciphered" on their slates. The dancing firelight, replenished now and then with a fresh pine-knot, cast a ruddy glow over the group and threw their shadows on the ceiling and back wall;

> And all the old, rude-furnished room
> Burst, flower-like into rosy bloom.[6]

Everything was intended for use: there was no attempt at ornament. There was no carpet, no wall-paper, no whitewash. The board walls were brown and bare; the mantelpiece, which could be reached only by standing on a chair, had nothing but the almanac and family Bible on top of it; there were no pictures, no works of art of even the rudest character. In the back part of the room were two beds, and these, together with an ancient bureau, with brass rings for handles to the drawers, two chests, or "chists"—in one of which reposed an antique, tight, old-fashioned suit of clothes which had been Uncle Billy's wedding-suit—and about twenty splint-bottomed chairs, comprised the furniture.

Hanging near the door was a small broken looking-glass wherein the beholder's face appeared in disjointed sections, and beneath it was a comb-case containing some broken combs. These were the toilet conveniences for the whole family. In the morning they went to the well and drew water, washed their faces and hands, dried them on a towel that hung in the kitchen, then came back and combed their hair, bestowing no more care on their personal appearance during the day. There was no clock to tell when bedtime came, but it announced itself in the yawns of the children, who grew sleepy after an hour or two spent in front of the fire, and were sent to bed by their mother. By this time Uncle Billy had got into a warm discussion with his older sons, not about politics or the state of the country—for they took no papers and knew little of the world beyond their horizon of woods—but about some local matter—whether the new foot-log was to be placed where the old one was or a little farther up the creek, or whether the white sow that broke into their turnip-patch belonged to Neighbor MacNary or to their own hogs, which ran wild in the woods. Still asserting his opinion, he rose up, hung his hat on a peg behind the door, divested himself of his outer garments and got into bed. He went on talking with occasional pauses until an aggressive snore proclaimed that he was continuing the argument in his dreams. Then the sons took themselves to the loft above, where the creaking of the floor and the rickety bedsteads announced that they were retiring for the night. The two younger children slept in a trundle-bed drawn from under their parents' bed, and two half-grown daughters occupied the other one in the room. Aunt Betsy, after nodding a while over her knitting, would rouse herself and cover the fire, and I would retire to my little shed-room at the back of the house.

The view from its one small, four-paned window over the deep valley, which at night was a gulf of darkness, to the white skeleton trees of the "deadening" and the sombre pine forest on the high ridge beyond, together with the murmuring voice of the stream, which was the only sound that broke the stillness when silence had fallen upon the household, was not particularly cheering to one inclined to homesickness.

Everything about this establishment was done in the most primitive manner. The cloth for the woolen clothes of the family was spun and woven by the thrifty hands of the mother and her daughters, the coloring being obtained from dyes found in the woods around them, the bark of trees or nutshell. The washing was done in tubs on a slab bench by the well. The men's working garments were beaten in a pounding-barrel; the other clothes were rubbed between the hands. Wash-day, which was any time in the middle or latter part of the week, sometimes Saturday, came and went without the use of washboards, starch, bluing or clothes-lines. The clothes were stretched on the sharp points of the garden paling to dry, or on the "peazzer" rail, whence they occasionally blew down in the night, and the dogs slept upon them.

There were a few old books, mostly school-books—the children were bright and eager to learn, and made the most of their advantages— but no newspapers, no periodical literature, to bring news of the outside world. Sometimes on Sunday afternoons Uncle Billy took the deeds of his land—yellow, time-stained documents—out of the "chist" or bureau- drawer where they were kept, and read aloud in a monotonous voice the descriptions of the boundary-lines, in which there were such items as "thence east so many rods to a post oak, thence south so many rods to a black jack." This was the family classic.

At intervals a traveller passed along the road on horseback. The three dogs bounded up from their place on the "peazzer" and ran barking down to the gate; the children ran out to call them off, shouting, "Bull! Pup! Towse!" and Uncle Billy came out to ask the stranger or acquaintance to "'light and come in."

This family were an exception to the general cast of the neighborhood, but the exception was rather in their favor. They were considered the most enterprising and intelligent, had made various trips to Greensboro' to trade hams for flour and other articles, and into the upper counties of South Carolina to dispose of horses. Uncle Billy was the oracle of the neighborhood, the leader in school, meeting, and road affairs. A mile and a half distant in the woods, on the opposite side of the creek, were the meeting- and school-houses, the first a large, ancient barn-like building nearly a hundred years old, stained with pitch to protect it from the weather; the second small and comparatively new. Near by was the old graveyard, the sunken mounds overgrown with ground-ivy, which gave forth a pungent smell when crushed under the footsteps. To the meeting-house, through the woods, on horseback or on foot, came the people of the neighborhood on Sunday, the women wearing sun-bonnets stiffened with cornstalk splints, homespun dresses and woollen mitts— some of them chewing snuff-sticks—the men in butternut-colored clothing and wide-brimmed hats, most of them chewing tobacco. The ignorance of some was of a mild, negative type, and as it was combined with timid, shrinking manners, one saw nothing offensive in it; but in others it was aggressive: it took the form of assertion and self-conceit. One man, a type of the non-progressive class, was sceptical regarding the superior advantages of the outside world: he was "agin railroads and all sich," and refused to send his children to school to learn book-knowledge, which was contrary to "Scripter and to common sense." He scouted the theory that the world was round and that it turned over. Didn't "the Scripters" speak of the four corners of the earth? and if it had four corners, how could it be round? And if the world turned over, why didn't all the water in the ponds fall out? No sich book-nonsense for him or for his children! He had got along very well without eddication, and there was no need of the children knowing more than their father. His horizon was bounded by the pine forest about his rocky farm: he knew nothing of the great world beyond, and cared nothing for it.

The men of the neighborhood met at times to work on the roads that wound up and down the steep hills, to fill with pine boughs and earth the gullies which the last rain had washed in the soft red soil. The next rain only washed the gullies deeper, but the men had worked out their road-tax, and had exchanged "chaws" of tobacco and a vast lot of petty neighborhood gossip. These, together with the occasional meetings in regard to school-matters, were the only public gathering. The people

of this section did not vex their souls with politics. I doubt if some of
them knew, half the time, who was President. It was miles through the
pine forest to the nearest post-office, and that was a little village on a
stage-road that wound out of one infinity of distance and wound into
another. The people had little money, and little need of any. The various
articles of food, clothing and household use were produced on their farms
or obtained by barter. Wild game was to be had for the seeking, and fish
abounded in the mountain-streams. Sometimes the men and boys of the
neighborhood joined in a fox-hunt, and the deep musical bay of the hounds
resounded through the moonlit woods. But the chasing and catching of
hogs afforded exercise and excitement enough for even the most exuberant
vitality. The hogs ran wild for the greater part of the year, feeding in the
woods, and became very shy and fierce, sometimes developing tusks and
bristles. They were lank, lean and wild-eyed, and ran like deer when their
haunts were disturbed. Sometimes the hog-chasers saw other game—a fat
'possum up in a persimmon tree or a black bear in the thickets of the forest.

The families of this neighborhood, though living out of sight of
each other, were social in their tendencies, and found time to visit back
and forth in the long winter evenings. Sometimes the elders of one family
came after supper to stay till bedtime and chat with the elders of another.
Sometimes the young folks, with a pine-knot torch that cast light along the
path through the pine forest, went singing and laughing, accompanied
by two or three dogs, to spend a merry evening with their neighbors.
On these occasions the kitchen was given up to the young people, and it
resounded with their laughter and songs as they played games or practised
their favorite tunes. The blazing pine-knots on the hearth cast a bright
light over the room, the logs of the wall, the pole rafters overhead, and
the loom at the farther end. Every family had a loom, but not every
one a loom-house, and this cumbersome piece of furniture was generally
kept in one corner of the kitchen. Before the young people separated the
girl-visitors must have a peep at the piece in the loom to see what stripe
and colors it had. There was much good-natured rivalry between the
weavers, and she whose homespun dress displayed a new stripe and a
new combination of dyes was regarded with admiring envy by the others.
It was a matter of pride to have a variety of homespun dresses, each with
a different stripe or check.

As before remarked, not all the houses had a loft and a spare shed-
room, like Uncle Billy's. One that I visited was a cabin of a single room.
It contained three beds—one by the fireplace and two in the back part,

with folded bed-quilts piled on a chair between them. These quilts
when unfolded displayed patchwork pieced together with infinite pains—
bright scraps of calico in circles and squares, three-cornered bits, wavy
green vines sending out round red and round yellow flowers alternately,
angular flower-pots and stiff bouquets on a ground of white. These were
regarded with great pride, and were used only on extraordinary occasions.
The beds were commonly spread with colored homespun coverlets, part
wool and part cotton, with simple figures in the centre and a procession
of stiff, unnatural birds around the border.

   This family consisted of father and mother and three grown or half-
grown daughters. The old man and old woman smoked pipes, sitting on
opposite sides of the fireplace and grumbling at one another: the daughters
all dipped snuff, and the oldest one chewed. This daughter had by some
means found her way out of the woods a year or two before and gone to
Raleigh, where she had been chambermaid in an hotel. She brought back
with her a number of silly fashions and sickly graces, beside which the
rude manners and unsophisticated ignorance of her backwoods associates
appeared respectable. She wore tight corsets, cheap jewelry and a profusion
of artificial flowers: she rouged her cheeks, and appeared at meeting in
the first large hoops and first overskirt that had ever been introduce to these
primitive regions. She was regarded with wonder and envy by the other
young women, but their scant homespun dresses appeared to advantage
beside her hoops and flounces, and their clear white-and-red complexions
were much more attractive than her artificial bloom. She affected to
despise the rude fare and simple manners of her native backwoods, and
to sigh for the superior advantages of the capital; but it is questionable
whether a life spent among the healthy and natural influences of this
mountain-region, with few of the conveniences of civilization, would
not be better than all the privileges and possibilities of cities for one
like her who had conceived cheap ideals.

   The people I have been describing formed the better class of this
region. They were thrifty, temperate, industrious, scrupulous, as a rule,
to owe no man anything, and upright in their dealing. There was a lower
class, composed of "poor white trash," who owned no land, but lived as
renters or squatters in rude and filthy cabins. They were lazy, trifling,
worthless, without even the element of picturesqueness to relieve their
squalor. Their homespun dress was a muddy brown or gray in color; they
went barefoot or wore coarse, cowhide shoes; and their entire personal
appearance denoted an indolent acquiescence in their condition. Their

uncombed hair fell over their faces, and they had not even the ambition to put it back out of the way, but gazed through it with their lacklustre eyes. Their complexion was sallow or marred with pimples, and their teeth, lips and chins were discolored with tobacco-juice. No matter how poor they were, they always managed to have tobacco for chewing, dipping and smoking. The entire family, men, women and children, used tobacco in some form. The English language in their mouths was transformed into an uncouth dialect. The civilities, courtesies, even some of the decencies, of life were dispensed with; and as a relapse from culture is always more degrading in its influence and tendencies than a corresponding state of ignorance among a people who have never been elevated, so these degenerate Anglo-Saxons compared unfavorably with the native Indians, a few of whom still lingered in the mountains.

These mountains filled all the northern and western horizon. Gazing upon the blue and violet waves that melted into the sky, upon the nearer ranges that lifted their huge purple shoulders above the miles of pine forests, or upon the solitary domes that now draped veils of mist about their brows, now stood revealed in all their rugged and enduring majesty, one might think that their very presence would ennoble and uplift the lives spent at their base. But the eye sees, the soul receives, only what they bring with them the power of seeing and receiving; and these slatternly, fretful women, these ignorant, shiftless men, are blind to the beauty around them: their minds are sealed to the lessons of the sky and the mountains. What to an artist or a poet would be a perpetual inspiration is to them blank and meaningless.

"Through Cumberland Gap on Horseback"

James Lane Allen (1849–1925)

BURNSIDE – CUMBERLAND FALLS –
WILLIAMSBURG -BARBOURVILLE – PINEVILLE –
YELLOW CREEK KY – CUMBERLAND GAP TN

James Lane Allen grew up outside of Lexington, Kentucky. He earned his way through Transylvania University, graduated as valedictorian in 1872, and went on to serve in various positions as schoolmaster and college teacher. In the early 1880s, dissatisfied with teaching, he embarked on a writing career. (See Introduction for more on Allen's career and biography.) By the early 1890s, he had achieved critical and commercial success. Although his reputation has not survived, in his own day he was mentioned alongside Hawthorne and Hardy as among the best novelists of the century (Pattee 237–38).

Though considered a regionalist and local color writer, Allen wrote only one other piece about mountains ("Mountain Passes of the Cumberland," *Harper's,* Sept. 1890) in addition to the present selection. He did, however, go on to make a living by interpreting bluegrass Kentucky to easterners. Fourteen of his eventual eighteen volumes, mostly novels and short stories, were devoted almost exclusively to the bluegrass region. In 1893, Allen moved to New York City and, except for one occasion, never visited Kentucky again (Ward 42).

Harper's Monthly, June 1886

The illustrations that accompany the present selection were commissioned from some of the best-known artisans of the day. Edward Kemble (1861–1933) drew the "genre" sketches, or caricatured sketches of the mountain people, which appear here. Kemble was at the time newly famous for his illustrations of Mark Twain's *Adventures of Huckleberry Finn,* which had first appeared in print the previous year. California-based landscape painter and engraver Julian Walbridge Rix (1850–1903) produced most of the landscapes. Some of the landscape illustrations were also by Henry Wolf (1852–1916), an Alsatian-born wood-engraver who was well known at the time. Though Allen appears to suggest in the article that he is traveling with a sketch-artist as a companion, in fact there is no evidence that Kemble or Rix accompanied Allen on the journey.

I.

Fresh fields lay before us. We had left the rich, rolling plains of the blue-grass region in central Kentucky, and had set our faces toward the great Appalachian uplift on the southeastern border of the State. There Cumberland Gap, that high-swung gateway through the mountain, abides as a landmark of what Nature can do when she wishes to give an opportunity to the human race in its migrations and discoveries, without surrendering control of its liberty and its fate. Such way-side pleasures of hap and scenery as might befall us while journeying thither were ours to enjoy; but the especial quest was more knowledge of that peculiar and deeply interesting people, the Kentucky mountaineers. It can never be too clearly understood by those who are wont to speak of "the Kentuckians" that this State has within its boundaries two entirely distinct elements of population—elements distinct in England before they came hither, distinct during more than a century of residence here, and distinct now in all that goes to constitute a separate community—occupations, manners and customs, dress, views of life, civilization. It is but a short distance from the blue-grass country to the eastern mountains; but in traversing it you detach yourself from all that you have ever experienced, and take up the history of English-speaking men and women at the point it had reached a hundred or a hundred and fifty years ago.[1]

Leaving Lexington, then, which is in the midst of the blue-grass plateau, we were come to Burnside, a station on the Cincinnati Southern Railway some ninety miles away, where begin the navigable waters of the Cumberland River, and the foot-hills of the Cumberland Mountains.

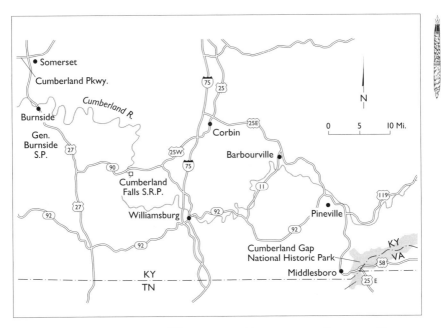

BURNSIDE – CUMBERLAND FALLS – WILLIAMSBURG – BARBOURVILLE – PINEVILLE – YELLOW CREEK KY – CUMBERLAND GAP TN. APPROXIMATE ROUTE OF JAMES LANE ALLEN, 1885.

Burnside is not merely a station, but a sub-mountainous watering-place. The water is mostly in the bed of the river. We had come thither to get horses and saddle-bags, but to no purpose. The hotel was a sort of transition between the civilization we had left behind and the primitive society we were to enter. On the veranda were some distinctly modern and conventional red chairs; but a green and yellow gourd vine, carefully trained across so as to shut out the distant landscape, was a novel bit of local color. Under the fine beeches in the yard was swung a hammock, but it was made of boards braced between ropes, and was covered with a weather-stained piece of tarpaulin. There were electric bells in the house that did not seem to electrify anybody particularly, and near the front entrance three barrels of Irish potatoes, with the tops off, spoke for themselves in the absence of the bill of fare. After supper, the cook, a tall, blue-eyed white fellow, walked into my room without much explanation, and carried away his guitar, showing that he had been wont to set his sighs to music in that quarter of the premises. Of a truth he was right, for the moon hung in that part of the heavens, and no doubt ogled him into many a midnight frenzy. Sitting under a beech-tree in the morning,

OLD FERRY AT POINT BURNSIDE. FROM JAMES LANE ALLEN, "THROUGH CUMBERLAND GAP ON HORSEBACK" *HARPER'S*, JUNE 1886.

I had watched a child from some distant city, dressed in white, and wearing a blue ribbon around her goldenish hair, amuse herself by rolling old barrels (potato barrels probably, and she may have had a motive) down the hill-side and seeing them dashed to pieces on the railway track below. By-and-by some of the staves of one fell in, the child tumbled in also, and they all rolled over together. Upon the whole, it was an odd overtopping of two worlds, and a promise of entertaining things to come. When the railway was first opened through this region a young man established a fruit store at one of the stations, and as part of his stock laid in a bunch of bananas. One day a native mountaineer entered. Arrangements generally struck him with surprise, but everything else was soon forgotten in an adhesive contemplation of the mighty aggregation of fruit. Finally he turned away with this note: "Blame me if them ain't the darnedest beans *I* ever seen!"

The scenery around Burnside is very beautiful, and the climate salubrious. In the valleys was formerly a fine growth of walnut,[2] but the principal timbers now are oak, ash, and sycamore, with some yellow pine. I heard of a wonderful walnut-tree formerly standing, by hiring vehicles to go and see which the owner of a livery-stable made three hundred and fifty dollars. Six hundred were offered for it on the spot; but the possessor, never having read of the fatal auriferous goose, reasoned that it would bring him a fortune if cut into many pieces, and so ruined it, and sold it at a great loss. The hills are filled with the mountain limestone—that Kentucky oolite of which the new Cotton Exchange in New York is built. Here was Burnside's depot[3] of supplies during the war, and here passed the great road—made in part a corduroy road at his order—from Somerset, Kentucky, to Jacksborough, over which countless stores were taken from central Kentucky and regions further north into Tennessee. Supplies were brought up the river in small steam-boats or through in wagons, and when the road grew impassable, pack-mules were used. Sad sights there were to be seen in those sad, sad days: the carcasses of animals at short intervals from here to Knoxville, and now and then a mule sunk up to his body in mire, and abandoned, with his pack on, to die. Here were batteries planted and rifle-pits dug, the vestiges of which yet remain; but where the forest timbers were then cut down a vigorous new growth has long been reclaiming the earth to native wildness, and altogether the aspect of the place is peaceful and serene. Doves were flying in and out of the cornfields on the hill-sides; there were green stretches in the valleys where cattle were grazing; and

"BLAME ME IF THEM AIN'T
THE DARNEDEST BEANS!"
FROM JAMES LANE ALLEN,
"THROUGH CUMBERLAND
GAP ON HORSEBACK"
HARPER'S, JUNE 1886.

these, together with a single limestone road that wound upward over a distant ridge, recalled the richer scenes of the blue-grass lands.

Assured that we would find horses and saddle-bags at Cumberland Falls, we left Burnside, and were soon set down at a station some fifteen miles further along, where a hack was to convey us to another of those mountain watering-places that are being opened up in various parts of eastern Kentucky for the enjoyment of a people that has never cared to frequent in large numbers the Atlantic seaboard.

Capps was the driver of the hack—a good-looking mulatto, wearing a faded calico shirt and a straw hat of most uncertain shape and variable colors.

NATIVE TYPES. FROM JAMES LANE ALLEN, "THROUGH CUMBERLAND GAP ON HORSEBACK" *HARPER'S,* JUNE 1886.

Capps stopped frequently on the road: once to halloo from the lofty ridge along which we were riding, down into a valley, to inquire of a mountain woman, sitting in her door with a baby in her arms, whether she had any "millons"; and again at a way-side grocery to get a bushel of meal from a man who seemed to be dividing his time pretty equally between retailing meal and building himself a new house. Here we asked for a drink of water, and got it—hot from a jug, there being no spring near. Capps knew a hawk from a handsaw when it came to talking about "moonshine" whiskey, and entered with some zest into a technical discrimination between its effects and those of "old Bourbon" on the head after imbibing incontinently. His knowledge seemed based on experience, and we waived a discussion.

Meantime the darkness was falling, and the scenery along the road grew wilder and grander. A terrific storm had swept over these heights, and the great trees lay uptorn and prostrate in every direction, or reeled and fell against each other like drunken giants—a scene of fearful elemental violence. On the summits one sees the tan-bark oak; lower down, the white oak; and lower yet, fine specimens of yellow poplar;[4] while from the valleys to the crests is a dense and varied under-growth, save where the ground has been burnt over, year after year, to kill it out and improve the grazing. Twenty miles to the southeast we had seen through the pale-tinted air the waving line of Sellico Mountains,[5] in Tennessee. Away to the north lay the Beaver Creek and the lower Cumberland, while in front of us rose the craggy, scowling face of Anvil Rock, commanding a view of Kentucky, Tennessee, and Virginia. The utter silence and heart-oppressing repose of primeval nature was around us. The stark white and gray trunks of the immemorial forest dead linked us to an inviolable past. The air seemed to blow upon us from over regions illimitable and unexplored, and to be fraught with unutterable suggestions. The full-moon swung itself aloft over the sharp touchings of the green with spectral pallor; and the evening-star stood lustrous on the western horizon in depths of blue as cold as a sky of Landseer,[6] except where brushed by tremulous shadows of rose on the verge of the sunlit world. A bat wheeled upward in fantastic curves out of his undiscovered glade. And the soft tinkle of a single cow-bell far below marked the invisible spot of some lonely human habitation. By-and-by we lost sight of the heavens altogether, so dense and interlaced the forest. The descent of the hack appeared to be into a steep abyss of gloom; then all at once we broke from the edge of the woods into a flood of moonlight; at our feet were the whirling, foaming rapids of the river; in our ears was the near roar of the cataract, where the bow-crowned mist[7] rose and floated upward and away in long trailing shapes of ethereal lightness.

The Cumberland River runs and throws itself over the rocks here with a fall of seventy feet, or a perpendicular descent of sixty-two, making a mimic but most beautiful Niagara. Just below, Eagle Falls drops over its precipice in a lawny cascade. The roar of the cataract, under favorable conditions, may be heard up and down stream a distance of ten or twelve miles. You will not find in mountainous Kentucky a more picturesque spot. The hotel stands near the very verge of the waters; and the mountains, rising one above another around, shut it in with infinite security from all the world.

CUMBERLAND FALLS. FROM JAMES LANE ALLEN, "THROUGH CUMBERLAND GAP ON HORSEBACK" HARPER'S, JUNE 1886.

MOONRISE ON CUMBERLAND RIDGE.
FROM JAMES LANE ALLEN, "THROUGH
CUMBERLAND GAP ON HORSEBACK"
HARPER'S, JUNE 1886.

While here, we had occasion to extend our acquaintance with native types. Two young men came to the hotel, bringing a bag of small, hard peaches to sell. Slim, slab-sided, stomachless, and serene, mild and melancholy, they might have been lotos-eaters,[8] only the suggestion of poetry was wanting, and they had probably never tasted any satisfying plant whatsoever. Their unutterable content came not from opiates, but from their souls. If they could sell their peaches, they would be happy; if not, they would be happy. What they could not sell, they could as well eat; and since no bargain was made on this occasion, they took chairs on the hotel veranda, opened the bag, and fell to. One of us tried to catch the mental attitude of the Benjamin of his tribe, while the other studied his bodily pose.

"Is that a good 'coon dog?"

"A mighty good 'coon dog. I hain't never seed him whipped by a varmint yet."

"Are there many 'coons in this country?"

"Several 'coons."

"Is this a good year for 'coons?"

"A mighty good year for 'coons. The woods is full o' varmints."

"Do 'coons eat corn?"

"'Coons is bad as hogs on corn, when they git tuk to it."

"Are there many wild turkeys[9] in this country?"

"Several wild turkeys."

"Have you ever caught many 'coons?"

"I've cotched high as five 'coons out o' one tree."

"Are there many foxes in this country?"

"Several foxes."

"What's the best way to cook a 'coon?"

"Ketch him and parbile him, and then put him in cold water and soak him, and then put him in and bake him."

"Are there many hounds in this country?"

"Several hounds."

Here, among other discoveries was a linguistic one—the use of "several" in the sense of a great many, probably an innumerable multitude, as in the case of the 'coons.

They hung around the hotel for hours, as beings utterly exempt from all the obligations and other phenomena of time.

"Why should we only toil, the roof and crown of things?"[10]

True to promise, the guide bespoken the evening before had made all arrangements for our ride of some eighteen miles—was it not forty?—to Williamsburg, and in the afternoon made his appearance with three horses. Of these three horses one was a mule, with a strong leaning toward his father's family. Of the three saddles one was a side-saddle, and another was an army saddle with refugee stirrups. The three brutes wore among them some seven shoes. My own mincing jade had none on. Her name may have been Helen of Troy (all horses are named in Kentucky), so anciently must her great beauty have disappeared. She partook with me of the terror which her own movements inspired, and if there ever was a well-defined case, outside of literature, in which the man should have carried the beast, this was the one. While on her back I occasionally apologized for the injustice by handing her some sour apples, which she appeared never to have tasted before, just as it was told me she had never known the luxury of wearing shoes. It is often true that the owner of a horse in this region is too poor or too mean to have it shod.

Our route from Cumberland Falls lay through what is called "Little Texas," in Whitley County—a wilderness some twenty miles square. I say route, because there was not always a road; but for the guide, there would not always have been a direction. Rough as the country appears to one riding through it on horseback, it is truly called "flat woods country," and viewed from Sellico Mountains, whence the local elevations are of no account, it looks like one vast sweep of sloping, densely wooded land. Here one may see noble specimens of yellow poplar in the deeper soil at the head of the ravines; pin oak, and gum and willow, and the rarely beautiful wild-cucumber.[11] Along the streams in the lowlands blooms the wild calacanthus,[12] filling the air with fragrance, and here in season the wild camellia[13] throws open its white and purple splendors. There are few traces of human presence in this great wilderness, except along the road that one comes to by-and-by; and it seems easy to believe that Williamsburg had a population of one hundred and thirty-nine in 1870, having increased fourteen souls in ten years. Since then, indeed, railway connection has caused it to double its population many times—once within the past two years.

There is iron in Whitley County so pure as to require some poorer ore to be mixed with it to smelt it successfully, while other requires only limestone to flux it; but we did not come upon "Swift's Silver Mine." From the Tennessee line south to the Ohio line north one may pass through counties that claim the location of "Swift's Silver Mine"—that El Dorado spot of eastern Kentucky, where, a hundred and twenty-years ago, one

INTERIOR OF A MOUNTAINEER'S HOME. FROM JAMES LANE ALLEN, "THROUGH CUMBERLAND GAP ON HORSEBACK" *HARPER'S,* JUNE 1886.

John Swift said he made silver in large quantities, burying some thirty thousand dollars and crowns on a large creek; fifteen thousand dollars a little way off, near some trees, which were duly marked; a prize of six thousand dollars close by the fork of a white oak; and three thousand dollars in the rocks of a rock house: all which, in the light of these notes, it is allowed any one who will to hunt for.

It was not until we had passed out of "Little Texas" and reached Williamsburg, had gone thence to Barbourville, the county seat of the adjoining county of Knox, and thence again into Bell County, that we stopped between Flat Lick and Cumberland Ford, on the old Wilderness road from Kentucky through Cumberland Gap. Around us were the mountains—around us the mountaineers whom we wished to meet intimately face to face.

II.

Straight, slim, angular, white bodies; average or even unusual stature, without great muscular robustness; features regular and colorless, unanimated but intelligent, in the men sometimes fierce, and in the women often sad; among the latter occasional beauty of a pure Greek type; a manner shy and deferential, but kind and fearless; eyes with a slow, long look of mild inquiry, or of general listlessness, or of unconscious and unaccountable melancholy; the key of life a low minor strain, losing itself in reverie; voices monotonous in intonation; movements uninformed by nervousness—these are characteristics of the Kentucky mountaineers. Living to-day as their forefathers lived before them a hundred years ago; hearing little of the world, caring nothing for it; responding feebly to the influences of civilization near the highways of travel in and around the towns, and latterly along the lines of railway communication, but sure to live here, if uninvaded and unaroused, in the same condition for a hundred or more years to come; utterly lacking the spirit of development from within; utterly devoid of any sympathy with that boundless and ungovernable activity which is carrying the Saxon race in America from one state to another, whether better or worse. The origin of these people, the relation they sustain to the different population of the central region—in fine, an account of them from the date of their settling in these mountains to the present time, when, as it seems, they are on the point of losing their isolation, and with it their distinctiveness—would imprison phases of life and character valuable alike to the special history of this country and to the general history of the human mind. The land in these mountains is all claimed, but it is probably not all covered by actual patent. As evidence, a company has been formed to speculate in lands not secured by title. The old careless way of marking off boundaries by going from tree to tree, by partly surveying and partly guessing, explains the present uncertainty. Many own land by right of occupancy, there being no other claim. The great body of the people live on and cultivate little patches which they either own, or hold free, or pay rent for with a third of the crop. These not unfrequently get together and trade farms as they would horses, no deed being executed. There is among them a mobile element—squatters—who make a hill-side clearing and live on it as long as it remains productive, when they move elsewhere. This accounts for the presence throughout the country of abandoned cabins, around which a dense new forest growth is springing up. Leaving out of consideration the few instances of substantial prosperity, the most of the people are abjectly poor, and they appear to have no sense of accumulation. The main crops raised on the patch are corn and potatoes. By the scant gardens will be seen little patches of cotton, sorghum, and tobacco; flax also, though less than formerly. Many make insufficient preparation for winter, laying up no meat, but buying a piece of bacon now and then, and paying for it by working. In some regions the great problem of life is to raise two dollars and a half during the year for county taxes. Being pauper counties, they are exempt from State taxation. Jury fees are highly esteemed and much sought after. The manufacture of illicit mountain whiskey—"moonshine"—was formerly, as it is now, a considerable source of revenue to them; and a desperate self-destructive sub-source of revenue from the same business has been the betrayal of its hidden places. There is nothing harder or more dangerous to find now in the mountains than a secret still.

Formerly, also, digging "sang," as they call ginseng, was a general occupation. For this, of course, China was a great market. It has nearly all been dug out now except in the wildest parts of the country, where entire families may still be seen "out sangin'." They took it into the towns in bags, selling it at a dollar and ten cents—perhaps a dollar and a half— a pound. This was mainly the labor of the women and the children, who went to work barefooted, amid briers and chestnut burrs, copperheads and rattlesnakes. Indeed, the women prefer to go barefooted, finding shoes a trouble and constraint. It was a sad day for the people when the "sang" grew scarce. A few years ago one of the counties was nearly depopulated in consequence of a great exodus into Arkansas, whence had come the news that there "sang" was plentiful. Not long since, too, during a season of scarcity in corn, a local store-keeper told the people of a county to go out and gather all the mandrake or "May-apple" root[14] they could find. At first only the women and children went to work, the men holding back with ridicule. By-and-by they also took part, and that year some fifteen tons were gathered, at three cents a pound, and the whole county thus got its seed-corn. Wild ginger was another root formerly much dug; also to less extent "golden-seal" and "bloodroot." The sale of feathers from a few precarious geese helps to eke out subsistence. Their methods of agriculture—if methods they may be styled—are of the most primitive sort. Ploughing is commonly done with a "bull tongue," an implement hardly more than a sharpened stick with a metal rim; this is often drawn by an ox, or a half-yoke. But one may see women ploughing with two oxen. Traces are made of hickory or papaw, as also are bed-cords. Ropes are made of lynn bark. In some counties there is not so much as a fanning-mill, grain being winnowed by pouring it from basket to basket, after having been threshed with a flail, which is a hickory withe some seven feet long. Their threshing floor is a clean place on the ground, and they take up grain, gravel, and some dirt together, not knowing or not caring for the use of a sieve. The grain is ground at their homes in a hand tub-mill, or one made by setting the nether millstone in a bee-gum, or by cutting a hole in a puncheon-log and sinking the stone into it. There are, however, other kinds of mills: the primitive little water-mill which may be considered almost characteristic of this region; in a few places improved water-mills, and small steam-mills. It is the country of mills, farm-houses being furnished with one about as frequently as with coffee-pots or spinning-wheels. A simpler way of preparing corn for bread than by even the hand-mill is used in the late summer and early autumn, while the grain is too hard for eating as roasting ears, and too soft to be ground in a mill. On a board is tacked a piece of tin through which holes have been punched from the under-side, and over this tin the ears are rubbed, producing a coarse meal, of which "gritted bread" is made. Much pleasure and doubtless much health do they get from their "gritted bread," which is withal a sweet and wholesome bit for a hungry man. Where civilization has touched on the highways and the few improved mills have been erected, one may see women going to mill with their scant sacks of grain, riding on a jack, a jennet, or a bridled ox. But this is not so bad as in North Carolina, where, Europa-like, they ride on bulls.

Aside from such occupations as have been herein pointed out, the men have nothing to do—a little work in the spring, and nine months' rest. They love to meet at the country groceries and cross-roads, to shoot matches for beef, turkeys, or liquor, and to gamble. There is with them a sort of annual succession of amusements. In its season they have the rage for pitching horseshoes, the richer ones using dollar pieces. In consequence of their abundant leisure, the loneliness of the mountains, which draws them thus together, their bravery and physical vigor, quarrels among them are frequent, and feuds are deadly. Personal enmities soon serve to array entire families in an attitude of implacable hostility, and in the course of time relatives and friends take sides, and a war of extermination ensues. The special origins of these are various: blood heated and temper lost under the influence of "moonshine"; reporting on the places and manufacturers of this; local politics; the survival of resentments engendered during the civil war—these, together with all causes that lie in the passions of the human heart and spring from the constitution of all human society, often make the remote and insulated life of these people turbulent, reckless, and distressing. But while thus bitter and cruel toward each other, they present to strangers the aspect of a polite, kind, unoffending, and most hospitable race. They will divide with you shelter and warmth and food, however scant, and will put themselves to trouble for your convenience with an unreckoning, earnest friendliness and good-nature that is touching to the last degree. No sham, no pretence; a true friend, or an open enemy. Of late they have had much occasion to regard new-comers with distrust, which, once aroused, is difficult to dispel, and now they will wish to know you and your business before treating you with that warmth which they are only too glad to show.

The women appear to do most of the work. From the few sheep, running wild, which the farm may own, they take the wool, which is carded, reeled, spun, and woven into fabrics by their own hands and on their rudest implements. One or two spinning-wheels will be found in every house. Cotton from their little patches, too, they clear by using a primitive hand cotton-gin. Flax, much spun formerly, is now less used. It is surprising to see from what appliances they will bring forth exquisite fabrics; all the garments for personal wear, bedclothes, and the like. When they can afford it they make carpets.

They have, as a rule, luxuriant hair. In some counties one is struck by the purity of the Saxon type,[15] and their faces in early life are often

very handsome. But one hears that in certain localities they are prone
to lose their teeth, and that after the age of thirty-five it is a rare thing
to see a woman whose front teeth are not partly or wholly wanting. The
reason of this is not apparent. They appear passionately fond of dress, and
array themselves in gay colors and in jewelry (pinchbeck),[16] if so be that
their worldly estate justifies the extravagance. Oftener, if young, they
have a modest, shy air, as if conscious that their garb is not even decorous.
Whether married or unmarried, they show much natural diffidence. It is
told that in remoter districts of the mountains they are not allowed to sit
at the table with the male members of the household, but serve them as
in ancient societies. Commonly, too, in going to church, the men ride and
carry the children, while the women walk. Dancing in some regions is
hardly known, but in others is a favorite amusement, and in its movements
men and women show the utmost grace. The mountain preachers oppose
it as a sin.

Marriages take place early, and they are a most fecund race. I asked
them time and again to fix upon the average number of children to a
family, and they gave as the result seven. In case of parental opposition
to wedlock, the lovers run off. There is among the people a low standard
of morality in their domestic relations, the delicate privacies of home life
having little appreciation where so many persons, without regard to age
or sex, are crowded together within very limited quarters.

The dwellings—often mere cabins with a single room—are built of
rough-hewn logs, chinked or daubed, though not always so. Often there
is a puncheon floor and no chamber roof. One of these mountaineers,
called into court to testify as to the household goods of a defendant
neighbor, gave in as the inventory, a string of pumpkins, a skillet
without a handle, and "a wild Bill." "A wild Bill" is a bed made by
boring auger-holes into a log, driving sticks into these, and over-laying
them with hickory bark and sedgegrass—a favorite couch. The low
chimneys, made usually of laths daubed, are so low that the saying,
inelegant though true, is current, that you may sit by the fire inside and
spit out over the top. The cracks in the walls give ingress and egress to a
child or dog. Even cellars are little known, their potatoes sometimes being
kept during winter in a hole dug under the hearth-stone. More frequently
a trap-door is made through the plank flooring in the middle of the room,
and in a hole beneath are put potatoes, and, in case of some wealth, jellies
and preserves. Despite the wretchedness of their habitations and all the

MOUNTAIN COURTSHIP.
FROM JAMES LANE ALLEN,
"THROUGH CUMBERLAND
GAP ON HORSEBACK"
HARPER'S, JUNE 1886.

rigors of a mountain climate, they do not suffer with cold, and one may see them out in snow knee-deep clad in low brogans, and nothing heavier than a jeans coat and hunting shirt.

The customary beverage is coffee, bitter and black, not having been roasted but burnt. All drink it from the youngest up. Another beverage is "mountain tea," which is made from the sweet-scented golden-rod and from winter-green—the New England checkerberry.[17] These decoctions they mollify with home-made sorghum molasses, which they call "long sweetening," or with sugar, which by contrast is known as "short sweetening." Of home government there is little or none, boys especially setting aside at will parental authority; but a sort of traditional sense of duty and decorum restrains them by its silent power, and moulds them into respect. Children while quite young are often plump to roundness, but soon grow thin and white and meagre like the parents. There is little desire for knowledge or education. The mountain schools have sometimes less than half a dozen pupils during the few months they are in session. A gentleman who wanted a coal bank opened engaged for the work a man passing along the road. Some days later he learned that his workman was a school-teacher, who, in consideration of the seventy-five cents a day, had dismissed his academy.

Many, allured by rumors from the West, have migrated thither, but nearly all come back, from love of the mountains, from indisposition to cope with the rush and vigor and enterprise of frontier life. Theirs, they say, is a good lazy man's home.

Their customs respecting the dead are interesting. When a husband dies his funeral sermon is not preached, but the death of the wife is awaited, and vice versa. Then a preacher is sent for, friend and neighbor called in, and the respect is paid both together. Often two or three preachers are summoned, and each delivers a sermon. More peculiar is the custom of having the services for one person repeated; so that the dead get their funerals preached several times months and years after their burial. I heard of the unspeakably pitiful story of two sisters who had their mother's funeral preached once every summer as long as they lived. You may engage the women in mournful conversation respecting the dead, but hardly the men. In strange contrast with this regard for ceremonial observances is their neglect of the graves of their beloved, which they do not seem at all to visit when once closed, or to decorate with those symbols of affection which are the common indications of bereavement.

Nothing that I have ever seen in this world is so lonely, so touching in its neglect and wild irreparable solitude, as one of these mountain graveyards. On some knoll under a clump of trees, or along some hill-side where dense oak-trees make a mid-day gloom, you walk amid the unknown, undistinguishable dead. Which was father and which mother, where are lover and stricken sweetheart, whether this is the dust of laughing babe or crooning grandam, you will never know: no foot-stones, no head-stones; sometimes a few rough rails laid around as you would make a little pen for swine. In places, however, one sees a picket-fence put up, or a sort of shed built over.

Traditions and folk-lore among them are evanescent, and vary widely in different localities. It appears that in part they are sprung from the early hunters who came into the mountains when game was

RIGHT: A MOUNTAINEER
DAME. FROM JAMES LANE
ALLEN, "THROUGH
CUMBERLAND GAP ON
HORSEBACK" *HARPER'S,*
JUNE 1886.

BELOW: A FAMILY
BURYING-GROUND. FROM
JAMES LANE ALLEN,
"THROUGH CUMBERLAND
GAP ON HORSEBACK"
HARPER'S, JUNE 1886.

FORD ON THE CUMBERLAND. FROM JAMES LANE ALLEN, "THROUGH CUMBERLAND
GAP ON HORSEBACK" HARPER'S, JUNE 1886.

abundant, sport unfailing, living cheap. Among them now are still-
hunters, who know the haunts of bear and deer, needing no dogs. They
even now prefer wild meat—even "'possum" and "'coon" and ground-
hog—to any other. In Bell County I spent the day in the house of an aged
woman—eighty years old, in fact—who was a lingering representative

of a nearly extinct type. She had never been out of the neighborhood of her birth, knew the mountains like a garden, had whipped men in single-handed encounter, brought down many a deer and wild turkey with her own rifle, and now, infirm, had but to sit in her cabin door and send her trained dogs into the depths of the forests to discover the wished-for game: a fiercer woman I never looked on.

III.

Our course now lay direct toward Cumberland Gap, some twenty miles southward. Our road ran along the bank of the Cumberland River to the ford, the immemorial crossing-place of early travel—and a beautiful spot thence to Pineville, situated in that narrow opening in Pine Mountain where the river cuts it, and thence through the valley of Yellow Creek to the wonderful pass. The scenery in all this region is one succession of densely wooded mountains, blue-tinted air, small cultivated tracts in the fertile valleys, and the lovely watercourses.[18]

Along the first part of our route the river slips crystal clear over its rocky bed, and beneath the lone green pendent branches of the trees that crowd the banks. At the famous ford it was only two or three feet deep at the time of our crossing. This is a historic point. Here was one of the oldest settlements in the country; here the Federal army destroyed the houses and fences during the civil war; and here Zollikoffer[19] came to protect the Kentucky gate that opens into East Tennessee. At Pineville, just beyond, we did not remain long. For some reasons not clearly understood by travellers a dead line had been drawn through the midst of the town, and not knowing on which side we were entitled to stand, we hastened on to a place where we might occupy neutral ground. The situation is strikingly picturesque: the mountain looks as if cleft sheer and fallen apart, the peaks on each side rising almost perpendicularly, with massive overhanging crests wooded to the summits, but showing gray rifts of the inexhaustible limestone. The river when lowest is here at an elevation of nine hundred and sixty feet, and the peaks leap to the height of twenty-two hundred. Here in the future will most probably pass a railroad, and be a populous town, for here is the only opening through Pine Mountain from "the brakes" of Sandy[20] to the Tennessee line, and tributary to the watercourses that center here are some five hundred thousand acres of timberland.

OLD CORN MILL AT PINEVILLE. FROM JAMES LANE ALLEN, "THROUGH CUMBERLAND
GAP ON HORSEBACK" HARPER'S, JUNE 1886.

The ride from Pineville to the Gap, fourteen miles southward, is one
of the most beautiful that may be taken. Yellow Creek becomes in local
pronunciation "Yaller Crick." One cannot be long in eastern Kentucky
without being struck by the number and character of the names given
to the water-courses which were the natural avenues of migratory travel.
Few of the mountains have names. What a history is shut up in these
names! Cutshin Creek, where some pioneer, they say, damaged those
useful members; but more probably where grows a low greenbrier which

cuts the aforesaid parts and riddles the pantaloons. These pioneers had
humor. They named one creek "Troublesome," for reasons apparent to
him who goes there; another, "No Worse Creek," on equally good grounds;
another, "Defeated Creek;" and a great many, "Lost Creek." In one part
of the country it is possible for one to enter "Hell fur Sartain," and get
out at "Kingdom Come." Near by, strange to say, there are two liquid
impersonations of Satan, "Upper Devil" and "Lower Devil." One day
we went to a mountain meeting which was held in "a school-house and
church-house" on "Stinking Creek." One might suppose they would have
worshipped in a more fragrant locality; but the stream is very beautiful,
and not malodorous. It received its name from its former canebrakes and
deer licks, which made game abundant. Great numbers were killed for
choice bits of venison and hides. Then there are "Ten-mile Creek" and
"Sixteen-mile Creek," meaning to clinch the distance by name; and what
is philologically interesting, one finds numerous *"Trace* Forks" originally
"Trail Forks."

Bell County and the Yellow Creek Valley serve to illustrate the
incalculable mineral and timber resources of eastern Kentucky. Our
road at times cut through forests of magnificent timbers—oak (black
and white), walnut (black and white), poplar, maple, and chestnut, beech,
lynn, gum, dogwood, and elm. Here are some of the finest coal-fields in
the known world, the one on Clear Creek being fourteen feet thick. Here
are exceedingly pure cannel-coals[21] and cooking coals. At no other point
in the Mississippi Valley are iron ores suitable for steel-making purposes
so close to fuel so cheap. With an eastern coal-field of ten thousand square
miles, with an area equally large covered with a virgin growth of the
finest economic timbers, with watercourses feasible and convenient, it
cannot be long before all eastern Kentucky will be opened up to the
great industries of the modern world. Enterprise has already turned
hither, and the distinctiveness of the mountaineer race has already begun
to disappear. The two futures before them are, to be swept out of these
mountains by the in-rushing spirit of contending industries, or to be
aroused, civilized, and developed.

Long before you come in sight of the great Gap, the idea of it
dominates the mind. At length, while yet some miles away, it looms
up, sixteen hundred and seventy-five feet in elevation, some half a mile
across from crest to crest, the pinnacle on the left towering to the height
of twenty-five hundred.

CUMBERLAND GAP. FROM JAMES LANE ALLEN, "THROUGH CUMBERLAND GAP ON HORSEBACK" *HARPER'S,* JUNE 1886.

It was late in the afternoon when our tired horses began the long, winding, rocky climb from the valley to the brow of the pass. As we stood in the passway, amid the deepening shadows of the twilight and the solemn repose of the mighty landscape, the Gap seemed to be crowded with two invisible and countless pageants of human life, the one passing in, the other passing out; and the air grew thick with ghostly utterances—primeval sounds, undistinguishable and strange, of creatures nameless and never seen by man; the wild rush and whoops of retreating and pursuing tribes; the slow steps of watchful pioneers; the wail of dying children and the songs of homeless women; the muffled tread of routed and broken armies—all the sounds of surprise and delight, victory and defeat, hunger and pain and weariness and despair, that the human heart can utter. Here passed the first of all the white race who led the way into the valley of the Cumberland; here passed that small band of fearless men who gave the Gap its name; here passed the "Long Hunters"; here rushed the armies of the civil war; here has passed the wave of westerly emigration, whose force has spent itself only on the Pacific slopes; and here in the long future must flow backward and forward wealth beyond the dreams of avarice. Beneath the shadows of the pinnacle—the limit of our journey reached—we slept that night in the Poor Valley of Tennessee.

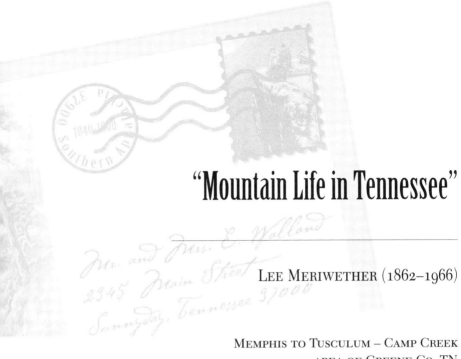

"Mountain Life in Tennessee"

Lee Meriwether (1862–1966)

Memphis to Tusculum – Camp Creek
area of Greene Co. TN

In the selection that follows, Lee Meriwether rides the last train out of Memphis as the Great Yellow Fever epidemic closes around the city in late summer 1878. As the train rolls east, it is greeted at every stop by armed guards refusing to let passengers off. Five hundred miles later, Meriwether disembarks in the idyllic setting of the Nolichucky Valley, in East Tennessee, near Tusculum, where his family is ensconced in a fever refugee camp. Leaving the fever nightmare behind him, he ventures into the mountains, where he meets the colorful mountain people whom he describes in the present selection.

The dramatic story Meriwether tells here has many of the elements of the yellow fever tale that had become a staple of the popular periodicals by the 1870s. (See Bonner, 179–93, for an example.) The story is also, alas, untrue. Or at least the dramatic framework has been invented for effect. In fact, Meriwether was only sixteen years old in 1878, the year of the Great Fever, when, from late summer into early fall, five thousand people died in the city of Memphis, while twenty-five thousand people fled the city.

Cosmopolitan, February 1888

Meriwether and his family took refuge not near Tusculum, but hundreds of miles from there, near Winchester, Tennessee, west of Chattanooga (Elizabeth Avery Meriwether 53). Though the story has been dramatized, however, the material is based in fact. Meriwether did visit the area he describes—not in the year of the fever, but rather some time around 1887, when he was traveling professionally, to gather labor statistics. This article thus presents accurate details and has documentary value. Meriwether presents here, for example, an analysis of the cost of labor in the southern mountains, and his observations on food and land prices and other living expenses are consistent with those he published in the Bureau of Labor Annual Report, 1887. This article also provides an interesting if only partly reliable account of a Nolichucky Valley camp meeting and foot washing.

Born in Columbus, Mississippi, Meriwether was educated in Memphis public schools. (His mother, Elizabeth Avery Meriwether, was devoted to the south but defied many of the predominant politics of her region, and has been called "an abolitionist-Confederate-suffragette" [McAlexander 106].) At the age of eighteen, Lee started a Memphis newspaper, the *Free Trader,* with his older brother. A year later he went abroad, employed by the Interior Department to collect labor data. He later published a first-person travel guide, in which he developed a persona for himself as "the Tramp" (*A Tramp Trip: How to See Europe on Fifty Cents a Day* [1887]). Meriwether worked the same "tramp" persona into subsequent magazine writing, including the present selection. The year following the appearance of this article, Meriwether published another version of the story he tells here, in a book entitled *The Tramp at Home* (1889).

Meriwether continued contributing to magazines and newspapers and wrote at least two novels. However, his output diminished as he became a prominent lawyer in St. Louis. Among other accomplishments, as Missouri's labor commissioner he helped initiate Progressive-era legislation outlawing exploitative company stores.

One morning several years ago I was standing on the veranda of a hotel in Fort Smith, Arkansas, waiting for the Indian Territory stage, when a telegram was handed me announcing the outbreak of yellow fever in Memphis.[1] A moment later the driver of the Indian stage turned the corner, cracking his whip, and drove up with a flourish in front of the hotel. But he did not number me among his passengers. I started for Memphis by the first, and, as it proved, by the last train; for, upon the appearance of dread Yellow Jack, the unfortunate city was ostracized and shunned like a leper. Trains after that week were permitted neither to enter nor depart.

For fifty miles, before the Mississippi River is reached, the road staggers along through a morass and a jungle. Even though resting on piles, the rails sag and sink in the mud as the heavy engine creeps along, its wheels dripping with the swamp waters below, its smokestack and top brushed by the forest limbs above. The night was dark and gloomy. Death lurked in the very air. The lights of Memphis that flickered faintly across the water seemed as if even they, like the fever, had a sickly, yellow hue. The passengers stuffed handkerchiefs, reeking with carbolic acid and other disinfectants, to their noses. Not a word was spoken, we crossed the river in silence and hurried, each of us, to our respective destinations. In that dread epidemic, the most terrible that ever afflicted any American city, thousands were cut down in the space of a few weeks. Many who crossed the Mississippi with me that night were dead within forty-eight hours. I was saved by flight.

My father and mother had just gone: I followed by the next train, the last that was permitted to leave during the epidemic. It was crowded with as frantic a set of beings as ever congregated together. Every seat was full. People sat on the coal-bins, on the stoves, or clung to the platforms and steps. From my position on the steps of the last car I saw crowds unable to obtain even that poor vantage ground. Such set out to *walk*. One poor woman was going along beside the track pushing a wheelbarrow on which were piled some blankets, provisions, and babies. The poor creature, of course, dropped by the wayside, overcome by fright and fatigue even, if not by the fever.

Five miles from the city we were put through a fumigating process, each person being placed in a room built for the purpose, that was stifling with fumes of sulphur and disinfectants. This ordeal over, medical certificates to the effect that we had been relieved of all yellow-fever germs were handed to each passenger, whereupon we scrambled back to our places and hastened away. Despite these certificates, armed guards stood at most of the towns through which the train passed, and discouraged with rifles and shotguns all attempts at landing.

At Stephenson, two hundred and sixty miles away, a passenger became prostrated. To be shut up in a car with a man dying of yellow fever was horrible. The bell was pulled, and the train came to a stop. But determined men stood at the station with guns and pistols, and swore they would shoot the man who attempted to land the patient. There was a hurried consultation. The passengers crowded into the next car; that with the yellow fever case was unoccupied and the train went flying on. The deserted patient, as I afterward heard, soon died. The villagers feared to approach him. With long poles they shoved the body out of the car, and gave it a scant burial where it fell beside the track. Notwithstanding their fear and caution, within ten days the fever was raging in that town, and scores of its people were dead or dying.

At midnight of the second day I found myself on the platform of a little station at the base of the Unika range of mountains.[2] A pouring rain was falling, but worn out with excitement and fatigue, I threw myself on the platform, and fell fast asleep in the rain. It seemed as if my eyes had scarcely closed when there was a rapping on the planks near my ears. It was inky dark. I could see nothing, and was about to try another nap when the rap was repeated. It came from *beneath* the platform, and a voice redolent with strong drink called through a knothole:

"I say, pard, why doncher crawl under here?"

It did not take long to act on this suggestion. In two minutes I had crawled down under the platform, and found a companion as well as partial protection from the rain. Of the two of us, the tramp soaked with whisky looked more respectable than the traveler soaked with rain and torn and tumbled from long journeying.

"Well, I swan, but you're in bad luck!" said the tramp, striking a match and surveying my bedraggled duster and almost disintegrated straw hat. "Where did you come from?"

The yellow fever refugee can not afford to sneer even at the nether side of a country railway platform. If I told this man whence I came, the probabilities were I would be "ousted." It was discreet to be mum. I put my hand to my ear and shook my head. At first the tramp seemed puzzled: then my meaning dawned upon him.

"Phew!" he said, "this here's a go. One o' them deaf and dumb mutes. What bedfellers we has to put up with, to be sure!" with which he threw down the match and went to sleep.

At break of day I was aroused by a hand on my shoulder. The tramp was crouching by me, making the most remarkable signs and gestures I ever witnessed.

"Come, me go getty breakfast," he said, waving his arm and dropping into pigeon English, as though he imagined the deaf could hear well enough if only the rules of grammar were sufficiently violated.

It was hardly of my choosing, but I was mistaken for a veritable American tramp, and it was necessary to act out the character. I accompanied my new-found friend to the nearest farm-house, where his really wonderful accomplishments as a liar secured us both a good breakfast. He assured the honest granger that I was an unfortunate brother whom he was taking to the deaf-and-dumb asylum. I had lost my hearing in a terrible explosion: our widowed mother depended on her two sons for support, but he, noble fellow, meant to work for the two of us while I learned the sign language in the asylum. So numerous did my misfortunes become under this adept liar's management that I began to feel sorry for myself, and with difficulty refrained from dropping the *role* of deaf mute and offering myself my own condolences. Half an hour later my self-sacrificing "brother" and I separated on the railroad track, he going one way, I starting the other. When he had disappeared round a curve, I returned to the farm where we had breakfasted, and knocked boldly on the door. The granger seemed surprised, but not glad to see me.

"I want to pay you for that breakfast."

The man was amazed—and no wonder: a mute thus suddenly restored to speech, and a tramp wanting to *pay* for his breakfast.

"You ain't dumb, then?" he said, when his first surprise was over.

"Not a bit of it, and I am not a tramp either; at least not a regular tramp. I want you to direct me to Tusculum."[3]

Near that remote hamlet—namesake of the great Cicero's villa— were my parents camped almost under the shadow of the high mountains. The old farmer refused to take payment for the breakfast, "'lowing we'uns had gin him as much fun as the grub was worth." He pointed out the road to Tusculum, whither I was shortly wending my way. When I first started, the distance was ten miles. After walking an hour a man whom I questioned said it was fifteen. A few miles further on, another said it was twenty. Notwithstanding this peculiar backsliding characteristic of East Tennessee mountaineering, I at length reached the camp, and was welcomed as one saved from the jaws of death.

In these mountains of the South men live and maintain strength and vigor on twenty cents or less a day. Chickens cost eight or ten cents apiece, eggs five cents a dozen, beef six or seven cents a pound. Buttermilk is fed to the hogs, while fruit and vegetables—corn, potatoes, cabbage— can be had almost for the asking. These are important facts, as Pennsylvania and other Northern manufacturers are learning. For the Southern workman, when living is so cheap, can afford to work for less wages than his brother in the North, where many large cities create heavy demands for food products, thus raising prices. The Chattanooga or Birmingham mill-owner pays lower wages than are paid in iron mills in the West and North; and the latter are beginning to feel the effects. At the same time it is to be remarked that though his wages are *nominally* less, in *reality* because of the cheapness of rent, food, and fuel, the Southern worker in iron receives higher wages than does the worker in iron in the North. I am almost afraid to say how very cheaply our camp of refugees lived. In the morning we would go to the cornfield, pluck a dozen ears of corn, which were boiled or converted into corn bread on the back of a hoe. With two round bowlders a pint or so of wheat was pounded until the husk cracked; this, with sugar and cream—that cost only a trifle— and the corn and fruit, made a breakfast an epicure might enjoy. The cost for the five of us could not have exceeded twenty cents a morning.

Tusculum becoming monotonous, despite its classical name, I bought a horse and started on a trip among the mountains. About ten miles on the way I overtook another horseman jogging slowly along. He was a lean, lanky fellow, with a hatchet face and long, stringy hair.

"Mornin', stranger," he said, as I rode up.

"Good-morning, sir."

"A powerful fine day, mister."

"Yes, it is a fine day."

"I meant a *good* day. It's the Lord's day."

I thanked him for this bit of information, and we rode on together, the lank man talking more or less on religion. Presently he said:

"Stranger, you'd better 'light an' look at your saddle."

"Why, what's the matter? Girth loose?" I leaned over and felt the strap; it was quite fast.

The lank man's hatchet face turned a shade redder.

"I've asked you to git down and look at your saddle," he repeated.

"I know you did; what is the matter with my saddle?"

"Mister, don't sit thar mockin' me on the Lord's day."

At this moment a man, bareheaded and dressed in a new suit of jeans, emerged from the thicket on the roadside.

"Mornin', stranger. I reckon you'll 'light an' look at your saddle, won't yer?"

"I've jist asked him," put in my companion, "an' he mocked me. He's got the old devil in him."

"Slow, Brother Kite, slow," said the other. "I reckon, Brother Kite, you're too fast. "Now," turning to me, "you'uns is a stranger heah, ain't yer?"

I nodded my head.

"Well, we'uns air holdin' meetin' heah to-day. Brother Kite asked you to 'light an' fix your saddle, an' come into meetin'.'" I understood. This was simply the form of invitation to church. Of course it was accepted.[4]

In the little log "meetin' house" were assembled some thirty or forty rude mountaineers, with their wives and families. Living in that pure air, one would expect to see fresh, healthy complexions, but I saw few. The women looked sallow and bilious, probably from unhygienic diet; the men red and some of them bloated from whisky. The women were dressed in bright-colored gowns and an astonishing variety of hats and feathers. The men, for the most part, were clad in their extra suit of jeans, and were proud in proportion as the crease in their trousers remained distinct and decided.

My road companion proved to be the preacher for whom the congregation were waiting. Having alighted and "looked" at his saddle, he walked down between the two rows of wooden benches, and climbing the rickety pulpit, shut his eyes and began a prayer that was punctuated every moment or two by loud groans from some one of the audience. When the prayer—fully a quarter of an hour long—ended, the preacher began a peculiar sermon. I learned afterward it was a funeral oration in memory of a member of the flock who had died *two years* before.

"We'uns all knew Sister Betts," the lank Brother Kite began, rolling his eyes down, showing the whites, and seemingly trying to examine the interior of his skull. "Sister Betts was *such* a good cook!" (emphasizing the word "such" with a groan). "She made *such* good coffee an' *such* good fried eggs and bacon. Many's the time I've spent the night at her house, an' she allus had the *best* corn bread, an' the *best* bacon an' the *best* eggs. We'uns all know, an' I knows in pertickler, Sister Betts warn't any slouch. But she's gone now, poor Sister Betts is gone from amongst us, an' thar ain't many left as kin ekal her in cookin' an' keepin' house."

In this strain he continued about an hour. At first the novelty was amusing, but novelty soon wore off. To while away time, I pulled out my scratch-book and began taking shorthand notes. Brother Kite was evidently not accustomed to being reported. His eagle eye detected me. Stopping abruptly in the midst of his touching tribute to Sister Betts' household virtues, he pointed his bony finger at me and said:

"Mister, ain't you got sense 'nough to know this heah's a meetin'? You'uns needn't come heah if you're 'bleeged to write."

I ceased writing, and the sermon proceeded. When at length Brother
Kite had exhausted the subject, his hearers, and himself, all three at the
same time, he descended from the pulpit, and I drew a sigh of relief.
The sigh was premature. There were no relays of audiences, but there
were relays of preachers. The hatchet-faced man who, bad luck to him!
had succeeded in persuading me to "look at my saddle," quit the pulpit
only to let another take his place: There were three of them in all, who,
with their powerful lungs, effectually prevented any napping between
the hour of nine in the morning, when the first one began, and one in the
afternoon, when the last one ended. Fortunately, Brother Kite was the
only one of the three who founded his sermon exclusively upon the corn
bread and bacon of the departed Sister Betts.

At one o'clock an hour's intermission for dinner was announced. The
women, in their red feathers and gingham gowns, rose first, and as they
filed down the aisles, bestowed curious glances at the "citified" stranger.
When they had made their exit, the men also arose. I was walking to the
tree where was tied my horse, when Brother Kite overtook me.

"You ain't a-goin', air you?"

"Yes, it is getting late."

"Pshaw! meetin' ain't half over. You'd better stay to foot-washin'. You
can eat dinner with Sister Phoebe. She asked me, an' I reckon she won't
keer if you come, too."

A ten-mile ride in the mountains gives one an appetite. Besides,
if these mountaineers really washed their feet, the operation must be
interesting. So the invitation was accepted. Mrs. Anderson, or "Sister
Phoebe," as the lank preacher called her, was a woman of about thirty-
five, round and plump and very hospitable.

"Brother Kite did jist right. I'm allus glad to see strangers. Come
down to buy land?"

There was something flattering in this query not unappreciated by
the yellow-fever refugee who, instead of contemplating land purchases,
was wondering if he would have money enough to carry him home when
the epidemic was over. But I nobly confessed the truth, and replied that
I was *not* "down to buy land."

"I am merely taking a look at your beautiful country."

"Yes, it is a mouty pretty country. A good many rocks, but some
of the land's *awful* rich. I've seed corn on my old man's place what was
twelve foot to the first ear. You kain't find no better corn country. I
don't care if it is me as says it."

"What's that land o' your old man's worth, Sister Phoebe?"

"Law, Brother Kite, *you* know land like that kain't be bought less'n thirty dollars an acre. If the stranger wants ter look at it, he kin ride home with me arter the meetin'."

The stranger expressed a desire to see this wonderful corn land, whereupon Brother Kite asked blessing, and dinner was begun, a cloth first being spread under the boughs of an oak and the provisions brought from the wagon. Though not personally acquainted with the deceased Sister Betts, I will venture to affirm that that paragon of household virtues did not surpass Sister Phoebe in at least the matter of cooking. The fried chicken and jelly, with corn bread and pure, rich butter, made a meal an epicure might have enjoyed. When it was over, Brother Kite and I were excused while the women folk packed up the dishes.

The men were standing around in knots, some gossiping, some trading, others feeding their horses.

"I hearn as you'd swapped off your mare for Black Nance," said Brother Kite, addressing one of the group of men who were chewing tobacco and whittling sticks with jack-knives.

"Yes, I did," was the laconic answer.

"Git any boot?"

"Reckon I did. You didn't 'low as I'd give Lucy for Black Nance 'thout any boot?"

"Waal, I didn't know," replied the preacher. "Black Nance's a mouty good little mare, Brother Harkins."

"So was Lucy; worth two of Nance, if she's worth a cent."

There was a pause, during which the preacher pulled out his knife and picked up a stick to whittle.

"I say," he said, when a stick was found to his satisfaction, "how'd you like to swap Black Nance for my Joe?"

Brother Harkins looked up with a quick glance.

"D'ye mean it, Brother kite?"

"Sartin."

"Waal, what'll you gimme boot?"

"Boot? Brother Harkins, you must be a funnin'. It's me as orter have boot; leastways the swap orter be even."

This dickering lasted some five or ten minutes; then they adjourned to where the two horses were hitched to the limbs of a cedar tree, and Brother Kite pointed out the fine parts of Joe, while Brother Harkins dilated upon the good qualities of Black Nance. The end of it all was, the preacher took Black Nance, giving for her his horse Joe and ten dollars "boot." Brother Harkins, I was afterward told, was the best horsetrader in the country. He is said to have once gone to "meetin'" with an old yellow cob, made several "swaps," and finally rode home on the *same* yellow cob and sixty-five dollars extra in his pocket. He had a knack of making you believe that *your* horse was of no account at all, while *his* was the finest animal in the mountains, and the very one suited to your purposes.

The horses all attended to and the "swapping" finished, the congregation filed back into church to wash one another's feet. Buckets of water were brought from the neighboring spring, while the three preachers sat on a platform with half-closed eyes, chanting a hymn, the masculine half of the assembly began taking off their boots and shoes, and—those who had them—also their socks. The women, at the same time, prepared the water and towels. These preliminaries over, the women left their quarters, crossed the aisle, and falling on their knees before the first row of men, began washing their feet in the cold spring water. The three preachers were served last. After every man in the congregation (excepting the writer) had had his feet washed and wiped, three women advanced to the pulpit with three buckets and began removing the mountain soil from the pedal extremities of the three divines.

Streams and pools of dirty looking water had begun by this time to form on the floor. The air, in addition, feeling close, I beat a retreat to the less curious but more salubrious region outside under the trees.

"You didn't wash your feet," said Brother Kite, severely, when the ceremonies had concluded.

"Oh, you are mistaken," I answered cheerily. "I washed them this morning."

"Mebbe so, but 'twouldn't 'a' hurt you to have washed 'em agin in the meetin'."

Sister Phoebe came up at this moment and renewed her invitation to inspect her husband's corn land. As my destination was no place in particular, I accepted the invitation, and was soon riding alongside her spring wagon, *en route* to a genuine mountain home.[5]

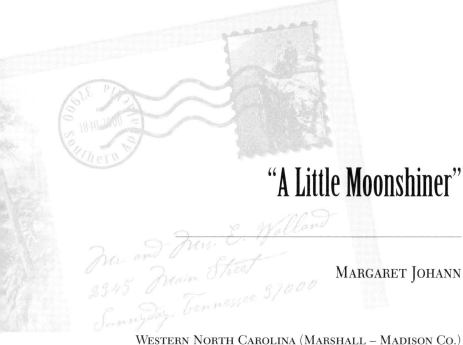

"A Little Moonshiner"

MARGARET JOHANN

WESTERN NORTH CAROLINA (MARSHALL – MADISON CO.)

Margaret Johann's article in the *Christian Observer* reflects a cultural phenomenon that has been called the "uplift movement," which took hold of evangelical communities in the north and influenced the development of the southern mountains around the turn of the twentieth century. David Whisnant describes the movement as "the consensus mythology of the mountains purveyed on the missionary guild lecture circuits throughout the liberal and Protestant northeast" (6). According to Whisnant, the uplift movement led not only to settlement schools and folk and craft revivals, but also, more broadly, to the creation of the southern mountaineer as that image emerged in the national consciousness in twentieth century.

Margaret Johann's article, reprinted here, shows a connection between the local color movement of the late nineteenth century and the uplift movement that followed on its heels. Johann's article is one part local color story to one part evangelism. It appeared as part of a regular department called "Story and Incident" in the *Christian Observer*. Founded in 1813, the *Christian Observer* was "the oldest religious weekly with a record of continuous publication"

Christian Observer, 21 July 1897

(Mott I 137) at the time Johann was writing. Published in Louis-ville, Kentucky, the paper was, in one sense, a church organ, "a paper for the whole Southern Presbyterian Church, in which ministers and others, in all parts of the Church, freely interchange views on ques-tions of general interest" ("Christian Observer" 141). Yet the paper has an ecumenical drift, and by the late nineteenth century it had "a circulation surpassed by very few papers in the Southern States" (141). Much of its popularity was likely due to the way its contrib-utors freely deployed local color and sentimental conventions to engage the emotions of its middle-class readers. The story here por-trays colorful mountain characters, including the "moonshiner girl" of the title, in a life-and-death drama. The ignorance and back-wardness of mountain inhabitants, as well as their inherent nobility, are exaggerated not only for dramatic effect, but also to stimulate evangelical sympathies.

In every form of the human
Some hint of the Highest dwells.[1]

It was the drummer's first visit to Randolph.[2] He watched the train that had brought him worm itself out of sight between the hills that walled in the narrow valley; then turned toward the town that crouched there as if ashamed of itself (as indeed it ought to have been) to be so mean where nature was so magnificent.

Its single street struggled crampingly along with the river on one side and a ridge of cliffs on the other. There was no room for dooryards, and the houses and shops, diminutive, ramshackle and weather-worn, rose abruptly from the narrow, illy-defined sidewalk upon which seemingly all the men and boys in the place were lounging.

Taking the middle of the street, he walked briskly along, swinging his gripsack and feigning unconsciousness of the fact that every pair of eyes along the route was upon him, brute as well as human, for the scuttling cats turned in covert and surveyed him; and the lean cows tied in "unimproved" plots regarded him with as much surprise as if he had been a field of grass.

This was a county capital, and he passed the court house,[3] with its stuccoed walls broken and defaced, and its entrance further disfigured with the inevitable crowd of idlers. A little beyond was a blackened pile of ruins. The sidewalk was unencumbered there, and he stopped and looked with the strange interest that people always manifest in the wreckage that fire leaves.

"That's the jail," adventured one of a group of little darkeys who had kept close to him ever since he left the station.

Enough of the walls was left standing to show that they had been rough brick, four-square, three-story, with rows of narrow barred windows on front and sides. The rear wall had shown an unbroken façade, for, though just at this place the hills receded somewhat, the building had been set quite close to them, allowing for a yard in front.

Across the way where swung the sign-board, "Drummer's Delight,[4] by Aaron Boggs," the landlord, apprised betimes of the presence of a stranger in town, stood waiting for him in his doorway, solicitous lest he should wander farther up the street and be inveigled into the "Traveller's Rest." But he was not disappointed. The drummer came across and called for dinner.

Having disposed of a generous quantity of fried chicken and hot soda-biscuit, he came out upon the "po'ch" prepared to add to his meager knowledge of Randolph whatever items his host might impart. He opined from Boggs' pronunciation that he was northern born, though from long residence in the Old North State he had acquired many southern phrases.

"Well, sir," said the landlord, after he had discovered his guest's line of merchandise, "you won't be able to do anything in this town today or tomorrow either, I reckon. Every man in Randolph that's good for anything, every one that can and will drive a nail or lift a stick of timber, has gone up into the mountains to lend a hand at Cindy Madcap's house. I'm no 'count, you see," shrugging a shoulder from which hung an empty sleeve, "but my son-in-law's gone and so's my team. It's a right smart pull up there. They carried every last item that's used in building a house, even down to a doorlatch, and three days' rations for man and horse. Maybe they'll be back tonight, but I don't look for them before tomorrow. A house such as they're going to build isn't thrown together in an hour. Of course it isn't going to be a mansion—three rooms, that's all—but it'll be a completer thing than the majority of those mountain people ever saw before. They never saw a house ceiled and walled inside with boards, as this is going to be."

"Cellar to it?" The drummer had not traveled in the South long enough to get used to human habitations balanced upon four corner piles of stones.

"No; but I'm plumb sure there'll be a heap of windows in it."

"'Cindy Madcap,' eh?"

"Well, that's what she calls herself, but they say it isn't spelled that way."

"Widow?"

"'Widow?' No-o-o! She's a little moonshiner girl—about as big as this pink;" he drew his own fourteen-year-old grandchild down upon his knee. "This, sir, is Miss Tennessee Whiteford. Her mother's all the chick we ever had. Her father's a clerk over at the court-house. He was raised in this country. Mighty fond of a dog and gun he was when he was a boy; and what he doesn't know about these mountains isn't worth finding out. That's how it is that when the Federal officers come round to hunt up the illicit distilleries they're pretty sure to swear Whiteford into their service.

"This is allowed to be the roughest county in North Carolina. Get a little way back from the river and there's mountain piled against mountain and hill against hill, with only gulleys and gorges, not valleys, between; and here and there in the seams, the mountain people live; less comfortably housed, most of them, than the wild beasts. A great many of them are moonshiners, as they are called, but, dear me, their competition with the great government distilleries isn't worth mentioning. I don't reckon they'd bother to make any more whiskey than they want to drink themselves if they weren't hunted so. A man'll keep a mighty tight grip on what he didn't care much about till some one tried to snatch it away from him. You see these people know nothing about government; their idea of the world is that it's the common home of the animal called man, and they can't understand why anyone has a right to interfere with their work. My son-in-law and I—wasn't that your mother calling, Tennie? Run and see."

Relieved of the child, the speaker laid one foot across the other knee and proceeded while thoughtfully outlining the sole of his boot with his jack-knife:

"Whiteford and I are not of exactly the same mind about dealing with the moonshiners. He's for hounding them even if they don't make more than a jugful in a year, but I'd let them alone unless they manufacture in considerable quantity."

He paused, and the drummer, having noticed a row of unlabeled bottles of various sizes and shapes standing within a cupboard in the office, wondered if any financial consideration might have influenced the narrator's sentiments.

"It's a little more than a month ago that an officer came and got Whiteford to help him ferret out Madcap's distillery. They went on horseback, of course. They found it, destroyed a barrel of his whiskey, and started to bring him down the mountain. He came with them quietly enough till they got out of the thicket and into a path that followed the rocky bed of a stream. There they came upon his cabin. Whiteford says 'twas better than the average home of these mountaineers—built of logs, and the branches of trees, and clay. A chimney of stones and dried mud ran half way to the roof, and was continued by a length of rusty stovepipe. You could stand outside, he says, and look through chinks in both walls into the woods beyond; and yet the mercury often reaches zero up there.

"As they approached the cabin Cindy came leaping through the woods like some wild, frightened thing. She sprang into the doorway and turned at bay by the side of her grandmother, a stolid old woman with a rusty snuff-box in her lap and a pipe in her mouth.

"'Madcap,' said the officer, 'as you've come with us so civilly, we'll allow you to go in and make any final arrangements you may think necessary. Is this all your family?'

"The old woman and the gal, that's all," said the moonshiner. He lifted himself into the doorway with no wrath, not even displeasure, showing in his countenance—these mountaineers have not what are called mobile features. But Whiteford knew something of moonshiner warfare, and he slipped from his horse and followed. None too close either, for when he stepped inside there was Cindy clinging to her father's arm with both hands and he trying to shake her off so as to get his old rusty rifle into position.

"'Cin saved ye,' chuckled the old woman. Then she rubbed her gums with snuff, refilled and lighted her pipe and puffed away with perfect unconcern.

"'Dad's drunk,' said the girl, raising frightened eyes to Whiteford's face, and the moonshiner said mildly, 'Be I?'

"Of course they didn't deal gently with him after that. They handcuffed him and ordered him to lead the way down the mountain, and he started off with no translatable expression on his face. They had not gone twenty rods when Cindy vaulted past the two horsemen. Her father was jolting clumsily ahead, for the road was rough and he missed

the balancing capacity of hands and arms. She put her arm through his
to steady him, and they went along so for a half-mile; then, at a place
where a tiny stream joined the larger branch, she sprang away and darted
up the hillside. Whiteford gave his bridle to his companion and followed
her stealthily. She traced the stream to where it trickled out of a seemingly
impenetrable mesh of scuppernong vines and rhododendron, and there
he lost sight of her. But he knew that somehow she'd got in behind that
thicket. So he pushed ahead, keeping close to where he knew the stream
must have a channel, mounted a brier-hidden knoll and peered down
upon a rocky platform walled in by nature's masonry of cliff and tangle.
A scent of whiskey mingled with the perfume of the woods, for here, too,
was an illicit distillery, though a powerful small one, consisting of little
more than a keg and a tin can.

"A man and a woman were there, lean and tall and hollow-eyed, types
of the mountaineers of this 'Land of the Sky,' and Cindy was there, too.

"'They've got dad,' he heard her say (she didn't need to explain, for the
moonshiner is used to being hunted), and then she stooped and dammed
the little stream with her hand to test its volume.

"'This yer ain't goin' to hold out much longer,' she said. 'You-all go
up to our place and look after granny, won't ye? There's right smart o'
water there, an' the ossifers won't hunt round there no longer, now dad's
done took.'"

"They reckoned they 'might's well' and then Cindy vanished. She
rejoined her father, and for five miles her feet sprang elastic from the
rough roadway. Then her steps began to lag, for, though she was used
to scrambling and climbing all day among the rocks and hills, this was
her first long tramp.

"Whiteford couldn't stand that. He's mighty soft-hearted where
little girls are concerned"—pinching the cheek of his granddaughter
who had returned to his side—"so he rode forward and tried to persuade
her to go back. Her father didn't have a word to say, just stood there like
he was deaf.

"'I'm goin' with dad,' said the child.

"Whiteford told her there were eight or nine miles more to travel and
besides that, her father was going to be locked up in jail.

"The girl's got as pretty a pair of shy brown eyes as any deer you
ever saw, and when she raised them to his and said simply, 'We all's
goin' to stay together,' and then took her father's hand and trudged

wearily on, Whiteford was nonplussed. It ended in their taking off Madcap's handcuffs and putting him and Cindy on Whiteford's horse.

"Young man, the ignorance of these mountain people is something hard to understand. When that party got into the high road and it began to wind down toward civilization, that girl struck a new world. Once when they passed a cabin where a child stood looking out at them through a glazed window she was so absorbed in astonishment that she lost her hold of her father and slipped off of the horse. After that they both walked.

"The girl had never before seen a house with a window in it! All along the road the dwellings with their dooryards, wells, farming implements, etc., poor and behind-the-age as they seem to you, were a marvel to her. The costumes of people seemed to amuse her and she laughed aloud at a parasol. Once, when they passed a school-house and a bevy of children came frolicking out, she just stood still bewildered. She was like a child born and reared in a mine, deep in the bowels of the earth, and suddenly thrust into the light of day, and sir, though it's hard to believe, there are hundreds up in those mountains no better off than she was.

"Nothing frightened her though, till they got almost down into town. They were jogging along that shelf you see up there when a train of cars tore out of the woods and came wriggling and shrieking along below them. I expect the poor little thing thought 'twas some huge fire-breathing serpent, for she almost went into convulsions. Whiteford just had to take her in his arms and pacify her, and even her father was sufficiently roused to take her hand in his. Whiteford took her other hand and led his horse and that's the way they came into town.

"But she was too timid to notice anything then. I hardly think she knew when they entered the jail. Her father was consigned to a cell, and as she wouldn't leave him, they had to lock her up with him. But the keeper's wife was kind to her and our little Tennie here, she didn't forget the little girl that probably saved her father's life, and so between them they succeeded, after a day or two, in coaxing the poor child out.

"You see that uppermost window in the wall facing this way? That was in Madcap's cell, and for a week that child couldn't be tolled out of sight of that window. And her father couldn't have been so indifferent as he seemed for he'd always sit where she could see him.

"Well, Tennie dressed her up a little, told her the names of things, and, as you may say, introduced her to civilization. Why, the girl thought that the flag on the court-house was a woman's apron hung out to dry, and asked what they hung it up so high for. The kitchen stove she stood in awe of, and she had to be taught the use of its utensils down to the very poker. After awhile she got used to most of the household furniture, but a pane of glass never ceased to be a marvel to her. If any sights were passing on the street she'd run inside to look at them through the window.

"Madcap had been in jail three weeks awaiting the action of the grand jury when posters were stuck up in town announcing a circus in Asheville. In North Carolina, sir, a circus will completely clean out all the towns within reach of it. There's no one here that's too learned or too refined to enjoy a circus, and, as for the poorer classes, mercy knows how they get the money to go with, but they do. Why, I've known small farmers—distressingly poor they are, most of them—get their families into the old farm wagon, carry them to the circus town, sell wagon, team and all for tickets, and walk back home as pleased as if they'd just come into a fortune.

"But Cindy wouldn't go, though she'd heard nothing but circus talked of for days. 'I'm goin' to stay where dad is,' she said.

"I left the old colored cook, Martha, in charge here, and the keeper of the jail left his hired man home to look after things. There were only eight prisoners—in for light offenses most of them—and they were all locked in their cells on the third floor. Besides these and the keeper's wife, who's delicate, and gave up to a headache at the last minute, there were only a couple of old women and a few little darkeys left in Randolph.

"Just about noon when, as ill-luck would have it, the man had gone to look after some stock on the farm—just behind that hill it is—an oil stove over which the keeper's wife was cooking her dinner, exploded. Her clothing took fire and she had to crush that out first and then I reckon lost her presence of mind, for by the time she gave the alarm the fire had gained considerable headway.

"Cindy was over here eating her dinner. Martha says, before she herself had time to think, the child stood in the door of the jail. But she couldn't get any further. They'd used a front room on the first floor for a kitchen and of course the flames took to the stairway first. That little thing never stopped to think. 'Twas kind of instinct such as is given to the wild critters. She just loped across the road again and into that shed there and out again with the axe.

"Do you see the remnant of that old pine tree just back of the ruin? It grows a little way up the cliff and it leans this way some. Its rough old trunk rose twenty feet or more without a branch. One of its scragged boughs leaned over the flat roof of the jail, and once before the child, just to show Tennie what she could do, had climbed up and got upon the roof. But she couldn't get up with the axe in her hand. Either the axe would fall or she'd slip back—cut and scratched herself pitifully too—and, if it hadn't been for old Martha, those eight men would have died there that day like rats in a trap in spite of little Cindy.

"Martha tied a clothesline round the girl's waist and fastened the other end of it to the axe, and she says it didn't seem more than a minute till Cindy had that axe swinging before her father's window.

"Of course he slashed his way out of his cell in no time and then— he proved himself his child's own father! For, though 'twas blistering hot up there by that time, and the flames had broke through in several places, he never took another step till he'd give every man up there the same chance to escape that he had himself. By hook and by crook they all got to the ground in safety—they had the rope you know—and then, sir, to a man those prisoners went to work to save what they could! They tore to pieces one or two partly-detached frame out-buildings and saved their contents; they carried water and put out the fire where it was following the fence towards the court-house, and when the train came in bringing the keeper and the sheriff every prisoner was waiting for them. It was funny to see how they'd hang around Cindy. If they couldn't be near her they'd keep an eye on her. But she kept close to her father.

"After the ruins had been viewed from every possible stand point the sheriff came up to little Cindy where she stood with her father beside a pile of wreckage, and said he:

"'Little girl, of all the things you've seen since you left the mountains, what would you rather have?'

"She raised that pair of deer's eyes to his face and says she:

"'This yer,' and put her hand on a charred window sash.

"'Not this?' he said touching it with his foot.

"'So's we-all won't have to keep the door open when it snows,' and then she added, kind of wringing her little hands together, 'It'ud be nice for granny.'

"The sheriff stood there for a moment with his eyes on the ground and then said in his quiet way:

"'You shall have it, Cindy, and a dozen more like it if want as many.'

"Well, sir, the sheriff of this county is a man, a good, sound practical, one. Of course we've all chipped in, but he's at the head of this building project, and the land the cottage will stand on is Cindy's own. It's bought, a generous plot of it—land up there can be had for twenty-five cents an acre—and the papers are made out. Whiteford is her guardian.

"The place is a little nearer to civilization than the old cabin, but yet it's wild enough to be homelike to them. As for the father, he'll get off easy for his little daughter's sake. Shouldn't wonder if he's never indicted. Whiteford says that the man was the worse for his own whiskey when they took him, though of course that's no excuse for his being so ready to defend himself, but we think that if he's looked after a little he'll go at some legitimate work—tobacco raising perhaps. At any rate both he and Cindy have acquired a few new ideas since they've been with us.

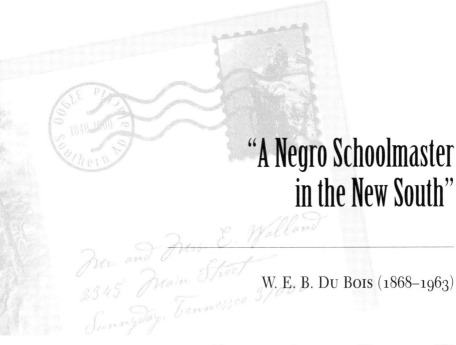

"A Negro Schoolmaster in the New South"

W. E. B. Du Bois (1868–1963)

Nashville – Lebanon – Watertown TN

T he following article is about a region of Middle Tennessee, west
of the Cumberland Plateau, that lies outside the geographical
area otherwise represented in this anthology. However, the region
shares some of the topographical characteristics of the mountain
south. As Robert Brandt describes the area, "Broken detached
pieces of the Eastern Highland Rim create ranges of rugged hills
that rise hundreds of feet above the valleys below" (172). The
article is included here for historical context, and for the perspective it provides on the local color–style travel writing about southern mountain inhabitants during the late nineteenth century.

William Edward Burghardt Du Bois was born and raised in
western Massachusetts. When he was seventeen, Du Bois rode the
segregated interstate rail cars from New York to Nashville, Tennessee, to attend Fisk University. Fisk, a coeducational institution
for blacks, was founded after the war by crusading Congregation-
alists and former abolitionists, most of whom were war veterans,
from the north. By the mid-1880s, Fisk was considered to be
among the best liberal arts colleges, black or white, in the south.

During the summers of 1886 and 1887, while he was enrolled
at Fisk, Du Bois taught school in rural Wilson County, fifty miles

Atlantic Monthly, January 1899

or so from Nashville. His pupils were rural blacks struggling through a historically difficult period. "The heroic futility of the two summers weighed upon him," writes Du Bois biographer David Levering Lewis. "He saw written across the faces deep in Wilson County the rebuked destinies of the black people who came singing, praying, and aspiring out of slavery" (70).

After graduating from Fisk, Du Bois went on to study at Harvard, where he earned an M.A. and, in 1895, a Ph.D. He also traveled and studied in Europe, and quickly established a reputation for himself as a scholar, writer, and orator. In 1898, he returned to Fisk as an honored guest, to deliver the commencement speech (entitled "Careers Open to College-Bred Negroes"). During that visit, he returned to the countryside where he'd taught school ten years earlier. Between the time Du Bois taught school in rural Middle Tennessee and the time he returned to deliver the commencement speech at Fisk, conditions for African Americans in the south had only gone from bad to worse. The period saw a steady rise in lynchings and other terrorist activity, while the system of formal and informal barriers to enfranchisement solidified into what came to be known as "Jim Crow."

The present selection is an account of Du Bois's return. This article was reprinted almost word for word in Du Bois's celebrated collection *The Souls of Black Folk* (1903) under the title "Of the Meaning of Progress." Du Bois is probably the best-known writer represented in this anthology. His long and prolific career began with newspaper contributions he wrote as a teenager, and ended with his death, in self-imposed exile in Ghana, at the age of ninety-five.

Once upon a time I taught school in the hills of Tennessee, where the broad dark vale of the Mississippi begins to roll and crumple to greet the Alleghanies. I was a Fisk student then, and all Fisk men think that Tennessee—beyond the Veil—is theirs alone, and in vacation time they sally forth in lusty bands to meet the county school commissioners. Young and happy, I too went, and I shall not soon forget that summer, ten years ago.

First, there was a teachers' Institute[1] at the county-seat; and there distinguished guests of the superintendent taught the teachers fractions and spelling and other mysteries,—white teachers in the morning, Negroes at night. A picnic now and then, and a supper, and the rough world was softened by laughter and song. I remember how—But I wander.

There came a day when all the teachers left the Institute, and began the hunt for schools. I learn from hearsay (for my mother was mortally afraid of firearms) that the hunting of ducks and bears and men is wonderfully interesting, but I am sure that the man who has never hunted a country school has something to learn of the pleasures of the chase. I see now the white, hot roads lazily rise and fall and wind before me under the burning July sun; I feel the deep weariness of heart and limb, as ten, eight, six miles stretch relentlessly ahead; I feel my heart sink heavily as I hear again and again, "Got a teacher? Yes." So I walked on and on,—horses were too expensive,—until I had wandered beyond railways, beyond stage lines, to a land of "varmints" and rattlesnakes, where the coming of a stranger was an event, and men lived and died in the shadow of one blue hill.

Sprinkled over hill and dale lay cabins and farmhouses, shut out from the world by the forests and the rolling hills toward the east. There I found at last a little school. Josie told me of it; she was a thin, homely girl of twenty, with a dark brown face and thick, hard hair. I had crossed the stream at Watertown, and rested under the great willows; then I had gone to the little cabin in the lot where Josie was resting on her way to town. The gaunt farmer made me welcome, and Josie, hearing my errand, told me anxiously that they wanted a school over the hill; that but once since the war had a teacher been there; that she herself longed to learn,—and thus she ran on, talking fast and loud, with much earnestness and energy.

Next morning I crossed the tall round hill, lingered to look at the blue and yellow mountains stretching toward the Carolinas; then I plunged into the wood, and came out at Josie's home. It was a dull frame cottage with four rooms, perched just below the brow of the hill, amid peach trees. The father was a quiet, simple soul, calmly ignorant, with no touch of vulgarity. The mother was different,—strong, bustling, and energetic, with a quick, restless tongue, and an ambition to live "like folks." There was a crowd of children. Two boys had gone away. There remained two growing girls; a shy midget of eight; John, tall, awkward, and eighteen; Jim, younger, quicker, and better looking; and two babies of indefinite age. Then there was Josie herself. She seemed to be the centre of the family: always busy at service or at home, or berry-picking; a little nervous and inclined to scold, like her mother, yet faithful, too, like her father. She had about her a certain fineness, the shadow of an unconscious moral heroism that would willingly give all of life to make life broader, deeper, and fuller for her and hers. I saw much of this family afterward, and grew to love them for their honest efforts to be decent and comfortable, and for their knowledge of their own ignorance. There was with them no affectation. The mother would scold the father for being so "easy;" Josie would roundly rate the boys for carelessness; and all knew that it was a hard thing to dig a living out of a rocky side hill.

I secured the school. I remember the day I rode horseback out to the commissioner's house, with a pleasant young white fellow, who wanted the white school. The road ran down the bed of a stream; the sun laughed and the water jingled, and we rode on. "Come in," said the commissioner,—"come in. Have a seat. Yes, that certificate will do. Stay to dinner. What do you want a month?" Oh, thought I, this is lucky; but even then fell the awful shadow of the Veil, for they ate first, then I—alone.

The schoolhouse[2] was a log hut, where Colonel Wheeler used to shelter his corn. It sat in a lot behind a rail fence and thorn bushes, near the sweetest of springs. There was an entrance where a door once was, and within, a massive rickety fireplace; great chinks between the logs served as windows. Furniture was scarce. A pale blackboard crouched in the corner. My desk was made of three boards, reinforced at critical points, and my chair, borrowed from the landlady, had to be returned every night. Seats for the children,—these puzzled me much. I was haunted by a New England vision of neat little desks and chairs, but, alas, the reality was rough plank benches without backs, and at times without legs. They had the one virtue of making naps dangerous,— possibly fatal, for the floor was not to be trusted.

It was a hot morning late in July when the school opened. I trembled when I heard the patter of little feet down the dusty road, and saw the growing row of dark solemn faces and bright eager eyes facing me. First came Josie and her brothers and sisters. The longing to know, to be a student in the great school at Nashville, hovered like a star above this child woman amid her work and worry, and she studied doggedly. There were the Dowells from their farm over toward Alexandria: Fanny, with her smooth black face and wondering eyes; Martha, brown and dull; the pretty girl wife of a brother, and the younger brood. There were the Burkes, two brown and yellow lads, and a tiny haughty-eyed girl. Fat Reuben's little chubby girl came, with golden face and old gold hair, faithful and solemn. 'Thenie was on hand early,—a jolly, ugly, good-hearted girl, who slyly dipped snuff and looked after her little bow-legged brother. When her mother could spare her, 'Tildy came,—a midnight beauty, with starry eyes and tapering limbs; and her brother, correspondingly homely. And then the big boys: the hulking Lawrences;

the lazy Neills, unfathered sons of mother and daughter; Hickman, with a stoop in his shoulders; and the rest.

There they sat, nearly thirty of them, on the rough benches, their faces shading from a pale cream to a deep brown, the little feet bare and swinging, the eyes full of expectation, with here and there a twinkle of mischief, and the hands grasping Webster's blue-back spelling-book. I loved my school, and the fine faith the children had in the wisdom of their teacher was truly marvelous. We read and spelled together, wrote a little, picked flowers, sang, and listened to stories of the world beyond the hill. At times the school would dwindle away, and I would start out. I would visit Mun Eddings, who lived in two very dirty rooms, and ask why little Lugene, whose flaming face seemed ever ablaze with the dark red hair uncombed, was absent all last week, or why I missed so often the inimitable rags of Mack and Ed. Then the father, who worked Colonel Wheeler's farm on shares, would tell me how the crops needed the boys; and the thin, slovenly mother, whose face was pretty when washed, assured me that Lugene must mind the baby. "But we'll start them again next week." When the Lawrences stopped, I knew that the doubts of the old folks about book-learning had conquered again, and so, toiling up the hill, and getting as far into the cabin as possible, I put Cicero pro Archia Poeta into the simplest English with local applications, and usually convinced them—for a week or so.

On Friday nights I often went home with some of the children; sometimes to Doc Burke's farm. He was a great, loud, thin Black, ever working, and trying to buy the seventy-five acres of hill and dale where he lived; but people said that he would surely fail, and the "white folks would get it all." His wife was a magnificent Amazon, with saffron face and shining hair, uncorseted and barefooted, and the children were strong and beautiful. They lived in a one-and-a-half-room cabin in the hollow of the farm, near the spring. The front room was full of great fat white beds, scrupulously neat; and there were bad chromos on the walls, and a tired centre-table. In the tiny back kitchen I was often invited to "take out and help" myself to fried chicken and wheat biscuit, "meat" and corn pone, string beans and berries. At first I used to be a little alarmed at the approach of bed-time in the one lone bedroom, but embarrassment was very deftly avoided. First, all the children nodded and slept, and were stowed away in one great pile of goose feathers; next, the mother and the father discreetly slipped away to the kitchen while I went to bed; then, blowing out the dim light, they retired in the dark. In the morning all were up and away before I thought of awaking. Across the road, where fat Reuben lived, they all went outdoors while the teacher retired, because they did not boast the luxury of a kitchen.

I liked to stay with the Dowells, for they had four rooms and plenty of good country fare. Uncle Bird had a small, rough farm, all woods and hills, miles from the big road; but he was full of tales,—he preached now and then,—and with his children, berries, horses, and wheat he was happy and prosperous. Often, to keep the peace, I must go where life was less lovely; for instance, 'Tildy's mother was incorrigibly dirty, Reuben's larder was limited seriously, and herds of untamed bedbugs wandered over the Eddingses' beds. Best of all I loved to go to Josie's, and sit on the porch, eating peaches, while the mother bustled and talked: how Josie had bought the sewing-machine; how Josie worked at service in winter, but that four dollars a month was "mighty little" wages; how Josie longed to go away to school, but that it "looked like" they never could get far enough ahead to let her; how the crops failed and the well was yet unfinished; and, finally, how "mean" some of the white folks were.

For two summers I lived in this little world; it was dull and humdrum. The girls looked at the hill in wistful longing, and the boys fretted, and haunted Alexandria. Alexandria was "town,"—a straggling, lazy village of houses, churches, and shops, and an aristocracy of Toms, Dicks, and Captains. Cuddled on the hill to the north was the village of the colored folks, who lived in three or four room unpainted cottages, some neat and homelike, and some dirty. The dwellings were scattered rather aimlessly, but they centred about the twin temples of the hamlet, the Methodist and the Hard-Shell Baptist churches. These, in turn, leaned gingerly on a sad-colored schoolhouse. Hither my little world wended its crooked way on Sunday to meet other worlds, and gossip, and wonder, and make the weekly sacrifice with frenzied priest at the altar of the "old-time religion." Then the soft melody and mighty cadences of Negro song fluttered and thundered.

I have called my tiny community a world, and so its isolation made it; and yet there was among us but a half-awakened common consciousness, sprung from common joy and grief, at burial, birth, or wedding; from a common hardship in poverty, poor land, and low wages; and, above all, from the sight of the Veil that hung between us and Opportunity. All this caused us to think some thoughts together; but these, when ripe for speech, were spoken in various languages. Those whose eyes thirty and more years before had seen "the glory of the coming of the Lord" saw in every present hindrance or help a dark fatalism bound to bring all things right in His own good time. The mass of those to whom slavery was a dim recollection of childhood found the world a puzzling thing: it asked little of them, and they answered with little, and yet it ridiculed their offering. Such a paradox they could not understand, and therefore sank into listless indifference, or shiftlessness, or reckless bravado. There were, however, some such as Josie, Jim, and Ben,—they to whom War, Hell, and Slavery were but childhood tales, whose young appetites had been whetted to an edge by school and story and half-awakened thought. Ill could they be content, born without and beyond the World. And their weak wings beat against their barriers,—barriers of caste, of youth, of life; at last, in dangerous moments, against everything that opposed even a whim.

The ten years that follow youth, the years when first the realization comes that life is leading somewhere,—these were the years that passed after I left my little school. When they were past, I came by chance once more to the walls of Fisk University, to the halls of the chapel of melody. As I lingered there in the joy and pain of meeting old school friends, there swept over me a sudden longing to pass again beyond the blue hill, and to see the homes and the school of other days, and to learn how life had gone with my school-children; and I went.

Josie was dead, and the gray-haired mother said simply, "We've had a heap of trouble since you've been away." I had feared for Jim. With a cultured parentage and a social caste to uphold him, he might have made a venturesome merchant or a West Point cadet. But here he was, angry with life and reckless; and when Farmer Durham charged him with stealing wheat, the old man had to ride fast to escape the stones which the furious fool hurled after him. They told Jim to run away; but he would not run, and the constable came that afternoon. It grieved Josie, and great awkward John walked nine miles every day to see his little brother through the bars of Lebanon jail. At last the two came back together in the dark night. The mother cooked supper, and Josie emptied her purse, and the boys stole away. Josie grew thin and silent, yet worked the more. The hill became steep for the quiet old father, and with the boys away there was little to do in the valley. Josie helped them sell the old farm, and they moved nearer town. Brother Dennis, the carpenter, built a new house with six rooms; Josie toiled a year in Nashville, and brought back ninety dollars to furnish the house and change it to a home.

When the spring came, and the birds twittered, and the stream ran proud and full, little sister Lizzie, bold and thoughtless, flushed with the passion of youth, bestowed herself on the tempter, and brought home a nameless child. Josie shivered, and worked on, with the vision of school-days all fled, with a face wan and tired,—worked until, on a summer's day, some one married another; then Josie crept to her mother like a hurt child, and slept—and sleeps.

I paused to scent the breeze as I entered the valley. The Lawrences have gone; father and son forever, and the other son lazily digs in the earth to live. A new young widow rents out their cabin to fat Reuben. Reuben is a Baptist preacher now, but I fear as lazy as ever, though his cabin has three rooms; and little Ella has grown into a bouncing woman, and is ploughing corn on the hot hillside. There are babies a plenty, and one half-witted girl. Across the valley is a house I did not know before, and there I found, rocking one baby and expecting another, one of my schoolgirls, a daughter of Uncle Bird Dowell. She looked somewhat worried with her new duties, but soon bristled into pride over her neat cabin, and the tale of her thrifty husband, the horse and cow, and the farm they were planning to buy.

My log schoolhouse was gone. In its place stood Progress; and Progress, I understand, is necessarily ugly. The crazy foundation stones still marked the former site of my poor little cabin, and not far away, on six weary boulders, perched a jaunty board house, perhaps twenty by thirty feet, with three windows and a door that locked. Some of the window glass was broken, and part of an old iron stove lay mournfully under the house. I peeped through the window half reverently, and found things that were more familiar. The blackboard had grown by about two feet, and the seats were still without backs. The county owns the lot now, I hear, and every year there is a session of school. As I sat by the spring and looked on the Old and the New I felt glad, very glad, and yet—

After two long drinks I started on. There was the great double log house on the corner. I remembered the broken, blighted family that used to live there. The strong, hard face of the mother, with its wilderness of hair, rose before me. She had driven her husband away, and while I taught school a strange man lived there, big and jovial, and people talked. I felt sure that Ben and 'Tildy would come to naught from such a home. But this is an odd world; for Ben is a busy farmer in Smith County, "doing well, too," they say, and he had cared for little 'Tildy until last spring, when a lover married her. A hard life the lad had led, toiling for meat, and laughed at because he was homely and crooked. There was Sam Carlon, an impudent old skinflint, who had definite notions about niggers, and hired Ben a summer and would not pay him. Then the hungry boy gathered his sacks together, and in broad daylight went into Carlon's corn; and when the hard-fisted farmer set upon him, the angry boy flew at him like a beast. Doc Burke saved a murder and a lynching that day.

The story reminded me again of the Burkes, and an impatience seized me to know who won in the battle, Doc or the seventy-five acres. For it is a hard thing to make a farm out of nothing, even in fifteen years. So I hurried on, thinking of the Burkes. They used to have a certain magnificent barbarism about them that I liked. They were never vulgar, never immoral, but rather rough and primitive, with an unconventionality that spent itself in loud guffaws, slaps on the back, and naps in the corner. I hurried by the cottage of the misborn Neill boys. It was empty, and they were grown into fat, lazy farm hands. I saw the home of the Hickmans, but Albert, with his stooping shoulders, had passed from the world. Then I came to the Burkes' gate and peered through; the inclosure looked rough and untrimmed, and yet there were the same fences around the old farm save to the left, where lay twenty-five other acres. And lo! the cabin in the hollow had climbed the hill and swollen to a half-finished six-room cottage.

The Burkes held a hundred acres, but they were still in debt. Indeed, the gaunt father who toiled night and day would scarcely be happy out of debt, being so used to it. Some day he must stop, for his massive frame is showing decline. The mother wore shoes, but the lionlike physique of other days was broken. The children had grown up. Rob, the image of his father, was loud and rough with laughter. Birdie, my school baby of six, had grown to a picture of maiden beauty, tall and tawny. "Edgar is gone," said the mother, with head half bowed,—"gone to work in Nashville; he and his father couldn't agree."

Little Doc, the boy born since the time of my school, took me horseback down the creek next morning toward Farmer Dowell's. The road and the stream were battling for mastery, and the stream had the better of it. We splashed and waded, and the merry boy, perched behind me, chattered and laughed. He showed me where Simon Thompson had bought a bit of ground and a home; but his daughter Lana, a plump,

brown, slow girl, was not there. She had married a man and a farm
twenty miles away. We wound on down the stream till we came to a gate
that I did not recognize, but the boy insisted that it was "Uncle Bird's."
The farm was fat with the growing crop. In that little valley was a strange
stillness as I rode up; for death and marriage had stolen youth, and left
age and childhood there. We sat and talked that night, after the chores
were done. Uncle Bird was grayer, and his eyes did not see so well, but
he was still jovial. We talked of the acres bought, one hundred and
twenty-five,—of the new guest chamber added, of Martha's marrying.
Then we talked of death: Fanny and Fred were gone; a shadow hung
over the other daughter, and when it lifted she was to go to Nashville
to school. At last we spoke of the neighbors, and as night fell Uncle Bird
told me how, on a night like that, 'Thenie came wandering back to her
home over yonder, to escape the blows of her husband. And next morning
she died in the home that her little bow-legged brother, working and
saving, had bought for their widowed mother.

My journey was done, and behind me lay hill and dale, and Life and
Death. How shall man measure Progress there where the dark-faced Josie
lies? How many heartfuls of sorrow shall balance a bushel of wheat? How
hard a thing is life to the lowly, and yet how human and real! And all
this life and love and strife and failure,—is it the twilight of nightfall
or the flush of some faint-dawning day?

Thus sadly musing, I rode to Nashville in the Jim Crow car.

SECTION IV

Yankee Explorations

TO THE HIGH PEAKS

Three Characters:
1. Narrator (Lewis)
2.
3.

Three Places:
1. WNC Railroad
2. Grandfather Mountain
3. The River

Three Events:
1. The Journey
2. "Globe" Misunderstanding
3. The hawk

Three Ideas:
1. Botany
2. Personified Mountain
3. The Waste left from the War, 311

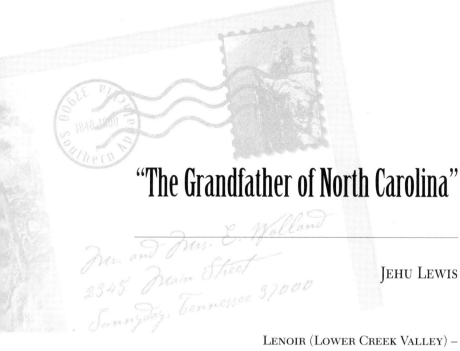

"The Grandfather of North Carolina"

JEHU LEWIS

LENOIR (LOWER CREEK VALLEY) –
JOHNS RIVER VALLEY – THE GLOBE –
GRANDFATHER MOUNTAIN NC

Childhood reminiscences in this article suggest that Jehu Lewis grew up in the northeast. Yet the article appeared in a magazine identified to some degree with the American west. The *Lakeside Monthly* was founded in January 1869 as the *Western Monthly* in the upstart city of Chicago. A writer in the first issue expresses the sectionalism that motivated the new magazine: "If we have earned the title of the Granary, let us strike for the Brainery of the nation" (quoted in Mott III 414). Yet only a few months after that first issue appeared, F. F. Browne took over the editorship and changed the name of the magazine, from the *Western* to the *Lakeside Monthly* in 1871, indicating a shift toward a more local metropolitan identity (Mott III 415).

The magazine attempted to recruit Bret Harte, whose western "local color" fiction was then all the rage in the east, as editor. The recruitment effort famously failed. Then came a series of small fires in the printing works, foreshadowing the Great Chicago Fire in October 1871. The magazine missed November and December after the big fire, but bounced back with its January fire edition

Lakeside Monthly, September 1873

(now a valuable collector's item). Subscriptions increased over the following year, but the magazine met its demise with the Panic of 1873. Black Friday came on September 19. In the ensuing season, the magazine lost a third of its subscribers (Mott III 415). The edition featuring Lewis's article on Grandfather Mountain was thus the magazine's last untroubled one. The very last issue appeared in February 1874.

Lewis traveled on foot, off-trail, at a time when recreational hiking was not yet popular in America. Rather than describing culture and local characters, in the mode of much of the writing of his time, Lewis writes here, instead, of flora, fauna, and topography.

The Western North Carolina Railroad traverses some of the finest scenery east of the Yo Semite, starting from old Salisbury, which is an easy connection with all main lines of travel in the country.

Fifty miles or less northerly from Salisbury, at a point on the Catawba River where join the counties of Catawba, Burke, and Caldwell, is Hickory Tavern. Here you may be so interested as to stay in the neighborhood for the season. But if you travel another northwesterly twenty miles, to the quiet old town of Lenoir, the seat of Caldwell county, when about half way, a bold summit, overtopping the surrounding mountains, dim in its thirty miles distance, but distinct and unmistakable in its lofty and striking outlines, will loom up before you.

If the mountain tops be cloudless you will see a gigantic silhouette, as of an old, old man, with wrinkled brow, drooping nose, and sunken mouth, lying calm and still, as though stretched on his bier, his dead, stony face cutting sharply against the tender blue of the sky. Hence the mountain's name. And from the moment you first trace the lines of the wonderful profile, the GRANDFATHER becomes a reality catching the eye, and even the heart, with its majesty touched with pathos.

Not always, however, can the outline be traced; for, often in the morning or evening, at mid-day, or for days and weeks together, those aged features are veiled with clouds—sometimes light and fleecy, but oftener dark and heavy—sending forth flashes, and thunder growls of warning that the storm-court is in session, wildly debating a descent upon the lowlands. At such times there is something awful in the stillness, the grandeur, and the closely-veiled mystery, and you watch, in reverential waiting, the lifting of the pall. Dwelling for months with the scene ever before you—sometimes catching a glimpse of disrobed greatness, as the first rays of the rising sun light up the rocky slopes and summit, or when

sinking, he leaves all those western ridges in deepest purple—you feel a
growing love for the grand lineaments of that still face, changeless as death
in the midst of change. You begin to long for a closer acquaintance, for
an opportunity to penetrate the mysteries of that blue distance, and for
a moment to stand on that far height and look down upon all the green-
topped hills and wooded, billowy mountains, to the utmost horizon.
Then, too, all through these mountains grow rare and beautiful plants:
such lovely forms of fern, club-moss, moss and lichen, that, if you are a
botanist—especially one in his first unassisted steps—you will look forward
eagerly to the starting on the wild tramp over the hills and through the
tangled forests to the path which loses itself upon the rugged sides of
the Grandfather.

All summer long my home had been a farm-house in Lower Creek
Valley, a few miles southwest of Lenoir. From the upper windows, and
from the hillside above the house, the Grandfather, or its cloudy covering,
was ever in view twenty miles away, over the pine woods which skirted
the farther side of the valley.

An opening of the hills a little to the left, where they sink away for
nearly a quarter of the horizon, gives a beautiful prospect of the John's
River hills, and beyond them the grand, level-topped wall of the Blue
Ridge, with here and there overtopping summits, like watch-towers on
the walls of a fortress. Most conspicuous of these is one on the extreme
left, an abrupt eminence, with perpendicular sides and flat top and known
by the too common name of Table Rock. A little to the right of it, and
not quite so high, is the celebrated and singular looking Hawk's bill, so
called from a fancied resemblance.

Due west, in the middle distance, is a round-topped eminence, one of
the John's River hills; and the path to the Grandfather leads to the banks
of that stream, at a point a little to the right.

Provided with a haversack of food and a portable press for botanical
specimens, I set out on the last morning of August. An indescribable
medley of weeds and plants, cultivated crops, and volunteer growth,
met my eyes as I passed through the fertile bottoms of Lower Creek.
Corn, well grown and heavy-eared, up which clambered, in spiral pathway,
small-flowered blue and scarlet and white morning-glories; great rank
cockle-burrs, with their speckled stems and pale-green leaves; the giant
rag-weed (*ambrosia trifida*), attaining a height of twelve feet; and an endless
variety of such compositae as delight in moist and fertile soils. Long
trailing vines, with pennate leaves—prone on the ground, slender and

straight in their course—prove, on examination, to be no other than that stately climber, the trumpet-creeper (*tecoma radicans*).[1] You can find it more fully developed, and in flower, in almost every old field and fence-row in Carolina and Virginia. Two rows of "mountain-rice"[2] added another item of interest. Very similar in appearance, though of smaller grain than that grown so extensively upon the coast, it perhaps requires less moisture for its successful culture, though never growing on what would be called a dry soil. You never see a whole field, or even a large part of a field, planted with it; only a row or two by the side of a ditch, or a little patch in some wet corner, where the soil is inclined to be stiff and heavy, as well as damp. Growers claim it does not succeed on very light soil, however well supplied with moisture. But botany makes me digress.

Up a gentle ascent from the bottoms, and then away, over red-gullied old fields and cultivated farms, and through forests of mixed growth of oak and pine, for ten miles, and I stood on the banks of John's River, just above the mouth of Mulberry Creek. It is a placid stream, at this place; but it comes down clear and cold from the mountains, and is wild and roystering enough in its upper course.

For some distance my route[3] lay right up the river. Sometimes the footpath ran along by the side of the highway, under the shadow of great spreading trees which overhung the water. Sometimes it wound along the face of a rocky hillside, while the wagon-road sought a more smooth and even way on the other bank of the stream. Many times, too, I had to cross the river; for there are bluffs which even the hardy mountaineers consider too steep and rough to afford a convenient or safe footpath.

The crossing is made on foot-logs—"benches," they are called in the lower course—where the stream is broad, and several pieces of timber, placed end to end, are supported on long legs: like exaggerations or caricatures of those slab benches which graced the log school-houses of the olden time. But, farther up, where the stream is narrow, often a single slender tree is felled across, resting, at either end, upon the high banks; while, far below, rages in its foam the dashing current on its rocky way. It requires a steady nerve to enable one to go up John's River in safety, and dry shod.

The valley of John's River is fertile, but narrow, and shut in by steep, rocky hills. In places, the hill-ranges fall apart, leaving broad acres of level farm lands; and, again approaching, leave but a narrow gorge, scarcely wide enough for a roadway beside the stream. A part of the valley, known as "The Globe," smiles with very fine farms, the owners of which are in quite easy circumstances, though much isolated from the outside world. How the valley came by its high-sounding name, I was unable to learn; but an anecdote is related, showing that it is sometimes a little inconvenient. A contested will was on trial in the District Court, the testator having been a resident of this valley, the judge hailing from a distant part of the Judicial District. A witness for the defence, testifying to the "sound mind and memory" of the deceased, concluded with the astounding assertion: "He was always considered the most intelligent man, and the best business man, in the Globe." A second likewise asserted the superiority of the deceased over every other man "in the Globe." "Hold!" cries the Judge, somewhat excited. "Tell us what you mean by 'the ablest man on the globe?' You certainly swear to what you do not know, and therefore your testimony cannot be received." The dignity of the court and the quiet of the audience collapsed simultaneously, when the counsel explained that "'The Globe' referred to is only a limited neighborhood, and not the whole mundane sphere, as your Honor supposed."

Leaving the course of John's River near the Globe post-office, my route[4] lay to the left, up the valley of a tributary that comes down from the direction of the Grandfather, whose lordly summit could be seen, at intervals, overtopping the lofty intervening hills. The nearest point seemed almost at hand—and certainly was not over five miles distant, as the crow flies; but the long, tedious windings of the bridlepath make up a distance more than double.

Night coming down, I sought shelter with a resident of the valley, a kind-hearted, but simple-minded and uncultivated "son of the soil."

In the fresh air of morning, my path lay across a small field, toward the mouth of a deep gorge, and past a great stone chimney, standing lone and stark, like a mute uninscribed monument to the memory of the household which once gathered round its blazing hearth. Such memorials are painfully common in every part of the Sunny South since the storm of war swept terribly over it. Whether this one marks the ruins of a home desolated thus, or only by the more stealthy process of desertion and decay, no signs tell; for grass and rank weeds overgrow the spot, the fences are gone, and all is still as though never a voice had been heard or never a heart had beat in joy or sorrow there.

After passing the gorge, I came upon a newly-made clearing, with a single log dwelling; and then for miles I saw neither house nor field nor any trace of man, save only the path, and the marks of axes upon trees by the wayside. The crest of a lofty ridge was at length attained, and then for a while—and it seemed a long while—there was the monotony of gnarled and stunted trees, scattered sparsely here and there, with low bushes— sometimes in clumps, or straggling thinly, with grass and wild flowers between, but oftener crowded in close thickets—hedging in the path with a tangled wall of gray and green. Then down a long, long sloping way to where the trees stood thick and tall, a mingled growth of hemlock, pine, oak, elm, ash, and tulip poplar, with little undergrowth, save here and there a group of giant kalmias beside the little brook that wound its murmurous way among the rocks and moss. A rare woody climber (*aristolochia sipho*)[5] overhung the path with its great, rounded, heart-shaped leaves, and wound its way high up among the branches of the tall trees.

The sound of an axe rang through the shadowy glen, and I emerged upon a clearing, where a few acres of tillable land had been opened to the sun. Two or three families were located here, in the heart of the wilderness, with no road to the outer world over which a wheeled vehicle of any kind could pass. Near one of the houses stood a wooden sorghum mill, with the refuse of last year's crop heaped up beside it. The owner and his wife, approaching the house with a basket of fine peaches, invited me to rest, and to partake of the fruit.

Quitting the grateful repose and cheerful sound of voices, I plunged again into the forest, by a dim trail, leading across a rocky level, which was one widespread mass of huge boulders. There was, evidently, some good soil beneath, for the trees were no fewer nor less stately for their apparent lack of standing-room. With a firm, determined grip their rugged roots clasped the rocks, and forced themselves into every crevice.

A half-wild sow with bristles raised, and champing jaws, stood eyeing me from a slight eminence; and, all at once, with a startling "guh! guh! guh!" a litter of pigs sprang up and away from my very feet. Funny little uncivilized looking things they were!—russet and iron-gray, and striped like a chipmunk—recalling thoughts of the famous "Striped Pig"[6] of Massachusetts, and how North Carolina had no need for any such Yankee expedient, so long as her legislators and her people held that whiskey should be free from all legal bonds of taxation or prohibition.

The crossing of Wilson's Creek,[7] one of the clearest, wildest, and most frolicsome of mountain streams, was made by picking my way among the boughs of a slender hemlock, fallen from the other side, till the top rested on the summit of a great rock, high above the reach of freshets. Laying hold of shrubs and roots of trees, to draw myself up the steep beyond, I reached the bridle-path, as it led up from the ford; and then followed the long ascent, the bush-grown crest and stunted trees, and green-walled, winding way—miles of loneliness, with no human trace, save only the dim trail—until, amid a thick growth of larger bushes, I came upon an old, decayed, broken-down fence, so old that the very field it had once enclosed had become a part of the forest, lacking only the gnarled and shaggy patriarchs which mark the primeval wilderness.

Below and beyond ran a broader road, bearing marks of having once been worn with wheels, in the years before the war, but evidently long deserted. It wound round a hillside, and then up to a lonely field on a height, from which I had, at a short distance, a full view of the gigantic profile of the Grandfather. I had supposed that so near a view would distort or destroy the resemblance to human features. The smoothness, it is true, was gone, and every rock and tree stood out full and clear; but the grand outlines were still the same. A few scattering wreaths of vapor were playing about the summit, driven and tossed by the sweeping winds; but, save these, the air was beautifully clear.

The first impression was one of surprise at the seeming nearness, and then one of disappointment that the mountain did not appear higher; but, resting and gazing, and measuring with mind and eye, there gradually came over me a sense of its overwhelming vastness, and my own exceeding littleness.

But never mind; to-morrow, God willing, small as I am, I shall stand above, and look down upon all that vastness.

Another half hour's walk, and a buckwheat field on the left occupied a depression on the ridge, known as the Grandmother Gap. The summit, which looks down upon it from beyond, is called, from its position, and not from any human resemblance, the "Grandmother." A single deep, narrow valley lies between her and her nobler consort. Through this valley flows one of the headwaters of Lindville[8] River. On its grassy banks, and almost hidden in the laurel thickets, I found a house in process of reconstruction. It had once stood in a field, far up in the mountains, but the owner preferring the valley, had with great labor, transported the material to this place. The family in the mean time were encamped in a rude shanty, enclosed on three sides and covered. A mason was at work laying up the great stone chimney, with mortar of tempered clay. A boy of ten or twelve years was strutting round in a pair of new red-topped boots, evidently the first he ever possessed. Much delighted at being noticed, he bounded away to guide me over the brook and though a meadow thickly set with timothy, to a cool bower of closely tangled rhododendrons, where a clear spring of water trickled from the hillside and fell into a basin scooped in the rock.

Accustomed, below the mountains, to water at a temperature of about 60 degrees, I was almost startled at the icy coldness of this spring. But not alone in the temperature of springs is to be found the evidence that this region belongs to a climatic belt far different from that of the Atlantic slope. I observed, in particular, the spontaneous growth of the cultivated grasses, overrunning every spot of open ground on hillsides as well as in the valleys, in strong contrast with the bare or sedge-grown roadsides and old fields, which I had learned, from wide observation, to associate inseparably with every idea of North Carolina.

The "two-leaved" and "three-leaved" species of pine, which had also seemed to belong to all Carolina soil, were no longer to be seen; but their place was filled by the white pine and hemlock, which, though abounding upon the Atlantic side of the Blue Ridge, are confined to the mountains and their immediate foot-hills. But, instead of the tall and stately forms I had been accustomed to see, I found them short and stocky, shaggy with dead and broken boughs, and gray with lichens. This appearance was so striking, that one of my first questions was, "What is the matter with your hemlocks over here?" The reply was, "Cold weather and the winds."

That the climate is moist as well as cool, is evident from the great abundance and variety of mosses and lichens to be seen on every hand.

The day was so far spent that I could not climb to the summit of the Grandfather and return before night, though the huge rocky mass frowned down upon me, apparently but a half hour's walk distant. So I thankfully accepted a blanket and a place at Bill Estee's camp-fire, for the evening was cool, and gave promise of frost.

In the crisp frosty air and paling starlight of early morning I was astir, hoping to gain the summit in time to see the sun rise. For a mile, a good road, cut through a dense growth of forest trees and rhododendrons, led up a winding ascent to an open field, from whence I looked forward and around, and perceived that I stood upon the *throat* of the Grandfather, while the chin towered, bold and rugged, above the forest before me. Entering the woods by a faint cow-path, I pushed forward in the dim light. Sugar maples, with sap-troughs at their roots, carried back my thoughts to the dear old days of early childhood; the sugar-making, and the play-houses we children used to make, carpeted with great flakes of moss from old logs and trees; the bark shelves of our cupboards carefully ranged with acorn cups and hickory-nut hulls; the sap-trough lined with softest moss, a resting-place for sister's home-made "Dollie." Though my feet stepped onward, my heart went back till all the years of hope and joy, of toil and sorrow, passed into nothingness, and I was a child again, breathing the sweet breath of spring, with birds and bees and earliest peeping flowers for my companions.

Half unconsciously, I had followed the trail till it became dim and dimmer, and at last disappeared. I had now to depend upon instinct and careful observation to guide me, for the mountain-top was hidden from view by the dense growth of trees. Marking well my way, I went on, breaking here a bush, blazing there a small tree with my knife, scattering sprigs of laurel with the white under surface of the leaves upward— anything by which I might retrace my steps; for, though I might not be on the best or easiest way thither, the mountain-top was a great thing, and not easily missed; but the cow-path in the forest was a very little thing, and might be very hard to find, without a clue leading to it.

An open space, a glimpse of the summit, and a formidable-looking blackberry thicket confronted me, apparently girdling the mountain. Having learned to fear the terribly sharp strong claws of the middle Carolina blackberry, I hesitated and drew back; but seeing no alternative except a retreat, and not being ready for that, I boldly attacked the barrier. To my great surprise I found the canes almost thornless. I could even part them with my hands, and receive no hurt.

After the briers, came a belt of black spruce and balsam firs, with striped maple, mountain ash, and other trees and shrubs of northern growth. These bushes, huge, sloping fragments of rock, and a rugged cliff, rose abruptly before me. Hurrah! That must be the summit! Climbing eagerly up the bare, rough rock, lo! It was only a jutting prominence on the mountain side, while beyond was a fearfully rugged, tangled wilderness of rocks and bushes; a huge pyramidal mass rose half a thousand feet above me.

The sun had risen, and I was fatigued and sore with the part already passed. Would it pay to go through all that toil, just for a brief half hour on yonder pinnacle? I would rest awhile and look around me. What a glorious prospect! A wilderness of wooded mountains, with only here and there a small opening where some settler had laid bare the soil. In the southeast I could trace the course of the Catawba and its tributaries by the snow-white fog line, slowly rising and melting beneath the rays of the sun, into the golden haze which dimmed and mellowed all the eastern landscape.

Sweeping the wide horizon with eager eye, the view was shut in at a short distance by the mountains to the north. The greater elevation of that pyramid top would place me above those obstructions. At this thought fatigue vanished, and with a cooling draught from a hollow of the rock, and a hurried breakfast from my haversack, I was strong for the task before me.

Climbing huge fragments of rock, only to swing myself down on the other side, by clinging to boughs of trees; creeping under arched passages and overhanging ledges; crawling on all- fours through thickets of laurel, so dense I could not see the sky above me; and again clambering over the tops of bushes, so closely matted as to bear me entirely up from the ground; I became so fascinated with my success in mastering such difficulties, as to several times forget to mark the way. Then I would have to retrace my steps and bring up the clue.

I met with frequent indications that bears abound in these mountains; and once, in crawling through the laurels, placed my hand side by side with the fresh impress of a great heavy foot. It could not have been many hours since Bruin trod the same path I was following; but so long as he did not return to dispute my passage, the way would serve us both.

Reaching the foot of the pyramid, the descent became more easy, though steep as an angle of 45 degrees. Balsam firs succeeded the bushes; and the absence of undergrowth gave more freedom of movement. Ascending rapidly, I soon emerged upon a steep bare rock, with scarcely enough roughness of surface to afford a footing. Cautiously climbing upward, hands lending aid to feet, a little level spot was at length attained, in a sunny nook within twenty or thirty feet of the top. There in the scanty soil were blooming a group of prairie flowers—three species which are common upon the prairies of Iowa. It was like meeting with three familiar friends, unexpectedly, in a foreign land—one of those joyful surprises which so often await the botanist in his rambles in out of the way places.

Passing though a rocky wall, I stood upon the brink of a precipice, which went down so steep I almost fancied I could cast a stone to the middle of the valley which skirts the mountain on the north; the depth so great that the trees, dwarfed by the distance, seemed almost like mosses at the bottom.

The only living thing in sight was a solitary hawk, poised on out-spread wings, hanging motionless for a moment over the abyss, and then sailing swiftly and noiselessly away.

Not a sound came up from those far depths; not a cloud marred the spotlessness of the crystalline sky; not a breeze swayed the bushes growing from the rifts of rock; all was still as the grave. I looked round and saw, on every side, the marks of violence and storm, and wondered at the utter calm.

A good, firm, easy way I found to mount the last remaining rock, the coping of the pyramid. But behold! it was not a pyramid at all. It was the projecting chin bone of the Grandfather!

To the northeast I could trace the elevations and depressions which fill out the whole of the profile. The nose about a mile, and the brow almost two miles distant, appeared to be near a hundred feet higher than the chin. Leaning upon the sharp crest, long I stood to gaze upon the vast panorama spread out around and below me. Bounding the prospect in the far southwest, I could see the towering summits of the Black; while all around, like green, tossing billows, lay the wooded mountains, and expanse of almost unbroken forest from highest crests to deepest valleys.

The narrow, fertile valley of the Catawba, with its cultivated lands, and the broad upland farms of Burke county showed faintly under the golden haze of the south and east, while far away toward Tennessee, were to be seen several farms upon the mountain tops; a few smaller clearings here and there in the valleys or on the sides of the mountains; but aside from these, the appearance was that of a wild, uninhabitable country.

One long, lingering gaze upon the landscape of grandeur and beauty: one reluctant, sad and final adieu, and bending my eyes upon the traced pathway, I began the descent.

Three Characters:
1. Narrator
2. Professor of Mineralogy
3. Mr. Haney

Three Places:
1. Warm Springs
2. Marshall
3. Mt. Mitchell

Three Events:
1. Arguing for food
2. No Hotel
3. Meeting up w/ Yankees + Mr. Glass

Three Ideas:
1. Flora + Fawna
2. Yankees buying out post-war desperation
3. Inconsistency of information

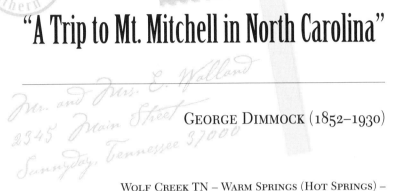

"A Trip to Mt. Mitchell in North Carolina"

GEORGE DIMMOCK (1852–1930)

WOLF CREEK TN – WARM SPRINGS (HOT SPRINGS) –
MARSHALL -ASHEVILLE – NORTH FORK
(SWANNANOA) VALLEY – MT. MITCHELL NC

George Dimmock was an active and long-standing member of the Boston-based Appalachian Mountain Club, which was founded in 1876 and later played an important role in developing the Appalachian National Scenic Trail. The club is still responsible for maintaining the "hut system" along the trail in the White Mountains, and in 2002 the group claimed more than ninety thousand active members. (See Introduction for more on the history of the AMC.) Early members of the club were mainly middle-class, educated, and urban. Like other AMC members hiking in the southern mountains at the time, Dimmock frames many of his observations on the southern Appalachians in terms of comparison with the White and Green Mountains of the northeast. Likewise, he compares the inhabitants of the region to the industrious Yankees of the northeast—and he is consistently disappointed. As Dimmock writes here, "that spirit of exploration, of appreciation of beauty in scenery, and of wonders in nature, and the active enthusiasm and love of travel which stimulates people in the North to form such associations as the Appalachian Club, and to explore their own vicinity, does not appear to exist in the South."

Appalachia, June 1877.

Dimmock writes from the point of view not only of an impatient Yankee but also of a budding scientist. In 1876, at the time he made the journey related in the present selection, Dimmock was finishing his A.B. at Harvard with honors in natural history. He would go on to become a noted entomologist. (His Ph.D. thesis, completed in 1881, was entitled "The Anatomy of the Mouth-parts and of the Sucking Apparatus of Some Diptera.") He later specialized in studying larval stages, a baffling topic for entomologists at the time. Among other accomplishments, he developed a method of bleaching the wings of lepidoptera known as the "Dimmock process," which prepares the specimens for study.

Read Feb. 14, 1877

As the White Mountains form an irregular knot of high peaks near the northern end of the Appalachian mountain system, so the Black Mountains, near its southern extremity, are in a cluster of not much less complicity. This Black Mountain group contains several of the highest mountains in the whole Appalachian system, and although my subject as announced limits me to a consideration of the highest one of these mountains, properly called Mitchell's Peak,[1] yet I wish to start with you to that mountain from the boundary line of Tennessee and North Carolina, where the railroad ends in that direction, and to leave you again at a railway station east of the mountains, in order that I may give you, first a general idea of the mountainous portion of western North Carolina, a region no less beautiful than the White Mountains, and secondly that I may explain how to get to Mt. Mitchell through a region where not one person in ten can tell anything about the roads which are more than a dozen miles from his own home.

The last station at the southern end of the Cincinnati, Cumberland Gap and Charleston Railroad, so far as it is at present completed, is Wolf Creek.[2] This is nearly on the boundary between Tennessee and North Carolina. The station has no companion-buildings within a radius of half a mile, and, at the end of a railroad, the time-table rate of which was four hours for a distance of forty miles (i.e., from Morristown, Tenn.), one feels a sense of loneliness as he takes a parting look from the stage window at rickety locomotive.

This was the fourth of last August. A professor of mineralogy from Pennsylvania was to be my companion a part of the way. We took dinner at a little hotel about three quarters of a mile from the station, and then went on by stage to Warm Springs,[3] a favorite summer resort for southern people. We were now fairly in the mountainous region, the flat valley of the French Broad River had been left behind, and, from the comparatively level strata of the rocks of eastern Tennessee, we had plunged into a turbulent sea of azoic formations.[4] The mountains about us were irregular in position and in structure. Between Warm Springs and Wolf Creek the French Broad river breaks through the Alleghany Mountains, which are called Smoky Mountains on the south and Bald Mountains on the north of the river.

Warm Springs consists chiefly of a large hotel,[5] where, as is usual at hotels in that part of the South, good meals are served. The springs, from which the place takes its name, are of a temperature of about 40° Centigrade, contain sulphur and are used for bathing. They spring up from the very edge of the river and even under its waters. Near the hotel are chalybeats[6] and other springs.

After spending the night and a part of the next day at Warm Springs, we started on the road to Marshall. We walked on all the afternoon, failing to secure any dinner, for the poor whites living along this road had either sold their corn for whiskey, as is customary with them, and would have no more till the new crop was harvested, or else they were ill-disposed to strangers. The latter supposition seemed less probable, for one can purchase a meal at almost any house in the South. We finally obtained a scanty supper at a log cabin, after its occupants had once refused to furnish us any, by asking about the mineral resources of the region, and talking mineralogy with them a little while. Upon the subject of precious minerals almost all the poor whites are monomaniacs. One of them will often have a few crystals of pyrites carefully wrapped up in a rag. He will slyly let you look at it and then tell you that he "reckons he can tell whar there's heaps on't," but never tells.

But if we could not feast our stomachs with corn-cakes,—or pones, as they are there called,—the standard food in that region, we could feast our eyes on the beautiful scenery which we passed.

The French Broad, here a stream of a hundred or two metres in breadth, dashed along between steep hills, often leaving little room for the road, and at every turn in the path some new combination-scene of the tree-clothed hills with the rushing torrent below surprised our eyes.

At a closer view there was little in the vegetation that differed strikingly from that of New England hills, except here and there one of the Magnoliaceae, a buckeye, a persimmon tree, or a chinquepin bush.[7]

Occasionally the little skinks and swifts, kinds of lizards, would rattle off through the brush, much in the same way and about as quickly as a striped squirrel dashes to its hole in the New England woods. The swift, a little striped lizard, is, by a strange perversion of language, called a "scorpion" in Virginia, Kentucky, Tennessee, and North Carolina, and its bite is greatly dreaded, while the skink, with sharper teeth and stronger jaws, is thought to be harmless.

When we arrived at Marshall, which is sixteen miles from Warm Springs, a new difficulty awaited us. It was about eleven o'clock at night and nearly every one had gone to bed. We were directed finally to the hotel, which was, to all appearances, a dwelling house. To it we went. Upon rapping, the gruff-looking proprietor put his head out of an up-stairs window. He evidently did not care for business, since he persist-ently denied that his house was the hotel. We afterwards learned however that it was. Fortunately we soon found a place to stop with Mr. Haney, keeper of the principal store in the village, and after we had made his acquaintance and learned how familiar he was with the vicinity, we did not lament being turned away from what proved to be a third class hotel, although the only one in the place. I would recommend any members of the Appalachian Club, who may be travelling in this region, to make the acquaintance of Mr. Haney and also of Dr. Hardwick, in Marshall. Both are intelligent men, know well the points of interest in the vicinity, and have no axe of their own to grind.

As my friend the professor could not go further with me, we spent a few days about Marshall, in search of mineralogical and entomological specimens. The whole country around Marshall, for about fifteen miles, is elevated, descending to the river and creeks by steep banks. Magnetite and other iron ores are abundant, but there are of course no coal-beds near, and no railroad within twenty-four miles, so the iron deposits are not at present of much value. Corundum[8] of good quality is found within a few miles of Marshall. The village itself has only a few hundred inhabitants.

At Marshall I hired the best team that could be obtained, and a driver, to go with me to Mt. Mitchell; and parted from my companion, the mineralogist. Such a team as I secured could scarcely be found in Massachusetts, and if it could, the Society for the Prevention of Cruelty to Animals would make an example of it. All one forenoon was required to get it in order, and when in order it went about four miles an hour. A suggestion to take some ropes along for repairs was scorned by my driver, yet the harness broke four times before night. Finally I camped at night about two miles west of Asheville, beside the road. The next morning I entered the town.

The road from Warm Springs to Asheville was seriously out of repair, because of a flood which had swept down the French Broad a few months before. The rest of our route to the base of Mt. Mitchell was not so difficult as the part we had gone over.

Asheville is one of the largest towns of western North Carolina, having 1500 to 2000 inhabitants, and supporting two newspapers. The town is only about thirty miles from the top of Mt. Mitchell, yet few of its inhabitants had ever been to the summit.

That spirit of exploration, of appreciation of beauty in scenery, and of wonders in nature, and the active enthusiasm and love of travel which stimulates people in the North to form such associations as the Appalachian Club, and to explore their own vicinity, does not appear to exist in the South. Many people who have lived their whole lives within fifteen miles of Mt. Mitchell never have visited its summit, and have no desire to do so.

At Asheville, which is about two thousand feet above the level of the sea, the valley of the French Broad widens and the town is surrounded by undulating farming land of good quality. The town itself is a very thriving one; has good buildings, and shows evidence of business prosperity. Pretty residences with neatly kept grounds and well repaired fences distinguish it from many other southern towns of about the same size.

Just above Asheville the French Broad is joined by Swananoa[9] Creek, a large mountain stream, beside which the road to the east goes for some distance.

Up this creek the scenery is again charming, alternating outspread valleys with narrow passes, and interspersing, now and then, little waterfalls in the creek.

The vegetation along this part of the Swananoa is similar to that of any New England Forest, but of a luxuriant growth. Just beyond Alexander's, a hotel twelve miles to the east of Asheville, we had to turn from the main road to the left. Soon we were in the entrance of that grand valley which extends up to the base of the highest peaks of the Black Mountains. Looking up towards its head the picture was similar to what it would be if one looked up an enlarged Tuckerman's ravine,[10] and the mountains about it had been clothed with trees to their very summits. The name Black Mountains, was given to these peaks because of the darkness of their summits as seen from a distance, with their heavy balsam forests.

On each side of the Swananoa valley the mountains grow higher, while the creek dwindles in size as we pass by one after another of its many little feeders. In this valley rains are numerous, and I was twice wet through during the day. At night I slept in a barn. The next morning, after going about a mile further, our horse showing signs of approaching dissolution, my driver engaged a mule to carry our baggage, and a colored boy to drive the mule. Pasturing the wreck of a horse which had brought us thus far, we packed the mule and started onward. Soon we reached the last house at the base of the mountain; the summit of Mitchell's Peak was still ten miles distant. Beyond the house there is nothing but a bridle path.

It was here that I first tried to ride a mule, and that under difficulty. The mule was not stubborn, in fact was as tractable as any animal could be, but the road was rough and often barricaded with trunks of fallen trees over which he had to step. I have often wished for my picture as I sat on that mule. I may have looked anxious as I trusted myself to the strange beast. Behind me was a large pack, and over it extended from my shoulders a rubber blanket, for it rained now and then. In one hand I grasped a frying pan and an umbrella, in the other the reins and a whip. A white slouched hat completed the picture.

At the base of the mountain the *Rhododendron maximum* was one of the striking features of the scenery. The large leaves of this Rhododendron are from eight to ten inches long, of a dark green, and hang downward around the tips of the twigs. How beautiful the trees must look when in full bloom, with their showy white flowers, for they often attain twenty feet in height!

Further up the mountain side the forest is of large trees, similar to those along the first two miles of the carriage road from the Glen House to the summit of Mount Washington. This kind of forest extends without much change up to the crest of Black Mountain, a height of perhaps five thousand feet. Here the forest changes, and the spruces, which are found up to the summits of all the Black Mountains suddenly appear.

Springs and running streams are not so numerous along the path as they are along the roads in the White Mountains, with which I so often compare the Black Mountains, presuming a greater familiarity with the former mountains than with the latter.

The source of the Swananoa is near the lower part of the mountain, beside the bridle-path. We saw no more springs until we reached the Black Mountain House,[11] several miles further on.

At this mountain house we overtook a party of ladies and gentlemen belonging to two families, by the name of Huey, from Hendersonville, N.C., a town to the south of Asheville. They were travelling with their own horses, and had hired one of the best guides to the mountain, Mr. Glass, to take their baggage on a pack-mule. Availing myself of this opportunity, I hired Mr. Glass to add my baggage to the load of his already heavily laden mule, and dismissed my driver and his mule. The young man whom I hired at Marshall wished to see the summit, so he continued on with us. The party which I joined at the Black Mountain House was made up of intelligent northern people, who had bought plantations in North Carolina since the war. Two of the ladies were interested in botany, and the rest of the trip was pleasanter on account of good company.

We lunched at the Black Mountain House, and then pushed on along the ridge, following the tortuous bridle path amongst wet spruces and gooseberry bushes,[12]—a queer vegetable combination,—for two and a half miles to Clingman's Peak. Hon. T. L. Clingman, a prominent North Carolinian, supposed for a time that he had discovered the highest of the Black Mountains, but afterwards Prof. Mitchell, of whom I shall have more to say later, was found to have discovered the highest peak, which all North Carolina people call Mitchell's Peak. Many of the published maps still call the highest point Clingman's Peak, although it is said that Mr. Clingman afterwards acknowledged that he was mistaken. I have adhered in my usage, as far as possible, to the names in common use in the vicinity of the mountains.

No good view can be obtained from Clingman's Peak on account of the trees, and, up to this time, the summit of Mt. Mitchell has not been in sight. Going down the bridle path, a little to the left of the ridge which extends from Clingman's to Mitchell's Peak, the summit soon comes in view; the pole erected upon it can be indistinctly seen in the cloudy haze. It is still two and a half miles distant, miles of rough and muddy path.

We were not long in getting over the two and a half miles of mire, for we had become more reckless as our goal came in view. Climbing a little knoll we were at the summit of Mitchell's Peak, the highest point in North America east of the Mississippi River.

But how high we were I am not certain, for there are many conflicting statements concerning the height of the different mountains of this group. Dr. Mitchell first determined the height in 1835 as 6476 feet; in 1844 he obtained a result of 6672 feet. In 1855 Mr. Clingman called it 6941 feet. In 1856 Prof. Guyot determined the height to be 6760 feet; the next year he made it 6701 feet. The map compiled by the United States Coast Survey, for the use of the army during the war, gives the height as 6711 feet. It is, however, evident from the measurements of Professor Guyot in 1857, that there are twelve peaks of the Black Mountains which exceed Mount Washington in height.

At the summit a visitor's attention is first attracted to a rectangular enclosure, of about ten feet by four, surrounded by a rude stone wall about a foot high. This marks the grave of Professor Elisha Mitchell, the supposed discoverer of the peak, who died while attempting to prove that it was this peak, and no other, which he had previously visited.

Professor Mitchell was a graduate of Yale college, of the class of 1813, afterwards a tutor at Yale. Finally, in 1818, he became a professor in the University of North Carolina, at Chapel Hill. Being a great admirer of nature, and a scientific student, he visited the Black Mountain, afterwards called Mount Mitchell, in 1835, then in 1838, in 1844, and in 1856.

On the 27th of June 1857, while attempting to descend the mountain on the north-west side, he was detained by a thunder storm till evening, and, as he was groping his way down the mountain, he pitched headlong over a precipice of some forty feet in height, and into a pool of water at its base, where on the 8th of July he was found. He was first buried at Asheville, but on June 14, 1858, his remains were removed, and reinterred on the summit of the peak,—which was then named after him,—with impressive ceremonies, participated in by the governor of the state, the officers and students of the state university, and a large assembly of North Carolina's most honored citizens. The land at the summit of the mountain was then presented to the trustees of the University of North Carolina. There amid the scenes he loved so well was placed all that remained of the discoverer of that noble mountain.

While I do not wish to enter into disputes concerning mountain nomenclature, I must here record my opinion that it was this peak, the highest of the Black Mountains, and no other, which was discovered by the man whose remains were buried in so fitting a grave at its summit, a grave, higher up, perhaps, than any other in the United States. My opinion that this is the peak Mitchell discovered is based on what I could learn among the mountains; from Mr. Glass, whose father helped in the search for Professor Mitchell's remains; from other guides, and from what I can find in the literature of the subject.

When we arrived at the summit it was almost evening, according to the northern use of the word; for "evening" at the South means between noon and sunset, while after sunset it is "night."

Notwithstanding the late hour, we succeeded in getting a view now and then of the surrounding mountains, for the rain, which had kept us so uncomfortable during our ascent, had now ceased. North of us extended a line of mountains almost as high as Mitchell itself. Around us, without much apparent system, were scattered peaks, all of considerable height, while far below, to the south, when the clouds broke away sufficiently, we could see the winding Swananoa, a string of pearls in the deep green forest. About us on the summit were trees and shrubs, similar in general appearance to those which one finds about half a mile below the upper limit of the trees on Mount Washington.

A few of the species of plants which I recognized as very common at the summit were, *Abies Frazeri*, Frazer's spruce; *Rumex acetosella*, dock sorrel; *Oxalis acetosella,* sorrel; *Sambucus pubens*, red-berried elder; *Cuscuta rostrata*; *Houstonia serpyllifolia*, a kind of bluets; *Impatiens pallida*, touch-me-not; *Rhododendron catawbiense*, *Saxifraga leucanthemifolia*, and species of *Rubus*, *Pyrus*, *Solidago*, *Prunus*, *Aster*, mosses and grasses. Butterflies, gay Papilios among them, flitted now and then about the flowers. The climate and the surroundings at the summit of Mount Mitchell, reminded me more of a camp half way up Mt. Washington than of one at its summit.

There is a log cabin and a shelving cave within a few rods of the summit, but, disdaining such civilized accommodations, I swung my hammock between two slender trees and enjoyed a night's rest rocked by the breezes.

The next morning I spent in viewing the scenery of the mountain summit, in analyzing plants and in catching insects. At noon I started down, arriving at Mr. Glass's house at four o'clock in the afternoon. The rest of the party who preceded me had already arrived, and the gentlemen were trout-fishing in the streams near at hand. The next morning, having accepted the kind proposal to ride back to Asheville with my new friends from Hendersonville, I paid and discharged my driver, who had succeeded so poorly in his contract to get me from Marshall to the summit of Mount Mitchell.

The Huey family had a carriage and spirited horses, and we easily reached Asheville that afternoon. The next day I took the stage to Henry's station, on the nearest railroad. Between Asheville and Henry's Station the highway passes over the Blue Ridge, at Swananoa Gap. At this gap a railroad to Asheville, finally to connect the Western North Carolina Railroad with the Cincinnati, Cumberland Gap and Charleston Railroad, is in progress, and at the crest of the Blue Ridge a temporary state-prison is located, its occupants being engaged in making a tunnel of seven hundred feet in length through the top of the mountain. When this railroad is completed, it will pass through some of the finest scenery in eastern America. To the east of the ridge, where the road bed is already finished, it writhes about like a snake to gain the elevation of the tunnel.

Henry's Station is but a few miles to the east of the crest of the Blue Ridge. The village consists of a poor hotel, a railroad station, and a few liquor saloons. On account of its natural surroundings, it is a place where one who admires beautiful scenery might wish to tarry, but man has so well succeeded in making the place itself repulsive, that I was glad to get out of it.

Having thus hurried you across the mountainous region of North Carolina in the way that I was hurried across it (for I was obliged to be at Charleston, South Carolina, at a particular time), I will briefly sketch out how to get to Mount Mitchell easily, hoping that a few, at least, of the members of the Appalachian Club may at some time profit from my hasty trip, on which I learned *how* to go to the Black Mountains.

From the east—assuming that the published railway guides give sufficient information in regard to getting to Henry's Station—the trip is short and easy. A daily stage runs from Henry's Station to Alexander's Hotel, near the place where the Swananoa Valley road leaves the main road. The entire route from Wolf Creek, on the Tennessee and North Carolina state line, to Alexander's, can be travelled by stage, and the scenery on the way is charming, but the roads are very bad, and it therefore takes longer than it does to go from the east. The expenses in going from Wolf Creek to Alexander's would be from six to ten dollars; from Henry's to Alexander's about two dollars.

The cheapest and most convenient way of getting transportation from Alexander's to the base of the mountain is to send a letter ahead to one of the guides, and have him meet you with a team at Alexander's. The cost of transportation is thus reduced to about two dollars for each person. At the base of the mountain a guide can be obtained for two days, with a horse or a mule, for packing or for riding, by paying five dollars. This gives one an opportunity to spend a night and part of the next day on the summit of Mount Mitchell.

To get to Henry's Station from Boston by rail, costs about forty dollars. The fare by rail from Boston to Wolf Creek would be about sixty dollars.

From the above general estimates one may get an idea of the cost of going to the mountain region of Western North Carolina, a region where living is much less expensive and the climate healthier, even during the summer, than at the White Mountains.

Three People:
1. The Narrator
2. Sam Walker
3. Bill Walker

Three Places:
1. Maryville
2. Chillhowee Gap
3. thunderhead Peak

Three Events:
1. The rest in the meadow
2. The thunderstorm
3.

Three Ideas:
1. Analogies w/ other mountain ranges
2. Backwardness - Hogs in the Street
3. Foooood

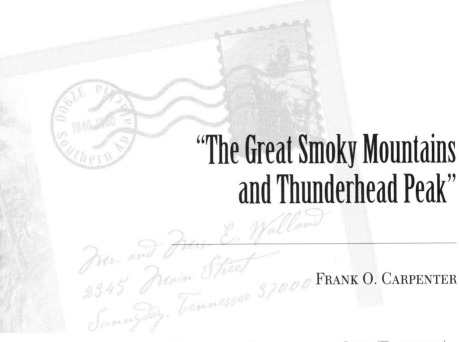

"The Great Smoky Mountains and Thunderhead Peak"

FRANK O. CARPENTER

MARYVILLE – TUCKALEECHEE COVE (TOWNSEND) –
THUNDERHEAD MOUNTAIN (GREAT SMOKY
MOUNTAINS NATIONAL PARK) TN/NC

F rank O. Carpenter was a teacher at the English High School in
Boston in the 1880s and 1890s. At the time of his hike into the
Smokies, he was also Councillor of Explorations for the Appalachian Mountain Club. Founded in 1876, the AMC later played an
important role in developing the Appalachian National Scenic Trail,
and is still responsible for maintaining the "hut system" along the
trail in the White Mountains. (See Introduction for more on the
history of the AMC.)

In 1897, eight years after the hike described in the present
selection, Carpenter co-founded the North Woodstock Improvement Association. With that group he helped to develop hiking
trails in the upper Pemigawasset Valley, in the area of New Hampshire's White Mountains south of Franconia Notch, Profile Lake,
and the Great Stone Face. He explored all the existing trails in the
upper Pemigawasset and produced a guidebook (1898), though
much of his work from that period was subsequently wiped out
when the watershed was heavily logged in the early twentieth
century (Waterman and Waterman 231).

Appalachia, December 1890.

Read Nov. 11, 1889

A massive chain of lofty mountains, two hundred miles long, forms the western boundary of the State of North Carolina. Known generically as the Smoky Mountains, it is nevertheless divided by deep river-gorges into five sections, each of which has its separate name. The most northerly of these is called the Stone Mountains; then follow the Iron, Bald, Great Smoky, and Unaka Ranges, of which the Great Smoky Mountains form the culmination. From the picturesque gap through which flows the French Broad River on the north to the narrow gorge where the Little Tennessee pours the waters of five counties through a gateway only eighty-five feet wide, the mighty wall extends for a distance of sixty-five miles, unbroken except in one place by the valley of the Big Pigeon.[1] Nineteen

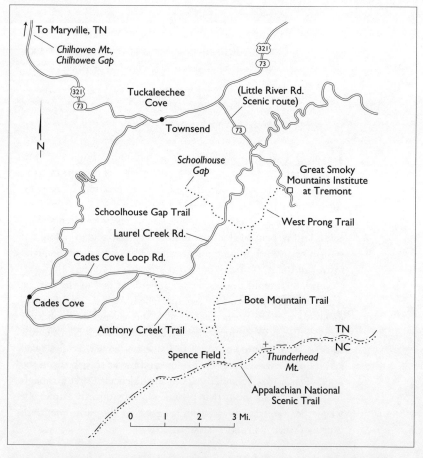

MARYVILLE – TUCKALEECHEE COVE (TOWNSEND) – THUNDERHEAD MOUNTAIN (GREAT SMOKY MOUNTAINS NATIONAL PARK) TN. ROUTE OF FRANK O. CARPENTER, 1888.

peaks over 6,000 feet, including (the highest) Clingman's Dome, 6,660 feet, Mt. Guyot, 6,636 feet, and fourteen more over 5,600 feet in altitude, connected by massive ridges and interspersed with peaks only a little lower than those mentioned, make a remarkable group of mountains.

A comparison may assist those familiar with the Presidential Range in the White Mountains. Imagine a range of mountains extending from Gorham to Plymouth containing a dozen peaks higher by several hundred feet than Mt. Washington, and twenty others as high as Mt. Adams, with many lesser spurs and ridges as high as Mt. Lafayette. This gives a fair idea of the Great Smoky Range.

In a few places, far apart, the old Indian trails have been made passable for wagons; but these roads cross the range through gaps at high elevations, never less than 5,000 feet, by long and difficult routes. Winding roads also follow the rivers through the deep narrow gaps, sometimes hardly wide enough for a road to find place between the mountain and river. Save for these slender bonds of communication, the people of North Carolina and Tennessee are separated by many leagues of unbroken forest and rugged mountain ridge.

The mountains are entirely wooded, except on a few summits, called "balds,"[2] where the treeless tracts are covered with luxuriant grass and patches of bushes breast-high.

Toward the southern end of the range stands a peak, the last of special prominence, known as "Thunderhead."[3] Stern and impressive, it lifts its giant head. Around it continually hover the great clouds, while the lightning flashes from it, and the thunder rolls and echoes about it as though it were the judgment-seat of mighty Jove himself.

During the past summer it was the good fortune of the writer to climb Thunderhead and to traverse a part of the range; and he submits to the Club the following account of his trip as germane to his duties as Councillor of Exploration.

Maryville, the county-seat of Blount County, Tennessee, is the most convenient starting-place for one who wishes to visit the most picturesque summits of the Great Smoky Range. Charleston is the nearest point on the Carolina side, but it requires an extra day's journey, at greater expense, to reach that place. Maryville is sixteen miles south of Knoxville, and is the present terminus of the Knoxville and Charleston Railroad. At Knoxville connections can be made with railroads running north, south, and west.

Maryville is a prosperous country town, of about 1,200 inhabitants. It has several churches, a court-house, two small colleges, and perhaps twenty stores, at which can be procured supplies needed for a camping-trip. These supplies must be carried, for the people in the mountain districts can only furnish corn meal and bacon. Several flour and saw mills do a good business; but somewhat of the old-time sleepiness still prevails, and the town is quiet as on a holiday. One characteristic sight is novel to a Northern eye. Scores of thin, fierce-looking, but mild-mannered hogs, of all sizes, run freely about the streets, sleep peacefully on the sidewalks or in the gutters, or move slowly with reproachful grunt out of the way of the passer. Pleasant views are obtained from several knolls near the centre of the town, from one of which the "Smokies" may be seen thirty miles distant beyond the high foot-hills of the Chilhowee Range. Maryville is a favorite stopping-place of Miss Murfree ("Charles Egbert Craddock"), and several of her stories have been written there,—"In the Clouds," "Thunderhead," etc. Mr. James Wilson, Surveyor, has an intimate acquaintance with the mountain region, and is most cordial and kindly to the visitor seeking information. One old building, a hotel,[4] once a famous resort, is very picturesque. It was built with wide double verandas, in the Southern style. Large pillars, three feet in diameter, made of laths covered with plaster, rise to the roof. The passing years have dealt hardly with the old hostelry. The great columns have lost their plaster here and there, the stucco walls are broken, while a wagon and blacksmith shop occupy the ground-floor, and send their echoes through the rooms once thronged with beautiful women and brave men. But as if mindful of its former glories, the old building holds itself erect and stately, like an old planter ruined by the war, still dignified and courtly in his threadbare clothes.

We reached Maryville Wednesday evening, July 24, 1889, and stopped at the Jackson House[5] (rates, $2.00 per day), a fairly comfortable hotel on the main street next to the old hotel just mentioned.

Thursday was rainy, and we made a few purchases and waited for the last letters before setting out for the woods. Friday was threatening, but we decided to start for a point at the base of the range where we could begin our ascent as soon as the weather should be favorable. At ten A.M. we were off, in a two-seated carryall, our destination being "Jake Freshour's" in Tuckaleeche Cove, twenty-five miles distant, where we expected to pass the night and get a guide. A "cove" is a valley that lies between two mountain ridges, generally ending in a point like a cove on the sea-shore.

The road from Maryville[6] is generally good, but the heavy rains of a month had made many washouts, and frequently the road made a sharp curve towards the high bank around some pools of red mud whose depth and tenacity no one seemed willing to test. The scenery along the way for the first five miles was pleasant, and on a bright day would be delightful. The red earth makes the abundant foliage seem brighter, and the changing views of hill and dale are attractive. Tall cornfields waved their plumes and rustled a greeting to us. Once the plump ears tempted us, and we picked a number, and ate them raw as we rode along. The kernels were just "in the milk," and were juicy and sweet as stolen fruit should be.

A short distance farther on, we reached Little River, which we followed the rest of our way, crossing it by fording several times. As we advanced, the scenery began to lose its New England appearance: Log-houses appeared, with a broad chimney at the end made of sticks and mud, the roof projecting in front to form a veranda roof. Sometimes we saw fastened to the shore a "dugout"[7] so long that it seemed as if it could reach the opposite bank if swung across the current. Several times the road crossed the stream by a ford so deep that the water came into the carryall as we jolted over the stony bottom.

About ten miles from Maryville we entered Chilhowee Gap. The Little River, which rises in the Smokies, has cut a passage for itself directly though the Chilhowee Range to a depth of a thousand feet below the summit. The scenery through the gap is of wonderful beauty, and the ride surpasses any the writer has enjoyed in New England. The road wound about the spurs on a narrow terrace high above the stream, while through the trees we caught many a glimpse of steep wooded slopes rising abruptly from the roaring stream, sometimes several hundred feet below us. It being daytime, we caught no sight of the "Harnt that walks Chilhowee."[8]

Beyond the gap, the road passed though several secluded valleys shut in on all sides by high ridges, and at last we came to Tuckaleeche Cove.[9] For several miles the river runs quietly along, a fertile intervale on one side, and on the other a rocky bluff in which are numerous caves which we were tempted to stop and explore. Some of them were used in war-times for hiding-places by the loyal Union farmers during rebel raids. We saluted one old man with a "Howdy" as we passed. Our driver told us it was Sam Walker, an old moonshiner whose daring defiance of the law had gained for him the title of "King of the Mountains."[10] We passed the "Tuckaleech" settlement, consisting of a small store, a church, and two or three houses a half mile apart, and reached Freshour's at four o'clock in the afternoon. Mr. Freshour is a well-to-do farmer, and very kindly; but owing to the illness of his wife, he could not keep us over night, and we decided to push on to the house of Bill Walker, the best guide in the section. After a hastily prepared supper of fried chicken, warm biscuit, and honey, we hurried on, following the directions of Mr. Freshour, who escorted us a short distance. We crossed Little River on the edge of an old mill-dam, and pushed on as fast as possible up stream. But the twilight was short, and soon it became evident that the narrow, indistinct path could not be followed in the dark. We found shelter for the night at the house of Mr. Myers beside the river, and wearied by the long, hard ride of the day, slept soundly in Myers's best bed, lulled to sleep by the murmur of the water, and the cry of a locust who had outlived all his fellows.

In the morning we paid the modest sum of twenty-five cents apiece for lodging and breakfast, and went on our way. Again we crossed the stream on a log-bridge and came to another cabin where a tall man was leaning idly against the door. "Howdy?" was his salute, to which we responded, "Howdy?" "What might your name be, stranger?" he asked. Repressing a desire to tell him it might be Smith but wasn't, we told him and asked his. "Myers," was the answer. We talked a moment, and went on. A quarter of a mile beyond, an old lady came from her cabin to see us. She was a Myers. A mile beyond, another Myers gave us a drink; and his brother was just beyond; while the barefooted woman who cooked for Walker, and Walker's son-in-law were named Myers.

The path to Walker's is only a mountain trail, zigzagging from side to side of the stream, and sometimes requiring careful attention to tell where it crosses on some fallen tree-trunk and threads its way among the thickets. There for the first time we saw the tangle of rhododendron which is called "laurel," and forms a dense thicket along all the mountain streams.

We reached Walker's at eleven o'clock,—a rude log-cabin at the highest point of the cove, situated on a high bank above the reach of floods. It is surrounded by a tiny farm of a few acres, with the forest within two hundred feet of the house. We found the guide at home. "Bill Walker," "Black Bill," and "Smoky Mountain Bill"[11] are the names by which he is usually known. He wears a large, bushy black beard, which gives him at first a rather fierce appearance; but he has a very large, warm, faithful heart. We stated our wish to engage him as guide for our trip. After some discussion and hesitation on account of some farm-work that was urgent, he consented to go. The afternoon was spent in preparations and in listening to stories of the mountains, among which it was interesting to find several showing a firm belief in the power of some persons to take on the form of animals for the purpose of injuring others, exactly like the European belief in werewolves. At nightfall we ate our supper of bacon, corn-pone, and honey, and after watching the stars through the wide cracks in the roof, we fell asleep.

The next morning the party started at eight o'clock for the summit of Thunderhead. It is not in sight from Walker's cabin, being eight miles distant behind the high, nameless foothills. Walker led; the writer came second, F—— third, and a young man named Stinnett[12] brought up the rear. We crossed the Little River, then traversed a steep, sloping field, and entered the woods. Two steep ridges were crossed before we reached the main slope of the "Smoky Mount'in." Many years ago a road was surveyed[13] and partly graded towards the top of Thunderhead, but it was given up. The storms have done their best to efface it; but there still remains a terrace, making a fairly easy path for several miles. We came upon this about half-way up, and followed it as far as it went.

The day was very hot. The sun seemed to exult in his release from his cloud prison, and shot at us his fierce rays, which the cucumber-trees[14] with their broad umbrellas of leaves tried in vain to ward off. Water was scarce; only twice in the eight miles did we find any. The Tennessee side of the Smokies, though entirely covered with forests, is rather barren and rocky, as compared with the Carolina side, which abounds in streams flowing beneath a luxuriant forest growth.

At the second spring we stopped for lunch. A fire was started, and the pone put to bake on a wide chip. Pone is the common food of the mountaineers. Corn meal is stirred up with water and a little salt, and the solid mass is put to bake, or rather to dry, on a board by the fire. When done, it is the most solid food imaginable. Sometimes, to make it more palatable and digestible (?), it is baked in the fat left after the bacon is fried. Sad experience teaches the necessity of becoming "acclimated" to this food before starting on a mountain trip in the south.

After lunch we climbed on, soon reaching the crest of the ridge, which we followed. Occasionally a welcome breeze fanned our faces; and beyond a great ravine, rose the dark summit of Thunderhead. We reached the end of the road, and then followed a stony trail through the rhododendron bushes, which rose far above our heads. A few late clusters of blossoms remained, some of which we gathered and carried for a while. Steadily, but rather slowly, we climbed up, for the air in the narrow path under the tangled laurel was very hot and enervating. About three o'clock we came to the open pasture on the top of the ridge,[15] and with delight threw ourselves down to rest, 5,000 feet above the sea. Hundreds of cattle, horses, sheep, and hogs roam at will during the summer over the ridges, which afford the finest grass for grazing, and grow fat without further care or attention than the occasional visits of the herdsman to "salt" them. Those on the summit came charging down upon us, led by curiosity and desire for salt, but soon returned to their grazing. The ridge where we were was shaped like an enormous saddle, and the light fresh green of the grass like a saddle-cloth extending a hundred rods down to the dark green forests increased the resemblance.

The view was inspiring. Though clouds still veiled many of the farther peaks, yet the ridges and peaks rose across great ravines in an endless array as far as the eye could follow. Infinite were the gradations of color,—from the black summits where it still rained, through violet, purple, and gray, mingling and blending with the harmonious browns and greens of the foliage, under the touch of the Master Artist. Towards the west the sunshine wrapped the mountains in mantles of golden mist set with turquoise and opal and pearl.

At last we reluctantly took up our packs, for our camping-place was several miles distant, and followed a herder's path along the ridge. One lonely little cabin stood a few rods down the slope, used by the herdsmen in charge of the cattle on the range. The herder came to the door, and shouted a few indistinguishable words. We shouted and waved our hands in answer, and hurried on. Twenty minutes' walk brought us to a rock on the highest summit of Thunderhead, 5,520 feet high, where we stopped a few minutes to rest, and watch the great ridges as they grew dark, while the deep shadows climbed out of the ravines.

The view from the summit is a very far-reaching and impressive one. In every direction great ridges with noble peaks rise successively till the eye wearies from trying to follow them in their varied changes. To the south the Warrior Bald of the Nantchalach[16] Range rises behind the intervening foot-hills. Northward stretches the main line of the Smokies, with its scores of lofty peaks. Clingman's Dome is in the near foreground, ten miles away. Toward the east the dark-green summits of the Balsam Range shut off the view beyond several great ravines and valleys. West over the summits of the Chilhowee Range lying close at hand the Cumberland Mountains of Tennessee crowd the horizon line, and blend with the blue and the clouds. Picturesque rocky summits like those of New England are missing from the view; but the strong, rugged ridges, deep ravines, and majestic peaks, all covered with a mantle of green and brown in infinite gradations of light and shade, make a view the beauty and grandeur of which will long be remembered.

As we left the peak, the almost omnipresent thunder growled in menace. A mile north of the peak we came upon a brook nearly on the summit of the ridge where we planned to camp. Soon we had a fire kindled, for we found plenty of wood. Some bark from a few trees that would peel, made a camp for shelter against the storm which drew closer and darker every minute. The coffee was made, the pone baked and eaten (though the writer's appetite for it was soon satisfied), the fire piled with wood, and we lay down to sleep a little, if possible, before the rain should come. A few hours we slept restlessly, while the distant thunder echoed among the hills.

About midnight the storm burst upon us. Long wreaths of cloud like ghosts floated through the trees; then the darts of the lightning pierced them, and the battle of the air had begun. Rain-drops sped through the trees like bullets, sheets of flame showed long vistas through the trees where cloud and lightning fought for the mastery; while high over all, from the peak of Thunderhead far above us, rolled the awful echoes of the artillery of the sky. For hours the battle raged, while we crouched under our frail shelter, awed to silence by the tempest about us.

At length the gray dawn struggled through, and the hosts of night and storm slowly retreated. We at last broke camp and went on our way, still under the influence of the new experience; and hereafter, whenever we hear the roll of the thunder, we shall think of that wonderful night on Thunderhead, and seem to see the majestic peak standing, stern and unshaken, while the spirits of Fire, Water, and Air fought about it the battle of the Giants.

Notes

Introduction

1. The area covered in this book corresponds to many definitions of what is now called southern Appalachia. The geographic definition adopted here is nearly the same as that adopted for the study area by Donald E. Davis. See Davis, 6–8, for a history of various definitions of the region. Except for its southern end, the Great Valley of Virginia has been excluded from this book. Though the nineteenth-century travel literature on that area is enormous, and though parts of the Great Valley are included in some definitions of southern Appalachia, it has been excluded because the history of settlement and tourism there is very different from that of the mountainous regions further south (Koons and Hofstra xvii).

2. There is no existing definitive bibliography of travel writing on Appalachia from this period. However, taken together, the bibliographies and notes from Collins, Edwards, Klotter, and Shapiro cite much—though not all—of a surprisingly large body of travel writing about southern Appalachia that appeared primarily in large-circulation, illustrated American magazines in the middle to late nineteenth century, both before and after the Civil War, increased during the Gilded Age (the late 1870s and 1880s), and tapered off towards the end of the 1890s.

3. According to the National Park Service, air pollution has reduced visibility in the Smokies by 60 percent in the past forty years alone.

4. The time period covered here, 1840 to 1900, starts after the Cherokee removal and ends with the end of an era of travel writing about the southern mountains.

Though many Appalachian studies scholars use World War I to mark the end of an era in southern Appalachian culture and development, this anthology ends at 1900 for the following reasons: During the mid-1890s, America's large-circulation magazines shifted from being supported primarily by subscription revenues to being supported by advertising revenues. This economic shift led to a shift in the content of the magazines: articles became shorter; increasing numbers of pages were devoted to advertising (Ohmann 99–106). That change in turn led to the decline of the extended domestic travel article. Also, by the mid-1890s, the large-circulation magazines had adopted half-tone reproductions of photographs for their illustrations. The era of the woodcut engraving came to an end (Grafton vii). As one historian of print technology writes, "Within a decade of the introduction of photomechanically produced relief blocks in the mid 1880s the whole [wood engraving] industry was dead" (Griffiths 25). The demise of wood engraving further contributed to the demise of the illustrated travel article. In addition, around 1900, a second wave of industrialization and natural-resource extraction swept southern Appalachia. For example, the last of the old-growth forests in the highlands of the Smokies and Unakas were cut only after Champion Coated Paper Company, later Champion International, acquired large holdings there, starting around 1901. As a result, the actual subject matter of this writing—lush, old-growth forest—disappeared. Tourism to some parts of the southern Appalachians suffered a decrease because of the cutting. Tourism to the Black Mountains all but halted in the early 1900s, for example, as large-scale logging denuded much of the range (Schwarzkopf 82).

    In addition, the period covered by this anthology straddles the Civil War era because extensive pleasure travel in the southeast was increasing before the Civil War, though the war suppressed that activity, and travel did not fully recover until the early 1870s (Schwarzkopf 35–49; 93–113).

5. The literature on the picturesque is vast. See Rainey, 26–30, for an overview.

6. In fact, travel to the southern mountains came to be viewed as an expression of loyalty to the Confederate cause. See DeBow as an example of how travel in the southern mountains was equated with loyalty.

Sketches of Georgia

[George Cooke]. "Sketches of Georgia." *Southern Literary Messenger* 6 (Nov. 1840): 775–77. [Original note: "From the pen of an artist of distinction, and a true lover of the sublime and beautiful in nature, who has made an extensive tour through the comparatively unknown territory of our Southern Sister. He presents some interesting features in Georgia scenery. —*Ed. Mess.*"]

1. *Chatahooche:* Chattahoochee.

2. *Highwassee:* Hiwassee.

3. *Naucooche:* Nacoochee.

4. *Guy Rivers:* William Gilmore Simms, from the popular novel, *Guy Rivers: A Tale of Georgia* (1834).

5. *Toccoa:* Toccoa Falls is located on the campus of Toccoa Falls College, near the town of Toccoa.

6. *Tallulah:* In 1913, the creek was dammed, shutting off the "cataracts" of the falls. Later the water was diverted through the 5,300-foot Terrora tunnel. In 1993, as an experiment, the water was allowed over the dam to flow through the Tallulah Gorge, for advanced whitewater kayakers. Since then, the falls below U.S. Highway 441 have been turned on a few weekends per year for recreational purposes. Cooke's painting of the falls, entitled *Tallulah Falls,* is owned by the Georgia Museum of Art at the University of Georgia, Athens. See Keyes, 89, for a reproduction of the painting.

7. *Tugalo:* Tugaloo.

8. *"How profound . . . vent":* Byron, *Childe Harold's Pilgrimage* 4.70.5–9.

9. *those of the Velino:* Velino Falls, created by the Romans, in the Terni region of Italy, where the Velino River cascades into the Nera.

10. *beauty of Toccoa with the sublimity of Tallulah:* Cooke is borrowing from a discourse about "the sublime and the beautiful" initiated by Edmund Burke's *Philosophical Enquiry into the Origin of Our Ideas of the Sublime and Beautiful* (1757).

11. *mound:* Nacoochee mound, near the intersection of Georgia Highways 75 and 17, south of Helen, in White County.

12. *Jeptha's daughter:* "Jeptha's Daughter" is title of one of Byron's lyric poems collected in *Hebrew Melodies* (1815). The poems were reproduced in American gift books produced in New York in the 1840s. The daughter of Jephthah (so spelled in the King James Bible) was sacrificed by her father after he returned from war (Judges 11.29–40).

13. *Iphigenia:* In accounts by Euripides and others, Iphigenia is sacrificed by her father, Agamemnon, before he goes off to war.

14. *Clarksville:* Clarkesville, Seat of Habersham County.

15. *Dahlonegar:* Dahlonega.

16. *Appenines:* Mountains in central Italy.

17. *"Where Eden . . . stateliest view":* Adapted from Milton, *Paradise Lost* 4.132–42.

18. *"Ocean . . . tost":* From "Night I," by Edward Young (1683–1765).

19. *No. 52:* Probably number 1052. See Lanman's version of the same story, in this volume. Also see "Gold Mining in Georgia," 510.

20. William Gilpin's *Observations on Several Parts of Great Britain, Particularly the High-lands of Scotland, Relative Chiefly to Picturesque Beauty, Made in the Year 1776* was first published in 1789. Jane Austen makes Gilpin's enthusiasm for remote, mountainous regions an object of fun in *Sense and Sensibility* (1811).

21. *branch mint:* See Lanman, this volume, note 3.

22. *Pere la Chaise:* Famous cemetery in Paris.

23. *turning the current:* Perhaps a reference to hydraulic mining. See Lanman, this volume, note 4.

24. *wealth of this country is but indicated:* Cooke's informant turns out to be mistaken. Even as Cooke was writing, just as the mint was completed and the last of the Cherokees removed, the gold began to play out. Mint production peaked in 1843. In 1849, with news of the California gold strikes, many miners left Georgia. The mint closed in 1861, the region's gold production having been a disappointment. Sporadic mining has continued since then, but the region's gold production has consistently failed to meet expectations (David Williams 117–23).

25. *"Walton Company":* Georgia gold rush historian David Williams writes, "About the Walton Company, I don't have any specific information, but I suspect that it was one of any number of companies that were failing around Dahlonega in the 1840s as the easily accessible placer gold was playing out" (personal correspondence, May 30, 2002). See David Williams, 117–23, for an account of gold mining around Dahlonega during this era.

26. *case of fever:* Yellow fever epidemics were a regular problem in the southeast during the 1830s and 1840s, especially during the summer, in the piedmont and coastal areas. Fever epidemics are one reason the mountains were attractive vacation sites. See introduction to Meriwether, in this volume, for more about yellow fever.

Dahlonega

Charles Lanman. "Dahlonega (Letters from the Alleghany Mountains; Editors' Correspondence: Dahlonega, [Geo.] April 20, 1848)." *Daily National Intelligencer,* 3 May 1848, 3.

1. *brought to light by recent explorations:* In 1838, near the Nacoochee mound, outside Helen, American gold miners uncovered a subterranean village of more than thirty log houses, which were well preserved and showed evidence of having been notched by sharp metal tools. It is possible the works were made by Spanish gold seekers who came with or after DeSoto's expedition. How-

ever, more recent excavations suggest that Indians of the southeast may have built such structures. See David Williams, 8–9 and 126, note 11.

2. *politely banished:* See Mooney, 130–35, for an account of the brutality of the Cherokee removal.

3. *branch Mint:* With the coming of the Civil War the mint was closed in 1861 and never reopened. In the 1870s, title for the building was transferred to the trustees of the newly established North Georgia Agricultural College. The main building burned to the ground in 1879. Today, Price Memorial Hall, the administration building for North Georgia College, stands on the basement walls of the old mint (David Williams 120–21).

4. *ravined by atmospheric agents:* Perhaps a reference to hydraulic mining, a highly destructive method whereby all timber and topsoil were removed and water cannons were used to wash the exposed subsoil down a series of flumes. Some environmental historians say that hydraulic mining was first used widely here before the Civil War and became known as the "Dahlonega method" (Donald Davis 156). However, others say that the method was first developed out west and was brought to Dahlonega only after the Civil War (David Williams 120–21).

5. *turned into a new channel:* In Lumpkin County, for example, a 33-mile aqueduct system was used to carry water to the mining operation (Donald Davis 156).

6. *54 40:* The 54° 40' north parallel marked the line to which the Democrats under President James K. Polk wished to annex the Oregon territory. "54 40 or fight!" was an expansionist rallying cry for Democratic supporters of Polk during the election of 1844. Joseph Gales and William Seaton, the editors of the *National Intelligencer,* were prominent opponents of Polk's expansionism.

7. *Camel's hump:* A distinctive mountain in the northern Green Mountains of Vermont, now Camel's Hump State Park.

8. *Charlottesville:* An error. The mint in Charlotte, North Carolina—like the mint in Dahlonega—discontinued operations in 1861 when it was taken over by Confederates.

9. *"What . . . worthier!":* Adapted from Byron, *Childe Harold's Pilgrimage* 4.185.5–6.

On Lookout Mountain

Oliver Bell Bunce. "On Lookout Mountain (with Illustrations by Harry Fenn)." *Appleton's Journal* 6 (26 Aug. 1871): 238–42.

1. *Leigh Hunt was a Cockney:* English journalist, essayist, critic and poet, Hunt (1784–1859), along with Keats and Hazlitt, were considered members of the "Cockney School" of British Romantic poets, whose work was often

distinguished from the "Lake School" poetry associated with Wordsworth. Hunt and the Cockney school were sometimes associated with humble origins and low breeding, and they were much maligned by reviewers in *Blackwood's* magazine.

2. *Ku Klux Klan:* Bunce downplays the significance of the Klan when writing for his northern audience. However, in March 1871, only a few weeks before Bunce and Fenn visited Chattanooga, the North Carolina legislature impeached Governor William Woods Holden for his earlier cracking down on statewide Klan activity. Even as Bunce and Fenn were making their way south through the mountains, the U.S. Congress responded to the North Carolina legislature by passing an anti-Klan bill, which gave the U.S. president power to place "rebellious" areas in the south under federal control. That bill has been credited with subsequent decline in Klan activity, though the Klan would later be revived in various forms. At the time, the Ku Klux Klan was a group of ex-Confederates, first organized in Pulaski, Tennessee, in May 1866 to oppose Reconstruction policies and federal governance in the South, and to promote white supremacy. Klan members used terrorist methods, dressing in white hoods to maintain secrecy while symbolically posing as Confederate dead.

3. *seven States:* Rock City still uses the slogan "see seven States," though visibility has diminished considerably, especially during the summer, and such views are now rarely, if ever, obtained.

4. *Hooker:* Joseph Hooker, Union General who, during the battle of Chattanooga, coordinated the assault on Lookout Mountain, referred to later as "the battle above the clouds."

5. *Bragg believed himself secure:* On the eve of the battle of Chattanooga, Confederate General Braxton Bragg sent troops to Knoxville, leaving Lookout Mountain with minimal defenses.

6. *"Marchioness":* In Dickens's *The Old Curiosity Shop,* the nickname given by Dick Swiveller to the half-starved servant kept locked under the stairs by the villainous Brasses. Swiveller later marries her.

7. *Day and Martin:* Day and Martin was a prominent British manufacturer of boot blacking.

8. *Rock City:* The area was developed in the 1930s and promoted with a well-known advertising campaign, whereby barns along U.S. highways were painted with the slogan "See Rock City." Rock City and Rock City Gardens still attract many tourists today.

9. *Lulu Falls:* Lulu Falls, 130 feet high, is just below Lulu Lake, about seven miles south of the incline railway on Lookout Mountain.

10. *"wears his heart . . . peck at":* From Shakespeare's *Othello* 1.1.67–68.

The Industrial Region of Northern Alabama, Tennessee, and Georgia

Julian Ralph. "The Industrial Region of Northern Alabama, Tennessee, and Georgia." *Harper's* 90 (Mar. 1895): 607–26. Excerpt reproduced here: 607–15. The article was reprinted in *Dixie; or Southern Scenes and Sketches,* Harper, 1896.

1. *Selkirks:* mountain range in Northwest Idaho and Canada.

2. *Chickamauga and Mission Ridge:* In September 1863, Confederates won the battle of Chickamauga Creek, seizing Missionary Ridge, Lookout Mountain, and the Chattanooga Valley. In November, a Union victory on Lookout Mountain at Chattanooga set the stage for Sherman's march through the south the following spring.

3. *"sleepers":* railroad sleeper cars.

4. *remarkable creation:* This incline railway first began operation in 1887. A second incline railway was opened in 1895, and shortly thereafter the first ceased operation. The 1895 incline railway is still in operation today.

5. *the whole world kin:* "One touch of nature makes the whole world kin." Shakespeare, *Troilus and Cressida* 3.3.184.

6. *sage writer:* This may be a reference to Henry Woodfin Grady (1850–1889), one-time editor of the *Atlanta Constitution* and author of "The New South," a famous address made in 1886 before the New England Club of New York and widely circulated in print. In that address Grady made essentially the same argument that Ralph makes here: that the south was good for investment because race relations and education were improving. (See Grady, 37–38.) Grady was widely quoted by both southerners and northerners interested in reconciliation and economic development.

7. *Rockwood:* The City of Rockwood, Tennessee, sprang up after the Civil War. During the war, Union officer John T. Wilder had noticed signs of iron ore in the area around Walden's Ridge. After the war, he returned with northern financial backing and founded Roane Iron Company in 1868. Wilder later purchased land and built a hotel on Roan Mountain, Tennessee/North Carolina.

8. *Bessemer:* The town of Bessemer, Alabama, outside Birmingham, is named after Sir Henry Bessemer (1813–1898), English inventor of the Bessemer conversion process for making high-grade steel. Ralph writes that the name of the town is "misleading" because the ore mined nearby was not of the phosphorus-free, high-grade type that is best suited to the Bessemer process.

9. *A mine of Bessemer ore:* A reference to the Cranberry Mine, in Cranberry, North Carolina. Cranberry ore was shipped by narrow-gauge railway to Johnson City, Tennessee. (Ralph's text is in error when it says "Johnson City, *North*

Carolina.") See Charles Dudley Warner's account of the Cranberry Mine, in this volume.

10. *Tennessee, Coal, Iron and Railway Company:* Know as TCI, the conglomerate was consolidated after the Panic of 1893 into "the largest single holder of ore lands and furnace plants in the U.S." (Woodward 299). Around the time of Ralph's visit, the company was breaking a miners' strike in 1894 with the aid of Alabama Governor Thomas G. Jones's militia (Woodward 266–67). In 1907, TCI was acquired by U.S. Steel, bringing J. Pierpont Morgan to the height of his monopoly control.

11. *labor in this great industrial section:* Ralph's labor observations are biased and incomplete. A substantial portion of TCI labor in Alabama was performed by leased convicts. TCI working conditions varied, but were "usually awful and sometimes murderously so" (Mancini 107).

12. *Baring failure:* In late 1890, the great English banking house of Baring Brothers collapsed, after failing to collect on speculative loans, many in South America. The collapse led to financial panic in Britain, resulting in liquidation of British investments in the United States. The Baring collapse was one of the developments that would lead to the Panic of 1893 and the resulting four-year financial depression in America, the worst in the country up to that time.

13. *Such changes:* Ralph's economic analysis is basically accurate, though he is overly optimistic about the time that will be required for change. For more than a generation to come, the region would remain what C. Vann Woodward calls a "Colonial Economy" (291–321)—that is, a third-world style economy, based on the extraction of raw materials that are transported elsewhere for manufacture.

14. *I. D. Imboden:* See Eller, 48–49, for an account of the promotional activities of former Confederate General John Daniel Imboden, whom Eller calls "among the earliest and most ardent promoters of coal and iron development in the southern mountains."

15. *district of like area in the world:* These predictions were to prove inaccurate. The iron deposits in the region were neither as extensive nor as pure as developers had hoped. Meanwhile, the opening of the Gohebic and Mesabi ore ranges in the upper Great Lakes basin in the following decades lead to a decline of the relative importance of iron and steel in the southeast.

A Week on Walden's Ridge I

Bradford Torrey. "A Week on Walden's Ridge I." *Atlantic Monthly* 75 (May 1895): 605–13.

1. *Walden's Ridge:* Walden's Ridge is a spur of the Cumberland Plateau that rises northwest of Chattanooga (labeled on some maps as Walden Ridge). The section of the ridge above Moccasin Bend is known today as Signal Mountain. Here the Cumberland Escarpment juts up from the river. In the 1880s and early 1890s, many of Chattanooga's most prominent families kept summer homes on Walden's Ridge. The region would soon become better known to northeastern readers through the writings of Emma Bell Miles, who grew up on Walden's Ridge, and whose poems and essays about the mountains and mountain people appeared in magazines such as *Harper's, Lippincott's,* and the *Century* during the first decade of the twentieth century. A collection of her writings, *The Spirit of the Mountains,* was published in 1905.

2. *truth-tellers first:* A reference to the type of literary realism then being promoted by W. D. Howells and others.

3. *"the dramatic element in scenery":* "And yet the weather, the dramatic element in scenery, is far more tractable in language, and far more human both in import and suggestion than the stable features of the landscape." Robert Louis Stevenson, "Talk and Talkers" (1882; chapter 10 of *Memories and Portraits,* 1900).

4. *"new road":* The new "W" road, so-called because dramatic switchbacks up the escarpment resemble a *W,* was opened in December 1893, only five months before Torrey's visit. It is now Signal Mountain Boulevard (Tennessee Highway 8/U.S. 127).

5. *long-leaved pines:* Considering current ranges, the pine Torrey refers to here is probably loblolly, *Pinus taeda,* rather than long-leaf, *Pinus palustris.*

6. *short of ripe:* The persimmon is notoriously bitter until completely ripe. An old southern gag is to offer an unsuspecting northerner an unripe persimmon. See the anecdote related at the beginning of the article by Louise Coffin Jones, in this volume.

7. *stay on the Ridge:* As he relates later in this article, Torrey's hotel is in Fairmount.

8. *Crawford Notch:* In New Hampshire's White Mountains, Crawford Notch had, by the time of Torrey's writing, been a popular resort area for northeasterners for more than fifty years (Waterman and Waterman 80).

9. *fringe-tree: Chionanthus virginica,* which usually grows no more than forty feet high, is "a raving beauty when in mid-spring it is loaded from top to bottom with the airest, most ethereal yet showy flowers" (Peattie 556).

10. *magnolia:* Perhaps the cucumber tree, *Magnolia acuminata,* but may also be one of the two other deciduous magnolias that bloom in May in the southern mountains: *M. tripetala, M. macrophylla.*

11. *Falling Water Creek:* Falling Water Creek runs off the Cumberland Escarpment below Fairmount.

12. *cross-vine: Anisostichus capreolata.*

13. *bimetallist:* A joking reference to the "free silver" controversy that had been an American political issue since the financial panic of 1873. Financial interests in the east favored a gold monetary standard; indebted agrarian interests in the south favored a silver standard—that is, the making of coins in silver as well as in gold—to promote inflation of prices for agricultural products. The latter position was sometimes called bimetallism. Free silver would be a major issue in the presidential campaign of 1896, when William Jennings Bryan captured the Democratic presidential nomination with his "cross of gold" speech, in favor of silver coinage.

14. *"image and superscription":* In the Gospel of Mark, Jesus picks up a coin and asks, "Whose is this image and superscription?" (12.16). A version of this story also appears in Luke 20 and Matthew 22.

15. *idle silence:* St. Ambrose: "Not only for every idle word but for every idle silence must man render an account."

16. *mosquitoes:* Mosquitoes are less frequent in the southern mountains, which have never been glaciated, than in the northeast, which has been heavily glaciated. Glaciated terrain holds standing water in which mosquitoes breed.

17. *yellow fever:* See introduction to Meriwether, in this volume, for more on yellow fever.

A Winter in the South

David Hunter Strother ["Porte Crayon"]. "A Winter in the South (4th paper of 6)." *Harper's* 16 (Jan. 1858): 167–83.

1. *Ceres:* Roman goddess of grain. The point of this first stanza is that mountains are agriculturally poor. The next two stanzas say, in effect, that mountains are beautiful, though barren. The poem reflects a standard romantic discourse about mountain landscape.

2. *P. P. Cooke:* Philip Pendleton Cooke (1816–1850), Virginia gentleman, lawyer, and poet; frequent contributor to the *Southern Literary Messenger.* There he published a poem entitled "The Mountains" (May 1846), from which Strother excerpted this and the other poetic passages that follow in this article. Cooke was cousin to John Pendleton Kennedy, popular romance novelist who also wrote a collection of fictionalized travel sketches, *Swallow Barn; or, A Sojourn in the Old Dominion* (1832), the second edition of which (1851) was illustrated by Strother. See Sweet, xiii, for more about Strother's connections to Kennedy's family.

3. *Bald mountain:* Numerous mountains in the southern Appalachians have been called "Bald mountain." (See Woolson, note 1, in this volume.) The Bald

Mountain visited by the Strother/Larkin party is on the border of Unicoi County, Tennessee, and Yancey County, North Carolina. The Appalachian National Scenic Trail runs across its summit. The highest point is often labeled "Big Bald Mt."

4. *"Right hardy . . . watch and ward"*: P. P. Cooke. See note 2, above.

5 *countries that have been so inked over . . . in Europe and America*: At the time of Strother's article (1858), the mountain resorts of the northeast, the Catskills, the White Mountains, and the Berkshires, were already swarmed with landscape painters. (See Dona Brown, 41–75.) The southern Appalachians (and, to a lesser extent, the Adirondacks) thus provided comparatively "virgin" territory for painters and illustrators, as well as for tourists.

6. *'A thing of beauty is a joy forever'*: Keats, *Endymion* 1.1.

7. *sturdy pioneer of the Black*: Tom Wilson, of Mitchell County, the Black Mountains. In the previous installment, the adventurers were guided by Wilson on Mount Mitchell.

8. *Roane*: Roan Mountain.

9. *Davy Grier*: Pat Alderman provides an account of David "Hog" Greer, the "Hermit of Big Bald" (33). Alderman's sources include Unicoi County gravestones, and conversations he had with Unicoi County residents in the 1960s.

10. *experience on the Black Dome*: In the previous installment, the characters summitted Mount Mitchell without suitable provisions.

11. *mountain torrent*: Spivey Falls, on what is now called Spivey Creek, along U.S. 19W (Spivey Mt Rd). The falls are on the Tennessee side of the state line. The road now follows the route that the party took down the mountain.

12. *"Skin for . . . life"*: Job 2.4.

13. *sugar-camp*: A place where sugar maples are tapped to produce maple syrup.

14. *Tumbling Fork*: Spivey Creek.

15. *painters*: Panthers. The panther is also called cougar or mountain lion. The last confirmed sightings in the southern Appalachians occurred at the end of the nineteenth century; however, reports of cougar sightings in the region have been on the rise since the late twentieth century (Nash 13).

16. *Kan Foster*: "Kan" is short for Kanada. See Alderman, 28, for an account of Foster.

17. *"Chuckey"*: Nolichuckey River.

The French Broad

Constance Fenimore Woolson. "The French Broad." *Harper's* 50 (Apr. 1875): 617–36.

1. *Bald Mountain*: Now called Rumbling Bald Mountain, in Rutherford County, about twenty miles southeast of Asheville, north of Lake Lure. In 1874, the year of Woolson's visit, from January to early summer, the mountain rumbled

and shook with enough force to rattle dishes in the nearby valley. The shocks dislodged boulders and opened fissures. Newspaper reporters came from around the country and across the Atlantic to observe what they thought would be a volcano. In 1940, scientists found that the rumbling was caused by "boulders breaking loose from the tops of subterranean crevices" (Sakowski, *North Carolina* 143.)

2. *Undine:* Or "Ondine," in folklore, a female water sprite that could acquire a soul by marrying a human being. The figure was popular in nineteenth-century French fiction, as well as in sculptures and paintings of the period, and was featured in a popular opera by E. T. A. Hoffmann, *Undine* (1812-14).

3. *strand:* "One day I wrote her name upon the strand," a sonnet by Edmund Spenser (1552–1599).

4. *Beaucatcher Knob:* Beaucatcher Knob was a northern knob of Beaucatcher Mountain, east of downtown Asheville. In the years after Woolson's article, the area was rapidly built over with residences (including "Zealandia," a castle-like estate built by John Evans Brown in 1889—part of which remains on the ridge today). However, the knob was largely destroyed and many of the residences removed to make way for the "Beaucatcher cut," a roadcut for the I-240 bypass east of town. College Street runs from downtown, beneath the mountain, through Beaucatcher Tunnel, south of the cut.

5. *Elisha Mitchell:* (1793–1857) minister, educator, scientist, died attempting to resolve a dispute about the altitude of the mountain subsequently named after him. His body is buried at the peak, near the observation tower. See Dimmock, this volume.

6. *6711 feet:* In 1930, the U.S. Geological Survey measured Mount Mitchell at 6,684 feet, now considered the official height (Schwarzkopf 78).

7. *"And the building . . . pure gold":* Revelation 21.18.

8. *Eagle Hotel:* The hotel stood on the east side of what was formerly Main Street, now Biltmore Avenue, just south of Eagle Street, which was named after the hotel's side entrance. The hotel was established in 1814 by Irish immigrant James Patton. Originally built of frame, it was later enlarged with brick. In 1934, the hotel was torn down when the east side of Main Street was widened.

9. *rocs that aided Sinbad the Sailor:* An allusion to an episode from *A Thousand and One Nights.* In Arabic legends, the roc, or *rukh,* was a gigantic bird with two horns on its head and four humps on its back.

10. *Alexander's:* Alexander's was a well-known hotel and stock stand along the old drover's road, part of which is now Highway 251. See Wellman, 42, 44.

11. the *Bald, the volcano:* See note 2, above.

12. *Guyot:* Arnold Henry Guyot (1807–1884), Princeton professor of geology, measured peaks throughout the Appalachian range. See Frome, 95–113, for a narrative account of Guyot's work in the southern mountains.

13. *"only talking for Buncombe":* "The definition of 'buncombe' (spelled also bunkum and contracted to bunk), as meaning anything said, written, or done for mere show, had its origin in a speech made in the Sixteenth Congress by Felix Walker, Representative from the district of which Buncombe County was a part. The address was a masterpiece of fence-sitting, and when a colleague asked the purpose of it, Walker replied: 'I was just talking for Buncombe'" (Federal Writers' Project, North Carolina 138–39).

14. *Antinous:* A favorite of Roman emperor Hadrian, known for his beauty.

15. *Warm Springs:* In the 1880s, the name of the town was changed to Hot Springs.

16. *Mountain Island:* This island is visible from the Appalachian Trail, where the trail crosses Lover's Leap Ridge, trail—north of Hot Springs.

17. *Macdonald's novels:* George MacDonald (1824–1905), Scottish novelist, poet, and preacher.

18. *Boughton's pictures:* George Henry Boughton (1833–1905).

19. *Cesnola collection:* In 1865, General Luigi de Palma Cesnola, a naturalized Italian American, became the U.S. consul to Cyprus, and there acquired antiquities. When he left Cyprus in the 1870s, he took many objects, which formed part of the original collection of the Metropolitan Museum in New York.

20. *they called it . . . after their captain, whose name was French:* Woolson's Romer is probably wrong about the etymology of the river's name. Another explanation is that early hunters and explorers called the river "French Broad" to indicate that it flowed to the Tennessee and Mississippi Rivers and into the lands granted to the French in 1763 Treaty of Paris. The river was thus distinguished from the "English Broad" rivers that flow off the eastern slopes of the Blue Ridge to the Atlantic (Dykeman 15–16).

21. *ruined culverts . . . spirit whistle:* In 1868, officials from the Western North Carolina Railroad absconded with four million dollars' worth of bonds from the company treasury. The state purchased the company in 1875 (the year Woolson's article was published). The Swannanoa tunnel was completed in 1879, bringing the Western North Carolina Railroad from the east into Buncombe County and, the following year, into Asheville. Three years later, the section of the East Tennessee, Virginia, and Georgia railroad between Knoxville and Paint Rock, through the French Broad gorge, was completed. The railroad was built with convict labor provided by the state. It is estimated that more than five hundred convicts died constructing that section of the railroad (Sakowski, *East Tennessee* 232).

22. *to Greeneville:* U.S. 25 to North Carolina Highway 208 to Tennessee Highway 70.

23. *Paint Rock . . . picture writing:* A red coloration is still visible on Paint Rock, though claims about Indian picture writing are uncertain (Wellman 14–15).

The Yares of the Black Mountains

Rebecca Harding Davis. "The Yares of the Black Mountains." *Lippincott's* 16 (July 1875): 35–47. Reprint in *Silhouettes of American Life.* New York: Scribner's, 1892.

1. *a railroad . . . given over too:* In 1868, officials from the Western North Carolina Railroad absconded with four million dollars' worth of bonds from the company treasury. The state took over the project, and the railroad was completed through the Swannanoa tunnel in 1879. See Woolson, note 21, in this volume.

2. *Desbrosses Ferry:* Lower west side of Manhattan.

3. *Digger Indians:* A derogatory term applied indiscriminately to Native Americans, with no ethnological basis.

4. *Air-Line Railroad:* Emerging after the Civil War, air lines used through-bills of lading and a pool of railway cars to operate a continuous railway line over a multitude of seemingly independent railroads. See Nelson, 58–62, for a discussion and map.

5. *an inn . . . sheltered by great trees:* This inn fits the description of the old Eagle Hotel, formerly on Eagle Street in downtown Asheville. See the picture on page 138, and see Woolson and Warner, both in this volume.

6. *along beside the . . . Swannanoa River:* Here the fictional characters follow a route the road along the North Fork of the Swannanoa, into the North Fork Valley, a popular tourist route both before and after the war. See Dimmock, this volume, for another account of the same route.

7. *sons of Anak:* In Numbers, giant inhabitants of Canaan.

8. *Kirk's Loyal Rangers:* George W. Kirk was a Union colonel whose headquarters were in East Tennessee, and who specialized in guerilla raids into the North Carolina mountains. See Dykeman, 99–123, for a narrative of Kirk and the conflicts in the mountains during the war, and an overview of the sorts of stories on which Davis bases the Yares' troubles.

9. *Salisbury and Andersonville:* Both notorious Confederate prisons received extensive coverage in the national media during and after the war. The Salisbury Prison was the only Confederate prison in North Carolina. National Cemetery on Military Drive in Salisbury has a monument to the estimated 11,700 Federal prisoners that are buried there in eighteen long trenches.

10. *Albert Richardson:* Albert D. Richardson was a popular newspaper correspondent for the *New York Tribune* who was in the Salisbury Prison and wrote about his escape.

11. *Major Gee:* Major John H. Gee was the commandant of the Salisbury Confederate Prison in 1864–65, when thousands of prisoners died of starvation and disease while awaiting exchange. After the war, Gee was imprisoned, tried, and acquitted on charges of cruelty and murder. The case was widely publicized at the time.

On Horseback II

Charles Dudley Warner. "On Horseback II." *Atlantic Monthly* 56 (Aug. 1885): 194–207.

1. *Mines at Cranberry:* Cranberry Mine, three miles from the Tennessee border, on Cranberry Creek. Ore in the twenty-two-mile vein, known for its purity, was free of sulphur and had high percentages of magnetic oxide of iron and metallic iron. By the end of the 1920s, the vein was largely depleted.

2. *cucumber tree: Magnolia acuminata,* a deciduous magnolia, indigenous to southern Appalachia, whose long white flowers bloom in May.

3. *Tatem his household cemetery:* A reference to a man in whose house the travelers had dined earlier in the day. As related in the previous installment, the man had tombstones in his sitting room.

4. *"Weary . . . work's expir'd":* Shakespeare, Sonnet 27.

5. *White birches:* Warner was perhaps seeing *Betula pendula,* a cultivated white birch. The white birch, or paper birch, common in New England, *Betula papyrifera,* occurs only rarely in the southern mountains, and only above 5,500 feet.

6. *Roan Station:* Now the town of Roan Mountain, Tennessee, at U.S. Highway 11E.

7. *This railway . . . wonders of the world:* The East Tennessee and Western North Carolina Railroad was formed in 1866 and began operations between Cranberry and Johnson City, Tennessee, in 1881. Later known as the "Tweetsie Railway," it discontinued regular freight and passenger excursions by 1940. In 1957, its remnants were used to establish the Tweetsie Railroad amusement park near Blowing Rock, North Carolina.

8. *this Mitchell County:* Roan Station, which Warner describes here, was actually located in Carter County, Tennessee, across the state line from Mitchell County, North Carolina. Warner's description of southern mountain inhabitants as excessively violent had become, by the time of his writing, at the height of

the Gilded Age, a stock convention. For a counter-view, see Silber, "What Does America Need?"

9. *Teniers:* David Teniers the Younger (1610–1690), Flemish court painter, known for genre scenes of peasant feasts and dances.

10. *House of entertainment:* In 1877, General John T. Wilder, owner of seven thousand acres of Roan Mountain, directed the building of a twenty-room spruce-log hotel. In 1885, one year after Warner's visit, Wilder opened the much larger Cloudland Hotel. A few years after that, the original hotel, which Warner describes here, was torn down.

11. *White Hills:* New Hampshire's White Mountains.

12. *Grey's lily:* Gray's lily, *Lilium grayi,* named after botanist Asa Gray, appears only on southern balds and blooms in late June through July.

13. *rhododendron:* The catawba rhododendron, *Rhododendron catawbiensis.*

14. *Old Mark Langston:* The title of an 1884 novel by Richard Malcolm Johnston (1822–1898), a "local colorist" whose fiction was set in the middle Georgia of his youth.

15. *Eagle Cliff:* Eagle Cliff is about a quarter of a mile out on the ridge past what is now called Roan High Bluff.

16. *High Bluff:* The location Warner describes is not what is today called High Bluff. Most likely Warner was on what is now called Grassy Ridge. Yet he might have been at Round Bald, Jane Bald, or Grassy Ridge. All of those summits are north of the old hotel site and provide 360° views consistent with the one Warner describes here.

17. *caracole:* A half turn to right or left executed by a mounted horse.

18. *"How heavy . . . my joy behind":* Shakespeare, Sonnet 50.

19. *"What . . . tend?":* Sonnet 53.

20. *not a drop of liquor:* Muriel Sheppard later observed that, "of course Warner could not get liquor when no one knew him. In the same period Henry Franklin's grandfather, who entertained travellers at Linville Falls, used to keep a bucket of apple brandy sitting on the porch with a dipper in it" (110).

21. *Nollechucky:* The North and South Toe join to become the Toe, which is called the Nolichucky after it crosses the state line into Tennessee.

22. *"Tired with all these . . . my love alone":* Shakespeare, Sonnet 66.

23. *Big Tom Wilson:* Celebrated hunter and mountain guide, known for finding the body of Elisha Mitchell, after Mitchell fell to his death in 1857. Warner visits Wilson in the Black Mountains, in the installment following the present selection—*Atlantic Monthly* 56 (September 1885): 388–98.

24. *Vanderbilt's wealth:* William Henry Vanderbilt (1821–1885) was heir to the steamship and railroad fortune built by his father, Cornelius ("Commodore") Vanderbilt (1794–1877). In 1881, William Henry completed construction on a 58-room mansion on Fifth Avenue in Manhattan, the most lavish house in the city at the time. This is probably the house to which Warner refers in this discussion. In 1888, three years after Warner's article appeared in the *Atlantic*, William Henry's son, George (1862–1914), visited Asheville for the first time. Taken by the beauty of the region, George began planning for what would become Biltmore Estate, including a 250-room mansion that was completed, just south of Asheville, in 1895.

A Strange Land and a Peculiar People

William Wallace Harney. "A Strange Land and Peculiar People." *Lippincott's* 12 (Oct. 1873): 429–38.

1. *amygdaloid:* Basaltic rock containing small cavities filled by nodules or geodes of different minerals.

2. *water-oaks:* "Water oak" is not a common name in this region. Harney may have been referring to *Quercus imbricaria* or *Q. phellos.*

3. *syenite, volcanic tuff and scoria:* Syenite is a kind of grey, igneous rock; tuff is porous rock, associated with volcanic ash; scoria is loose, cinder-like lava or slag.

4. *Lincoln:* In the late nineteenth century, Lincoln came to be identified with mountain people in the national consciousness. Partly this was a result of a deliberate strategy to use the figure of Lincoln as an identity for mountaineers. By 1903, for example, the letterhead for Berea College, the Kentucky college redefining its mission to serve mountain people, read, "In Lincoln's State—For Lincoln's People" (Klotter 845–46).

5. *shoats:* Young hogs.

6. *Wolford's regiment:* First Cavalry Regiment, Kentucky Volunteers, U.S. Army.

7. *Cophetua:* Tennyson's poem "The Beggar Maid" retells the story from Elizabethan ballads of King Cophetua, who searches for a pure wife, finds her in the form of a ragged beggar girl, and offers his crown in return for her love.

8. *preux chevalier:* Brave knight.

9. *Captain Jack:* "Captain Jack" was one of the leaders of the Modoc Indians, who held off the U.S. Army for several months, in winter and early spring 1873, in the middle of a north California lava field. In April, Captain Jack killed General Edward Canby. The story and the actions which ensued were widely covered in the national media at the time.

10. *ubiquitous Jew:* Harney articulates a view that was popular during Reconstruction in both the north and the south. The idea that Jews supported the Confederacy allows a criticism of Confederate leadership while saving face for southerners. See Jaher, 196.

11. *General Johnston:* Confederate General Joseph E. Johnston (1807–1891), commander of Department of the West, December 1862 to December 1863.

12. *Jonesborough:* Jonesboro, Georgia, south of Atlanta, east of the Flint River. The references here are to Sherman's progress through the south to Atlanta, following the fall of Chattanooga at the end of 1863.

In the Backwoods of Carolina

Louise Coffin Jones. "In the Backwoods of Carolina." *Lippincott's* 24 (Dec. 1879): 747–56.

1. *"The Land of the Sky":* Christian Reid's novel *The Land of the Sky,* serialized in *Appleton's,* 1875–76, first used this term to refer to the western North Carolina highlands. The term was soon adopted as a marketing phrase for the area.

2. *Guilford Courthouse:* Now Guilford Courthouse National Military Park. A nod to Revolutionary War sites is customary for the nineteenth-century genteel traveler, especially for the female traveler (Baym 131).

3. *Saratoga:* A "Saratoga trunk"—named after Saratoga Springs New York, a popular vacation destination—is large enough to pack for a season, and was known as the despair of porters.

4. *journey to the mountains:* The route Jones describes is consistent with the major route west from Greensboro, which is now followed by U.S. 421, still called the Boone Trail because it roughly parallels the traditional course taken by Daniel Boone from the piedmont into the mountains.

5. *thankful for these accommodations . . . as a pampered Sybarite:* "Sybarite" is from Sybaris, an ancient Greek city in southeastern Italy, renowned for pleasure-seeking and luxury in classical times. In her 1883 article, Jones writes of accommodations that had been provided for a "refined and educated young girl"—probably Jones herself—by a mountain family: "Her only chance for washing in the morning was in a trough which stood in the yard. In this the whole family washed their faces and hands, and from it the horses drank, not to mention ducks and other barn-yard fowls. Once she asked for a utensil which could serve as a wash-bowl, and was given a skillet containing some greasy water: after that she went back to the family wash-trough" ("In the Highlands" 385).

6. *And all . . . rosy bloom:* From "Snow-Bound: A Winter Idyl" by John Greenleaf Whittier (1807–1892).

Through Cumberland Gap on Horseback

James Lane Allen. "Through Cumberland Gap on Horseback." *Harper's* 73 (June 1886): 50–66.

1. *hundred and fifty years ago:* Here and throughout the article, Allen tends to overstate the backwardness, isolation, and racial distinctness of the people of the region. See Silber, "What Does America Need?" 246–51, for a succinct discussion of how northern writers and audiences alike in the late nineteenth century desired to see the mountain communities as "primitive" and isolated pockets of pure Anglo-Saxon racial heritage.

2. *formerly a fine growth of walnut:* Because it is a coveted hardwood, *Juglans nigra* was exported from Virginia as early as 1610. A rage for walnut furniture between 1830 and 1860 led to heavy exploitation, and by the end of that period the tree was comparatively rare in the east (Peattie 123).

3. *Burnside's depot:* Ambrose Everett Burnside (1824–1881), Union general during the Civil War. As commander of the Department of the Ohio, he made his headquarters here to launch his occupation of Knoxville and east Tennessee in 1863. Federal troops built the corduroy road through the town, at the confluence of the Cumberland River and its south fork. Earlier called Point Isabel, the town was renamed for Burnside.

4. *yellow poplar: Liriodendron tulipifera,* also known as tulip poplar or tuliptree.

5. *Sellico Mountains:* Jellico Mountains.

6. *Landseer:* Sir Edwin Henry Landseer (1802–1873), British painter.

7. *bow-crowned mist:* In the full moon Cumberland Falls is said to have a "moon bow," a spectrum formed in the mist. The old hotel on a ledge above the falls was called the Moonbow Inn.

8. *lotos-eaters:* Tennyson's poem "The Lotos-Eaters" (1832) is based on the episode from the *Odyssey* wherein Odysseus lands among the mythical occupants of North Africa whose diet of lotos brings indolence and forgetfulness.

9. *turkeys:* The wild turkey had been largely extirpated from New England by late colonial times (Matthiessen 66). Allen's northeastern audience would be impressed to know that turkeys were common in Kentucky.

10. *"Why should . . . things":* From Tennyson's "The Lotos-Eaters."

11. *wild-cucumber: Magnolia acuminata,* or cucumber tree, a deciduous magnolia.

12. *calacanthus:* Probably *Calycanthus floridus,* or sweet shrub.

13. *wild camellia:* Probably *Stewartia malacodendron,* a rare native shrub.

14. *mandrake or "May-apple" root: Podophyllum peltatum* was sometimes known as the American mandrake because its root, like the root of a European mandrake,

suggests a human shape. The plant is poisonous except in small doses, but North American Indians are thought to have used it for a laxative, and for other medicinal purposes. Allen's anecdote is a rare account of the plant having export market value.

15. *Saxon type:* This vague racial assessment of the mountain people is generally inaccurate. See Silber, "What Does America Need?" 245–46.

16. *(pinchbeck):* Artificial gold

17. *New England checkerberry: Gaultheria procumbens* is also called teaberry.

18. *Yellow Creek . . . lovely watercourses:* The Yellow Creek watershed was extensively polluted through much of the late-nineteenth and the twentieth century, though since 1980 a group called Yellow Creek Concerned Citizens has worked to reduce the pollutants.

19. *Zollikoffer:* Confederate Gen. Felix K. Zollicoffer fell at the battle of Logan's Cross Roads, January 19, 1862. This battle cleared the way for the Union advance into East Tennessee.

20. *"the brakes" of Sandy:* Since at least the 1930s more often called "breaks of the Sandy." At a gap in the valley of the Big Sandy River, a rocky five-mile stretch of the river descends about 350 feet. "In a succession of waterfalls and rapids—called 'jumps' by the natives—the river plunges over and around boulders that fill the bed of the stream" (Federal Writers Project, *Kentucky* 437). The word used in the nineteenth century, "brakes," refers to canebrakes, areas in river flats where native cane grew. (See Donald Davis, 29.)

21. *cannel-coals:* Varieties of bituminous coal that burn with a bright flame.

Mountain Life in Tennessee

Lee Meriwether. "Mountain Life in Tennessee." *Cosmopolitan* 4 (Feb. 1888): 456–60.

1. Memphis suffered yellow fever epidemics in 1867, 1873, and, worst of all, in 1878. Beginning in the late hot summer of that year, the epidemic raged into late October. During that time, more than 5,000 people died, and more than 25,000 fled the city. (Fewer than 20,000 remained, 14,000 of whom were blacks.) The bodies were perceived to be infectious, so many lay rotting in the streets where they fell. Crime ran out of control. Memphis was so ravaged by the epidemic that the city charter was revoked until 1893. Yellow fever is a deadly disease associated with the tropics. Acute forms can have an 85 percent mortality rate. At the time of Meriwether's article, people did not understand how yellow fever was transmitted. Nor did they know that the carbolic acid and disinfectants they used to ward off the fever had no effect. Only in 1900, twelve years after this article was published, was it established that the disease is carried by mosquitoes.

2. *Unika range of mountains:* The Unakas. Meriwether's fictionalized narrator disembarks at either Morristown or Bull's Gap.

3. *Tusculum:* East of Greeneville, near the Nolichucky River, Tusculum is the site of Tusculum College, then called Tusculum Academy, founded 1818. In *The Tramp at Home,* Meriwether visits Tusculum, drawn there by a circular that advertises the Academy's "ancient library." When he arrives he finds the circular is hucksterism and the library worthless (74).

4. *This was simply the form of invitation . . . accepted:* In *The Tramp at Home,* Meriwether includes essentially the same anecdote that appears here, with the following explanation: "The saddle girths are strapped very tight to keep the rider from sliding over his horse's tail in climbing the steep mountains. It is usual, when not riding, to loosen the girth to relieve the horse; hence the form of invitation to get down from your horse and stop a 'while' is ''light and look at your saddle'" (78).

5. en route *to a genuine mountain home:* The abrupt ending suggests that another installment was planned. This story was never resumed in the *Cosmopolitan,* probably because of the magazine's business circumstances. A month after this article appeared, in March of 1888, the magazine's publishing firm, only two years old at the time, failed and changed ownership. Publication was discontinued that summer, and the magazine nearly folded (Mott IV 481). It was soon revived, however, and publication continues to this day. Meriwether continues the account of life in East Tennessee—without the fictional pretext of the yellow fever evacuee—in *The Tramp at Home,* chapter 8, "Among Southern Farmers—continued" (82–88).

A Little Moonshiner

Margaret Johann. "A Little Moonshiner." *Christian Observer* 85 (21 July 1897): 700–701.

1. *In every form . . . the Highest dwells:* From "The King's Picture," a poem by Helen L. B. Bostwick (1826–1907).

2. *Randolph:* A fictional name; there is no North Carolina county seat named Randolph. However the setting of this story is almost certainly the town of Marshall, seat of Madison County, North Carolina, northwest of Asheville on the French Broad River. A few months after this story appeared in the *Christian Observer,* a nonfiction article describing the same area appeared in the widely circulated, New Jersey–based, interdenominational *Missionary Review of the World.* See D. L. Pierson.

3. *court house:* The old Madison County courthouse was heavily damaged by flooding in 1902. The present courthouse was built in 1906.

4. *Drummer's Delight:* Like "Traveller's Rest," a common name for a hotel serving traveling salesmen.

A Negro Schoolmaster in the New South

W. E. B. Du Bois. "A Negro Schoolmaster in the New South." *Atlantic Monthly* 83 (Jan. 1899): 99–105.

1. *teachers' Institute:* The Wilson County Teachers' Institute in Lebanon was one of many established by Tennessee counties, at the prompting of the state, in the 1870s. Teacher training in Tennessee was mostly left to the counties until after state normal schools were established in 1909 (Lawlor and Lawlor 110–11).

2. *schoolhouse:* A building that is said to be the old Wheeler school where Du Bois taught has been removed to Fiddler's Grove Historical Village, at the Ward Agricultural Center, in Lebanon. Docents there will tell visitors about Du Bois.

The Grandfather of North Carolina

Jehu Lewis. "The Grandfather of North Carolina." *Lakeside Monthly* 10 (Sept. 1873): 218–24.

1. *tecoma radicans:* Now named *Campsis radicans.*

2. *"mountain rice":* Probably *Zizania aquatica,* but perhaps a naturalized, cultivated version.

3. *my route:* State Bicycle Route 2 (Old Johns River Road) and Highway 90 roughly follow Lewis's route up the Johns.

4. *my route:* From here Lewis follows present-day Highway 1362 (Anthony Creek Road) up Gragg Prong and later Anthony Creek.

5. *aristolochia sipho:* Dutchman's pipe, *Aristolochia macrophylla.*

6. *"Striped Pig":* An anti-tax movement in Massachusetts before the war went by the name of "the Striped Pig Party."

7. *crossing of Wilson's Creek:* Lewis here seems to be following the route of present-day Highway 1514.

8. *Lindville:* Now spelled Linville.

A Trip to Mt. Mitchell in North Carolina

George Dimmock. " A Trip to Mt. Mitchell in North Carolina." *Appalachia* 1 (June 1877): 141–51.

1. *Mitchell's Peak:* During the period from 1850 to 1870, the names of the major peaks in the Black Mountains were shifting and uncertain, as Dimmock discusses later in this article. Likewise, there was ongoing dispute about which peak was, under any name, the highest. See Schwarzkopf, especially 73–78. The peak Dimmock refers to here as Mitchell's Peak is almost certainly what

is now known as Mount Mitchell, the highest peak in the eastern United States. In 1930, the U.S. Geological Survey measured Mount Mitchell at 6,684 feet, which is now considered the official height (Schwarzkopf, 78).

2. *Wolf Creek:* On the French Broad River at the state line. The rail line, later called the East Tennessee, Virginia, and Georgia railroad, was completed between Knoxville and Asheville, through the French Broad gorge, in 1882.

3. *Warm Springs:* Renamed Hot Springs in 1886.

4. *azoic formations:* For a good description of the geology of the region, written for the nonspecialist, see Chew.

5. *hotel:* Built in 1839, the hotel burned in 1884.

6. *chalybeats:* Waters containing salts of iron.

7. *chinquepin bush:* The Allegheny chinkapin, *Castanea pumila.*

8. *Corundum:* Aluminum oxide, a common mineral with industrial applications.

9. *Swananoa:* Now spelled Swannanoa.

10. *Tuckerman's ravine:* In New Hampshire's White Mountains.

11. *Black Mountain House:* The Mountain House was built by William Patton in 1851, along a spur ridge off Potato Knob. After the war, it gradually fell into disrepair.

12. *gooseberry bushes:* The northern gooseberry, *Ribes hirtellum,* is not found in the southern mountains. Dimmock may have seen *Angelica triquinata,* or filmy Angelica, which is found in the high-elevation southern spruce-fir forest.

The Great Smoky Mountains and Thunderhead Peak

Frank O. Carpenter. "The Great Smoky Mountains and Thunderhead Peak." *Appalachia* 6 (Dec. 1890): 138–46.

1. *valley of the Big Pigeon:* Established forty-six years after this article was written, the Great Smoky Mountains National Park has its northeast boundary at the Pigeon River.

2. *"balds":* Along the crest of the Smokies here run southern "balds"—high-altitude ecosystems that are without forest cover, though they are well below the treeline. Scientists are not entirely certain about the origin of the balds (Lindsay 3). And twentieth-century travel writers have been fond of referring to the mystery of the balds' origin. In fact, however, it has been established that most if not all the balds in the regions were cleared for grazing, almost certainly by people of European origin (Margaret Lynn Brown 281–83). Grassy and heath balds such as those near Thunderhead were maintained, if not created, by large-scale cattle and other stock grazing in the years before the park was established (Houk 63–77).

3. *"Thunderhead"*: Thunderhead Mountain (5,527 feet) is visible above Cades Cove in the Great Smoky Mountains National Park, west of Clingman's Dome on the park's high ridge, along the state line.

4. *a hotel*: In 1842, William McTeer built what was initially called the College Inn and was advertised after its opening as the Citizen's Hotel. Ten years later, Montgomery McTeer built a porch over the sidewalk with the massive pillars. "Thus it became the 'Verandah Hotel' in 1852 and was the official stage stop during the years that Montvale Springs was entertaining the aristocracy of the South" (Burns 75). In 1894, the building was removed to make way for the Broadway Methodist Church.

5. *Jackson House*: Three-story brick Jackson House Hotel built in 1886 by George C. Jackson. In 1919, after the property changed hands several times, it was renamed the Blount Hotel (Burns 76).

6. *road from Maryville*: Carpenter's route roughly follows present-day U.S. 321/ Tennessee Highway 73 from Maryville to Townsend. From just north of Chilhowee Gap to Tuckaleechee Cove, Carpenter's route follows the old Walland highway, which in turn parallels U.S. 321/Tennessee 73 across the Little River.

7. *"dugout"*: A dugout canoe, or pirogue, carved usually from an old-growth tulip poplar, in the Cherokee fashion.

8. *"Harnt that walks Chilhowee"*: "The 'Harnt' That Walks Chilhowee," by Mary Murfree (aka "Charles Egbert Craddock") was first published in the *Atlantic Monthly* in 1883. It was reprinted in *In the Tennessee Mountains* (1884), a very popular book that is said to have inaugurated the vogue for mountain "local color."

9. *Tuckaleechee Cove*: Tuckaleechee Cove is now the town of Townsend, named after a lumber mill built in 1902 by W. B. Townsend. The chamber of commerce promotes Townsend as "the peaceful side of the Smokies," though tourist development has increased here dramatically in the past decade.

10. *"King of the Mountains"*: See Meriwether, *The Tramp at Home,* 82–88, for an account of Sam Walker.

11. *"Smoky Mountain Bill"*: A cattleman and occasional bear trapper, William M. Walker also kept bees and made oak buckets and barrels, earning enough money to send several daughters to Maryville College. A stroke disabled him in 1918 and, according to the family story, forced him to sell his land to Wilson B. Townsend, the lumberman whose name the town in the cove now bears. Townsend visited Walker at his cabin not long after his stroke, "and persuaded the mountain man to sign away 96 acres, 'more or less,' for $1,500 cash and a promise not to cut the great trees on Thunderhead Prong. The old man sold his land for a song, one family member lamented, and the lumber company 'sang it.' Walker died one year later. Townsend kept the promise until his own death in 1936, after which the Little River Lumber Company took all the

trees on Thunderhead Prong" (Margaret Lynn Brown 55). In some accounts, Walker is referred to as "Big Will" ("Walker Valley History" 301).

12. *a young man named Stinnett:* Bill Walker is said to have had three wives at once, the third of whom was named Moll Stinnett. Stinnett's children with Walker were named Stinnett ("Walker Valley History" 301).

13. *a road was surveyed:* Probably what is now called Bote Mountain Trail, the old Anderson road, named for the founder and former president of Maryville College, the Reverend Isaac Anderson, who promoted the construction of this road from Tuckaleechee Cove up to the state line. The road was built by "Indian labor" in the 1840s, in order to open the backcountry to missionaries (Dunn 84–85). Carpenter went through Schoolhouse Gap from Tuckaleechee Cove to get to the road. Today, hikers in the Great Smoky Mountains National Park may reach the road via Anthony Creek Trail, from the ranger's station parking lot at Cades Cove. At the intersection with the Appalachian Trail, Carpenter's route follows the AT across Spence Field, at the ridgeline, to Thunderhead.

14. *cucumber-trees: Magnolia acuminata,* a deciduous magnolia, indigenous to Southern Appalachia, whose long white flowers bloom in May.

15. *open pasture on the top of the ridge:* This is near where the Appalachian Trail now intersects Bote Mountain Trail, at an area called Spence Field. Not considered an "historic" bald, Spence Field was first cleared probably in the 1870s or 1880s (Lindsay 6–7). The area has been allowed to grow in, and hikers today will not see the wide, open meadows of Carpenter's day. However, vistas can still be obtained, including a 360° view from Rocky Top, at the edge of Thunderhead Ridge.

16. *Nantchalach:* Nantahala.

Bibliography

Alderman, Pat. *Greasy Cove in Unicoi County: Authentic Folklore.* Johnson City, TN: Overmountain, 1975.

Allen, James Lane. "Henry Mills Alden." *Bookman* 50 (Nov. 1919): 330–36.

———. "Local Color." *Critic* 8 (9 Jan. 1886): 13.

Ames, William E. *A History of the* National Intelligencer. Chapel Hill: U of North Carolina P, 1972.

Ammons, Elizabeth, and Valerie Rohy. Introduction. *American Local Color Writing, 1880–1920.* Ed. Ammons and Rohy. New York: Penguin, 1998. vii–xxxi.

Andrews, Kenneth R. *Nook Farm: Mark Twain's Hartford Circle.* Cambridge: Harvard UP, 1950.

Appalachian Mountain Club. *AMC White Mountain Guide, 25th Edition.* Boston: AMC, 1992.

Appleton-Century Company. *The House of Appleton-Century.* New York: Appleton-Century, 1936.

Arthur, John Preston. *Western North Carolina: A History (from 1730 to 1913).* Asheville: The Edward Buncombe Chapter of the Daughters of the American Revolution, 1914. Rpt. Johnson City, TN: Overmountain, 1996.

Ashe, Samuel A'Court. *History of North Carolina.* Vol. 1, Greensboro: C. L. Van Noppen, 1908. Vol. 2, Raleigh: Edwards and Broughton Printing Co., 1925.

Ayers, Edward L. *The Promise of the New South: Life After Reconstruction.* New York: Oxford UP, 1992.

Ayers, Harvard, Jenny Hager, and Charles E. Little, eds. *An Appalachian Tragedy: Air Pollution and Tree Death in the Eastern Forests of North America.* San Francisco: Sierra Club Books, 1998.

Bailey, Brigitte. "The Panoptic Sublime and the Formation of the American Citizen in Cooper's *Wing-and-Wing* and Cole's *Mount Etna from Taormina, Sicily.*" *James Fenimore Cooper: His Country and His Art; Papers from the 1997 Cooper Seminar (No. 11)*. Ed. Hugh C. MacDougall. Oneonta: The State University of New York College at Oneonta, 1997. 7–13.

"Balsam Trail—Mt. Mitchell State Park." 12–page booklet. Elisha Mitchell Chapter National Audubon Society. N. C. Dept. of Environment and Natural Resources. Mt. Mitchell State Park, Burnsville, NC (828–675–4611). Undated [approx. 2001].

Baym, Nina. *American Women Writers and the Work of History, 1790–1860*. New Brunswick: Rutgers UP, 1995.

Benedict, Clare. *Voices out of the Past*. Vol. 1 of *Five Generations, 1785–1923: Being Scattered Chapters from the History of the Cooper, Pomeroy, Woolson and Benedict Families, with Extracts from Their Letters and Journals, as Well as Articles and Poems by Constance Fenimore Woolson*. 3 vols. Ed. Benedict. London: Ellis, 1929.

Bermingham, Ann. *Learning to Draw: Studies in the Cultural History of a Polite and Useful Art*. New Haven: Yale UP, 2000.

Berthold, Dennis. "Miss Martha and Ms. Woolson: Persona in the Travel Sketches." *Constance Fenimore Woolson's Nineteenth Century: Essays*. Ed. Victoria Brehm. Detroit: Wayne State UP, 2001: 111–18.

Billings, Dwight B., and Kathleen M. Blee. *The Road to Poverty: The Making of Wealth and Hardship in Appalachia*. Cambridge, UK: Cambridge UP, 2000.

Billington, Ray Allen. *Frederick Jackson Turner: Historian, Scholar, Teacher*. New York: Oxford UP, 1973.

Bobo, William M. *Glimpses of New York City by a South Carolinian (Who Had Nothing Else To Do)*. Charleston: J. J. McCarter, 1852.

Boime, Albert. *The Magisterial Gaze: Manifest Destiny and American Landscape Painting, 1830–1865*. Washington, DC: Smithsonian Institution P, 1991.

Bonner, Sherwood [Katherine Sherwood Bonner McDowell, aka Katherine McDowell]. *A Sherwood Bonner Sampler, 1869–1884: What a Bright, Educated, Witty, Lively, Snappy Young Woman Can Say on a Variety of Topics*. Ed. Anne Razey Gowdy. Knoxville: U of Tennessee P, 2000.

Born, Wolfgang. *American Landscape Painting: An Interpretation*. New Haven: Yale UP, 1948.

Bottorff, William K. *James Lane Allen*. New York: Twayne, 1964.

Boudinot, Elias [Buck Watie]. "An Address to the Whites, Delivered in the First Presbyterian Church [Philadelphia], on the 26th of May, 1826, by Elias Boudinott [*sic*], A Cherokee Indian." *Cherokee Editor: The Writings of Elias Boudinot*. Ed. Theda Perdue. Knoxville: U of Tennessee P, 1983. 65–83.

Branch, Michael P., and Daniel J. Philippon. *The Height of Our Mountains: Nature Writing from Virginia's Blue Ridge Mountains and Shenandoah Valley*. Baltimore: Johns Hopkins UP, 1998.

Brandt, Robert. *Touring the Middle Tennessee Backroads.* Winston-Salem: Blair, 1995.

Brewer, Alberta. *Valley so Wild: a Folk History.* Knoxville: East Tennessee Historical Society, 1975.

Briden, Earl F. "Kemble's 'Specialty' and the Pictorial Countertext of *Huckleberry Finn.*" *Mark Twain Journal* 26.2 (Fall 1988): 2–14.

Brodhead, Richard H. *Cultures of Letters: Scenes of Reading and Writing in Nineteenth-Century America.* Chicago: U of Chicago P, 1993.

Brown, Charles H. *William Cullen Bryant.* New York: Scribner, 1971.

Brown, Dona. *Inventing New England: Regional Tourism in the Nineteenth Century.* Washington, DC: Smithsonian Institution P, 1995.

Brown, Margaret Lynn. *The Wild East: A Biography of the Great Smoky Mountains.* Gainesville: UP of Florida, 2000.

Brown, Richard D. *The Strength of a People: The Idea of an Informed Citizenry in America, 1650–1870.* Chapel Hill: U of North Carolina P, 1996.

Bryant, William Cullen. See Bunce and Bryant.

Buck, Paul Herman. *The Road to Reunion, 1865–1900.* Boston: Little, Brown, 1937.

Bulkley, Peter B. "Identifying the White Mountain Tourist, 1853–1854: Origin, Occupation and Wealth as a Definition of the Early Hotel Trade." *Historical New Hampshire* 35 (Summer 1980): 106–62.

Bunce, Oliver Bell. *In the Woods with Bryant, Longfellow and Halleck.* New York: Hurd and Houghton, 1866.

———, and William Cullen Bryant, eds. *Picturesque America, or, The Land We Live In: A Delineation by Pen and Pencil of the Mountains, Rivers, Lakes, Forests, Waterfalls, Shores, Cañons, Valleys, Cities, and Other Picturesque Features of Our Country.* 2 vols. New York: Appleton, 1872–74.

Burns, Inez. *History of Blount County, Tennessee, from War Trail to Landing Strip, 1795–1955.* Nashville: Tennessee Historical Commission, 1957.

Burrows, Edwin G., and Mike Wallace. *Gotham: A History of New York City to 1898.* New York: Oxford UP, 1999.

Cameron, William E. *The World's Fair: Being a Pictorial History of the Columbian Exposition; Containing a Complete History of the World-renowned Exposition at Chicago.* Mansfield, OH: Estill, 1893.

"Charles Egbert Craddock." *Critic* ns 2 (14 Mar. 1885): 127. [Rpt. of "A Literary Surprise," the *Boston Herald* revelation that Craddock is Mary Murfree].

Charvat, William. "Poe: Journalism and the Theory of Poetry." *The Profession of Authorship in America, 1800–1870 (The Papers of William Charvat).* Ed. Matthew J. Brucolli. Columbus: Ohio State UP, 1968. 84–99.

Chew, V. Collins. *Underfoot: A Geologic Guide to the Appalachian Trail.* 2nd ed. Harpers Ferry: Appalachian Trail Conference, 1993.

"Christian Observer." *Encyclopedia of the Presbyterian Church in the United States of America: Including the Northern and Southern Assemblies.* Ed. Alfred Nevin. Philadelphia: Presbyterian Encyclopedia Publishing, 1884. 141–42.

Coffin, Levi. *Reminiscences of Levi Coffin, the Reputed President of the Underground Railroad.* 3rd ed. Cincinnati: Robert Clarke, 1898.

Coffin, Louise. See Jones, Louise Coffin.

Cohen, Hennig, and William B. Dillingham, eds., intro. *Humor of the Old Southwest.* New York: Houghton Mifflin, 1964.

Cole, Thomas. "Essay on American Scenery." *American Monthly Magazine* ns 1 (Jan. 1836): 1–12.

Collins, Carvel. "The Literary Tradition of the Southern Mountaineer, 1824– 1900." Diss. U of Chicago, 1944.

Colton, Henry E. "Picturesque America: Farm on the French Broad, and Hickory-Nut Gap, with Illustrations by Harry Fenn." *Appleton's* 4 (17 Dec. 1870): 737–38.

———. "Picturesque America, Part I: Mountain Island." *Appleton's* 5 (7 Jan. 1871): 15–18.

———. "Picturesque America, Part III: Reem's Creek." *Appleton's* 5 (4 Feb. 1871): 135–37.

———. "Western North Carolina." *Appleton's* 5 (20 May 1871): 587–88.

Comparato, Frank E. "D. Appleton & Company." *Publishers for Mass Entertainment in Nineteenth Century America.* Ed. Madeleine B. Stern. Boston: Hall, 1980. 16–25.

Craddock, Charles Egbert. See Murfree, Mary Noailles.

Cuthbert, John A., and Jessie Poesch. *David Hunter Strother: "One of the Best Draughtsmen the Country Possesses."* Morgantown: West Virginia UP, 1997.

David, Beverly R. "The Pictorial *Huck Finn:* Mark Twain and His Illustrator, E. W. Kemble." *American Quarterly* 26.4 (Oct. 1974): 331–51.

———. "Visions of the South: Joel Chandler Harris and His Illustrators." *American Literary Realism* 9.3 (Summer 1976): 189–207.

Davis, Donald E. *Where There Are Mountains: An Environmental History of the Southern Appalachians.* Athens: U of Georgia P, 2000.

Davis, Rebecca Harding. "By-paths in the Mountains." *Harper's* 61 (July–Sept. 1880): 167–85; 353–69; 532–47. [3-part illustrated series]

———. "Here and There in the South." *Harper's* 75 (July–Nov. 1887): 235–46; 431–43; 593–606; 747–60; 914–25. [5-part illustrated series]

———. *Life in the Iron Mills; or, The Korl Woman.* Ed. and intro. Tillie Olsen. New York: Feminist Press, 1972.

Davidson, Donald. *The Tennessee, Vol. I: The Old River, Frontier to Secession.* 1946. Nashville: Sanders, 1992.

Dean, Sharon L. *Constance Fenimore Woolson: Homeward Bound.* Knoxville: U of Tennessee P, 1995.

[DeBow, J. D. B.]. "Southern Travel and Travellers." *DeBow's Review and Industrial Resources, Statistics, Etc.* 3rd ser. 1 (1856): 323–29.

Du Bois, W. E. B. *The Souls of Black Folk: Essays and Sketches.* Chicago: McClurg, 1903.

Dunaway, Wilma. *The First Frontier: Transition to Capitalism in Southern Appalachia, 1700–1860.* Chapel Hill: U of North Carolina P, 1995.

———. "Speculators and Settler Capitalists: Unthinking the Mythology about Appalachian Landholding, 1790–1860." Pudup, Billings, and Waller 76–102.

Dunn, Durwood. *Cades Cove: The Life and Death of A Southern Appalachian Community, 1818–1937.* Knoxville: U of Tennessee P, 1988.

Dykeman, Wilma. *The French Broad. Illustrated by Douglas Gorsline.* Newport, TN: Wakestone, 1992. Rpt. of Holt Rinehart Rivers of America Series. 1955.

Eby, Cecil D., Jr. *Porte Crayon: The Life of David Hunter Strother, Writer of the Old South.* Chapel Hill: U of North Carolina P, 1960.

Edel, Leon. *Henry James: The Middle Years, 1882–1895.* New York: Lippincott, 1962.

Edwards, Everett Eugene. "References on the Mountaineers of the Southern Appalachians." *U.S. Dept. of Agriculture Bibliographical Contributions no. 28.* Washington, DC: U.S. Dept. of Agriculture Library, 1935.

Eller, Ronald D. *Miners, Millhands and Mountaineers: The Industrialization of the Appalachian South.* Knoxville: U of Tennessee P, 1982.

"Equal to L.A.: Groups Call Smokies Most Polluted Park." *Johnson City {TN} Press.* 24 Sept. 2002: A1+.

Evans, Curtis J. *The Conquest of Labor: Daniel Pratt and Southern Industrialization.* Baton Rouge: Louisiana State UP, 2001.

Exman, Eugene. *The Brothers Harper.* New York: Harper and Row, 1965.

Faragher, John Mack. *Daniel Boone: The Life and Legend of an American Pioneer.* New York: Holt, 1992.

Federal Writers' Project, Georgia. *Georgia: A Guide to Its Towns and Countryside.* Athens: U of Georgia P, 1940.

Federal Writers' Project, Kentucky. *Kentucky: A Guide to the Bluegrass State.* New York: Hastings, 1939.

Federal Writers' Project, North Carolina. *North Carolina: The WPA Guide to the Old North State.* 1939. Intro. William S. Powell. Columbia: U of South Carolina P, 1988.

Federal Writers' Project, Tennessee. *Tennessee: A Guide to the State, Compiled and Written by the Federal Writers' Project of the Works Projects Administration for the State of Tennessee.* New York: Viking, 1939.

Federal Writers' Project, Virginia. *Virginia: A Guide to the Old Dominion.* New York: Oxford UP, 1940.

Fields, Annie Adams. *Charles Dudley Warner, by Mrs. James T. Fields.* New York: McClure, Phillips, 1904.

Fishkin, Shelley Fisher. *From Fact to Fiction: Journalism and Imaginative Writing in America.* Baltimore: Johns Hopkins UP, 1985.

Foreman, Grant. *Indian Removal: The Emigration of the Five Civilized Tribes of Indians.* Norman: U of Oklahoma P, 1932.

Frome, Michael. *Strangers in High Places: The Story of the Great Smoky Mountains.* Knoxville: U of Tennessee P, 1980.

Gascoigne, Bamber. *How to Identify Prints: A Complete Guide to Manual and Mechanical Processes from Woodcut to Ink Jet.* London: Thames and Hudson, 1986.

Gaston, Kay Baker. *Emma Bell Miles.* Signal Mountain, TN: Walden's Ridge Historical Association, 1985.

Godwin, Parke. *The Life and Works of William Cullen Bryant, in Six Volumes—Vol. 1–2: A Biography of William Cullen Bryant with Extracts from his Private Correspondence.* New York: Appleton, 1883.

"Gold Mining in Georgia." *Harper's* 59 (Sept. 1879): 506–19.

Gossett, Thomas F. *Race: The History of an Idea in America.* Dallas: Southern Methodist UP, 1963.

Gould, Stephen Jay. *The Mismeasure of Man.* New York: Norton, 1981.

Graci, David. *Mt. Holyoke: An Enduring Prospect, History of New England's Most Historic Mountain.* Holyoke, MA: Holyoke Calem, 1985.

Grady, Henry Woodfin. *The New South and Other Addresses.* Ed. Edna Henry Lee Turpin. 1904. New York: Haskell, 1969.

Grafton, John. *The American West in the Nineteenth Century: 255 Illustrations from "Harper's Weekly" and Other Contemporary Sources.* New York: Dover, 1992.

Griffiths, Antony. *Prints and Printmaking: An Introduction to the History and Techniques.* Berkeley: U of California P, 1996.

Guilds, John Caldwell. *Simms: A Literary Life.* Fayetteville: U of Arkansas P, 1992.

Harper, Joseph Henry. *The House of Harper.* New York: Harper, 1912.

Harris, Sharon. *Rebecca Harding Davis and American Realism.* U of Pennsylvania P, 1991.

Hawthorne, Nathaniel. "The Ambitious Guest." *The Great Stone Face and Other White Mountain Stories.* New York: Houghton Mifflin, 1882. 31–42.

Headrick, Daniel R. *When Information Came of Age: Technologies of Knowledge in the Age of Reason and Revolution, 1700–1850.* Oxford: Oxford UP, 2000.

Houk, Rose. *Great Smoky Mountains: A Natural History Guide.* New York: Houghton Mifflin, 1993.

Howell, Benita J., ed. *Culture, Environment, and Conservation in the Appalachian South.* Urbana: U of Illinois P, 2002.

Inscoe, John C., ed. *Appalachians and Race: The Mountain South from Slavery to Segregation.* Lexington: UP of Kentucky, 2001.

"Introductory." *Appalachia: The Journal of the Appalachian Mountain Club* 1 (1876–78): 1.

Jackson, Helen Hunt. *A Century of Dishonor: A Sketch of the United States Government's Dealings with Some of the Indian Tribes.* New York: Harper, 1885.

Jaher, Frederic Cople. *A Scapegoat in the Wilderness: The Origins and Rise of Anti-Semitism in America.* Cambridge: Harvard UP, 1994.

James, Henry. "Miss Woolson." *The American Essays of Henry James, New Edition.* Ed. Leon Edel. Princeton: Princeton UP, 1989. 162–75.

Johns, Elizabeth. *American Genre Painting: The Politics of Everyday Life.* New Haven: Yale UP, 1991.

Jones, Jacqueline. *Soldiers of Light and Love: Northern Teachers and Georgia Blacks, 1865–73.* Chapel Hill: U of North Carolina P, 1980.

Jones, Louise Coffin. "In the Highlands of North Carolina." *Lippincott's* 32 (1883): 378–86.

[Jones,] Louise Coffin. "Mythology of the New Zealanders," *Ladies' Repository* [Cincinnati] 3 (May 1876): 441–44.

Justice, William S. and C. Ritchie Bell. *Wild Flowers of North Carolina (Garden Club of North Carolina).* Chapel Hill: U of North Carolina P, 1968.

Kemble, Edward W. "Illustrating Huckleberry Finn." *The Colophon: A Book Collectors' Quarterly* 1 (Feb. 1930): 45–52.

Kern, John Dwight. *Constance Fenimore Woolson: Literary Pioneer.* Philadelphia: U of Pennsylvania P, 1934.

Keyes, Donald D., ed., *George Cooke (1793–1849) {Exhibition Catalogue}, with Additional Essays by Linda Crocker Simmons; Estill Curtis Pennington; William Nathaniel Banks.* Athens: Georgia Museum of Art, 1991.

King, Edward. "The Great South: Among the Mountains of North Carolina." *Scribner's* 7 (Mar. 1874): 513–44.

Klotter, James. "The Black South and White Appalachia." *Journal of American History* 66 (Mar. 1980): 832–49.

Knight, Grant C. *James Lane Allen and the Genteel Tradition.* Chapel Hill: U of North Carolina P, 1935.

Koons, Kenneth E., and Warren R. Hofstra. "Introduction: The World Wheat Made." *After the Backcountry: Rural Life in the Great Valley of Virginia, 1800– 1900.* Ed. Koons and Hofstra. Knoxville: U of Tennessee P, 2000. xvii–xxx.

Lancaster, Paul. *Gentleman of the Press: The Life and Times of an Early Reporter, Julian Ralph of the* Sun. Syracuse: Syracuse UP, 1992.

Lanman, Charles. *Adventures in the Wilds of North America.* Ed. Charles Richard Weld. London: Longman, Brown, Green, and Longmans, 1854.

———. *Letters from the Alleghany Mountains.* New York : Putnam, 1849.

———. "Novelties of Southern Scenery." *Appleton's* 2 (16 Oct.–30 Oct. 1869): 257–61; 296–97; 327–29. [3-part series]

Lawlor, Virginia, and Richard Lawlor. "Schools and How They Grew." *History of Wilson County: Its Land and Its Life; Compiled and Written by History Associates of Wilson County.* Ed. Dixon L. Merritt. Nashville: Tennessee Historical Commission, 1961. 95–121.

Leach, Eugene E. "Charles Dudley Warner's 'Little Journey in the World.'" *New England Quarterly: A Historical Review of New England Life and Letters* 53 (1980): 329–44.

Ledford, Katherine. "'The Primitive Circle': Inscribing Class in Southern Appalachian Travel Writing, 1816–1846." *Appalachian Journal* 29.1–2 (Fall 2001–Winter 2002): 68–89.

———, and Kevin E. O'Donnell. "Travel Writing." *Encyclopedia of Appalachia.* Ed. Rudy Abramson and Jean Haskell. Knoxville: U of Tennessee P, forthcoming.

Lewis, David Levering. *W. E. B. Du Bois: Biography of a Race, 1868–1919.* New York: Holt, 1993.

Lewis, Ronald L. *Transforming the Appalachian Countryside: Railroads, Deforestation, and Social Change in West Virginia, 1880–1920.* Chapel Hill: U of North Carolina P, 1998.

Lindsay, Mary. *History of the Grassy Balds in Great Smoky Mountains National Park.* Management Report No. 4. Gatlinburg: GSMNP Uplands Field Research Laboratory, Apr. 1976.

Little, Charles E. *The Dying of the Trees: The Pandemic in America's Forests.* New York: Penguin, 1996.

Lounsbury, Thomas Raynesford. "Biographical Sketch of Charles Dudley Warner: Written for the Uniform Edition of His Collected Writings." *"Relations of Literature to Life" and "The People for whom Shakespeare Wrote"* (Vol. 15 of *Charles Dudley Warner's Collected Writings*). Ed. T. R. Lounsbury. Hartford: American, 1904. i–xxxviii.

Mancini, Matthew J. *One Dies, Get Another: Convict Leasing in the American South, 1866–1928.* Columbia: U of South Carolina P, 1996.

Marvin, Carolyn. *When Old Technologies Were New: Thinking about Electric Communication in the Late Nineteenth Century.* New York: Oxford UP, 1988.

Matthiessen, Peter. *Wildlife in America.* 1959. New York: Viking Penguin, 1987.

McAlexander, Hubert H. *The Prodigal Daughter: A Biography of Sherwood Bonner.* Baton Rouge: Louisiana State UP, 1981.

McCauley, Deborah Vansau. *Appalachian Mountain Religion: A History.* Urbana: U of Illinois P, 1995.

McDowell, Katherine. See Bonner, Sherwood.

McNeil, William Kinneth, ed. *Appalachian Images in Folk and Popular Culture.* Ann Arbor: UMI, 1989.

McPherson, James M. *The Abolitionist Legacy: from Reconstruction to the NAACP.* Princeton: Princeton UP, 1975.

————. *Battle Cry of Freedom: The Civil War Era.* New York: Oxford UP, 1988.

McKinney, Gordon B. *Southern Mountain Republicans, 1865–1900: Politics and the Appalachian Community.* Chapel Hill: U of North Carolina P, 1978.

Menand, Louis. *The Metaphysical Club: A Story of Ideas in America.* New York: Farrar, Strauss and Giroux, 2001.

Meriwether, Elizabeth Avery. *Recollections of Ninety-two Years, 1824–1916.* Nashville: Tennessee Historical Commission, 1958.

Meriwether, Lee. *The Tramp at Home.* New York: Harper, 1889.

Mitchell, W. J. T. "Imperial Landscape." *Landscape and Power.* Ed. W. J. T. Mitchell. Chicago: U of Chicago P, 1994. 5–34.

Mooney, James D. *Myths of the Cherokee: Nineteenth Annual Report of the Bureau of American Ethnology to the Secretary of the Smithsonian Institution, 1897–98; in Two Parts—Part I.* Ed. J. W. Powell, Bureau Director. Washington, DC: Government Printing Office, 1900. 3–576.

Moore, Rayburn S. *Constance Fenimore Woolson.* New York: Twayne, 1963.

Mott, Frank Luther. *A History of American Magazines 1:1741–1850; 2:1850–1865; 3:1865–1885; 4:1885–1905.* Cambridge: Harvard UP, 1967.

Murfree, Mary Noailles ["Charles Egbert Craddock"]. "The Dancin' Party at Harrison's Cove." *Atlantic Monthly* 41 (May 1878): 576–86.

————. *In the Tennessee Mountains.* New York: Houghton Mifflin, 1884.

Nash, Steve. *Blue Ridge 2020: An Owner's Manual.* Chapel Hill: U of North Carolina P, 1999.

Nelson, Scott Reynolds. *Iron Confederacies: Southern Railways, Klan Violence, and Reconstruction.* Chapel Hill: U of North Carolina P, 1999.

Novak, Barbara. *Nature and Culture: American Landscape and Painting, 1825–1875.* New York: Oxford UP, 1995.

O'Donnell, Kevin E. "The Artist in the Garden: George Cooke and the Ideology of Fine Arts Painting in Antebellum Georgia." *Crossroads: A Southern Culture Annual.* Ed. Ted Olson. Mercer UP, 2004. 73–96.

Ohmann, Richard. *Selling Culture: Magazines, Markets, and Class at the Turn of the Century.* New York: Verso, 1996.

Olson, Stanley. "Sargent at Broadway." *Sargent at Broadway: The Impressionist Years.* Ed. Olson, Warren Adelson, and Richard Ormond. New York: Universe/Coe Kerr Gallery, 1986. 11–25.

Overton, Grant. *Portrait of a Publisher and the First Hundred Years of the House of Appleton, 1825–1925.* New York: Appleton, 1925.

Paine, Albert Bigelow. *Mark Twain: A Biography.* 4 vols. New York: Harper, 1912.

Parks, Edd Winfield. *Charles Egbert Craddock (Mary Noailles Murfree).* Chapel Hill: U of North Carolina P, 1941.

Pattee, Fred Lewis. *The New American Literature, 1890–1930.* New York: Cooper Square, 1930.

Peattie, Donald Culross. *A Natural History of Trees of Eastern and Central North America.* 1950. Intro. Robert Finch. New York: Houghton Mifflin, 1991.

Pennington, Estill Curtis. "Time in Travelling: Intimations of the Itinerancy of George Cooke." Keyes 23–32.

Pfaelzer, Jean. *Parlor Radical: Rebecca Harding Davis and the Origins of American Social Realism.* Pittsburgh: U of Pittsburgh P, 1996.

Pierson, D. L. "The Mountaineers of Madison County, North Carolina." *Missionary Review of the World* ns 10 (Nov. 1897): 821–31.

Pierson, George Wilson. *Tocqueville and Beaumont in America.* New York: Oxford UP, 1938.

Pudup, Mary Beth, Dwight B. Billings, Altina L. Waller, eds. *Appalachia in the Making: The Mountain South in the Nineteenth Century.* Chapel Hill: U of North Carolina P, 1995.

———. "Introduction: Taking Exception with Exceptionalism: The Emergence and Transformation of Historical Studies of Appalachia." Pudup, Billings, and Waller 1–24.

Rainey, Sue. *Creating Picturesque America: Monument to the Natural and Cultural Landscape.* Nashville: Vanderbilt UP, 1994.

Reid, Christian. See Tiernan, Frances Fisher.

The Resources of North Carolina: Its Natural Wealth, Condition, and Advantages, as Existing in 1869; Presented to the Capitalists and People of the Central and Northern States. New York and Wilmington, NC: Bannister, Cowan & Company—Real Estate and Financial Agents, 1869.

Richards, T. Addison. *Appleton's Illustrated Handbook of American Travel.* New York: Appleton, 1857.

———, and William Richards. *Georgia Illustrated in a Series of Views—Drawn from Original Sketches by T. Addison Richards.* Penfield, GA: W. and W. C. Richards, 1842.

Richardson, Robert D., Jr. *Emerson: The Mind on Fire.* Berkeley: U of California P, 1995.

Rose, Jane Atteridge. *Rebecca Harding Davis.* New York: Twayne, 1993.

Rowe, Anne. *The Enchanted Country: Northern Writers in the South, 1865–1910.* Baton Rouge: Louisiana State UP, 1978.

Sakowski, Carolyn. *Touring the East Tennessee Backroads.* Winston-Salem: Blair, 1993.

———. *Touring the Western North Carolina Backroads, Revised ed.* Winston-Salem: Blair, 1995.

Schama, Simon. *Landscape and Memory.* New York: Vintage, 1995.

Schwaab, Eugene Lincoln. *Travels in the Old South, Selected from Periodicals of the Times.* Lexington: UP of Kentucky, 1973.

Schwarzkopf, S. Kent. *A History of Mt. Mitchell and the Black Mountains: Exploration, Development, and Preservation.* Raleigh: North Carolina Division of Archives and History, 1985.

Sears, John. *Sacred Places: American Tourist Attractions in the Nineteenth Century.* 1989. Amherst: U of Massachusetts P, 1998.

Shapiro, Henry D. *Appalachia on Our Mind: The Southern Mountains and Mountaineers in the American Consciousness, 1870–1920.* Chapel Hill: U of North Carolina P, 1978.

Sheaffer, Helen Woodward. "Rebecca Harding Davis: Pioneer Realist." Diss. U of Pennsylvania, 1947.

Sheppard, Muriel Earley. *Cabins in the Laurel.* Chapel Hill: U of North Carolina P, 1935.

Silber, Nina. *The Romance of Reunion: Northerners and the South, 1865–1900.* Chapel Hill: U of North Carolina P, 1993.

———. "'What Does America Need So Much as Americans?': Race and Northern Reconciliation with Southern Appalachia, 1870–1900." Inscoe 245–58.

Silver, Timothy. *Mount Mitchell and the Black Mountains: An Environmental History of the Highest Peaks in Eastern America.* Chapel Hill: U of North Carolina P, 2003.

Slotkin, Richard. *Regeneration through Violence: The Mythology of the American Frontier, 1600–1860.* Middletown, CT: Wesleyan UP, 1973.

Sondley, Forster Alexander. *A History of Buncombe County, North Carolina.* Asheville: Advocate, 1930.

Spurr, David. *The Rhetoric of Empire: Colonial Discourse in Journalism, Travel Writing, and Imperial Administration.* Durham: Duke UP, 1993.

Stanton, William Ragan. *The Leopard's Spots: Scientific Attitudes toward Race in America, 1815–59.* Chicago: U of Chicago P, 1960.

Stevenson, Robert Louis. *Memories and Portraits.* New York: Scribner, 1900.

Sweet, Timothy. Preface. *The Blackwater Chronicle: A Narrative of an Expedition into the Land of Canaan in Randolf County, Virginia.* By Philip Pendleton Kennedy; illustrated by David Hunter Strother. 1853. Ed. Sweet. Morgantown: West Virginia UP, 2002. vii–xxxvi.

Tichi, Cecelia. "Introduction: Cultural and Historical Background." *Life in the Iron-Mills.* By Rebecca Harding Davis. Ed. Tichi. New York: Bedford, 1998. 3–26.

Tiernan, Frances Fisher [Christian Reid]. "'The Land of the Sky;' or, Adventures in Mountain By-Ways, Chapter I." *Appleton's* 14 (4 Sept. 1875): 289–94. [The first of 18 chapters; installments appear almost weekly, through 19

Feb. 1876.] Rpt. *"The Land of the Sky," or, Adventures in Mountain By-ways.* New York: Appleton, 1876.

──────. "The Mountain-Region of North Carolina." *Appleton's* ns 2 (Mar. 1877): 193–204.

Torsney, Cheryl B. *Constance Fenimore Woolson: The Grief of Artistry.* Athens: U of Georgia P, 1989.

──────. Introduction. *Critical Essays on Constance Fenimore Woolson.* Ed. Torsney. New York: Hall, 1992. 1–14.

Toynbee, Arnold J. *A Study of History.* 12 vols. New York: Oxford UP, 1948–61.

Trachtenberg, Alan. *The Incorporation of America: Culture and Society in the Gilded Age.* New York: Hill and Wang, 1982.

Truettner, William H. *West as America: Reinterpreting Images of the Frontier, 1820–1920.* Washington, DC: Smithsonian Institution P, 1991.

──────, and Alan Wallach, eds. *Thomas Cole: Landscape into History.* Washington, DC: Smithsonian Institution P, 1994.

Veblen, Thorstein. *The Theory of the Leisure Class.* New York: Macmillan, 1899.

Vedder, Henry C. *American Writers of To-Day.* New York: Silver, Burdett, 1894.

Wade, Wyn Craig. *The Fiery Cross: The Ku Klux Klan in America.* New York: Simon and Schuster, 1986.

"Walker Valley History." *Connecting People and Nature—A Teacher's Guide: Environmental Education Lesson Plans from Great Smoky Mountains Institute at Tremont.* Ed. Ken Voorhis. Townsend, TN: Great Smoky Mountains Institute at Tremont, GSMNP, 2000. 301–5.

Wallach, Allan. "Making a Picture of the View from Mount Holyoke." *Bulletin of the Detroit Institute of Arts* 66.1 (1990): 35–46.

Ward, William S. *A Literary History of Kentucky.* Knoxville: U of Tennessee P, 1988.

Watie, Buck. See Boudinot, Elias.

Waterman, Guy, and Laura Waterman. *Forest and Crag: A History of Hiking, Trail Blazing and Adventure in the Northeast Mountains.* Boston: Appalachian Mountain Club, 1989.

Wellman, Manly Wade. *The Kingdom of Madison: a Southern Mountain Fastness and its People.* Chapel Hill: U of North Carolina P, 1973.

Whisnant, David E. *All That is Native and Fine: The Politics of Culture in an American Region.* Chapel Hill: U of North Carolina P, 1983.

Williams, David. *The Georgia Gold Rush: Twenty-Niners, Cherokees, and Gold Fever.* Columbia: U of South Carolina P, 1993.

Williams, Raymond. *The Country and the City.* London: Chatto and Windus, 1973.

Wilson, Jennifer Bauer. *Roan Mountain: A Passage of Time.* Winston-Salem: Blair, 1991.

Wolfe, Margaret Ripley. *Daughters of Canaan: A Saga of Southern Women.* Lexington: U of Kentucky P, 1995.

Wood, Ann Douglas. "The Literature of Impoverishment: The Women Local Colorists in America, 1865–1914." *Women's Studies* 1 (1972): 3–40.

Woodward, Comer Vann. *Origins of the New South.* Baton Rouge: Louisiana State UP, 1951.

Woolson, Constance Fenimore. "Crowder's Cove: A Story of the War." *Appleton's* 15 (18 Mar. 1876): 357–62.

Zeigler, Wilbur Gleason, and Ben S. Grosscup. *The Heart of the Alleghanies; or, Western North Carolina; Comprising its Topography, History, Resources, People, Narratives, Incidents, and Pictures of Travel, Adventures in Hunting and Fishing and Legends of Its Wildernesses.* Cleveland: Williams, 1883.

Index

Seekers of Scenery was designed and typeset on a Macintosh computer system using QuarkXPress software. The body text is set in 11/14 Adobe Garamond 3 with display type set in Birch and New Caledonia. This book was designed and typeset by Cheryl Carrington and manufactured by Thomson-Shore, Inc.